THINK and SOLVE

3

HAROLD CLARKE
ROBERT SHEPHERD

CAMBRIDGE
UNIVERSITY PRESS

Designed and illustrated by Celia Hart
Cover design by Chris McLeod

PUBLISHED BY THE PRESS SYNDICATE OF THE UNIVERSITY OF CAMBRIDGE
The Pitt Building, Trumpington Street, Cambridge CB2 1RP, United Kingdom

CAMBRIDGE UNIVERSITY PRESS
The Edinburgh Building, Cambridge CB2 2RU, United Kingdom
40 West 20th Street, New York, NY 10011–4211, USA
10 Stamford Road, Oakleigh, Melbourne 3166, Australia

First published 1984
Twelfth printing 1999

Printed in the United Kingdom at the University Press, Cambridge

ISBN 0 521 26973 3

Task 1

A

1 Add together nine, eleven and sixteen.

2 Take eighteen from thirty-seven.

3 Multiply seven by nine.

4 Apples are 8p each. How many can I buy with 40p?

5 John was given 45p. After spending 29p,
   how much would he have?

6 What number is one less than 200?

7 Divide 210 by 10.

8 Add 10 to 937.

9 How many tens are there in 350?

10 Write **4157** in words.

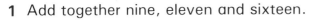

Th H T U
2 0 0 0
two thousand

B

11 Does 14 + 15 + 16 give the same answer
   as 9 × 5?

12 If $3^2 = 9$, how much is 5^2?

3^2 means 3 × 3,
3 squared.

13 How many centimetres are there in 1 ½ metres?

14 Is 4 a factor of 20?

15 How many weeks are there in a year?

16 What is the average of 13 and 17?

17 Sarah was 8 last year. How old will she be
   three years from now?

18 If it takes ¾ hour to paint one wall,
   how long should it take to paint two similar walls?

19 What is the cost of three books at 75p each?

20 Add together 500 grams and ½ kilogram.

Task 2.

1 How much is thirteen added to five and twelve?

2 What is the difference between thirty-six and twelve?

3 A box holds 5 crayons. How many crayons will there be in 6 boxes?

4 If a box of crayons cost 34p, what change will I get after buying one box with a 50p piece?

5 Share 24 by 3.

6 Add 10 to 498.

7 Write **2074** in words.

8 Divide 490 by 10.

9 Write **three thousand and twenty-seven** in figures.

10 Take 10 from 503.

B

11 How many millimetres are there in a centimetre?

Look for millimetres on your ruler.

12 What is four less than 9 × 4?

13 What is the next number?   2,   5,   8,   11,   ?

14 Is 6 a factor of 26?

15 Add ¼ to ½.

16 If I double a number, I get 48. What is the number?

17 Find the cost of 6 bars of toffee if 2 bars cost 15p.

18 If I buy two notebooks at 18p each, what change will I get from £1?

19 If a man walks at 5 km an hour, how long would it take him to walk 12½ km?

20 How many days are there altogether in June and July?

4

Task 3

1 What is the sum of eight, thirteen and fifteen?

2 Take nineteen from forty-five.

3 Share 36 by 4.

4 What are five lots of 14p worth?

5 How much change is there from 50p after spending 22p?

6 What number is five less than 600?

7 Divide 370 by 10.

8 Add 10 to 293.

9 Susan has saved £1.67. How much more does she need to have £2?

10 Write **5903** in words.

B

11 Is 57 a multiple of 3?

> $4 \times 3 = 12$
> $5 \times 3 = 15$
> 12 and 15 are Multiples of **3**

12 If $3^2 = 9$, how much is 4^2?

13 Mary is 3 cm shorter than 1 metre. How tall is she?

14 How many grams are there in ½ kilogram?

15 How many grams are there in 1¼ kilograms?

16 Seven times a number is sixty-three. What is the number?

> One kilogram = 1000 grams

17 How long is it from 3:30 p.m. to 5:15 p.m.?

18 If 30 bottles fill a crate, how many bottles are there in 2½ crates?

19 Add together 600 grams and ¼ of a kilogram.

20 If pencils cost 15p each, how many could I buy with £1.50?

Number-crunching

Write the numbers that will come out of these machines.

38 + 22
×10

600

1 25 + 15 ×10
2 7 × 6 ×10
3 26 + 12 ×10
4 7 × 5 ×10

5 13 + 37 ×10
6 9 × 5 ×10
7 27 + 28 ×10
8 8 × 7 ×10

These last four are for dividing.

9 34 + 36 ÷10
10 12 × 5 ÷10
11 70 + 50 ÷10
12 25 × 6 ÷10

A

1   Find the sum of fifteen and twenty-seven.

2   How much bigger is thirty-two than nineteen?

3   Multiply 12 by 5.

4   Six balls fill a box. How many boxes can be filled using 42 balls?

5   Graham had twenty-eight marbles, but then he lost twelve. How many has he now?

6   Write **five thousand, three hundred and sixteen** in figures.

7   Find the product of 57 and 10.

8   Add 100 to 738.

9   Write **2174** in words.

10 What is 10 less than 803?

B

11 What is the time?

12 What is the value of ³⁄₅ of £1?

13 Is 24 a multiple of 5?

14 Is this an equilateral triangle?

15 How many 5p coins make £1?

16 How much is   (½ of 60p) + (¼ of 80p)?

17 Add together ½ metre and 60 centimetres.

18 If it takes me 10 minutes to make a bed. How many beds can I make in an hour?

19 How much longer is 25 days than 2 weeks?

20 Double a number is 4 less than 10. What is the number?

Task 5

1 Find the sum of twenty-three and eighteen.

2 What is the difference between seventeen and thirty-five?

3 Share 48 by 6.

4 David buys 6 oranges at 9p each. How much does he spend?

5 Multiply 8 by 7.

6 Write **eight thousand, five hundred and twelve** in figures.

7 Multiply 405 by 10.

8 What is 10 less than the largest number here?
901,   782,   869.

9 How many tens are there in 430?

10 Write **4638** in words.

11 What is the next number?   24,   19,   14,   9,   ?

12 Is 38 a multiple of 4?

13 How many lines of symmetry has a square?

14 How many minutes are there in 1½ hours?

15 Each side of a square wooden frame measures
1½ metres. What is the total distance all round
the frame?

16 Mum is three times as old as Tina. If Tina is twelve,
how old will Mum be next year?

17 January 12th is on a Monday. On what day will
January 18th be?

18 How long is it from 8:30 a.m. to 10:05 a.m.?

19 If chocolate bars are 5 for 65p, how much does one
bar cost?

20 If I cut 2 metres of ribbon into 10 equal pieces,
how long will each piece be?

Task 6

1. What is the total of nineteen and thirty-two?
2. From 50p take 28p.
3. Two cakes cost 24p. How much will 4 cakes cost?
4. Find the product of 6 and 8.
5. How many teams of 4 can I make from 32 girls?
6. Multiply 108 by 10.
7. Write **1097** in words.
8. Take 10 from the smallest number here:
   567,   598,   581,   507.
9. Divide 1030 by 10.
10. Write, in figures, the number which is five more than one thousand.

11. How many minutes are there between 5:40 p.m. and 6 p.m.?

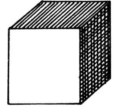

12. How many faces has a cube?

13. Is 45 a multiple of 3?
14. St Patrick's day is 17th March. What is the date a fortnight after that?
15. How many grams are there in 2 kilograms?
16. What fraction of £1 is 25p?
17. How long is it from 10:45 a.m. to 1:15 p.m.?
18. Grandad was 15 in 1941. When was he born?
19. A girl spent ¼ of her money in one shop and ½ of it in another. If she then had 50p left, how much did she start with?
20. A box of cheese contains 6 portions. How many portions are needed to fill 250 boxes?

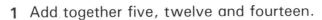

Task 7

A

1. Add together five, twelve and fourteen.
2. How much bigger is twenty-seven than twelve?
3. How many teams of seven can I make from 49 boys?
4. Multiply nine by eight.
5. How much will 5 cups of tea cost at 12p a cup?
6. Divide 310 by 10.
7. What is the number before 1899?
8. Add 100 to the largest number here: 717, 708, 721, 714.
9. Multiply 27 by 10.
10. Write **7206** in words.

> A prime number can only be divided by one or itself without leaving a remainder.

B

11. Is 17 a prime number?
12. If $4^2 = 16$, how much is 6^2?
13. If I face west, in which direction does my back face?
14. Is 8 a factor of 24?
15. How many 5p coins make 95p?
16. If I buy 8 pencils at 7p each, what change will I get from £1?
17. How much more is ½ a kilogram than 300 grams?
18. What is the average of 2, 7 and 3?
19. If I treble a number I get 24. What is the number?
20. If I cut 40 cm from a 2 metre plank how many centimetres will remain?

Darts

A dart in the outside ring doubles its score.

1 Which two pairs of opposite numbers add up to 24?

2 Which two pairs of opposite numbers have a difference of 5?

3 Which two pairs of neighbours add up to 23?

4 Which two pairs of neighbours have a difference of 14?

5 Start due north, and move clockwise seven places. What value has the opposite double?

6 Start due west, and move clockwise nine places. What value has the opposite double?

7 Start due east, and move clockwise, counting as you go until your number matches the value of the space. What is double the number opposite?

8 Eric and Jackie have five darts each. Who scores the most? By how many do they win?

ERIC	JACKIE
Double 17	Double 18
19	16
20	14
Double 13	Double 12
15	7

Task 8

A

1 Add together six, fourteen and twenty-two.

2 Take sixteen from thirty-nine.

3 How many children could each be given ¼ litre of orange juice from 5 litres?

4 Share 56 by 7.

5 What will 8 pencils cost at 8p each?

6 Add 100 to 1837.

7 From two thousand take 100.

8 Multiply 315 by 10.

9 Write **7124** in words.

10 Divide 880 by 10.

B

11 What is the next number?   27,   23,   19,   15,   ?

12 Michael ate ¾ of a bar of chocolate. What fraction was left?

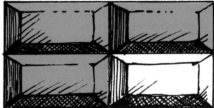

13 How many minutes are there between 6:10 a.m. and 7:10 a.m.?

14 Is 4 a factor of 46?

15 How many seconds are there in a ½ minute?

16 If January 29th is a Monday, what is the date of the following Friday?

17 A bottle of lemonade costs 35p. Can I buy 3 bottles with £1?

18 Which weighs more, 3 bars of soap at 150 g each or ½ kg of flour?

19 What is the cost of 6 tubes of sweets at 22p each?

20 How many bunches, each of 6 flowers, can I make from 180 daffodils?

12

Task 9

A

1 What is the total of nine, sixteen and twelve?

2 What must I add to sixteen to get 50?

3 Multiply thirteen by five.

4 If six eggs fill one box, how many boxes will 30 eggs fill?

5 Pencils cost 7p each. How much will 8 pencils cost?

6 Write **three thousand, two hundred and fifteen** in figures.

7 Multiply 103 by 10.

8 What is ten less than 1198?

9 Divide 720 by 10.

10 Write **7057** in words.

B

11 What is the next number?   3,   7,   11,   15,   ?

12 Is 36 a multiple of 9?

13 Diane ate $\frac{5}{8}$ of a chocolate bar. What fraction was left?

14 Is 7 a factor of 27?

15 How many millimetres are there in two centimetres?

16 What is a quarter of £2?

17 Jane had £1. She bought two tennis balls at 35p each. What was her change?

18 Fred walks at 5 kilometres an hour for 3 hours. How far does he walk?

19 A journey starts at 8:00 a.m. and takes 2½ hours altogether. At what time does the journey end?

20 What is the cost of 10 stamps at 18p each?

Task 10

A

1 What number is thirteen more than twenty-eight?

2 From forty-six take nineteen.

3 If oranges are 8p each, how much will 9 cost?

4 Share 39 by 3.

5 What is the product of 9 and 9?

6 Write **seven thousand, one hundred and seventy-two** in figures.

7 Multiply 351 by 10.

8 What is 100 more than 1983?

9 How many tens are there in 350?

10 Write **2106** in words.

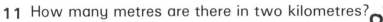

1 kilometre = 1000 m
1 metre = 100 cm

B

11 How many metres are there in two kilometres?

12 How many hours are there in ½ a day?

13 Is 4 a factor of 42?

14 How many grams are there in ¾ of a kilogram?

15 Is 47 a prime number?

16 Tea and biscuits cost 24p. How much will it cost for 5 people to have tea and biscuits?

17 A man has £8. He spends ¼ of it and gives 50p to his daughter. How much has he left?

18 How many 500 g bags of flour can be made from a 2 kg bag of flour?

19 How long is it from 4:15 p.m. to 6 p.m.?

20 How many 25 cm ribbons can the home-economics teacher cut from 3 metres of ribbon?

"Have you the time?"

Match the clock faces with the digital times.

Task 11

1 Add together twelve, eighteen and seventeen.

2 Take seventeen from fifty-one.

3 Multiply seven by seven.

4 If 6 eggs fill one box, how many boxes can be filled using 72 eggs?

5 Claire has 65p. If she spends 38p, how much will she have left?

6 Take 10 from 1207.

7 Add 1000 to 3027.

8 Multiply 309 by 10.

9 What is $\frac{1}{10}$ of 50?

10 Write **9025** in words.

11 Is 68 a multiple of 4?

12 What is the value of $2 \times 2 \times 2$?

13 How many metres are there in ¾ of a kilometre?

14 What are the factors of 39?

15 How many millimetres are there in 2½ cm?

16 Five more than a number is twenty-one. What is the number?

17 What is the average of 4, 7 and 10?

18 How long is it from 6:45 p.m. to 7:25 p.m.?

19 If a box of sweets holds 24 sweets, how many sweets are there in 3½ boxes?

20 Bananas are 12p each. How many can I buy with £1, and what change would I get?

Task 12

A

1 What number is nineteen more than thirty-seven?

2 What is the difference between 47 and 28?

3 Divide 42 by 3.

4 Add five to the sum of twelve and eighteen.

5 Nine pencils fit into a box. How many pencils will eight similar boxes hold altogether?

6 What number is ten less than two thousand?

7 What is the value of the six in 16.3?

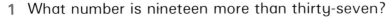

TU·t
18·2

8 What is the largest number you can make using the figures 2, 4, 1, 3 in any order?

9 What is $\frac{1}{10}$ of 560?

10 What is 418 worth to the nearest 100?

B

11 Robert drinks $\frac{3}{5}$ of the lemonade. What fraction is left for Nicola?

12 Find the value of $2 \times 3 \times 5$.

13 What is the next number?   2,   5,   9,   14,   20,   ?

14 How many right-angles are there in a full turn?

15 What is the perimeter of a square with each side measuring 3 cm?

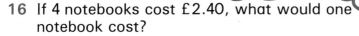

The snail crawls all the way round the square – the perimeter.

← 3 cm →

16 If 4 notebooks cost £2.40, what would one notebook cost?

17 James is 22 years younger than his Mum who is 29 next year. How old is James now?

18 A train journey takes 35 minutes. If the train leaves at 10:20 a.m., when will it arrive?

19 Find the cost of 25 pencils at 8p each.

20 How many kilograms do six packets of sugar weigh, if each one weighs 500 g?

Task 13

A

1. What is the sum of fifteen and seventy-six?
2. What is the difference between (2×11) and (5×7)?
3. How many teams of seven can I make with 56 children?
4. Packets of crisps cost 12p each. How much will 6 packets cost?
5. Take nine from the sum of fifteen and thirteen.
6. What is the value of the 7 in 41.7?
7. Write ³⁄₁₀ as a decimal.
8. Take one-tenth from 0.7.
9. What is 10 more than 21.3?
10. What is 1197 to the nearest 100?

```
u . t
0 . 2
²⁄₁₀
two tenths
```

B

11. What is the smallest number which is a multiple of 3 and of 4?
12. What is the next number?   4,   13,   22,   ?
13. Is 114 a multiple of 6?
14. Add together ⅓ + ⅓ + ⅓.
15. What is the next prime number after 17?
16. What is double five times nine?
17. If May 27th is a Wednesday, what is the date the following Wednesday?
18. If I must arrive at school at 8:45 a.m., when should I start my 20-minute journey?
19. How much altogether is (⅓ of 90p) + (½ of 80p)?
20. Which is worth more, and by how much,   ¼ of 60p or   ⅕ of 60p?

Task 14

A

1 Find the sum of forty-six and forty-five.

2 Take twenty-eight from fifty-seven.

3 What is the product of nine and seven?

4 Share 45 by 3.

5 What is the answer if I divide 208 by 4?

6 Write $\frac{5}{10}$ as a decimal.

7 What is 1503 worth to the nearest 100?

8 Write $\frac{7}{10}$ as a decimal.

9 Which is larger, 1.3 or 11?

10 Take 10 from the largest number here: 1147, 1741, 1714.

B

11 Find the value of 3 × 4 × 5.

12 If $\frac{3}{8}$ of those who stay to lunch have sandwiches, what fraction have school dinners?

13 What are the factors of fifteen?

14 What is the value of 7^2?

equilateral triangle

15 How big are the angles of an equilateral triangle?

16 How many days are there altogether in October and November?

17 Half of a box contains 18 chocolates, so how many chocolates are there in $\frac{3}{4}$ of a box?

18 What is the average of 7, 9 and 17?

19 If I cut 85 cm from a 3 m length of string, how many centimetres of string are left?

20 How long is it from 8:45 p.m. to 10:20 p.m.?

19

Odd one out

Which is the odd fraction in each line?
Is it in the triangle, rectangle, square or circle?
(Can you complete all these in 3 minutes?)

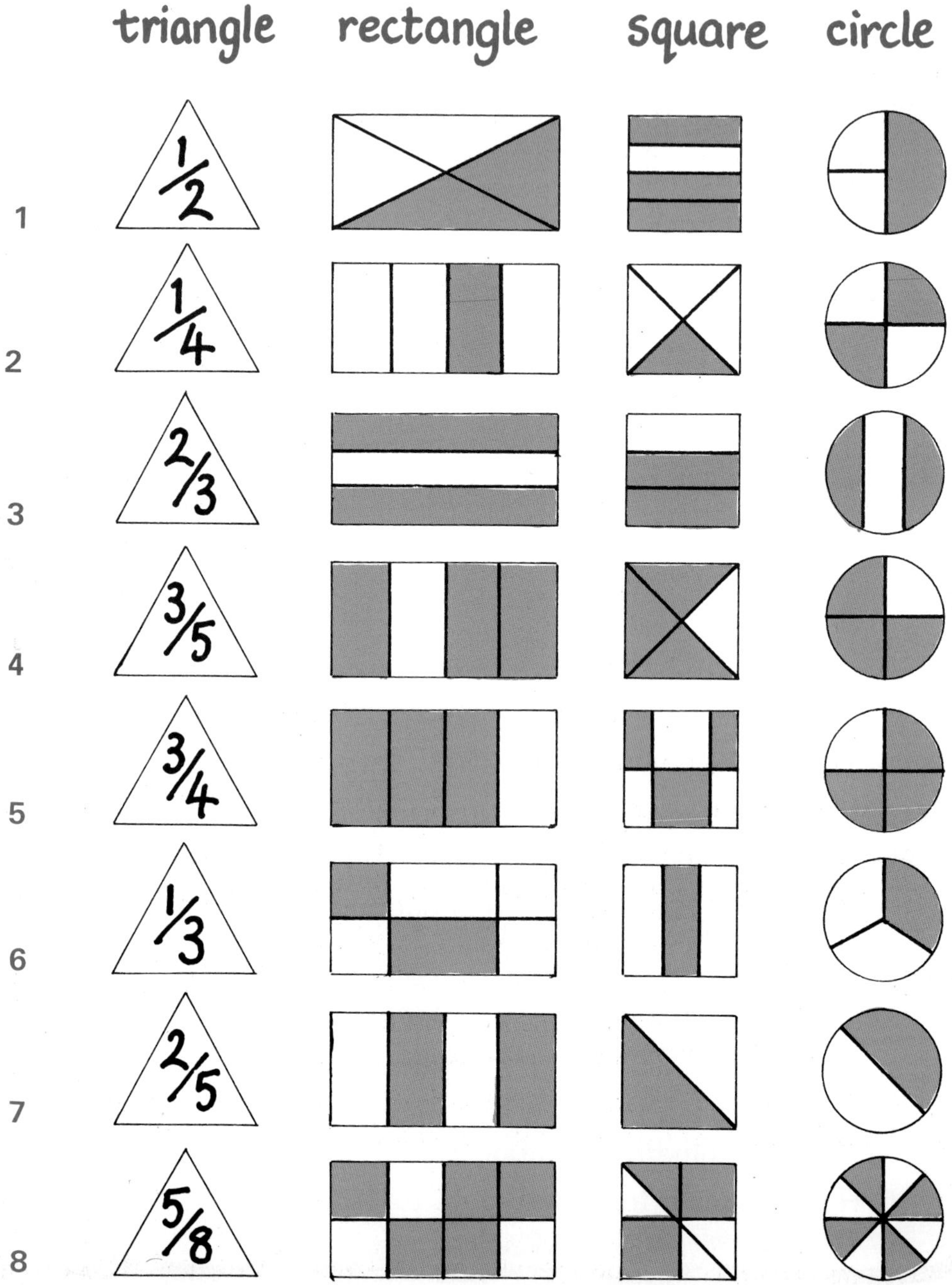

triangle	rectangle	square	circle

1 $\frac{1}{2}$

2 $\frac{1}{4}$

3 $\frac{2}{3}$

4 $\frac{3}{5}$

5 $\frac{3}{4}$

6 $\frac{1}{3}$

7 $\frac{2}{5}$

8 $\frac{5}{8}$

A

1 What is twenty-three more than sixty-six?

2 Take twenty-eight from 47.

3 The product of two numbers is 39. One of them is 3. What is the other?

4 What change do I get from 30p after spending 23p?

5 How much is seven lots of 12p worth?

6 Put these in order, smallest first: 9.3, 19, 2.7.

7 Take three-tenths from 1.4.

8 Add five-tenths to 1.1.

9 Write **two units and four-tenths** as a decimal.

10 What is 1343 to the nearest 100?

u • t
1 • 1
one • one
unit tenth

B

11 What is 4 p.m. as written on the 24-hour clock?

12 Which of these is a prime number?
7, 10, 15, 21.

13 How many millimetres are there in 3½ centimetres?

14 Find one number which is a factor of 35 and 49.

15 What is the perimeter of a 9 cm square?

16 What is the average of 18, 12 and 15?

17 Swimming costs 25p per person. How much will it cost for a class of 32 children to go swimming?

18 Julie has £5. She buys two pairs of socks for her Dad at £1.35 a pair. What change will she get?

19 Doubling a number gives the same result as adding 17 to 29. What is the number?

20 Judith cuts 4 ribbons, each 29 cm long, from a two-metre length. How much is left?

Task 16

A

1 Add together thirty-six and twenty-seven.

2 From 52 take twenty-nine.

3 13 × 6.

4 If a bus fare is 15p, how much will it cost to pay for 5 people?

5 Divide 57 by 3.

6 Write **four-tenths** as a decimal.

7 Which is larger, 0.7 or 1.3?

8 Add seven-tenths to 2.2.

9 Write **three and seven-tenths** as a decimal.

10 What is the value of the 5 in 21.5?

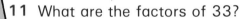

B

11 What are the factors of 33?

12 Is 91 a multiple of 7?

13 What is ¼ of 3?

14 A bag of sweets weighs 150 g less than 1 kg. How many grams does it weigh?

15 How many minutes are there in 3½ hours?

16 Find the cost of 8 choc-ices at 35p each.

17 If coffee costs 28p and biscuits 9p each, how much will it cost for 3 coffees and 2 biscuits?

18 What change will I get from £5 after buying the coffee and biscuits?

19 If a snail crawls 20 cm in a minute, how long will it take to crawl 2 metres?

20 How long is it from 15:00 to 17:15?

Task 17

1 What is the total of 37 and 53?

2 From forty-three take twenty-nine.

3 Multiply 13 by 4.

4 Divide 48 by 6.

5 If I cut 7½ cm from a 20 cm strip of card, how much is left?

6 Write **0.3** in words.

7 Put these in order, smallest first: 1.3, 0.9, 0.2.

8 What is 1493 worth to the nearest 100?

9 Write **four and two-tenths** as a decimal.

10 Take 100 from 219.3.

11 What is the next number? 47, 45, 42, 38, ?

12 Is 135 a multiple of 7?

13 How many degrees are there in a quarter of a turn?

14 What is 4:30 p.m. as written on the 24-hour clock?

15 How many centimetres are there in ⅕ of a metre?

16 School football matches take 80 minutes. When will the match end if it starts at 4 p.m.?

17 St George's day is April 23rd. What is the date a fortnight after that?

18 How many 200 g packets of sweets can be made from 1 kilogram of sweets?

19 If notebooks cost 29p each, how much will 5 cost?

20 A puppet theatre has 25 rows of seats, and each row has 12 seats. How many seats are there in the theatre?

Steam

SEA → 1 + 10 + 50
→ 61

What are these words worth?

1 STEM   3 SEAM
2 TEAM   4 TEAS

Try these

5 MEET
6 MASSES
7 ESTATES

If R = 25

What value have these?

8   MASTER
9   STAMMER
10 ARRESTS
11 EASTER
12 STREAMERS

Task 18

1 Add together fourteen and forty-seven.

2 What is the difference between thirteen and fifty-one?

3 What is the product of 15 and 4?

4 How many groups of 6 can I make from 54 children?

5 Oranges cost 7p. How much will 8 cost?

6 Write $^{6}/_{10}$ as a decimal.

7 What is the value of the 2 in 21.3?

8 What is 1093 worth to the nearest 100?

9 Write **3.7** in words.

10 Write **14 744** in words.

11 Is 23 a prime number?

12 Can you find one number that is a factor of 12 and 21?

rectangle

13 How many lines of symmetry has a rectangle?

14 How many 2p coins are there in £1.50?

15 What is the perimeter of a rectangle 2 cm by 6 cm?

16 If I buy 13 chews at 5p each, what change will I get from £1?

17 Wendy's pocket money is £2. How much would it be if it were increased by one-tenth?

18 A train travels at 88 km per hour. How far will it have travelled in half an hour?

19 Three more than a number is the same as twice five. What is the number?

20 If I cut a 150 g slice from a 1½ kg cake, how many grams are left?

Task 19

A

1 What is twenty-three more than forty-eight?

2 Take 29 from 67.

3 Ice-creams cost 24p each. How much will three cost?

4 Four cakes fill a box. How many boxes can be filled with 64 cakes?

5 How many sweets do I need to give 21 girls 5 sweets each?

6 A batsman needs 7 runs to complete his century. How many runs has he scored?

7 Put these in order, smallest first: 2.5,   3.4,   1.9.

8 What is the value of the 7 in 12.7?

9 Write **two and nine-tenths** as a decimal.

10 Write **47.3** in words.

B

11 What is the next number?
   57,   59,   63,   69,   77,   ?

12 Is 87 a multiple of 3?

13 What fraction of two dozen is 3?

Dozen ↔ 12

14 What are the factors of 16?

15 How many centimetres are there in 30 millimetres?

16 When 5 is added to half of a number, the answer is 9. What is the number?

17 If Peter buys 3 ties at £1.50 each, what change will he have from £5?

18 Cardigans need 7 buttons each. How many cardigans can be fitted with 105 buttons?

19 I have to make a 35-minute journey and must arrive at 11 a.m. At what time must I start the journey?

20 Tins of beans cost 27p each. What change will I get from £1 after buying 3 tins?

Task 20

A

1 Emma has twenty-nine marbles. If she wins 32 more, how many will she have?

2 Take nineteen from eighty-four.

3 The product of two numbers is 72. If one is 6, what is the other?

4 Share 49 by 7.

5 Find the total of 4 lots of fifteen added to 3 lots of eight.

6 Add 1.3 to 2.4.

7 Put these in order, smallest first: 1.2,   2.3,   1.1.

8 Write **sixteen and one-tenth** as a decimal.

9 Take one thousand from thirty thousand. Write the answer in figures.

10 Take 10 from 91.3.

B

11 What is half of a half?

12 What is 21:00 as written on the 12-hour clock?

13 What are the factors of 18?

14 How many grams are there in 2¼ kilograms?

15 How many metres is ⅕ of a kilometre?

16 How long is it from 4:15 p.m. to 6:30 p.m.?

17 Mugs cost 39p each. After buying two mugs, what change will I get from £1?

18 Entry to the museum is 35p per person. How much will it be for 5 people?

19 How many kilograms will 5 packets of tea weigh if one packet weighs 400 g?

20 How many 20 cm lengths of ribbon can be cut from 3 metres of ribbon?

Task 21

1 Karen had 142 stamps. How many did she have after buying a packet of 28 stamps?

2 What is the difference between 82 and 29?

3 If bananas are 12p each, what is the cost of 6 bananas?

4 A florist has 66 tulips to put in bunches of 6 tulips. How many bunches can he make altogether?

5 If five times a number is 65, what is the number?

6 Put these in order, smallest first:
1109,   1119,   1191,   1190.

7 Add 2.1 to 3.7.

8 Add 3.1 + 10.

9 Write $\frac{7}{10}$ in words.

10 Write **fifteen thousand and seventy-five** in figures.

11 How long is it from 10:45 a.m. to 1:15 p.m.?

12 How tall is Joe if he is 25 cm shorter than 1½ metres?

13 What is the largest number that is a factor of 16 and 28?

14 What is 9 p.m. on the 24-hour clock?

15 What is the next number?   31,   27,   22,   16,   ?

16 How many 200 ml cups can I fill from one litre of milk?

1 litre
1000 millilitres

17 Add together ¾ kilogram and 500 grams.

18 How much change will I get from £5 after buying 6 pens at 75p each?

19 How long is it from 14:00 to 15:15?

20 Share 60p so that Jill gets twice as much as Tim. How much does Tim get?

Copy out each set of links.
Put in all the missing numbers.

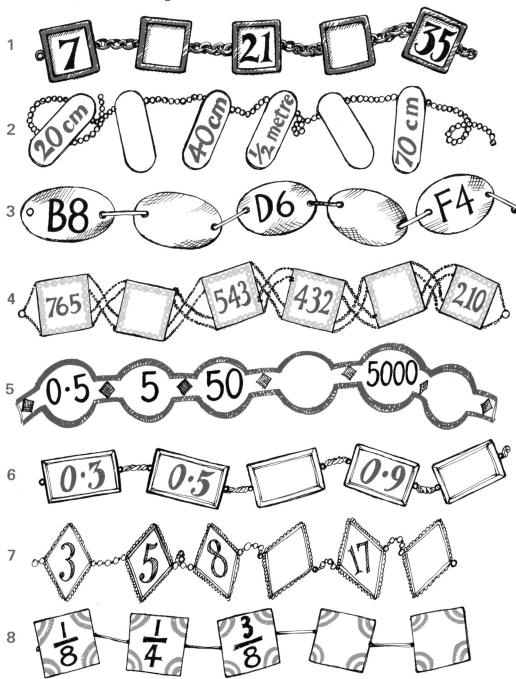

1. 7 ☐ 21 ☐ 35

2. 20 cm ☐ 40 cm ½ metre ☐ 70 cm

3. B8 ☐ D6 ☐ F4

4. 765 ☐ 543 432 ☐ 210

5. 0·5 5 50 ☐ 5000

6. 0·3 0·5 ☐ 0·9 ☐

7. 3 5 8 ☐ 17 ☐

8. $\frac{1}{8}$ $\frac{1}{4}$ $\frac{3}{8}$ ☐ ☐

A

1 Mary was given 47 stamps to add to her collection of 51. How many stamps did she have then?

2 Take 29 from 82.

3 Find seven lots of twelve.

4 Divide 81 by 3.

5 From the sum of 29 and thirty-two, take 14.

6 Put these in order, smallest first:
2722, 2272, 2227.

7 What is 1763 to the nearest 100?

8 Write eight-tenths as a decimal.

9 Take three-tenths from 5.7.

10 Take ten from 36.7.

B

11 How many days were there altogether in January and February 1984?

12 What is 11 p.m. as shown on the 24-hour clock?

13 Is 45 a multiple of 5 and of 9?

14 What is the perimeter of a rectangle 4 cm long and 2 cm wide?

isosceles triangle

15 How many equal sides has an isosceles triangle?

16 David had to share fifteen £5 notes with his two brothers. How much did they each receive?

17 What is the average of 14, 8 and 11?

18 One-half of a number is 3 less than 16. What is the number?

19 Add ½ of £2 to ¼ of £3.

20 What fraction of 1 kilogram is 750 grams?

Task 23

A

1 Increase 39 by 84.

2 What is the difference between 7×7 and 8×9?

3 What is the product of six and thirteen?

4 Fifteen tins of beans fill a box.
How many boxes will 45 tins fill?

5 How much change will be received from 70p after spending 28p?

6 Add 2.4 to 3.7.

7 Write three-tenths as a decimal.

8 Put these in order, smallest first:
1811, 1818, 1181, 1118.

9 Write 2984 to the nearest 100.

10 Take 0.8 from 4.5.

B

11 What is the next number? 42, 37, 31, 24, ?

12 Write 5:30 p.m. as shown on the 24-hour clock.

13 How many corners has a cube?

cube

14 What is the perimeter of a 5 cm square?

15 How many millilitres are there in a litre?

16 If March 13th is on a Tuesday, on what day is March 21st?

17 A carton of cream holds ¼ litre. How many litres of cream are needed to fill 20 cartons?

18 20 is one less than a quarter of a certain number. What is the number?

19 In a class, ¾ of the children stay for dinner.
If 8 children go home for dinner, how many stay at school?

20 It is 207 km from my home to York. If I travel 68 km towards York today, how much further must I go tomorrow in order to reach York?

A

1 What is the sum of 86 and 37?

2 What change do I get from 60p after spending 32p?

3 The product of two numbers is 84. If one of the numbers is 7, what is the other?

4 Grapefruit cost 14p each. How much will six cost?

5 Add sixteen to the product of eight and four.

6 Put in order of size, with the smallest first:
2.9,   2.3,   2.4,   2.8.

7 Add 0.6 to 0.4.

8 Add 3.8 + 10.

9 Write in words the number 18 704.

10 Write $^{15}/_{10}$ as a decimal fraction.

B

11 How would 3 p.m. be shown on the 24-hour clock?

12 If I face N.E. in which direction does my back face?

13 How many faces has a cube?

14 Which is larger, 27 mm or 3.5 centimetres?

15 How many days are there altogether in June and July?

16 Add ½ kg to 150 grams. How much more is needed to make a kilogram?

17 What is the average of 13, 18 and 14?

18 Three more than half a number is ten. What is the number?

19 If I cut 13 cm from ½ a metre, how many cm are left?

20 What fraction of 30 is ten?

(3 < 7)

Fill in the correct sign,

❮ or ❯

1. 7 × 5 ...... 6 × 6
2. 9 cm × 6 ...... ½ metre
3. 21 − 9 + 8 ...... 2 × 11
4. 17 × 3 ...... 13 × 4
5. ½ kg ...... 450 g
6. 7.5 ...... 7⁶/₁₀
7. 35 mm ...... 3.7 cm
8. 330 g ...... ⅛ kg
9. £0.25 ...... 4 × 7p
10. 1½ m ...... 137 cm

❮ means less than.

❯ means greater than.

Task 25

A

1 What is 62 more than twenty-seven?

2 How much more than 37 is 45?

3 Multiply 19 by 3.

4 How many 12p pencils can I buy with 60p?

5 The sum of two numbers is 27. If one number is thirteen, what is the other?

6 Which is bigger, 1.7 or 0.8?

7 Add 4.6 + 4 tenths.

8 Write seventeen-tenths as a decimal.

9 50p × 10 = £ .

10 Take 0.6 from 6.5.

B

11 Is fifteen a multiple of three and of five?

12 If $3^3 = 3 \times 3 \times 3 = 27$, what is the value of 2^3?

13 What is 7 p.m. on the 24-hour clock?

14 How much is ½ + ½ + ½?

15 How many degrees are there in ½ of a right-angle?

16 What change from £5 is there after buying three 85p books?

17 A car travels at 72 km an hour. How far will it go in 1½ hours?

18 If 3 toffees cost 15p, how much will 2 cost?

19 A journey starts at 10:45 a.m. If it lasts for 35 minutes, when does it end?

20 If 50 g of cheese costs 35p, how much does 250 g cost?

Task 26

1 Pat had 39p, but then she earned an extra 55p for cleaning a car. How much did she then have altogether?

2 How many must be added to 57 to make 86?

3 Seven times a number is 91. What is the number?

4 How many teams of six can be made from 54 boys?

5 Find the value of three times 31p.

6 Write 0.3 as a fraction.

7 Put these in order, smallest first:
1472, 1427, 1742, 1724.

8 Add one unit to the largest number here:
0.4, 4.1, 4.7, 1.7.

9 Take five from five thousand.

10 30p × 10 = £   .

11 What is the perimeter of a square of sides 6 cm?

12 What is the next number?   64,   32,   16,   8,   ?

13 How many edges has a cube?

14 What number is halfway between 17 and 25?

15 Is 48 a multiple of 2 and of 3?

16 Pencils cost 9p, and rubbers cost 7p. How much will it cost to buy a pencil and a rubber for 5 people?

17 What fraction of a metre is 30 cm?

18 If I double a number and add 5, I get 23. What is the number?

19 If July 27th falls on a Thursday, on what day is August 2nd?

20 How many centimetres are there in ¼ of 3 metres?

Task 27

A

1. Lee has 129 conkers. If he found 37 more, how many would he have then?
2. What is the difference between 145 and 39?
3. What is the product of seventeen and five?
4. Divide 184 by 4.
5. Increase 27 by 145.
6. £6.00 + 10p =   p.
7. Add 7 tenths to 6.5.
8. How many tenths are there altogether in $2\frac{3}{10}$?
9. Write 0.7 as a fraction.
10. Write the number that is 100 more than 18 977 in figures.

B

11. What are the factors of 33?
12. How much is $1\frac{1}{2}$ + $1\frac{1}{2}$ + $1\frac{1}{2}$?
13. What is the perimeter of a rectangle 6 cm long and 5 cm wide?
14. What is 1:30 p.m. on the 24-hour clock?
15. How many metres are there in 300 cm?
16. One sheet contains 50 stamps.
    How many stamps are there altogether on 9 sheets?
17. What is the average of 20, 30 and 16?
18. How long is it from 2:40 a.m. to 4:00 a.m.?
19. What fraction of £3 is 30p?
20. What change from £10 will I get after buying 4 pairs of socks at £1.35 a pair?

Task 28

A

1 What is 27 more than 135?

2 What is one-half of 6^2?

> 5^2 means five squared = 5×5

3 If ice-creams cost 27p each, how much would 3 cost?

4 If five times a number is 75, what is the number?

5 What is twice the sum of twelve and ten?

6 Write 0.8 as a fraction.

7 From the largest of these subtract the smallest:
  1.3, 3.7, 2.3, 1.4.

8 How many tenths are there in 1.9?

9 Write **42 176** in words.

10 Add 3.3 to 5.2.

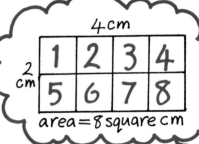

4 cm
2 cm

| 1 | 2 | 3 | 4 |
| 5 | 6 | 7 | 8 |

area = 8 square cm

B

11 What is the area of a rectangle 4 cm long and 3 cm wide?

12 Write down a number which is a factor of both 10 and 8.

13 What is the next number? 1½, 3, 4½, 6, ?

14 ⅓ of 60 cm + ½ of 60 cm.

15 How many kilometres are there in 2500 metres?

16 A 50p coin weighs 13.5 g. What would four 50p coins weigh?

17 What is ³⁄₁₀ of a metre in centimetres?

18 Add ½ of £5 to ¼ of £3.

19 How many minutes are there from 10:30 a.m. to 11:46 a.m.?

20 How many degrees do I turn when I move clockwise from facing north-east to south-east?

Count the cubes

How many small cubes are there in each group?

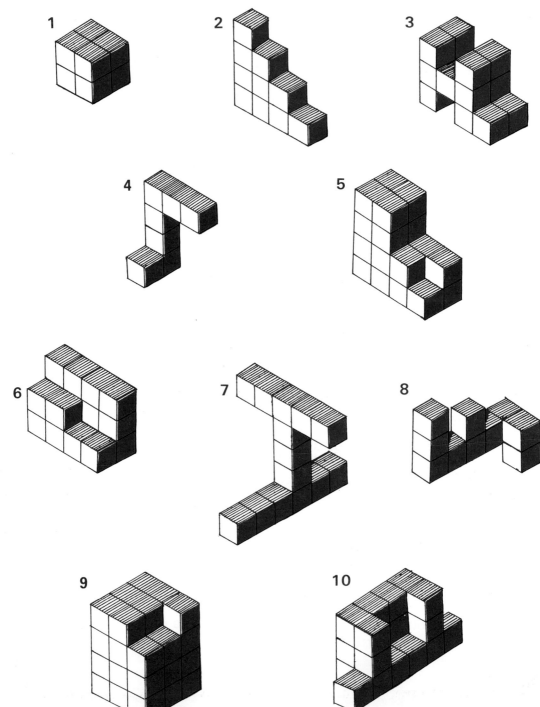

Task 2.9

1 Gary collects conkers and has a collection of 107. If he later finds another 29, what will be his total collection?

2 Take one from 8^2, and divide the result by 7.

3 Find the cost of 6 newspapers at 18p each.

4 Divide the sum of 14 and 13 by three.

5 Add sixteen to the sum of 45 and 19.

6 Write nineteen-tenths as a decimal.

7 Put these in order, smallest first:
2018,   2108,   2801,   2118.

8 Add together 2.9 and 3.0.

9 How many tenths are there in 3.9?

10 Multiply 0.4 by 10.

11 Write down the set of prime numbers that are less than ten.

12 What is the smallest number that is a multiple of 2 and of 3?

13 How many minutes are there in 120 seconds?

14 What is 8:15 p.m. on the 24-hour clock?

15 What number is halfway between 13 and 17?

16 A kilogram loaf is cut into 25 slices. How much will 5 slices weigh?

17 What fraction of £5 is 50p?

18 Kate saves 20p a day, starting on May 25th and ending on June 4th. How much does she save?

19 Add ¼ kg to 700 grams. How much more is needed to make a kilogram?

20 A clock is ten minutes fast. What is the correct time if it reads three minutes past ten?

1. What is the total of 43 and 29?

2. The sum of two numbers is 47. If one of the numbers is 18, what is the other?

3. Nine times a number is 108. What is the number?

4. What is six times 25?

5. One box can hold six tins. How many boxes can be filled from a load of 84 tins?

6. Add together 2.3 and 5.1.

7. Divide 25.0 by 10.

8. Add five-tenths and $\frac{3}{10}$.

9. Multiply 0.7 by 10.

10. Take 15 from 20 000 and write the answer in words.

11. What is the perimeter of an equilateral triangle with sides of 5 cm?

12. How many days are there altogether in November and December?

13. How much is ¾ of £4?

14. What is the lowest common multiple of 3 and 8?

15. How many millimetres are there in 4.2 cm?

16. A bar of soap weighs 350 g. How much will 7 bars weigh altogether?

17. 4 pens cost 25p. How many could I buy with £1.50?

18. If a square tile is 15½ cm wide, how long is a row of 6 tiles?

19. Add together ¼ of £2 and ½ of £3.

20. If a packet of 25 envelopes costs 40p, how many envelopes would I get for £2?

Routines and Orgies

Routines and Orgies

The Life of Peter Cundill

Financial Genius, Philosopher, and Philanthropist

CHRISTOPHER RISSO-GILL

McGill-Queen's University Press   Montreal & Kingston • London • Ithaca

© The Cundill Foundation 2014

ISBN 978-0-7735-4472-7 (cloth)
ISBN 978-0-7735-9687-0 (ePDF)
ISBN 978-0-7735-9688-7 (ePUB)

Legal deposit fourth quarter 2014
Bibliothèque nationale du Québec

Printed in Canada on acid-free paper that is 100% ancient forest free
(100% post-consumer recycled), processed chlorine free

McGill-Queen's University Press acknowledges the support of the
Canada Council for the Arts for our publishing program.
We also acknowledge the financial support of the Government of
Canada through the Canada Book Fund for our publishing activities.

Library and Archives Canada Cataloguing in Publication

Risso-Gill, Christopher, 1948–, author
        Routines and orgies : the life of Peter Cundill, financial genius,
philosopher, and philanthropist / Christopher Risso-Gill.

Includes index.
Issued in print and electronic formats.
ISBN 978-0-7735-4472-7 (bound). – ISBN 978-0-7735-9687-0 (ePDF). –
ISBN 978-0-7735-9688-7 (ePUB)

1. Cundill, Peter. 2. Capitalists and financiers – Canada –
Biography. 3. Philanthropists – Canada – Biography. 4. Value
investing. I. Title.

HG172.C85R58 2014   332.092   C2014-904927-7
                                            C2014-904928-5

The commonest, one might call it the natural, rhythm of human life is routine punctuated by orgies. Routine supports men's weakness, makes the fatigue of thought unnecessary, and relieves them of the intolerable burden of responsibility. Orgies, whether sexual, religious, sporting, or political, provide that periodical excitement which all of us crave.

ALDOUS HUXLEY, *Beyond the Mexique Bay*

Huxley is brilliant; he invites us to think of history in terms of politics, economics and sociology, yes, but also in terms of psychology and physiology.

PETER CUNDILL

Contents

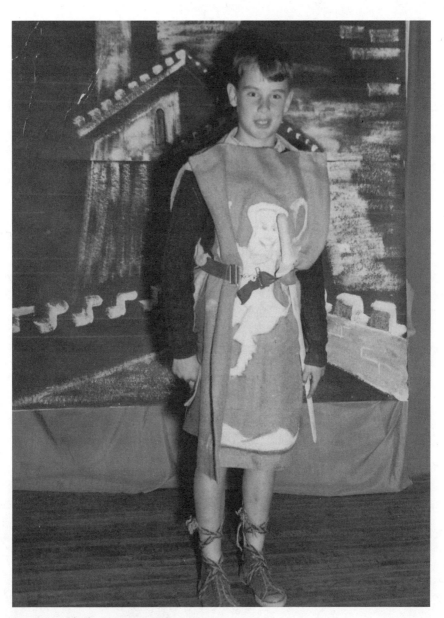

Peter in Macbeth costume

Frank Cundill in Black Watch
uniform

The famous outfit

On the campaign trail
with Michael Meighen,
1960s

The outfit again

Frank, Peter, Grier, and Ruth in Vancouver

Hang gliding in California

Best man at Ian and Victoria Watson's wedding in London

Conquering Everest for Canada

Relaxing on Everest

The fire on Everest

With Sir Edmund Hillary (at left)

Running with Joannie in Vancouver

Shooting partridges in Wiltshire

BENJAMIN GRAHAM
7811 EADS AVENUE
LA JOLLA, CALIFORNIA 92037
TEL (714) 459-7056

Apr. 31, 1975.

Dear Mr. Cundill,

       Ansering your letter of Apr. 10, I regret to say that I do not have available here the financial results of Graham-Newman Corp.

       However, I know that for a number of years before 1956 Moody's Financial manual included us in its list of investment companies, and gave annual figures for distributions and year-end asset values of our shares. You should not have much difficulty in obtaining these figures.

       I wish you success with your investment fund to be operated under the policy you describe. May I express some reservations about your limiting your holding to "ten to fifteen securitties"- first because You may have difficulty in acquiring the number of shres of each companies you will need, and secondly because I have more faith in really wide diversification than in the value of "extensive research."

Sincerely,

Mr. Peters Cunhill,
Vancouver, B.C.

Ben Graham

P.S. Warning: I am a very bad regular correspondent.

Letter from Benjamin Graham

Peter's Picasso (photograph: courtesy of Bonhams)

Running the New York City
Marathon, 1982

With Joanie at Evelyn's wedding

Exploring the Battle of the Bulge in the Ardennes

Peter and Joanie with Defiantly

Routines and Orgies

Introduction

THIS BOOK IS a biography not an investment manual, but those seeking insights into the thinking of one of the greatest value investors of all time will find it has much to offer. It is more by way of an epic, describing a journey that spanned more than seventy years, most corners of the globe and a broad array of human endeavour – commercial, artistic, romantic, and adventurous. It is a tale of hard-won professional development, extraordinary challenges faced and survived – sometimes only barely so.

It is supported by forty-four years of meticulously kept daily journals, written in tiny script, which are intimate, utterly frank, self-admonishing, and confessional. They encompass every aspect of what Peter Cundill justifiably referred to as his "wonderful life" – his professional career with all its vicissitudes, his numerous love affairs, and his sporting achievements, including twenty-two marathons, and his passion for the kind of physical challenges that not only test endurance but also confront the participant with moments of stark terror usually associated with war or natural disaster.

The journals explore depression and self-doubt. They tell not just of successes but also of failures and the lessons learned as a result; and they serve the function of a "commonplace book" in which Peter noted passages from his extensive reading, commented on them, and often developed the ideas they prompted. His interests spanned a diversity of disciplines, springing from a genuinely insatiable curiosity, a characteristic he regarded as a vital component in every aspect of life and especially his professional life.

The journals also exhibit a thoroughly open intelligence. Peter was ready to try almost anything and prepared to work to achieve success in any venture, or in the acquisition of any skill he decided to undertake. Mastery often came at real personal cost because, as he freely confessed, he was far from being naturally gifted at everything, and especially not in directions that required physical co-ordination in addition to the courage and determination that he possessed in abundance. What counted always was the learning process. The importance of continuing to learn throughout life was a recurring theme.

In his daily entries Peter often laughs at himself. His comments on others are usually trenchant and perceptive, but never cruel and rarely unkind. Most of his closest friendships were formed early; nevertheless, an enormous tapestry of friends and acquaintances throughout the world emerges over the years and they play a significant role in the development of his career; friends often led to investments and investments to friendships. Within the investment world, Peter met and visited with most of the great and the good – as well as some of the less than good – and his unrivalled capacity for international networking was clearly a hugely important component of his success.

His truly punishing travel schedules attest to his unremitting efforts to immerse himself in the culture and ethos of any country in which he contemplated an investment. In this he can, quite literally, alongside John Templeton, Charles Brandes, Mason Hawkins, and Prem Watsa, be said to have pioneered the international approach to value investment, particularly in respect to North America, which, at the outset of Peter's career in the 1960s and the early 1970s, could fairly have been described as bordering on the parochial. His approach to some degree mirrored that of the old-style merchant banker for whom it was as important to sniff the air and feel the texture as to study the numbers. An understanding of local issues and politics – imbibing the culture and character of the people – became essential to Peter's confidence in investing in sometimes unfashionable, outlandish, or just apparently unpromising locations; even when the numbers appeared compelling, if he became uncomfortable with the "feel," he would pass on an investment.

Peter's ways of "getting the feel" were to some extent unorthodox, even eccentric. The starting point in a new city was almost invariably a long run, often two hours or more, through the streets – people watching, taking in the flow of the city's life, even getting lost. Afterward, shorter runs around the town became part of the daily routine. Pre-planned and arranged calls would follow the first outing, and Peter would then rapidly assess which of the individuals he had met were likely to prove of ongoing value and were consequently worth developing as relationships. Sometimes, as he did in Hong Kong, London, Paris, and New York, he would rent an apartment and settle in for a stay of a few months, giving himself ample opportunity to visit individual companies and to get under the skin of the financial community. Even when he was only staying for a few days, his practice was to select a victim, usually an investment broker-age house, a money manager, or an investment bank, and beg the use of an office on their premises. There, with access to the technical back-up and communications resources necessary for his detailed analytical work, he would hunker down, receive visitors, and absorb the cut and thrust of their daily commercial life. The result of this approach was the cultivation of an almost uncanny instinct, a nose for a good potential investment, and a corresponding sense of unease when confronted with one that looked logically and statistically appealing, but simply did not smell right.

Peter's instinct was always firmly grounded on the Graham and Dodd principles of value investment that for thirty-five years were the back-bone and nervous system of his strategy. This form of grounding, in combination with attention to detail and endless patience, was the key to his magic. He believed that, while the necessary characteristics may be present to a varied extent in each individual, they can be developed and honed in almost anyone. The reader may conclude that this is too modest an assessment.

With his peripatetic existence – residence in London from 1985 onward and offices in Bermuda and eventually Hong Kong – it might be supposed that Peter's Canadian roots would weaken or gradually be transplanted, but this never happened. He remained inordinately proud of being Canadian and passionately interested in everything about his country, from politics and economics to the arts and education, to all of which he lent tangible support, which continues through The Peter Cundill Foundation. The names of great Canadian achievers, many of whom he knew or had known, were always on the tip of his tongue, often with an anecdote to match. And tellingly, within his journals, as lyrically and admiringly as he would describe far-flung places, he would often compare them nostalgically either with Vancouver or the province of Quebec, especially Montreal. In his heart he remained a Montrealer, and a gathering of Canadians, with a bit of Montreal, Toronto, or Vancouver gossip, never failed to delight him.

Peter had the unusual characteristic both of liking women's company and being totally at ease in an all-male environment. There were few instances in which a girlfriend or a serious love affair did not mature into a friendship; all were appreciated and none forgotten. Among his male friends there will not be many who have not confided in him and found a ready and sympathetic ear in times of joy and trouble. And there are many of both sexes who have received substantial material support when it was most needed, as well as wise advice and the discovery that doors they had imagined to be firmly shut somehow opened effortlessly to them.

The Peter Cundill Foundation, which now controls Peter's very considerable wealth, has supported and will continue to support a wide and international range of charities from sporting and academic, to artistic and educational, with a focus on youth. The Cundill Prize in Historical Literature, administered by his alma mater, McGill University, is the largest of its kind in the world, but it is only one example of his philanthropy.

In his professional journey Peter became more than a highly regarded and immensely successful mutual fund manager who made fortunes for others as well as himself; he was also a teacher and mentor, generous with his time and fully prepared to share his experience with aspiring new practitioners. This dedication to his profession, to the encouragement of its new blood and the propagation of the principles of value investing on the foundations laid by Graham and Dodd, would have been continuing today, and this book would have been an autobiography, had Peter not been struck by the affliction of Fragile X-associated Tremor/Ataxia Syndrome (FXTAS), a neurological disease whose symptoms closely resemble those of Parkinson's but is far less amenable to treatment.

The story of Peter's life is now, of course, concluded but, as I was working with him daily on this and the previous book, I came to realize that his finest hour was in fact in his brave struggle with his deteriorating disability. He was entirely without self-pity, good-natured and full of humour, and determined never to surrender to hopelessness or despair.

As Peter would have wished, I have been careful to continue the exposé of his investment approach which was initially explored in my previous book, *There's Always Something to Do*. However, in this book the reader will find much more than that and make the acquaintance of a remarkable, generous, multi-faceted and complex man whom I had the privilege, for over thirty years, of calling a friend.

PART · ONE ·

Some Family History

EARLY ONE MORNING in the spring of 1946, in a tiny, isolated cottage near the Laurentian village of Saint-Sauveur, about sixty miles from Montreal, a little boy, not quite eight, with fair hair and penetrating pale blue eyes, walked resolutely downstairs. Fully dressed, washed, and scrubbed, with his hair neatly brushed, he turned into the living room and, without an instant's hesitation, strode up to face the tall, uniformed officer standing beside his mother. Looking him squarely in the eye, he extended his right hand and said with courteous finality: "It's been very nice to meet you, Sir. You can leave now and I wish you a good journey home." The little boy was Peter Cundill and the man was his father, Frank, whom the boy had knowingly met for the first time only the previous evening.

This meeting might well never have taken place. Together with thousands of other Canadians, Frank Cundill had volunteered in 1939 at the outbreak of the Second World War. As an ex-officer cadet, he had tried to enlist in the Navy but had been brusquely informed that at thirty-seven he was far too old. Nevertheless, he persisted and eventually obtained a commission in the Black Watch, the oldest and most distinguished of Canada's Scottish regiments.

Frank Cundill was posted to a holding camp in Newfoundland and in August 1940, he and his battalion were shipped across the Atlantic. His wife and baby son of course remained in Canada. He was immediately thrust into a rigorous combat training program, largely in the rugged northern highlands of Scotland, and soon became involved in testing some of the "commando" tactics being pioneered by two eccentric, daredevil highland chieftains who were then popular with Winston Churchill: Lord Lovat and Colonel William Stirling, of Kier. As a result, early in 1942, a company of the battalion that, despite his age, included Lieutenant Cundill, was seconded to the Royal Regiment of Canada to prepare for the planned raid on Dieppe.

Having earned a reputation as a tough and effective instructor during the training in the highlands, he was given the task of organizing the regiment's final combat preparations. In an exercise using live ammunition he was shot through the back of his knee, putting him "hors de combat." To his disappointment, the task force of six thousand predominantly Canadian infantry embarked on 19 August 1942 without him. This may well have saved his life. The Dieppe raid was a catastrophe; when withdrawal was finally ordered, the expeditionary force had suffered casualties of nearly four thousand, well over half the entire complement. Although Frank's wound healed, he was classified as unfit for combat duty and sent back to Canada as a training officer.

Peter was fortunate to know his father at all and, in spite of its somewhat surreal beginning, their relationship developed into a much valued camaraderie. However, that happened much later. While it is a testament to his parents' good judgment and sense of humour that the incident in the Saint-Sauveur living room became a family legend, for a sensitive little boy who had never until then experienced anything less than his mother's undivided attention, the family's reunion was undoubtedly a traumatic experience. It ushered in a lonely period of adjustment and perhaps accounted for a lifetime of difficulty in forming committed relationships with women.

Records show that Peter's Cundill ancestors had been settled in England in the moors and dales of North Yorkshire since at least the fourteenth century. As Peter's story unfolds, it becomes clear that Yorkshire folk and Yorkshire institutions were of immense importance to him, especially at some critical moments early in his career. Yorkshire people have a reputation for innovation, rugged independence, and firm opinions and values, with an uninhibited sense of fun and the ridiculous – all characteristics that Peter inherited. They are also notoriously clannish; hence perhaps the importance for Peter of having an established Yorkshire background with solid Yorkshire antecedents.

A village named Cundall still sits today in the rolling arable land of the North Riding of Yorkshire – the name derives from the Old English word *cynedoel* ("royal dale"). With their predominantly blue eyes and fair hair, the settlers were almost certainly of Norse/Viking stock. Through the generations, the Cundills became prosperous farmers who leased from families of aristocratic landowners and were largely self-sufficient, raising cash crops to pay their rent. They employed their own servants and farm labourers, and their daughters married well into the families of other yeoman farmers and prosperous tradesmen who owned their own small businesses – blacksmiths, millers, shopkeepers, and innkeepers – in the surrounding towns and villages. They were sufficiently well off to set up their younger sons in trade and provide their daughters with dowries for comfortable marriages.

Peter was directly descended from a William Cundill (b. 1740), an impoverished yeoman farmer who maintained a few acres in Lincolnshire, just across the border with Yorkshire. His youngest son, John (b. 1784), inspired by the fiery oratory of John Wesley, founder of the Methodist church and a local Lincolnshire man, left the homestead to take up a career as a Baptist preacher. When John married in 1813, the couple moved to Chatham, a town dominated by massive naval dockyards in southeast England at the mouth of the Thames. He was ordained at the Calvinist Baptist Chapel three years later and promptly published a highly inflammatory pamphlet denying the existence of the Trinity. When his first wife died in childbirth – and perhaps also because he was finding Chatham a little too hot for comfort after the publication of the pamphlet – he moved to a ministry in the wealthy market town of Saffron Walden in Essex, where he remarried, producing two sons, Francis and John. By 1825 he had moved back up to Yorkshire and established himself as a Chapel preacher and schoolmaster in Hull, which was then enjoying a resurgence as a seaport serving the whaling industry and the cod-fishing fleets that trawled the Newfoundland banks.

The Cundill family settled into a decent house on the edge of the city looking out across green fields. But their comfort was short-lived. John died in 1826 of injuries sustained by a boiler explosion on a new steam-powered ferry in the Humber Estuary as he returned from preaching in a nearby town. He left the two boys, one barely a year old, and his young wife, Rebecca, who found herself in seriously straitened circumstances, notwithstanding a report in the *Hull Advertiser* that "a large sum has been raised for the family of Cundill." As a consequence, young Francis, Peter's great-grandfather, lived in dire poverty beside the belching chimneys of the potteries. His mother managed to teach him to read and write, but he was otherwise self-educated, making copious use of the circulating libraries of the day and developing an abiding interest in botany. As his daughter recalled years later, he was able to recite "yards" of Shakespeare, Wordsworth, and Tennyson with "dramatic delivery and fine modulation" and he had "an encyclopaedic knowledge of plants and trees."

Francis was apprenticed to a chandler near the docks in Hull. Having undergone a Dickensian regimen of long grinding work hours, he took off seafaring as soon as his mother died. Starting as a deckhand, he rose to the rank of purser, visiting most of the world's major mercantile ports. After almost twenty years of voyaging he returned to England and the great transatlantic port of Liverpool, where he worked for a time at a company engaged in the North American export trade. Finally in 1858 he took ship again, this time with a license to act as an import agent in his pocket. He sailed up the St Lawrence to disembark at Montreal, and there he settled.

Montreal in the 1860s was a thriving cosmopolitan centre universally regarded as the queen of Canadian cities. In 1850 the whole of British North America could claim a mere sixty-six miles of railway track, and within a decade it boasted over 1,800 miles. It was the decade in which the true foundations of Canadian industry and commerce were laid, and the country was consequently opened for the exploitation of the enormous reservoirs of natural resources in the west and the north that the world's rapidly industrializing economies were demanding in ever-increasing quantities. Montreal was Canada's main port of entry for the transatlantic flow of goods and people, and the railway paved the way for the development of new towns to accommodate growing populations in remote rural communities. The first Montreal to Toronto rail service was launched in 1856, and the St Lawrence and Atlantic Railway Company's line, between Montreal and Portland, Maine, an ice-free port, made it possible for commercial and passenger traffic to continue uninterrupted throughout the long winter months.

It was at this propitious moment – just before the discovery of gold in British Columbia and the new country's acquisition of vast resource-rich northern territories – that Francis Cundill, Peter's great-grandfather, chose Montreal to make his home, his career, and in due course his fortune. The years of seafaring, the apprenticeship in Hull and shipboard service out of Liverpool, and the centuries of traditional Cundill family involvement in trading and retailing in the market towns of North Yorkshire had clearly not been wasted.

By the early 1860s Francis had emerged as a successful importer, trading under the name Francis Cundill and Co., sole agents for a number of prestigious London-based companies that manufactured a broad range of products – from pickles to perfumes and hairpieces – all calculated to appeal to the increasingly prosperous citizens of Montreal and its new satellite towns. In addition, he had secured the agency for Jacob Wrench and Co., major British seed merchants who supplied the pioneer wheat farmers moving westward into the Prairies. Already by 1861 Francis was sufficiently established to be able to convince Emily Parkinson, the daughter of a wealthy Liverpool merchant – and perhaps more important, her family – that she should marry him at the second time of asking.

Between 1861 and 1875 the couple had six children. The business was thriving and the family homes became larger and better appointed to accommodate the growing brood and numerous staff. Peter's grandfather, another Francis, was born in 1866 when the family moved to a large, comfortable and newly built villa at the top of Avenue Durocher, not far from the Victoria Bridge, which now connected the island of Montreal with the east side of the mainland. The choice of this location may have been expedient: the new bridge carried the only rail link from Montreal south to New York City, making it a commercially convenient location for Francis's now-substantial trade.

The children of the Avenue Durocher household were educated at home as their father had been, although in their case it was no ad hoc affair at their mother's knee. Governesses taught them the basics: mathematics, English grammar and literature, history and natural history as well as some Latin. A lady from France, rather than a French Canadian, taught them that language. Mrs Cundill herself attended to the religious side and made no concessions to their father's non-conformist background. The children were brought up as proper little Anglicans as befitting the best Anglo-Montreal society. Of the four who survived into adulthood, the two older girls became teachers themselves and the youngest, evidently having thoroughly absorbed the principles of polite Protestantism, married an Anglican clergyman who eventually became a bishop.

Although Francis junior was offered the chance to attend McGill University, by now an internationally reputed institution, he did not take it up. Judging from his subsequent career, getting to grips with business right away likely appealed to young Francis. For an ambitious young man in a city whose population was growing from 50,000 in 1850 to more than 300,000 toward the turn of the century, opportunities must have appeared limitless. Montreal was then unquestionably the commercial and financial hub for the booming economy of the whole of the newly formed Dominion of Canada.

Thus Francis junior served his own apprenticeship in the family business. He had an enquiring mind, with a sharp commercial instinct and the personality to make full use of the trading connections established by his father. But he was really looking for an opportunity on a more ambitious scale than Francis Cundill and Co.'s general import trade, profitable though that was. In 1874 he came across a paper by Dutch chemist Jacobus van 't Hoff – later the first winner of the Nobel Prize for chemistry. It drew attention to some of the lesser-known properties of camphor, produced from the Camphor Laurel tree, then grown in abundance on the island of Formosa. The Chinese had been exploiting its medicinal and embalming properties for thousands of years, but it was now increasingly used in industry, for medicinal purposes, and as the functional ingredient in insect and moth repellents. Francis junior saw great possibilities in the craze for camphor.

Through Francis Cundill and Co.'s international connections, he made contact with some of the powerful British trading houses that effectively ruled Hong Kong, and succeeded in establishing links with camphor producers. Backed by his father's capital, he began to import camphor on his own account. With the main manufacturing and consumer base for the industrial production of camphor products in the United States, logic dictated that, as his business grew – as it rapidly did – Francis should relocate to the main port of entry for his new trade. In 1895 he moved to New York.

He was an immediate commercial and social success. In 1898 he married Ann Hampson, the daughter of a wealthy Quebec family that had settled in Canada a century earlier when the loyalist communities of the newly independent United States had fled north into British territory. Francis junior soon became the "King of Camphor," with a formidable reputation, both in New York and Montreal, as a shrewd businessman and a canny investor. By the time Peter's father, Frank, was born in 1902, the second of five children, the family had a house in Manhattan – a huge, baronial, German-built villa with five reception rooms set on the fashionable "heights" of Staten Island looking out toward the newly erected Statue of Liberty – as well as a seaside home in Connecticut.

A few months after Frank's birth, the first-generation Montreal Cundill died, having made a remarkable transition from extreme poverty in the potteries district of Hull, to wealth, status, and respectability in his adoptive country – a shining example of what might be achieved with the grit and industry he inherited from his old-world Yorkshire background. The original import business having by then been eclipsed by the success of Francis junior's camphor trade, the Camphor King wound down the Canadian company, and his mother moved with his sisters and a reduced household to a more convenient home in downtown Montreal. The New York business continued to thrive and expand, and the growing family enjoyed the charmed existence made possible by a tycoon's wealth. There Francis remained during the First World War, going on to profit from the extraordinary economic and financial boom of the early postwar years in America. By 1920, at the age of eighteen, Frank, ultimately Peter's father, had decided that he wanted a career in the navy and was enrolled in the Royal Naval College of Canada near Halifax, Nova Scotia; when it was closed two years later, he continued his training for a commission at its successor in Esquimalt, British Columbia. But a naval career was not to be.

Despite the booming times in New York, Francis soon faced trouble in the camphor market. While the world focused on the conflict in Europe, China had been steadily sinking into chaos following the extinction of Imperial rule in 1911. Chinese merchants had become unreliable and the price of natural camphor in Western markets was volatile and unpredictable. Synthetic camphor could also now be produced on economically competitive terms. By the mid-1920s the impact of these factors on Francis Cundill's business became critical and by 1927, after a series of poor trading judgments in the natural camphor market, his capital and credit were exhausted and he was forced into bankruptcy.

The impact was devastating for the whole family; their fairy tale life vanished overnight. Peter's father, Frank, was by then just twenty-five.

Because of his family's deteriorating financial position he had not been able to follow his chosen career in the navy and had witnessed the decline and eventual crash at first hand as he worked alongside his father. His view of his father as imprudent – even reckless – in his stubborn refusal to recognize that "terms of trade" had changed permanently led to an estrangement from which father and son never recovered. Fortunately neither old Mrs Cundill's assets nor Frank's mother's Hampson inheritance had fallen victim to the debacle of Francis's affairs, and the family held together in adversity. Mrs Cundill senior promptly provided them all with a home back in Montreal.

The Cundill children were quickly gathered back into Montreal society under the auspices of their mother and their grandmother. The two who were most damaged by the disaster were Francis and Frank. Francis retained much of his old charm and remained a convivial companion, but his commercial confidence and pride were deflated, and the long shadow of the bankruptcy sapped any will to launch a comeback. He led an unremarkable and aimless social existence and drifted slowly into alcoholism. He died in 1942, falling out of a window while inebriated.

For Frank, whose career had seemed clearly mapped out either as a naval officer with private means or in a successful family business, disappointment and shame over the bankruptcy were compounded by seeing his father's decline. But in Frank's case, the commercial and trading instincts, such a strong element in the Cundill family genes, quickly reasserted themselves. After a short stint as a cowboy and rodeo rider in Alberta, he returned to Montreal and found himself a job as a stockbroker with the Montreal firm of Kingstone Mackenzie. Eventually, with his mother's help, he bought a seat on the Canadian Stock Exchange and was soon launched on an entrepreneurial career as a stock trader.

It was not, of course, the ideal moment. The Wall Street crash of 1929 had repercussions for every market in the world and especially on New York's nearest northern neighbour. Strangely, however, Frank Cundill actually prospered under these conditions, building up a good client base and showing a natural flare for the business of sole trading in stocks. Nevertheless, it was nearly ten years before he felt financially secure enough to propose to Ruth Grierson, Peter's mother.

Ruth Grierson's family were of Scots origin on both sides – Grierson and Lawson – border raiders and cattle thieves, as well as hill farmers, landowners, and lawyers. The Griersons enjoy the distinction of having an ancestor who was killed at the Battle of Flodden in 1513 in the company of King James IV of Scotland. Peter's branch of the Grierson family emigrated to New England in the 1680s, probably fleeing the anti-papist sentiment that swept Britain in the aftermath of the defeat of King James II's Catholic army by his Protestant nephew William III at the Battle of the Boyne. They settled first in Boston, likely having first disassociated themselves from Catholicism, as there is no evidence that they followed anything but the Protestant persuasion thereafter. There they prospered, owning a smithy and a flour mill.

The Lawsons came of slightly grander stock – Scottish gentlemen and landowners. The first to reach New England was Henry Lawson, who arrived at Boston with the Winthrop fleet in 1631, escaping arbitrary taxes and heavy-handed attempts to impose uniformity of religion in Scotland. Henry Lawson obtained a land grant from John Winthrop, who held the governorship of the colony under the Royal Charter purchased from the cash-strapped Charles I. The family prospered as farmers, industrial entrepreneurs, and shipowners with a growing interest in the cod industry of the Grand Banks. John Lawson, Henry's descendant, became so involved in the cod industry that by the time Halifax was founded in 1749, following the fall of Quebec, he and his family had left Boston for the new city to be closer to the heart of the trade. By the end of the American War of Independence, the Lawsons were a well-established Nova Scotia family.

After the War of 1812 John's son, also John, purchased enormous quantities of prize vessels and goods captured by licensed privateers and the Royal Navy, which were auctioned off in Halifax. When the quantity became too large for the Canadian colony alone to absorb, John Lawson successfully petitioned to be allowed to export to the United States. Since the majority of these goods had been the property of American citizens in the first place, one can only imagine that he enjoyed the irony. By the time he died he owned shares of an iron foundry, the Shubenacadie Canal, and a whaling vessel as well as part of the Halifax cod-fishing fleet.

John's son, Peter's great-grandfather, the Hon. William Lawson, born in 1772, was the founding director and first president of the Bank of Nova Scotia. As Peter later discovered, his portrait hangs prominently in the boardroom at the bank's head office in Halifax. As a member of the House of Assembly, William had introduced the bill to provide the necessary charter for a public bank and guided it through against some persistent opposition.

By 1857 branches of both families had migrated to Ottawa, Canada's newly designated capital city, and when Frank Grierson married Frances Lawson in 1898, the Lawsons especially had become extremely well-connected insiders within the political power structures of the day. Frank, Ruth's father, was something of a maverick, well educated and well read, but a free thinker very much concerned with social issues. He was that attractive combination of strapping outdoorsman full of woodland lore, gifted sportsman, and intellectual, if a very left-wing one. He fought in the First World War, enlisting in the ranks rather than as an officer, and rose to the rank of sergeant on his own merits. He was blessed with an insatiable appetite for exploring the world around him, which he transmitted in full to his daughter and through her to Peter.

On Frank's return from the Western front in 1917, the Canadian government was grappling with conscription, a highly sensitive issue, especially among French Canadians. Frank Grierson was co-opted to run wilderness training programs for conscripts, which he did with an enthusiasm that came as an unwelcome surprise to many of the participants. He was in his element undertaking forced marches, carrying full equipment in the harshest winter weather, leading from the front. His regime prompted one victim to remark that he would likely be less in danger of fatal accident in the trenches.

But the war soon ended, as did the role Frank so relished, and a job stable enough for him to reinvent himself as a family man had to be secured. Through Lawson influence, and no doubt with some help from Prime Minister Borden, who was Ruth's godfather, a secure and reasonably well-remunerated civil service job was found for him. However, as events unfolded, it became clear that the new job could not satisfy Frank's restless energies or harness his increasingly left-wing ideals. When he took up the cudgels for a cause he did so with ruthless determination, and without concern for what his sponsors or in-laws might consider desirable or appropriate.

He was successful in two major initiatives: instigating the unionization of the Canadian Civil Service and fighting to secure adequate
pensions for disabled war veterans and war widows. Troublesome
though he may have been over the pension issue, it was hard for any
political party to dispute the justice of the cause. The unionization of
the civil service was another matter. From the government's point of
view it was highly undesirable, a step on the slippery road toward what
came to be known as the "British disease" – the dominance of con-
frontational, militant unions – and Frank Grierson himself was viewed
by many of Ottawa's political elite as a troublemaker. To his Lawson
in-laws he had betrayed the family trust and their good offices on his
behalf. The rupture was irreparable.

Frank's re-establishment as a full-time father and husband, however,
was an undisputed success story. For children he was a natural hero;
funny, gregarious, full of energy, and a great communicator; willing and
able to transmit his own enthusiasms as well as to enter unselfconsciously
into a child's world, with stories, games, songs, and fantasies. His daughter, Ruth, adored him and he inspired in her the limitless curiosity that
she was eventually to pass on so comprehensively to Peter. She was sporty,
intellectual, artistic, and highly independent of mind, and channelled her
own considerable energy and ambition through her children.

As might be expected with a father like Frank, her education, conventional as it may have been in school, was highly original in the home.
Dolls and frilly frocks were not for her; camping expeditions and the
great outdoors had far greater appeal. She had a refined musical taste
and played the piano stylishly and well. What her father instilled in her
was his own principle of taking on every endeavour with the determination to excel, to aspire to be the best, and to win.

Through her mother's Lawson connections, Ruth benefited from
daily exchange with the all important political and diplomatic figures
in Ottawa. With a highly respected ex–prime minister as her godfather,
her entrée was assured, and this access from early childhood made her
familiar, almost one of the family, within the circles that brokered
power and influence. As a natural debater with decided opinions of her
own, she was an ideal participant in the political salons of the day and,
had she been born a generation or two later, might herself have become
a politician.

Ruth would have made the perfect "blue stocking," but rather than go to university, which had been possible for women at McGill since the 1880s, she became private secretary to Vincent Massey. A distinguished lawyer, Massey became Canada's first fully accredited ambassador to the United States and ultimately Canada's first Canadian-born governor general. It was the kind of job to which Ruth was ideally suited. Massey was also president of Massey Harris (later Massey Ferguson), manufacturers of farm machinery, and a close friend of William Lyon Mackenzie King, the prime minister. His homes and his offices were venues for continuous streams of visitors who represented the commercial, political, and intellectual elite of Canada, as well as the senior members of the diplomatic corps. Ruth could hardly have imagined a more stimulating place to be, and Massey seems to have taken full advantage of her enthusiasm and energy, as well as her organizational talents.

In 1932 Massey became president of the National Liberal Foundation of Canada, further extending his political influence and importance and, with the return of the Liberal government under Mackenzie King in 1935, was appointed Canadian high commissioner in London. Before his departure he recommended Ruth to the new governor general, Lord Tweedsmuir, perhaps better known as John Buchan, the bestselling writer of *The Thirty-Nine Steps* and a host of other successful novels. And so Ruth joined the governor general's staff.

Ruth's social life revolved predominantly around sport. She was much sought after as a doubles partner at the Rideau Tennis Club, where she played on several teams. Not surprisingly, it was on the tennis court that she met Frank Cundill. They were married in 1938 and Ruth moved from Ottawa to her new husband's hometown of Montreal. It was there, in October of that year, that Peter was born.

2

An Unusual Childhood

THE EARLY YEARS of married life were a letdown for Ruth. She had supposed, with reason, that she had married into a moneyed family, so that, despite her husband's rather modest earned income as a stock trader, she could expect the means to maintain the comfortable standard of living she had always enjoyed. But the money in the family belonged to Frank's Hampson relations, including his mother, and to old Granny Cundill. It had not yet filtered down to Frank's generation, and in a family where the women were blessed with exceptional longevity it would be thirty years before it did. The ladies were decidedly careful, if not actually parsimonious, and they too may have borne scars from the Camphor King's bankruptcy and the memory of Frank senior's reputation for reckless commercial gambling on the market. Consequently purse strings were not appreciably loosened after the wedding, and the couple's married life began in an extremely modest apartment in the town of Baie d'Urfé, not even very close to Montreal. Ruth became pregnant almost at once.

Leaving Ottawa and relinquishing a job that passionately interested her was a sacrifice for Ruth. She had relished the stimulation of the political and diplomatic circles of the day in what remained very much a man's world – domesticity was not her natural bent. The Montreal society of which the Cundills were part, although congenial, was by contrast quite restricted. The anglophone community was already beginning to feel isolated and perhaps sidelined, if not yet actually beleaguered. Also it was essentially a society with a commercial rather than a political focus, and the city had already begun to surrender to Toronto its pre-eminence as Canada's financial hub. Ruth was unexpectedly parachuted into a relative backwater without sufficient means to be a leading light in it.

Further money problems were occasioned by Frank's weakness for a flutter on the horses. Ruth was never anything but outspoken and it is easy to imagine that the apartment in Baie d'Urfé rapidly became less cosy than a love nest. For Frank, the outbreak of the war may have come

as a heaven-sent opportunity to get away, with patriotism as a cast-iron
alibi. But a lieutenant's pay was insufficient even to keep up with the
small rent in Baie d'Urfé; the apartment was given up, almost certainly
with little regret on either side. However, the alternative of army accommodation proved even less satisfactory. There was simply not enough
money to rent anywhere that Ruth deemed suitable, and she was unwill-
ingly driven to beg rooming space from a number of her in-laws. She
rarely saw Frank during the war, and the family was not properly
reunited until he was finally demobbed in 1946. In the intervening years
Peter and Ruth lived a peripatetic, though not entirely uncongenial existence, but without a home they could in any sense call their own.

They were frequent guests of Peter's Hampson grandmother and a
variety of aunts and uncles, both in Montreal and in the beautiful Murray
Bay area, northeast of Quebec City overlooking the St Lawrence River –
a refreshing refuge from the steamy heat of Montreal at the height of
summer. The cottage near Saint-Sauveur, the scene of Peter's first postwar
meeting with his father, was only a temporary arrangement, although a
real boon because an old family friend had made it available at a pep-
percorn rent and they at least had it to themselves. Nestled deep in the
Laurentian Hills and surrounded by lakes, it was a summer paradise and
a skiing mecca in winter. However, during the long frozen months the
cottage had a minor disadvantage: it was heated only by a wood-burning
stove downstairs.

Peter had a vivid recollection of a frightening night at Saint-Sauveur
when he was a small boy. A howling mid-winter gale suddenly blew his
bedroom window open. Try as he might, the skinny little boy did not
have the strength to close it. He shouted repeatedly for his mother, to no
avail. Too scared to go downstairs in the dark, Peter tried to tuck himself
back into bed, but he just went on shivering under the blankets as the
room temperature plunged below freezing. Fortunately, with the window
banging, and snow gusting in onto his bed he was unable to get back
to sleep. Finally he did tiptoe down, only to find Ruth reading peacefully by the stove. Had he fallen asleep under those conditions, there
might well have been no biography to write. But the winters had their
charm, Peter remembered, on days when the clear skies and brilliant
sunshine turned the forest and countryside into a sparkling fairyland and
he would crunch his way through the snow to the village store to buy

fresh-baked bread for breakfast. His distinctive elflike ears were often nearly frostbitten by the time he got home again. Hitching a ride on a forester's jingling sleigh was not only fun, it was a welcome relief. The independence and adventure of those early morning expeditions gave him experiences he treasured for life.

In the best tradition of Jean-Jacques Rousseau, Ruth encouraged Peter to run somewhat wild, but she saw personally to his schooling, teaching him to read and trying desperately to train him to be right-handed. Her determined efforts were a torment he never forgot. That aside, she was always at hand to encourage him and answer his innumerable questions and she read to him at length: *Hiawatha*, *A Christmas Carol*, speeches from Shakespeare, *The Last of the Mohicans*, *The Odyssey*, *Alice in Wonderland*, and a children's version of Plutarch's *Lives* with illustrations by Walter Crane, including one of the death of Brutus, which impressed Peter deeply. Left to his own devices Peter read the Hardy Boys books, *Lassie*, *Bambi*, and Ernest Thompson-Seton's animal stories, and played for hours with his painted lead soldiers, devising battles with cannons that fired matchsticks. It was a solitary existence, with few friends his own age, but a life that fostered curiosity and a certain reflective introspection. Ruth's insistence that Peter keep a journal led to much resentment because she subjected the results to criticism, never praise. Her frustrated ambitions translated into a string of vicariously held aspirations for Peter which meant that his least failures were met with anger and severe punishment.

In these nomadic war years, Peter and Ruth spent part of the time in Toronto with his aunt and uncle, Joan and Peter Scott. "Uncle Pete" willingly engaged his nephew in outdoor ball games that Ruth did not play. (Later, as chairman of Wood Gundy investment bankers, he was an influential supporter of his nephew's professional development.) Summer journeys to Peter's grandmother's house at Cap à l'Aigle overlooking Murray Bay offered another adventure. The train trip from Montreal took a full day, with a change in Quebec City, and between trains, mother and son stretched their legs around the ancient ramparts. With their gun emplacements and old cannons, the walls enchanted this small boy already smitten by his armies of toy soldiers. At the citadel, which offers an uninterrupted view across to the Plains of Abraham, Peter's enduring fascination with history was awakened as he listened, wide-eyed, to the story of General Wolfe leading his five thousand men up the narrow cliff path in the dead of night, to take the Marquis de Montcalm completely by surprise the following morning, thereby transforming Canada's future forever.

Young though he was, Peter clearly remembered the bustle and excitement surrounding the May 1944 Quebec City Conference that was taking place as the family made its way to Murray Bay. The sessions were hosted by Prime Minister Mackenzie King and attended by Franklin Delano Roosevelt and Winston Churchill, as well as both of Ruth Cundill's ex-employers, Vincent Massey and Lord Tweedsmuir. As they afterward learned, these were the final planning meetings between the two principal allies for the D-Day landings a month later. But Peter's strongest recollection of these trips was an occasion when the burly porter in charge of the Pullman car from Montreal to Quebec City allowed the little boy – impeccably dressed in a grey flannel suit and with neatly brushed flaxen hair – to stand beside him and collect tickets as the passengers boarded the train.

Murray Bay is often referred to by its old French name, La Malbaie, which, the story goes, it acquired from Samuel de Champlain as he was exploring the St Lawrence River in 1608. Champlain had moored his ships in the bay for the night, unaware that as the tide goes out the bay empties completely. He woke up the next morning to find his vessels beached and, realizing there was no alternative but to wait for the next high tide, exclaimed: "Ah, la malle baye!" – and it stuck. Toward the end of the nineteenth century the area was rediscovered as a summer resort destination for the "high society" of Montreal and New York, who arrived by steamers known as "floating palaces." A luxury hotel and a golf course were built, and magnificent summer residences sprang up along the Chemin des Falaises with splendid views of the St Lawrence. The area became fashionable through the influence of the Taft family and particularly William Howard Taft, the United States president, who declared that the air was "as intoxicating as champagne, but without the headache in the morning." The Tafts were soon joined by the Cabots, and the cream of Boston and New York society followed suit. Murray Bay became known as the "Newport of the North" and by some was considered even more exclusive.

The Mrs Cabot who was a figure in Murray Bay society in Peter's youth was an enthusiast of amateur dramatics, mostly of the Gilbert and

Sullivan genre, but she occasionally turned her hand to more serious drama. When Peter was eleven she attempted a mid-summer production of *Macbeth*, to which all the visiting socialites were bidden. Peter was not expecting to participate other than as a spectator, but destiny waited in the wings. The role of Banquo was being played by a very pretty, although highly strung, young lady who was already nervous at the prospect of being murdered by Macbeth's thugs. Matters were made worse in rehearsal when the strapping lads cast as the assassins set about their work with real vigour. They were no doubt bursting with testosterone and over-excited at the prospect of manhandling such a pretty girl under theatrical license. However, this sensitive Banquo drew the line and refused ever to be murdered again. As Mrs Cabot's eye roved across the hall in search of a substitute, it fell upon Peter among the onlookers at the rehearsal. In a flash of inspiration, she co-opted him to be murdered instead. He made his stage debut with a walk-on role and eight spoken words. The stage directions for the scene are:

[*The murderers set upon Banquo.*]
BANQUO
O, treachery! Fly, good Fleance, fly, fly, fly!
[*Dies. Exeunt murderers.*]

Peter maintained that he received rave reviews.

The Murray Bay summers were full too of the kind of sporting activity that was to become a big part of Peter's life. Tennis in particular was a family pastime. Both his parents were excellent players and his aunt Phoebe Grierson had been a Canadian mixed doubles champion. It never took much to rouse Peter's competitive instincts and tennis was quickly adopted as something at which he intended to excel.

Peter's enduring memories of these annual visits still moved and thrilled him over sixty years later: the daily passage of the two enormous Canadian Steamship Lines vessels, bringing visitors to and from Montreal and the U.S. Eastern seaboard, passing each other in mid-stream with their horns blasting and echoing round the bay, accompanied by the shouts and greetings of the excited passengers; Sunday visits to the tiny Anglican church of St Peter on the Rock at Cap à l'Aigle – a charming building of latticed pine, painted red, with white gothic windows and

roofed with black cedar that gave the interior a sweet scent, oddly min-
gled with the tang of the creosote primer. Many years later Peter was to
help generously with much-needed restoration.

By 1947 life had begun to resume a more conventional course in the
Cundill family. Peter's father had been demobbed, his mother became
pregnant again with his brother, Grier, and the family had settled into a
modest but comfortable rental apartment on the upper floor of a
Victorian house at Wood Avenue in Westmount. With the family's help
Peter was able to start immediately at Roslyn, a school for boys at the
foot of Mount Royal, and then, aged twelve, to move on, as a day boy,
to Lower Canada College, set in its fine seven-acre campus along the
Avenue Royale. There he was competent enough academically; but he
really began to shine on the sports field, particularly at football, making
it onto the senior squad, as well as being the highest scorer on the basketball team.

As Peter's features firmed up and began to mature into their distinctive
adult lines, they earned him the nickname "Lips," which the basketball
team caricature ably illustrates. His final football season was brought
to an abrupt halt by a serious back injury in which he suffered a burst
kidney, but even this did not stop him from carrying on with basketball.
As Peter himself related, Stevie Penton, the headmaster of Lower Canada
College, was a good friend and a wise judge of character. By the end of
Peter's year in the Lower Sixth form, Penton deemed that another year
at LCC risked redoubling "Lips's obvious swagger," making him too
bumptious for comfort. On Penton's advice, Peter's parents settled for
the option of sending him to McGill University a year early, where it was
felt that he might profit from having some of the excess stuffing knocked
out of him. Peter's *valete* notice in the LCC magazine of 1956 tells its own
story, suggesting that the headmaster was probably right.

FP CUNDILL
"It's Peter Cundill time."
"Lips" is an influential member of the class, and the most active.
He doubtless holds some sort of record for the number of
extracurricular activities he engages in. Needless to say he is our
Eaton's Junior Executive. His quarterbacking season was unfortu-
nately cut short by a hefty kick in the back which burst a kidney

and cracked his spine. But "Lips" was walking around after only one day's absence and he went on playing basketball and ended up first place scorer. As class captain, he seems to enjoy imposing his will on others, though he has had to stand up to the worst razzings Carrique can muster up.

So ended Peter's childhood and early education.

3

Rites of Passage

PETER RECEIVED A Bachelor of Commerce degree from McGill University, which at that time offered modules in financial accounting. He saw the discipline as elegant and intellectually stimulating – the commercial end of mathematics, with a subtly nuanced language that allowed initiates to read between the lines. It pointed him toward professional qualification as a chartered accountant and suggested an ultimate career direction in the investment industry rather than a big accounting firm. His father fully supported the idea; Frank had remarked that Peter had better not be a gambler like him, or at least, if he were going to be, he'd better have a professional qualification to fall back on. It was sound advice. Although Peter never had to adopt the fall-back position of becoming a practising accountant, there would be moments when it seemed it might be necessary.

In his four years at McGill, he continued his sporting activities, although not with the prowess he might have anticipated. Principal Penton had been right on the mark; McGill proved to be a considerable challenge, as Peter experienced what it is like to go from hero to zero overnight. Character-building it may have been, but it was also deflating, and his ego took a considerable knock, culminating in the humiliation of his failing a module in history, of all subjects. He passed the retake with distinction but it cost him a trip to Europe and a summer of painting the railings around the McGill campus. He emerged a perhaps wiser, though considerably less confident young man, and physically he was bordering on the podgy. Nor had his encounters with women been conspicuously successful. In those years, nice girls held back unless marriage was in prospect, and often even then.

However, his time at McGill had cemented one lifelong friendship and formed another. Peter and Michael Meighen first met when they were both twelve, when the Cundill family moved into a house that had previously belonged to the Meighens in Parkside Place, adjacent to Mount

Royal Park. The boys had enjoyed a friendly acquaintanceship ever since, but they became staunch friends at McGill. Michael's father was a successful lawyer from a well-known political family – his grandfather Arthur Meighen had succeeded Sir Robert Borden as prime minister of Canada. The two families were certainly familiar with each other and knew each other by reputation as well as having friends and acquaintances in common. But from their university days Michael and Peter's lives became intertwined on more than a superficial level. Their friendship was to endure until Peter's death, encompassing a long and close business association, and political and philanthropic activities, as well as many a fine party. Each of them contributed in large measure to the career success of the other.

George MacLaren was another great friend from Peter's undergraduate days. His family had been influential in Quebec since the early nineteenth century, founding not only MacLaren Power and Paper, then one of Canada's top hundred companies, but also the Bank of Ottawa and the Ontario Central Railway. George was not interested in joining the family business but, on top of being excellent company with a great sense of humour, he had a questing mind, incisive legal acumen, and sound commercial instincts. By the time the MacLaren company was bought out by Noranda in 1981, George was a successful commercial lawyer and businessman. Sharing Peter's love of Montreal and the province of Quebec, George eventually went on to occupy the influential post of Quebec's agent general in London. Once again, friendship and business life were to be interwoven over the years.

Immediately after graduation in 1960, Peter joined a group of McGill and University of British Columbia graduates on the SS *Homeric*, an Italian liner that plied the northern Atlantic route to Southampton and Le Havre. On board, the graduation was once again comprehensively celebrated. Fortunately the seven-day crossing was relatively calm and the sea air and deck quoits blew away the cobwebs. Gerry Williams, an English friend from McGill, met him at London's Victoria Station and whisked him off for a weekend at his family home in Kent, where the partying continued.

That Monday, reality took over, and he began work. After a night at a thoroughly grim bed-sit in a dingy London suburb and an uninspiring English breakfast at a "greasy spoon," Peter took the "tube" into the City,

London's financial heart. Thanks to the good offices of his uncle Pete Scott, who had made the arrangements with Wood Gundy, then the premier Canadian broking and investment banking presence in Europe, Peter would receive the princely sum of twelve pounds a week – at the top end of the going rate for graduates in the City. But no other concession was made to the family connection; he was promptly dropped in at the deep end and given the task of overseeing the London branch's stock-positioning book. After six weeks he was "promoted" to the role of junior dealer, a far more exciting job, particularly as the Canadian stock market was then enjoying a boom in mining shares, notably the more speculative and volatile ones.

Lunchtime for senior people in the City of London at that time was a two-to-three-hour affair starting with aperitifs and finishing with port or brandy and cigars. Even at more junior levels the concept of a sandwich at the desk was unheard of; whether traders, office clerks or post room staff, everyone expected to leave their office for at least an hour every day for a "pie and a pint" – which on a Friday might well become two or three. So Peter often found himself at midday, handling the dealing desk on his own. Since most clients were also out lunching, this was normally a quiet and reflective occupation, consisting of flicking through the pink pages of the *Financial Times* or even some less august publication. However, on one occasion the phone rang unexpectedly and the voice at the other end shouted, "Quick, gimme a price in Steep Rock." Peter, the junior dealer, did not hesitate. "Six to a half," came smartly out. "A thousand sold to you," said the voice. When the other dealers returned from lunch, they were aghast; Peter had been unaware that he was not empowered, or for that matter licensed, to trade. There was no question of "undoing" the bargain – that would have been regarded as highly unprofessional – but it had to be covered, and swiftly. Fortunately for Peter, the team succeeded in closing it out with a respectable profit; otherwise his nascent career in securities might have been abruptly curtailed.

In his six months with Wood Gundy, Peter picked up a great deal about how and why London operated as the dominant financial centre in Europe. The technology, as well as the business practices, had in many ways changed little from the late nineteenth century. Most of the trading still took place in Threadneedle Street on the floor of the Stock Exchange. The market makers in individual stocks and bonds, the "jobbers," still strolled through the alleyways in black top hats and striped trousers, swinging their tightly furled umbrellas. The pubs and the eateries, like the George & Vulture and Sweetings, the famous fish and oyster bar, retained their Victorian character and club-like ambience.

Wood Gundy had carved out a special niche in one peculiarly arcane market: the trading of "premium dollars." Under the exchange control system of the time, British institutions that wished to buy overseas securities were obliged to buy their foreign currency from a finite pool provided by the Bank of England. The exchange rate for these "dollars" was directly determined by supply and demand, since any sale of foreign investments increased the pool and the purchase of them shrank it. It was a volatile and highly technical market – and potentially highly profitable. The architect of Gundy's involvement was Ian Steers, who was to be the initiator of his firm's immensely successful participation in the Eurobond market that began to emerge three years later in 1963. Peter and Ian immediately liked each other and became firm friends, as they remained, developing a stimulating business relationship of enormous value to them both.

Shortly after Christmas, spent in the country with the Williams family, Peter crossed the channel for the second part of his European work experience. At that time the trip took at least eight hours – even longer if the going was rough. But Peter was thrilled to watch the "white cliffs" shrinking as the coast of France approached and to see the contrast in the landscape between the cosy apple orchards of Kent and the rolling plains of Northern France, with the prospect of Paris ahead of him. Through Gerry Williams's brother Paul, he was offered shared accommodation on a yacht, the *Maltouka*, which was moored in the Seine directly opposite the Eiffel Tower. It was, of course, a fantastic venue for parties and the three "flatmates" who shared it took full advantage. They were even allowed to sail the boat up and down the river whenever they chose, which would be quite out of the question today.

Peter's Parisian *stage* was rather a grand one. From the yacht he walked to work along one of the city's most magnificent routes – up the Avenue Matignon, past the windows of the renowned fashion houses, to the Rond-point des Champs-Élysées and then along the Rue Royale, past the red awning of Maxim's restaurant, into the Rue St. Honoré and through to the Place Vendôme. His new office at Morgan Guaranty was

across the square from the Ritz Hotel in a spectacular building, originally
constructed in the early eighteenth century as an aristocratic residence
and later occupied by Benjamin Franklin when he was ambassador to
the court of Versailles for the fledgling United States of America – an
association that Morgan Guaranty, naturally enough, relished.

After a short stint on the ground floor as a teller, Peter was promoted
upstairs to the research department, whose task was to make equity
investment recommendations in U.S. stocks and bonds to the banks and
insurance companies clustered along the nearby Boulevard Haussmann.
The most interesting aspect of it for Peter was the freedom to browse
through the Morgan Guaranty files, which covered all their French relationships, both with their institutional clientele and, perhaps even more
intriguingly, with the wealthiest families of France and Belgium.

Two events from his Paris stay left an especially lasting impression.
He was fortunate to obtain tickets to one of Edith Piaf's last public performances at the historic Olympia, the city's famous music hall. The
diminutive Piaf, already suffering from the cancer that was to kill her
two years later, was well aware that this season would probably be her
last. With every ounce of her remaining strength she gave her beloved
Parisians the performances of her life, even collapsing on stage in one of
the last shows. Peter was bowled over by the power and passion of the
voice that emanated from this tiny creature – *le moineau*, the "sparrow."
She truly seemed to express the raw spirit of the city that lay beneath its
supremely elegant surface. The emotion of the experience brought Peter
to tears, and he never forgot it.

The other event turned out to be one of the major, enriching discoveries of Peter's life. His twice-daily walks led him past the Jeu de Paume in
the Tuileries Garden, the old royal tennis court attached to the palace of
the Louvre. Before becoming a gallery for the world's most renowned
collection of Impressionist paintings, the building had served as the first
debating chamber of the French Revolutionaries. One afternoon, having
nothing better to do, Peter wandered in. The vibrant shimmering colours,
revealingly frank portraits and luscious landscapes of the unique trade-
marks of the Impressionist revolution sparked his lifelong passion for
art. From then on, no matter how busy or crowded his schedule, Peter
would make a point of visiting and revisiting the important galleries of
every city in which he found himself, especially those that housed fine

Impressionist works. Viewing a city's collections became part of the process of getting under the skin of a place – an essential element of his investment approach.

A frequent guest at the parties on the yacht was Patricia Welbourn, another McGill graduate of Peter's vintage, who was in Paris improving her French. She was being courteously – but relentlessly – pursued by a personable young Frenchman who fancied himself something of a Don Juan and clearly had amorous expectations. Patricia, however, was a well-brought-up young lady and this was still only 1960. Consequently, although attracted to the young man and a little flattered by the Gallic exuberance of his pursuit, she remained unconquered. Toward the end of her stay, her admirer suggested a trip to Spain *à deux* before her return to Canada. A visit to Spain was appealing, but the *à deux* part was slightly unnerving, so Patricia turned to Peter, whose three-month work placement was also about to end. Would he like to join the expedition, she asked, to make the twosome a threesome, with the idea that his presence might dampen her suitor's ardour a little? Peter was delighted at the chance and quite content to play quasi-chaperone, and so they set off together for Barcelona and the Costa Brava. The French beau, although disgruntled at first, had the grace to adjust to the arrangement and seemed prepared to have a good time anyway – which they did.

The bullfighting season was just opening, and there was more music and pageantry than usual to camouflage the gore and no need to pay premium prices for seats in the shade. Franco's Spain had one major advantage for the dollar tourist: whatever the politics, it was extremely cheap, so the three of them were able to hit the nightclubs and flamenco bars to their hearts' content and gorge on the stupendous array of *tapas* and accompanying libations. And it was warm enough for a visit to the beach – which was where they had their encounter with the Guardia Civil. None of the three spoke Spanish and the staccato delivery of the Guardia instructions had them mystified to begin with. But the officer kept pointing at Patricia and shaking his head. It eventually dawned on them that a bikini did not provide sufficient covering of her shapely figure to meet the standards of public decency in "old Spain." They beat a hasty retreat, but they did notice that the officer's gaze lingered on Patricia for some time.

As the trio progressed back up the coast toward Barcelona, Peter made friends with a young Argentine, a fellow tourist who spoke excellent

English. He proposed himself as the group's interpreter and guide for a visit to Madrid. Peter leapt at the idea, but Patricia had to get back to Paris to catch her flight home. The good-byes were said quite tenderly, as Peter was by this time smitten by Patricia, and she enjoyed his company. Their relationship eventually developed into Peter's first real love affair and ultimately into a lifelong friendship. In the meantime, he and his new Argentine friend hopped onto the train for Madrid to continue the Spanish adventure. Both of them were still well in funds, not thanks to any attempts at economy but purely because the favourable exchange rate made for bargain prices. So they made straight for the Ritz, Madrid's most palatial hotel, set amid luxuriant gardens and practically overlooking the famous Prado Museum. They treated themselves to a splendid room for $10.00 a night.

Their first morning was the Thursday of Easter week. After an uproarious night on the town doing the rounds of the bars of the Plaza Mayor, the carousers woke to a thudding sound from the street below. As it intensified, they roused themselves and, slightly unsteadily, made their way to the shuttered windows. What met their eyes was a procession of hooded individuals, looking not unlike the Ku Klux Klan, following the statue of a heavily bejewelled and crowned Madonna, enthroned and borne aloft on a float to the sombre beating of drums. As the procession came closer and Peter could focus more clearly, he was able to make out the most arresting and shocking part of the spectacle. The majority of the hooded processors were flagellating themselves with barbed flails and wailing, presumably for the forgiveness of their sins.

The flagellation was no mere ritual pretense; the white cloaks were torn open at the back and stained with blood. It was an annual penitential rite, a remnant from the Inquisition – the procession of the faithful who wound their way to the Plaza Mayor for an *auto-da-fé*, dragging along the supposedly heretical victims destined for live burning. With their grandstand view, the two lads watched spellbound as the hooded cloaks went out of sight and the drums and wails faded away. After they had witnessed that display of self-mortification, the barbarism of the bull ring seemed less inexplicable. Peter came to see it as the highpoint of the trip because it offered an "insight" – a word that frequently recurs in his journals, by which he meant a sharpened perception about people, places, and investment opportunities.

The low point of the trip soon followed. As in all Roman Catholic countries, Good Friday is traditionally a day of fasting on which no meat is consumed, and travellers have frequently found that they ignore this stricture at their peril. Peter's journey back to Paris was a blur punctuated by dashes for the lavatory. He had foolishly elected to eat chicken.

4

The Early Journals: A Sampler

AFTER HIS YEAR away Peter returned to Montreal to begin what was to be a lifelong association with Price Waterhouse. He worked through his Chartered Accountancy articles and wrote his exams, not without having to resit a module. By the spring of 1963, still waiting to learn if he had qualified, he had moved out of the family home in Parkside Place, set himself up independently in a shared apartment, and joined the investment firm of Greenshields, a respected stockbroker and dealer with headquarters in Montreal. Having completed the beginner's obligatory round of departments, from back office and postroom through to Institutional Equity Sales and Investment Banking, Peter was keen to join the Special Projects Department, which covered mortgages and real estate finance. He had already been noticed by Frank Trebell, Greenshields' general manager in Montreal, who was prepared to support this move.

During this time, Peter made a momentous decision. On 16 August 1963 he began to write the journal that he then kept faithfully, day by day, for over forty years. However discouraging his mother had been about the style and content of his juvenile efforts, he must have acquired some of the true diarist's discipline. And he had learned that a *private* diary could potentially be one's best friend – an uncritical confidant for one's frustration and pent up emotion, and a sounding board for the pros and cons of life decisions. The exercise can be a habit-forming, even addictive pastime, and Peter was naturally disposed to establish strict routines that he respected, barring compelling reasons to change.

The first entries are not in any way remarkable, but four brief asides give an indication that this journal was unlikely to be dull. They offer clues as to what preoccupied Peter then and continued to do so throughout his life. Here is some of what he wrote in those early jottings:

– ½ million Americans own stocks and that's more than the whole population of Canada!

– I ran for about half an hour before work. Played tennis with John Bridgeman. Lost – must improve. It's not a battle of technique but of the mind.
– I'm reading Erich Fromm's "The Art of Loving." He says that sexual desire can be stimulated by very strong emotion, even the wish to hurt. Love is just one of these emotions. I think I'm very susceptible to that one. Talked about Fromm with JB and my book.
– There's been an elephant in the fridge, trampling on the peanut butter and I wish he had smaller feet.

His most natural tendency was to write about investment matters, drawing useful inferences from his reading. Sport and fitness were frequent features, including the competitive instinct and the drive to excel. The nature of human love, sexual attraction and sensuality, especially in the context of his personal sexuality, was another preoccupation, and he was a critical observer of human behaviour and habits. But the censure of the "elephant," whoever that may have been, is tempered with characteristic humour and tolerance. Perhaps most striking of all is the reference to "his" book already in the very first pages of the journal.

His interest in art also appears early on, as he explores the role of the journal in his life. Of the exhibition of the great French impressionist sculptor Auguste Rodin that came to Montreal that year, he observed: *The Rodin exhibition was truly impressive. It makes me really want to do my exercises. The muscles all strain; the emotion is immense. I noticed the fine technical detail. These sculptures really pulse. It's the first time that any sculpture has really excited me. I'm convinced that to achieve real greatness an artist needs above all to have passion but at the same time immense discipline, concentration, patience and an unshakeable determination to become a master of his craft. To some extent all that must be desirable in one's own profession as well.*

Do I, in fact, hear myself when I think? I believe that I think better through writing my thoughts down. Perhaps I anticipate a biography as I watch my own development. If so I'll need to make something interesting of myself first.

Peter's journal also documents the vicissitudes of his social life, particularly his relations with women, which by now had begun to liven up considerably. The dearth of conquests was the paramount factor in his determination to shed his puppy fat, to become fit and eventually super-fit. At this point his views on women were not clouded by romance, and he subjected several of the girls he met to some acute analysis. *Had dinner with V and others. She is bright but she seemed to be apologizing for Vancouver, which according to her is a cultural backwater. At 24 she is so conventionally upper-class. She's quite pretty but she just wants to marry the boy next door back home. Big deal!! And yet I ask myself why would I not give myself heart and soul to one woman exclusively – basically I'm shy of girls, although sex often seems to be the reward of those who don't actually go looking for it.*

In early September the news came through that he was fully qualified as a chartered accountant, one of only 675 who had passed out of 1,260 candidates. Almost as soon as the celebrations were over, Peter pressed for an interview with Michael Boyd, in charge of Greenshields' Special Projects department. Peter was dubious about the outcome: *Perhaps I was too sharp and too profane, but I felt I had to get my point across and clear the air.* Whatever his tactic, it must have been successful. A week or so later he became a member of the Special Projects team. The explosion of energy sparked by his having a defined role, as well as some real responsibility and the chance to shine, comes across at once. *Starting tomorrow, I'm going to do deals. I shall start talking to lawyers etc. and doing deals. Call everybody. Use the mortgage list.*

Peter's commercial instincts also started to take on a sharper and more deductive perspective, beginning, as though instinctively, to focus on possible investment ideas. *U.S. Treasury Silver is being sold at $1.293 per troy ounce; the price at which the value of the metal in a U.S. Silver Dollar is equal to its monetary value. The most important factor in the silver market must be the phenomenal growth potential in its industrial uses rather than the more traditional jewellery and decorative art markets. To me this looks like mispricing based on misconception.* This from a twenty-four-year old novice nearly two decades before the Hunt brothers tried to corner the silver market and drove the price up to over $50 an ounce.

Peter's search for a basis of investment judgment or a forecasting mechanism that could measure the relative merits of different investment ideas also forms a thread in the early journals. He became interested in the "Elliot Wave" principle and the possibilities of charting as a price-predictive tool. As a fellow chartered accountant, Peter was predisposed to give Elliot some credence: *Human endeavour does appear historically to move in cycles. It is much influenced by fashion and the herd instinct – boom leads to bust, bubble to burst – but whether these phenomena can be analysed mathematically and then extrapolated to give indications of the timing of such trends in the future is quite another matter. What seems incontrovertible is that there are times when things ... reach price levels out of all proportion to their present or future economic value and there are times when the very same things sink to price levels significantly below their intrinsic value. The difficult problem is in recognizing these water-sheds, in having the ability to think clearly and objectively in the midst of the surrounding euphoria or panic. Perhaps Elliott's theory may be one way of helping one to do this.*

As we shall see, Peter later dismissed Elliott as a useful tool for investment decisions. In fact he ended up having no faith in any form of macro-forecasting, directing his attention almost entirely to the particular instead. Reading between the lines, he appears to be already on the verge of becoming a convert to value investment principles. *No investor can properly come of age until the statistics that he works with mean something to him. They must live, and the inferences that he draws from them must begin to be intuitive. One should constantly be on the look-out for statistical bargains and then apply common sense to determine whether they are real bargains.*

Styles and techniques of management and negotiation also started to feature significantly in the journal around this time. Frank Trebell triggered one line of reflection by remarking that in order really to succeed in any business one needed to develop the instincts of an owner rather than just an employee. The point was not lost on his protégé. Peter Scott, by now chairman of Wood Gundy, also began to interest his nephew from a managerial standpoint. *Uncle Pete very much has the ability to see what really matters through the excitement of daily events. He has the uncanny knack of going to the heart of a problem immediately and he employs about a dozen people to supply the answers.*

And Peter had begun to develop a realistic appreciation of the importance of taking the trouble to get to know his colleagues and business associates on more than a merely superficial level. *I want to know as much as possible about those I'm doing business with; their motivation, their desires and their demons, their abilities and their resources. If others remain unaware of my own that leaves me with a competitive advantage.*

This perspective led him to the realization that one should respect the capacities and morality of colleagues even if one did not like them personally or spend leisure time in their company. For companionship there would always be friends, who might or might not be workmates. Peter began to think about what really constitutes job satisfaction and whether for him this meant power, or money, or both; or possibly something entirely different. His early questioning is revealing. *Do I want my job to become my obsession, I'm not sure? What I do know is that I want to do something which will engage my spirit and all my faculties; my very being, and why should this not be my profession?*

Peter's characteristic, self-admonitory exhortations soon became a feature of his journals, and from this point on they tell us much about the lifestyle and the habits he believed he should cultivate, and in what directions he felt he needed to improve. *Work at a variety of things; keep active in mind, spirit and body. So; learn to drive, improve your squash, improve your French, get the insurance company going and learn to cook properly.*

How did he do? He did eventually learn to drive, mainly because he was embarrassed at having to rely on friends, but fortunately for himself and the public at large he never came to love it and, as soon as he had the means, he opted for chauffeur-driven car and limousine. He worked doggedly at French, taking hours of conversation classes with a stupendously unattractive French lady, and making copious notes on vocabulary and colloquial expressions – and the occasional obscenity – and at the end of it all, he was able to deliver more or less competent speeches in French. The cooking, however, was shelved in favour of restaurants at the earliest opportunity, much to his friends' relief. He lists some pretty unspeakable recipes: *Put too much molasses in the lamb casserole – tried to improve it by adding mint sauce and lots of pepper – just made it worse but everyone ate it after they got drunk. My stomach is awful today.*

Peter's athletic interests began to broaden in new directions, to squash and racquetball as well as tennis and, surprisingly, for the first time even though his father had tried to enthuse him as a boy, to skiing. Now he became a lifelong fan. *Skied out at Marquise Hill; magnificent sport. I learned to use the poles as pivots and put weight on the downhill ski … Skied at Avila. I've got the bug. Back to the Meighens' for turkey supper and then drove home elated on a starry night.*

Running, of course, remained a big feature, and the first of many such descriptions appeared, illustrating his sensitivity to natural beauty as well: *I ran with a beautiful view from the La Malbaie shore across to the Cabot Property. Cloud together with sun brings everything to life so that it hits you in the face.*

Among his commentaries on his social life are reports on dinners, concerts, parties, and movies in the company of a stream of attractive young women. His tastes were becoming more sophisticated. *Lunch at the Regent Club, where I had a Black Velvet for the first time; Guinness and champagne, half and half. Well worth the experiment and combined with the oysters it apparently does wonders with the libido – not that I'm much in need of stimulation in that department.*

The lack of a steady girlfriend began to disturb him more and more. His deliberations on the subject were always those of an instinctive gentleman, albeit one with quite an arsenal of pent-up frustrations, there being no indication so far that the permissive society had yet reached Montreal. *They say that to be successful with women one must not seem to care too much. (Nuts!! I think somehow that's wrong.) One ought to care and to be responsible.*

However, an entry from shortly afterward may explain a lot about Peter's apparently half-hearted dating. The Costa Brava holiday as Patricia Welbourn's escort and chaperone turned out to have meant a good deal more to him than just a passing fancy on vacation: *Heard that Patricia's father died. I called her. She has been in Edmonton since October 23rd and leaves in January to return to London. She hopes to come back to Montreal in April or June. I was terribly excited to hear her voice. I think I've had had a bucketful of emotion for the day.*

Another intense emotional response was elicited by a more public death that occurred a few days later: *President Kennedy was shot and killed today and it has affected nearly everyone in Canada, perhaps more than if our own Prime Minister were assassinated. What is obvious is the way we count ourselves as part of America. And then there are the endless rumours that have begun to fly around almost immediately after it happened; Russian communist and Cuban conspiracies as well as the mafia and the CIA ... I suppose crisis acts as a stimulant to every man. I know I enjoy it in a macabre sort of way. I heard a young fellow say, "I wanted to go into my room and cry"; I felt like that too.*

He logged accounts of concerts and the broad range of books he was reading: John Masters on tiger hunting, Jacques Cousteau on deep sea exploration, John Dos Passos, Dostoevsky, and Victor Hugo, as well as numerous anthologies of poetry, Edward Fitzgerald's translation of *The Rubaiyat of Omar Khayyam*, and the works of Spinoza. Nor did his interest in Impressionism wane. As soon as he returned to Montreal, Peter made it his business to learn about the movement in Canada and he discovered the work of Maurice Cullen, one of the first Canadians to adopt Impressionist techniques. He commented that Cullen's haunting and evocative painting of a Quebec farmhouse reminded him of his time in Saint-Sauveur.

Peter's observation and eye for detail had undoubtedly been sharpened by his time in Europe, and his wry, sometimes slightly black sense of humour was maturing: *The War Memorial in Westmount reminded me that peaceful sculptors get plenty of work after a good war!*

His habit of scrutinizing people and objects with eye-piercing attention led to a brief nugget of self-counsel: *Don't look so intently into people's eyes; it frightens them.*

5

New Challenges

THE ENERGY PETER had given Special Projects in the first few months seems to have paid a dividend. In the New Year of 1964 the group was working flat-out on an ambitious project that was the brainchild of Michael Boyd and his associate Terry Scott. In the United States, mortgage insurance had been established by the National Housing Act as far back as 1938, providing the legal basis for the auction of mortgages and the foundation of the Federal National Mortgage Association – Fannie Mae. Canada, however, had no such legislation. A number of Canadian institutions, including Greenshields, had successfully joined forces to promote a Private Member's Bill in Parliament to allow for the creation and funding of an entity to be known as the Mortgage Insurance Company of Canada (MICC).

Once the bill passed, a business plan with solidly researched projections to back it up was needed. As an indication of Boyd's newfound confidence in Peter's capacity and diligence, the new team member was put in charge. The requirement was for quarter-by-quarter forecasts encompassing a whole decade – an extremely laborious task in the middle of the 1960s without spreadsheets or Excel. However, armed with a brand new, but nevertheless antedeluvian, Olivetti adding machine that made grinding noises as it worked, Peter set about the job with a will. The project progressed rapidly and MICC was formed with a small amount of seed capital prior to the main financing. All the forecasts had to be cross-checked by professional actuaries as well as by Coopers & Lybrand, who were to sign off on the completed business plan. Peter was so closely involved that he was soon seconded to the fledgling company; in effect he became its first employee.

By mid-May the plan was ready for its unveiling. Peter was asked speak to the numbers – a nerve-racking assignment for a newly qualified twenty-five-year-old. Nevertheless, his presentation to the group, which included Greenshields' president, Canada's minister of finance,

the president of Alcan, and a senior executive director of the Bank of
Nova Scotia, earned him an invitation to lunch in the directors' dining
room, and the proposal received the go-ahead. Peter's job in fundraising
would be to ensure that Greenshields contributed as little of its own capital as possible but at the same time secured as large a stake in the new
venture as could be prised out of the other partners. The point was not
lost on Peter, and the eventual list of shareholders speaks for itself:
Alcan, the Bank of Nova Scotia, Air Canada, the CN Pension Fund, and
Greenshields – a minnow by comparison with the others, but nevertheless
with a holding of a little over 10 percent.

The successful closure of the MICC financing was followed immediately
by one of those fortuitous occurrences that sometimes alter an entire
career path. Boyd and Steel decided their reputations were well enough
established, mainly on the strength of the MICC deal, to go independent
and start their own firm as a merchant banking and corporate finance
boutique. Their sudden departure from Greenshields left Peter running
Special Projects on his own.

Without Trebell's support, this assignment would likely have been a
short-term caretaker role. But soon after the departures, Trebell and Peter
had a talk. Peter, excited to the point of intoxication by the chance to
spread his wings, offered to continue in Special Projects as long as he had
a bit more control and a lot more money. It is easy to imagine that Peter's
brash approach amused Trebell as much as it impressed; in any event he
was already prepared to support the young firebrand, although he wisely
counselled patience on the question of substantially increased remuner-
ation: *FDT is an excellent negotiator. I was much too dispassionate, but
I'll thank him in September if the reward is adequate.* In his youthful
exuberance, Peter may just have missed the point.

For the next ten years, Trebell was a dominant influence on Peter and
an inspiring role model. A man of relatively humble background with little formal education, he had enormous personal charisma and was a
brilliant salesman. His meteoric rise from office boy to general manager
of Greenshields in Montreal by the age of thirty-two had been entirely
due to his undoubted talents and his prodigious hard work. He was a
consummate motivator with a fine instinct for picking and backing good
people and was already, despite his youth, a well-respected figure in the
financial communities of Montreal and Toronto. His weak administrative

skills, blind spots in business ethics, and sheer hubris – character flaws that were to bring about his downfall – were not yet apparent. Nevertheless, as the story of their relationship unfolds it becomes clear that Peter's debt to Trebell was considerable, not least because, during their long association, the younger man learned much about the factors that can lead to commercial nemesis. These lessons were of immense value when he eventually built his own investment business.

In the meantime, at an age when most of his contemporaries were still pen-pushing apprentices, Peter found himself running a groundbreaking new venture for Greenshields. Since he reported directly to Trebell, and Special Projects was not widely understood within the firm, Peter soon acquired an aura of glamour and mystique that he was not slow to cultivate. In reality, he genuinely worked very hard indeed: *the finished Central Mortgage tender at one-thirty this morning, eyes bugging out.*

Greenshields were obviously impressed with Peter's efforts as head of Special Projects; he got his raise, from $7,600 to $9,000. And new mortgage deals were closing in quick succession, including that of Le Château Apartments, which made headlines all over town. He was also acquiring some experience of the personnel issues whose effective handling is so critical to management success. One member of his team was causing particular concern. Peter mistrusted him and had suspicions about his motives, although he acknowledged his competence. Peter's way of solving the problem was direct, if unconventional – and unlikely to find its way into any human resource manual: *I'm going to go and get drunk with him and see what his issues really are.*

This approach must have worked, for the journal never mentions the problem again. In fact, of course, the method recognized a fundamental principle of Peter's thinking about relations with all the people who worked for him: the personal chemistry has to be in balance. He came to believe that debate and even outright disagreement are quite acceptable and sometimes desirable, but friction at a personal level needs to be addressed without flinching, because unchecked it can lead to thoroughly unproductive squabbling. *You can only command loyalty if you take the time and make the effort to understand the people around you. You must be observant enough to recognize and share in their concerns.*

As so often happens, when one aspect of life begins to fall into place the other parts have a tendency to follow suit. Peter's August holiday at his grandmother's house in Cap à l'Aigle overlooking beautiful Murray Bay was relaxing and regenerative, and he recorded a day which, although solitary, sounds delightful: *Slept late, until no sleepiness left. Hefty breakfast, swam at granny's beach, started to read Jung, sawed wood, fished with the spinney and caught two nice perch, then practised with the fly – keep the rod a little more vertical and out, but not too fast. Ran in the twilight, lots of birdsong as they began to roost, steak dinner.*

The problematic lack of a girlfriend had been rectified. From that moment on Peter never looked back, even though the learning curve with the fairer sex was somewhat roller-coaster, as he frequently acknowledged: *If you make zero effort to talk to your women other than when you have urgent need of them, I suppose you can expect them to feel neglected, hurt, undervalued. Learn to be warm and pay them proper attention.*

In conjunction with this new confidence, Peter found his public image had significantly improved – mothers and daughters no longer regarded him as a rather wild adolescent to be treated with extreme caution, but as an eligible bachelor perhaps worth serious consideration. Now a different kind of problem arose – to marry or not to marry? – and it prompted much heart searching and internal debate over the next few years. *Gave D. dinner and we talked about our relationship. I said that I didn't think I would marry her and that I was prepared in all fairness to stop seeing her, although I would prefer to continue to see her on a semi-casual basis.* It was characteristically straightforward, but an unlikely winning formula for any ongoing liaison; he got his marching orders a few days later.

But another relationship showed signs of improvement. Peter's feelings for his father had reached their nadir during Peter's time at LCC: even though the family home at Parkside Place in Westmount was only a few blocks away, he had chosen to board part-time. At McGill also, he had lived away from home. In truth, the relationship had never really recovered from its awkward start. Peter had consistently rebuffed Frank's efforts to approach him, having, as he put it, "taken the decision to go it alone after the war when I was seven or eight," ignoring his parents as much as possible. However, now that he was independent, Peter's attitude to his father had softened appreciably.

Frank was a good all-round athlete – a fine shot, a keen fisherman, and a first-class skier – in many ways a man's man after Peter's own heart. Until now Peter had never been enthusiastic about any of these hobbies. However, on a duck-hunting trip they made together to Oshawa, Peter's competitive instinct – never far below the surface – was triggered. During the morning, to his disgruntlement, Peter missed every bird he fired at, but he described the afternoon in glowing terms: "shot like a crazy man till I was almost sick with the sheer thrill of killing. I fired 73 rounds and picked up fourteen duck – no-one had told me that the limit was five." They dined on duck at the house of Frank's old friend Britton Osler, and then played three-handed bridge with lots of cognac. Peter's verdict was simple: *I shall never, ever forget this wonderful day's hunting and the companionship with Dad.*

6

Vancouver-Bound

BEHIND THE SCENES, another plan was taking shape that was to transform Peter's life again. While climbing the ladder at Greenshields, Frank Trebell had met Maurice Strong, also a rapidly rising corporate executive, and by now CEO of the large Thomson-controlled conglomerate Power Corporation, and the acquaintance had matured into a friendship as well as an active business association. By early 1965 Trebell felt that his career at Greenshields had reached its useful limit and it was time to emulate Strong and undertake something entrepreneurial on his own account; Strong in turn admired Trebell personally, especially given his achievements and the similarity of their backgrounds. Trebell's restlessness coincided with Power Corp's consideration of how best to reorient itself to reduce exposure to separatist trends in Quebec, initiate a greater involvement in financial services, and raise its profile in Western Canada. It seemed a propitious moment for a change.

Vancouver was then seeing the beginnings of the immigration of Hong Kong Chinese that was to gather pace as the expiry date of the British lease approached, and real estate values, stagnant since the mid-1950s, were starting to rise again. The real estate market attracted Trebell, as he could clearly see the potential of using leverage in a low-interest-rate environment in the context of a rising market for commercial property. With his antennae tuned, he soon heard of the possibility of acquiring a well-respected, although distinctly undynamic, trust company in Vancouver, the Yorkshire Trust.

The Yorkshire, as it was locally known, was a venerable Vancouver institution founded in the 1880s by George Norton, an accountant from the textile-rich town of Huddersfield in Yorkshire. On a visit to the United States and Canada to seek out investment opportunities, Norton had immediately seen Vancouver's potential based on its location and British Columbia's wealth in minerals and forest products, and he correctly forecast a real estate boom. The Yorkshire Trust Company was consequently formed with Yorkshire-based shareholders, the largest of whom was Norton himself, for the purpose of channelling investment into commercial real estate and other suitable ventures that might emerge by virtue of its local presence. From there the Yorkshire had grown substantially.

After the founder's death, the Norton family had retained its controlling interest. However, by the 1960s British Labour governments had raised taxes on investment income to the point where, for those with substantial unearned income, the tax take was over 100 percent on the marginal increment. For the Nortons, dividend income from the Yorkshire Trust was positively unwelcome. They transferred their real estate assets into a private unlisted investment company, instructed the management of the Yorkshire that they would prefer not to make a profit, and let it be known that they were minded to sell outright to the right buyer.

When the Yorkshire executives then representing the Norton interests, Peter Kaye and company chairman Harry Boyce, were in town, they mentioned over lunch at Greenshields that their company might be for sale. Trebell quickly convinced Strong that, at the right price, the Yorkshire would be worth buying. The plan was for Strong to put him in as chief executive to revitalize the moribund institution and use it as a vehicle for other acquisitions in financial services. Trebell's interest was, of course, in the deal-making capability that the acquisition offered, and he needed someone to undertake the day-to-day management. Peter, with his understanding of the mortgage and real estate market, was the obvious choice, and Trebell promptly set about persuading him to move to Vancouver as his executive assistant. After a day on the beach and lunch and drinks on Trebell's sundeck, Peter was sold. The timing of Trebell's offer was not misjudged. Even though Peter had only been heading Special Projects for a short time, he too was beginning to feel the need to broaden his horizons. Vancouver would offer just that opportunity.

The Yorkshire deal proceeded at breakneck speed. Peter conducted the due diligence virtually single-handedly, with an attention to detail that was decidedly not Trebell's forte, and it soon became clear that, while Yorkshire Trust might not be dynamic, it had enormous potential. It was in its own right a mini-financial conglomerate: under the umbrella of a single holding company it combined a licensed trust company with an enviable reputation and a solid local client base; a savings and loan company with a copper-bottomed mortgage portfolio; a licensed securities company; and a small but profitable insurance company. It was also obvious that, although it was not then being run to the advantage of its UK shareholders, it was certainly benefitting its local executives, and some "good housekeeping" might have a favourable impact on the bottom line.

Given Strong's ambitions for Power Corporation in Western Canada, the Yorkshire had all the characteristics of an ideal vehicle, and the board quickly consented to negotiations. To Peter's intense annoyance, Trebell promptly jumped the gun: not only did he resign from Greenshields himself, but he also revealed that Peter Cundill was leaving too. Peter's trust in Trebell took a nasty, if temporary, knock. However, by then it was too late to turn back, and he had to hope that this was either an aberration out of character with Trebell's normal behaviour, or just a slip of the tongue. In fact, as he would discover, it was a straw in the wind: Trebell's tongue never slipped by mistake and he could be economical with the facts where it suited his purpose.

When Peter formally tendered his own resignation a few days later, he was pleased to find no ill feeling; the firm was used to its alumni spreading their wings and was generally keen to maintain all its connections as part of the greater Greenshields family. To underline the point, they gave Peter an extra bonus cheque for $1,500 – a "silver handshake." He and Trebell immediately flew to Vancouver with the lawyers, and Trebell redeemed himself in the eyes of his new executive assistant by handling the financial negotiations with Boyce and Kaye sensitively and effectively.

As a backdrop to these developments, Peter's love affair with Patricia Welbourn had been making considerable progress, and in the early summer she threw Peter a very fast ball: *Women are nothing if not practical realists, Patricia has decided she wants to get married. She can be petty and selfish in small things, but I think marvellous on the big issues. If nothing else happens at least I know now what it's like to be in love. Am I ready for the domesticity of us living our lives together for the foreseeable future?*

In the end the answer was no, but not without a great many twists and turns and some uncomfortable self-analysis. By his account, he finally told her he loved her but was not yet ready to marry. From hers, she appears to have been having considerable doubts as to whether Peter was temperamentally suited for matrimony. In any event, before he left Montreal they had a painful parting.

Within ten days the Yorkshire deal was agreed in principle. By then, Peter had met and formed an immediate bond with Maurice Strong, seen his first ballet, and had a debut swim in the Pacific. There was one other encounter, which seemed of little importance at the time: *Met George Norton who is a very shy man. We held a rather forced conversation.* However, Norton, reserved rather than shy, had made a positive assessment of young Cundill and noted his Yorkshire heritage with satisfaction. Some years later he was to remember that first encounter favourably – immensely to Peter's advantage at a key moment in the development of the Cundill Value Fund.

Peter was articulate in his disdain for what he found on the ground at Yorkshire. One of the old guard of executives was: *snivelling, devious, weak, selfish, untrustworthy and incompetent, with irremediable defects as a businessman.* Overall, it was a far cry from the measured professionalism of Greenshields: *The Yorkshire office is a madhouse inhabited by some talented but very erratic young men who peddle real estate as though they were drunk with life in a city which they imagine has never had a boom or, more importantly a bust before. They have a mad boss, who spends money like water, living like the ruler of an empire in terminal decline, and who cheers them on as their sometimes dubious exploits make the headlines. Fortunately, although the word is no longer fired but de-hired, it amounts to the same thing and that is what will happen. Still, I'm more than ever beginning to think I may be sitting on a gold mine.*

The closing on the Yorkshire deal took place on Peter's twenty-seventh birthday and the consideration agreed in the end was at Book Value of just over $4 million with no premium. This, given the longevity and reputation of the business, was a remarkable deal for the purchasers. It was a red-letter day too because Peter also received the news that he had passed the Chartered Financial Analyst exam in one of the first groups ever to qualify.

His birthday entry sounded an introspective note: *A young man ought to express what he thinks deep down at least once. I believe that the*

major influences on my life so far have been:
– The fact that my family, though well connected, was poor.
– I essentially rebelled against parental authority from the time Dad got back from the war and it got worse when Grier was born.
– For a while I became a self-satisfied, arrogant snob and I was probably unsuccessful with women because of that and not my looks or physique. I've changed my physique anyway and I'm glad of that, but I have also begun to confront the other hang-ups, especially my relationship with Dad.

The ink was scarcely dry on the Yorkshire acquisition agreement before Peter was voicing concerns about Trebell in his new role as a chief executive. With Boyce still in place as chairman, Trebell, as the Yorkshire Group president, was actually less well positioned to dictate policy than he had been at Greenshields, and had to resort to persuasion to get things done, particularly when dealing with internal vested interests. Peter believed the financial deal that had been negotiated was unbeatable, but Trebell had made some serious errors of judgment in the negotiations around his own role and the extent of his executive authority. He had been too impatient to master the detail and consequently had failed to see all the implications of what he was agreeing to. Nevertheless, the glint of golden opportunity still had Peter enthralled enough to proclaim his loyalty to Trebell as a *magnificent business man.*

It is difficult to tell what the greater energizer was: the feeling of complete sexual freedom stimulated by the advent of the contraceptive pill, or the excitement of wide-ranging responsibility in the new business. Certainly, Peter was thinking a lot about business method and strategy. His departure point was that the minimum requirements for a sound business were solid financing, thorough technical competence, experienced management, plenty of flexibility disciplined by a clear strategy, and good forecasting with "a sprinkling of luck." He was still confident that the Trebell/Cundill combination could produce the required management skills, and had some interesting things to say about forecasting: *Forecasting ought not to claim to be able to predict what will actually occur in the fullness of time. Its purpose is to provide the road signs, especially to indicate the cul-de-sacs, that can help the management to direct the business toward well thought out goals. It should provide enough statistical information to be able to set a profitable course, with limited risk and with the means to assess it on a continuing basis, adjusting it where necessary. Management should only regard forecasting as part of their toolbox. It is both lazy and stupid to treat it as the primary basis for determining a business plan.*

And what qualities are needed for an effective business leader? Making time for people, even when very short of it; as far as possible telling things as they are, without spin or gloss; talking with people rather than lecturing them; listening without preconceptions and always keeping your door and your mind open. There was one additional nuance: *You must invent a weakness, even were you foolish enough to suppose that you don't have them; not a serious weakness but a human frailty that others can empathize with.* (In Peter's case there was no need to invent the frailty, and it did not, in those days, wear trousers.)

But after eight months he noted that all was far from plain sailing: *We have started to expand and reorganize the business and we face losses as a result; we must, nevertheless, hold our nerve and press on. I am worried about being an executive assistant whose only formal authority is to give advice. Frank called me a "rude young man" yesterday – perhaps we've been working in too close proximity. Sometimes I feel I'm fighting a losing battle, but I'm still having a wonderful time trying!*

He was also disappointed at the absence of concrete support from Power Corporation for the investment they had apparently so much coveted; they had provided no short-term financing, opened no doors. Not a single trust account had been pushed in the Yorkshire direction. There had been no nominations to the boards of any of the Western Canadian companies where Power Corp had influence or outright control, and no attempt to foster a merchant-banking relationship, which might have proved fruitful, given the combined skills of Trebell and Peter.

There was a perfectly logical explanation: the vision had simply been lost. Maurice Strong had attracted the attention of Prime Minister Lester Pearson, who lured him into government to head Canada's External Aid Office, and in 1966 he resigned as president of Power Corporation. Since Strong had been the driving force behind their financial services initiative in Western Canada and had the relationship with Trebell, at his departure the project lost its priority in the Power Corporation agenda.

And then, as though in tandem, Peter's emotional life seemed to be unravelling: *What am I to do? There are now three women with whom I am intimately involved: one sitting on the sidelines, one just lost and at least one with potential. I have spent a lot of time in being "involved" in the past few weeks. Not that I have been neglecting my work, or sports, but certainly my intellectual life has suffered. Is this the sort of life I really want?*

A week or two later his time-allocation problem was rather abruptly resolved; Patricia announced her engagement to somebody else and so did another of his string of girls. His reaction does not, however, suggest any slipping into "the slough of despond." The journal registers a touch of pique and more than a little bravado: *You're a leader and now a boss. Your two tasks are office and Course (CFA Part III). Add in some more athletics and a new girl.*

His athletics had by no means been suffering. He had taken up riding, earned his scuba diving certificate, and was playing tennis, squash, or racquet ball almost every day as well as running. He also spent a long weekend at Powell River, where he and an unspecified friend, undoubtedly male, drove "like lunatics" up terrible roads, getting stuck halfway up the mountain and needing to be rescued by truck. They caught and ate trout, drank copiously, tottered precariously onto a log boom, and ran beside the "white water," followed by ravens. When Peter flew back to Vancouver, he still had the energy to have drinks with another friend, take a "new girl" out for dinner and home with him, stay up until four in the morning, and be at work by eight-thirty the following day – after a run.

Another weekend, on the spur of the moment, he took it into his head to drive down to San Francisco alone, glorying in the views of the Pacific coast through Oregon and his first sight of the redwoods in California – and chasing a red MG convertible driven by a tanned platinum blonde. Having reached his destination, he just slept for five hours and drove straight back, fortunately with no passenger to be subjected to his erratic driving.

At the same time, Peter frequently travelled back to Montreal to visit old friends and see his parents. After a lunch at the Ritz-Carlton with his mother, he acknowledged his vast debt to her: *She has made a huge contribution to my intellectual life; to books and to music and to the realization of how few people there are who are truly enthralled by the*

world around them, with the desire to understand it. This awareness,
which I owe to her, is deeply enriching.

His relationship with his father also continued to become more companionable. They set off on another shooting expedition, this time to the
resort area of Montebello, in search of the Hungarian partridge. Frank
brought along his champion pedigree pointer, the Baron von Dobie, and
the three walked all day through fields of buckwheat and cornflower,
edged with fine old elms. With the Baron's help they found a few coveys.
On the first occasion as the Baron froze rigid, pointing to perfection, the
birds rose in a flurry and Peter fired both barrels, to no effect. The Baron
watched as the birds disappeared over the horizon and then very slowly
turned back toward Peter, curled his lip with aristocratic disdain, and
snarled derisively. Peter did later manage to down a partridge, and at
dusk they made their way back to Montreal for a celebratory dinner.

As for his relationship with Trebell, almost from the start Peter had
been frustrated with his secondary role as executive assistant. Although
it may have been intended as a kind of probation to judge Peter's readiness
for an independent executive job, it was more likely motivated by
Trebell's preference for keeping him on a tight rein. Whatever the motivation, Peter quickly outgrew the job. Less than a year after the Yorkshire
acquisition, he was appointed vice-president of Yorkshire Financial
Corporation, the holding company, general manager of the Savings and
Loan Company, and treasurer of the Trust Company, taking on day-to-
day supervisory control of over $100 million of assets.

As a Christmas bonus, Trebell funded a trip to Hawaii. The holiday
appears to have been an unremarkable haze of bars and nightclubs,
sports, and girl-chasing. As he sat on the beach on the final evening, the
balance sheet leaned toward lassitude: *It has not been a bad year. Passed*
the CFA exams and the scuba course. Work is beginning to pay off. There
were lots of girls. I travelled a good deal and learnt more. On the other
hand I'm tired of the swinger's life. I must find some real love again and
laugh at myself a little more. I think I shall take up flying, it will be a
new skill and may be worthwhile.

7

Apprenticeship on the Move

ON PETER'S RETURN from Hawaii he set about implementing the changes he had been pushing Frank Trebell to make. In what he referred to as "the night of the long knives," fourteen people were fired and before the end of the month he had made his first acquisition, a small real estate brokerage firm with a team of excellent and, most important, ethical salesmen. But Peter had hardly begun to put his stamp on the dimensions of this new job when another sizeable project landed in his lap.

William Bennett, the Social Credit premier of British Columbia, had become frustrated by the stranglehold that Toronto and Montreal exercised over bank lending in his province. In the absence of home-grown chartered banks in Western Canada, even the most insignificant of loans required approval from the head offices of banks based in the East. This struck Bennett as both inefficient and something of an affront, given the province's rapid economic growth and its huge resource base. He had succeeded in passing the parliamentary bill for the incorporation of the Bank of British Columbia at the end of the previous year, and he was looking for advice on how it might best be structured and developed.

Trebell had already made it his business to cultivate Bennett and his government and, as president of the Yorkshire, he was in fact in charge of British Columbia's oldest and largest native financial institution, though it was not, of course, a chartered bank. Bennett, himself a shrewd businessman, could see the potential in merging his new bank with the Yorkshire. But first he needed to turn the Bank of British Columbia into a fully operational entity as quickly as possible, and he did not wish to trust an Eastern-controlled institution to advise on moving ahead and dealing with potential regulatory issues. He turned to Trebell, who immediately agreed to take on the consultancy and just as quickly passed it over to Peter to do the work.

It was a huge undertaking, breaking new ground. Complete forecasts and pro forma accounts had to be prepared, as well as material for presentations to the province's major corporations. The memorandum of objectives that Peter prepared for the bank's provisional board of directors underlines the political drive behind its creation. One major objective reads: "To supply banking expertise in the field of foreign exchange and other aids to foreign trade with special emphasis on the Pacific trading area." And it is not surprising to find that the first item under the section about plans is devoted to foreign banking: "British Columbia is a major trading province and is particularly oriented toward the Pacific trading area. The suggestion is that immediate correspondent relations be established with the major banks in Tokyo and Hong Kong as well as San Francisco with the appointment of a representative of the bank in each of those areas."

Peter accomplished the entire project in less than six months, at the same time as carrying out his executive functions at the Yorkshire. The networking opportunities it provided were exceptionally valuable. He became familiar with all the captains of industry, and the heads of the major institutions throughout the province, and perceptions of him within the business community were transformed. No longer the relatively obscure *parvenu* from Montreal, he was now a "coming man" whose opinion was worth something and whose career deserved attention. The portals of the Vancouver Club were immediately opened, and he was invited to join the Vancouver Foundation and the Garibaldi Olympic Development Association, which at the time was trying to structure a bid to hold the winter Olympics at the newly developed ski resort of Whistler. Peter's rapidly expanding list of business connections in Canadian and international circles would open many other doors.

———————

Simultaneously, however, Peter's estimate of Trebell's capacity to run the Yorkshire business began to concern him so much that he seriously considered resigning and moving to New York or Toronto, where he was being courted by another firm. His frustration spills out onto the pages of the journal: *Trebell is last of the complete bull-shitters. He has lost all control of this business. It is completely fallacious to drivel about making quick decisions. Quick decisions are only needed when the whole deal has been properly controlled, structured and double-checked.*

With Trebell's indiscriminate, poorly planned expansionary schemes and reluctance to control costs or reduce staff, the Yorkshire was haemorrhaging cash. His reliance on Power Corporation as a lender of last resort and provider of short-term funds had proved illusory, even when Maurice Strong had been in control. Now that Paul Desmarais, whose family had recently acquired the controlling interest of Power Corp from the Thomsons, was in charge, Peter could see a sale of the Yorkshire in the cards, and his doubts about his boss intensified.

Peter's investment preference had already moved away from the property, bond, and mortgage markets that were Trebell's special penchant, in favour of equities, which he now believed to be the most profitable long-term financial instruments. He carefully set down his principles: *My overriding objective is to make money for my clients and to make this business profitable by employing and associating with thoroughly competent people, proper financial controls, attention to detail, a determination ... to be decisive; no speculative ventures either for the clients or the company ... Trust and teamwork are vital combined with the ability to think independently ... coolly assessing the realities and pursuing values that are not transitory. I now believe that it is in equity markets that solid value may be most readily found among what is neglected, unfashionable and apparently boring.*

To work in this way, he had formed a mutual fund called the Yorkshire Growth Fund under the umbrella of the Yorkshire Financial Corporation. He chose Mike Ryan, a colleague whose judgment he respected, to run its investments under the guidance of an investment committee chaired by Peter himself, an arrangement that allowed him considerable control over portfolio selection and strategy. The first investment that Peter selected was Bethlehem Copper, a home-grown British Columbia company founded by Herman "Spud" Huestis, a legend among Canada's great mining innovators.

Dissecting annual reports had already become Peter's Sunday evening recreation, and Bethlehem Copper's report was more intriguing than most. At that time, the inexorable rise in the price of copper in response to demand from emerging markets, especially China, had not yet begun. What struck him was that Bethlehem shares were actually trading at the price of the cash on the balance sheet and there was no debt; the mining operations were profitable and backed up by long-term supply contracts with blue-chip corporations. His fund started to buy the shares, finishing up with a holding whose average cost was $4.50 per share.

The fact that commodity stocks were on very few institutional "buy" lists did not bother Peter. He argued quite simply that if he was buying cash with cash and the rest of the company was thrown in for nothing he had little to fear. In effect, he had unwittingly made a classic Benjamin Graham–style value investment. Four months later the shares had doubled and after six months the fund began to take profits at $13.00.

Peter's hunch that Power Corporation might be keen to be rid of its investment in the Yorkshire was now borne out, but he greeted the event with a certain relief. The incoming investor group, which included Canadian Forest Products and Crédit Foncier Franco-Canadien, was to prove more valuable in the near term than Power Corporation, particularly to Peter himself. At the same time he was keenly aware that without the moderating influence of Strong, and with Power Corp's 25% shareholding in the Yorkshire now split into smaller parcels and the Norton interest as dormant as ever, there was no one left in a position to restrain Trebell's buccaneering instincts: *Do not get conned by Trebell into doing anything that is incorrect or not strictly above board.*

In spite of the workload, 1968 had not lacked its diversions. He had learned to sail in Barbados and gone on to Bermuda prospecting for business. His first call in Hamilton was at the Bank of N.T. Butterfield to visit John Talbot, a McGill contemporary. Their close friendship and business association culminated in John's becoming a trustee of The Cundill Foundation and a director of The Peter Cundill Trust.

There were love affairs too. He met Barbara Kelly, Miss Canada 1967, and successfully managed to dodge her chaperone. Over forty years later, she still visited Peter regularly when she came to London. And there was also "Bev," a statuesque red-headed ski fanatic whom Peter described as "a cocktail of life, laughter, anger, sentimentality, bitchiness and passion – much passion." He briefly considered marriage, but she was socially awkward and he found her obsession with skiing and ski-groupies too confining; but if nothing else, she worked wonders on his skiing technique, helping him "master the powder."

He enjoyed a riotous weekend in Mexico City with his friend Ian Watson, a diminutive stockbroker with a great sense of fun and an almost limitless capacity for partying, all of which concealed a fine intellect, enormous ambition, and a formidable capacity for hard work. And, just before Christmas, Peter notched up another skill; his pilot's license arrived.

Christmas itself was surprisingly lonely. Peter went on his own to the Christmas Eve service and, moved to tears by the readings and the carols, took communion for the first time in years. Later that evening he walked by himself along the beach drinking Scotch until the loneliness was numbed. He surfaced after the festivities with a renewed feeling of optimism and mused that, although the entire fortnight might have been thoroughly immature, *there is a choice of courses in life; either to seek equilibrium or to enjoy the heights and suffer the depths.*

———————————

The new year brought Peter's first extended exploratory trip, one that was consistent with objectives of British Columbia's new bank, and illustrative of travels that followed in the years of peripatetic research to come. He had met Yuge-San, the local head of Nippon Steel, in a serendipitous encounter characteristic of many that he would turn into life-enriching experiences over the years. Peter was keen to gain first-hand knowledge of Japan's culture and its postwar development, and was fascinated by the exquisite exhibitions of Japanese courtesy. Yuge-San in turn was delighted to talk to someone who was genuinely interested, and before returning to Tokyo at the end of his time in Vancouver, he invited Peter to make a visit, which he would arrange. By the time Peter received confirmation that Yuge-San was ready and waiting to see him, he had decided to turn the expedition into a round-the-world trip.

After a stopover in Hawaii with his friend Peter Webster, an LCC contemporary, he arrived in Tokyo in mid-March and immediately knew he had entered a world that, on all but the most superficial levels, had nothing in common with any of his previous experience. Japan was to become such an important part of his investment career that his journal entry is worth quoting: *My first impression was of a busy, bustling, construction crazy city, glazed and diffused through an orange sky … The Otari hotel has over 1,000 rooms and a sushi restaurant. Yuge-San took me for drinks and dinner... then downtown for a steam bath – relaxing even when the masseuse was walking on me. As Yuge-San observed it was a pure steam bath, like a Turkish bath ... not an "obscene" one ... I was struck with the contrast between the frenetic movement all around me and the stillness of the people's quiet courtesy – also by the Western influence evident everywhere, which I had not quite expected. This is a major economic power!*

On his first morning, Peter inaugurated the exploration runs that became part of his routine whenever he arrived in a new city. At first light he paced his way through streets through crowds of early-arriving office workers and then, as the sun came out, ran on through the peaceful gardens of the Imperial Palace, where the first of the famed cherry blossom were in bloom.

His first insight into the world of Japanese corporate culture, in a formal meeting Yuge-San had arranged with the Nippon Mining finance department, was complemented by his host's invitation to take tea at the home of his mother and sister, an occasion for the elegance of porcelain, green tea cakes and exquisitely embroidered kimonos. Even today in Japan it is virtually unheard of for a business man to introduce another male who is not a relative, still less a foreigner, into his family circle. Yuge-San was offering his Canadian friend a unique experience, trusting in Peter's ability to respond appropriately. He clearly passed muster because that evening he was also honoured with an invitation to Yuge-San's home to meet his wife and two young children for a graciously served sukiyaki dinner and an unusually in-depth conversation.

Peter was fascinated by the interaction between corporate and domestic life in this newly discovered economic powerhouse. He felt he could ask questions that would be completely inappropriate in Western society, and he learned that Yuge-San's salary, despite his seniority, allowed little, after necessities, for luxuries, and all family leisure activities and holidays were arranged by Nippon as a form of corporate pursuit. The traditional system was clearly paternalistic in an almost feudal way, and Peter saw its role in keeping labour costs down and enabling Japanese industry to be price-competitive. The corporation, including all its employees and their families, represented a kind of extended family, with all the implied old-fashioned mutual obligations. In spite of the abundant evidence of Western influence in Japanese consumer culture, ancient ways were still prevalent.

Peter took the "bullet" train to Kyoto on the following day, through snow-capped mountains and past the vast coastal oyster beds. On a run along the canal and then to the Hirano shrine, the oldest in Kyoto founded in the eighth century, he found himself almost alone, with the sun filtering through the mist onto the cherry blossoms, giving the scene a kind of eerie beauty. The intense quiet and the tranquillity of the shrine crept over him, instilling a sense of the presence of kindly spirits wishing him well. The old Expo site at Osaka, by contrast, lacked magic entirely – *muddy, dank smelling, clammy, wet, filled with distinctly second-rate ghosts and undistinguished architecture.* But the experience struck a nostalgic note in Peter over what he saw as an irrecoverable, lost opportunity: *I wish that when I was a boy I'd learnt to hunt with my Pa when he asked me. He is one of the best. I can still learn to shoot better than I do, but I've lost the chance to really learn about the woods, the smell of the earth and the primeval instinct for the chase through the wild.*

Peter's next stop was Hong Kong, another city that was to become a major part of his life. He found its brash, go-getting, slightly louche brand of British colonialism, combined with the exotic flavours of the Orient, quite irresistible. He was met by a Jardine Matheson limousine and taken out "on the town" by Latham Burns, the sophisticated, charming and hard-drinking president of the Canadian investment bank Burns Brothers and Denton. *This is an enormous and fascinating metropolis of just over 4 million people ninety-nine percent of whom are Chinese – but entirely governed by the Brits. It smells of people at close quarters, excrement and cooking.*

He packed in everything a three-day visit would allow. The sparse population of Hong Kong Island by comparison with the intensely crowded city astonished him. His tour of Hong Kong's New Territories took him right up to the Chinese border, where the guards stared suspiciously across at the British army patrols. Again, he was charmed by the landscape with its richly clad low hills, paddy fields and tiny unspoiled fishing villages, one nestled below an exquisitely beautiful Taoist Temple. He noted particularly that the people were *poor, poor, poor,* although apparently blissfully happy.

In Bangkok, next on the itinerary, he had an impression of the contrast between the new wealth that had spawned the abundance of vehicles that clogged the inadequate road systems, and the poverty along the dirty *klongs* (canals). Paradoxically, the car drivers looked exhausted and frustrated, whereas the *klongs* were alive with activity, happy smiles and laughing children. Though not easy to define, true progress seemed to have little to do with Western ideas of wealth and comfort and all to do with the joy of living. How to harness the possibilities? *This trip is giving me a whole new set of perspectives. I see Canada now as affluent but really tiny. If these mainland Asian countries, especially China, were ever to get their act together like Japan, they could take on the whole of North America and the rest of the developed world without even blinking. There must be investment opportunities here and in mainland China – maybe through Hong Kong.*

As it turned out, the political writing was already on the wall, and the first proxy trial of strength between China and the United States was drawing to its humiliating close. From the hotel swimming pool in the Bangkok twilight he could hear the roar of the B-52 bombers taking off for their nightly bombing raids on North Vietnam: brutal, indiscriminate, and ultimately futile. The initial hammer blow to American prestige in Asia was shortly to follow with the precipitate abandonment of Saigon. On the plane on his way to London two days later Peter reflected that, despite its appeal for those able to exploit it, there was little to admire about colonialism, particularly of the muscular variety.

Impressions from the Asian experience prompted all kinds of musings about his personal ogres, and his thoughts on the nature of fear reverberated in Peter's life from then on. *I'm a jealous man with women and I fear this in myself because it can so preoccupy me that I lose my effectiveness in other directions. I have a real terror of doing a bad job, but this has a positive side effect as a spur to performance. My shyness and awkwardness with things unfamiliar can make me brash and egocentric and I fear this characteristic too. I think ambition is healthy, but it can also be a corrupting influence which can obscure good intentions. I really want to lead a useful life, to learn, not only to make but to keep friends and to feel that I am succeeding in filling my life with rich experience at all times. In a way I do fear for my ability to control my ambition properly, to channel it in a positive direction.*

The homeward journey through London was broken by a stopover in Athens, once again a first visit, and Peter was up at the crack of dawn to run, crossing over from the Hilton to the park beneath the Acropolis, past the resplendent Temple of Olympian Zeus bathed in pink light, relishing simple things like the clean air of the early morning with the smell of new-mown grass and the profusion of daisies around the roots of the ancient olive trees. He was able to go right inside the empty Parthenon, feel the heat radiating from the ancient marble, appreciate the lightness of the enormous columns, and peer through them out across the waking city. His people-watching was acute, as ever: *Greek women don't seem to be very attractive and the men mostly look flabby and unfit. I was expecting Maria Callas look-alikes – very disappointing.*

In London he made straight for the British Museum to see the marbles that Lord Elgin had stripped from the Parthenon frieze. The recognition that he was contemplating art of the highest order came with a wry political comment: *I know of nowhere other than this collection where in so short a walk one can explore all the rich contrasts of artistic culture; Egyptian jewellery versus Aztec carvings, mysterious Thai Buddhas and nearby a tender Lycian sculpture of a woman with high rounded breasts leaning gracefully forward. It must, of course, be the result of Britain's vast worldwide land grab and looting in the eighteenth and nineteenth centuries.*

It was nearly ten years since he had last been in London, and the impact of the "swinging sixties" was apparent everywhere. And here for the first time his journal mentions Annabel's ... of which more to come: *The King's Road now has a Safeway, but London is still only partly efficient. I didn't think I'd have to spend so much time in a Laundromat and the public telephone system is still awful, but I went to a private members night club called Annabel's (after the owner's wife) where there were absolutely the most beautiful, stylish women I have ever seen. This is a superb city.*

After the weekend he made his way directly into the City to call on Ian Steers, who was now heading up a much-enlarged Wood Gundy office with a staff of seventy – *the boys all looked the same – competent as hell!* And he was able to establish another of his long-term routines: working out of the Gundy office.

Notwithstanding the irritatingly somnolent attitude of the Norton family to their equity interest in the Yorkshire, Peter felt the relationship with them ought to be cultivated rather than ignored. He took the British Rail service north to Huddersfield and put up at the George, *an old hostelry of doubtful origins*. He found George Norton seated behind a handsome partner's desk in a darkly panelled room with three straight-backed chairs, an unlit fireplace, and a window ajar. In his heavy but impeccably tailored grey flannel suit, he seemed impervious to the absence of heating on that wintry spring morning. The accountancy firm of Armitage & Norton had a staff of three hundred, all of whom knew Norton as Mr George. Peter found him surprisingly well informed as well as extremely appreciative of the visit. The other staff members to whom he was introduced struck him as highly competent with a well-honed command of tax issues both corporate and private. The office may have appeared Victorian, but the people definitely were not.

Norton invited Peter to the Huddersfield Club for lunch – a privilege rarely accorded visitors. It was a tangible token of Peter's acceptance into a trusted fold, and he was duly introduced to other members of the city's wealthy but ultra-conservative business community. After sherry they adjourned to the dining-room, where, at the communal club table, they dined on "Brown Windsor" soup and the traditional roast sirloin of beef carved at the table – to Peter's surprise, the famous Yorkshire pudding came as a separate course afterward. Dark porter beer was served in silver tankards; Mr George had his own, engraved with the name of his grandfather – the same Norton who had visited Vancouver in the 1880s. The conversation touched on Peter's economic views on Asia, the advantages of Hong Kong as a tax haven, and real estate markets in Canada and the United States. He left with the impression that for all its ingrained parochial customs, the Huddersfield community had a healthy international outlook.

By the time he arrived back in Vancouver Peter had been away for nearly six weeks. He had paid a great many calls and either cemented or laid the foundations for a number of relationships which, although it was not always apparent at the time, were to become mainstays of his professional life. The trip had served to toughen up some of the softer edges of his character and this was probably fortunate given the troubled waters he was about to navigate.

You need to get into some situations which make your gut tight and your balls tingle. I think I can now afford a few hates: I hate people who are imprecise and I hate those who want to create chaos and mayhem in the world. I believe in change, but measured and controlled. I do see that the establishment needs the avant-garde – what is brand new challenges complacency and anyway, in a consumer society where obsolescence is vital to progress, only stasis is frightening.

8

Going It Alone

I'm looking at the moon with new eyes now and much curiosity. There are going to be incredible changes in the next forty years of my life and I look forward to them whatever they may be and I hope to have many more high points. Yesterday, sailing in a brisk wind was one; it combined a feeling of mastery of the elements and of man-made materials with an understanding of how they can interrelate. There is a really sensual pleasure in the illusion that one is dominating the sea and chasing the clouds, with some additional spice from the occasional prickle of fear.

Soon after the moving experience of watching the 1969 moon landing on a weekend in Alaska, he was preparing for another major trip, this time around Southern Europe, North Africa, and the Middle East. In his recently acquired role as treasurer of the Garibaldi Olympic Development Association (GODA), his goal was to drum up support for a Winter Olympics at Whistler from the more obscure members of the International Olympic Committee.

Also on the horizon was another major corporate assignment. In November of the previous year the Commonwealth Trust Group, British Columbia's only other important homegrown financial institution, had been put into administration and its assets frozen by the Supreme Court. Concerned that $50 to $80 million of funds had been put to improper use, the RCMP had seized all its records so as to conduct a full investigation. The upshot was to put the entire group into liquidation and to guarantee the depositors' funds, so as not to cause further damage to the province's regulatory reputation.

From the onset of the crisis, Premier Bennett had been in close touch with Frank Trebell and at one stage a rescue merger of Commonwealth Trust with the Yorkshire had been considered. However, now that a liquidator was to be appointed, Bennett turned to Peter, who had gained his confidence from the previous work on the Bank of British Columbia. As serious negotiations proceeded over the terms of Peter's appointment,

Trebell tried to pre-empt any danger of Peter venturing off on his own by increasing his salary by 40 percent. Of course, in the end Peter did go solo, but not in the direction his boss anticipated.

Leaving the final negotiations to be settled by Trebell, Peter departed via CP Air on the first stage of the GODA road show. His first meeting was in Casablanca, with Jean Brussart, the European member of the GODA committee who had organized the itinerary and was to be Peter's guide for the trip. They were graciously received by the Moroccan delegate of the International Olympic Committee and entertained for dinner at his home in the old quarter of the city, a *wonderful mozarabic mansion five stories high surrounding an open central courtyard with a fountain*. Peter took it as a good omen to be told that the word *cundil* in Arabic meant "lantern" or "beacon." The nightclub to which they repaired struck him as a perfect time-warp: *Country and Western, Moroccan girls in miniskirts jitterbugging with each other and a belly-dancing performance reminiscent of "Champs Show Bar" on a poor night*. At breakfast the next morning, their host expressed his qualified support – which Peter felt might become unqualified were he to receive an all-expenses-paid invitation to visit Vancouver.

In Tunis the minister of defence, Mohamed Inzali, gave them a sympathetic hearing and an excellent lunch, and assured them of his support at the vote the following May. Peter had his doubts: Inzali had never even seen snow and understood nothing at all about winter sports. But the "Guard of Honour" saluted them smartly as they left, and Peter duly acknowledged it as if he were a visiting head of state. He also was nursing doubts about Brussart's diplomatic skills: *B. is a typical French colonial, condescending and patronizing with the Arabs and with an ill-concealed, unreasoning hatred of the United States. It is simply a waste of time hammering on about our technical capability with these people. I can see their eyes glazing over.*

Notwithstanding his reservations, it was hard not to appreciate the generosity of the Arab hospitality. The colonel responsible for military sport arrived for them the next morning in a spacious old air-conditioned Mercedes with a flag on the hood. They drove out to the ruins of ancient Carthage, lying just as barren as it had been after the Romans sacked it, enslaved the entire population, and ploughed up the site, sowing it symbolically with salt so that it would never rise and threaten Rome again.

At the resort of Hammamet they enjoyed a leisurely seaside lunch before flying via Tripoli to Cairo, where they were met by the secretary of the Pan Arab Football Federation. He intrigued Peter by explaining that most Arabs did not play soccer but Round Ball, a game in which the players are allowed to use their hands. He seemed a little vague about the rules, but it was apparently a fairly rough game in which the spectators sometimes lent a hand if their team was losing.

The secretary whisked them over to the Cairo stadium to meet a Monsieur Touney, a past chairman of the Egyptian Olympic Committee and a member of the International Olympic Committee. He listened carefully and asked good questions, but was completely non-committal. They were escorted to lunch by the minister for youth and then given a tour of the pyramids, the bazaar, and the Mohamed Ali Mosque inside Saladin's citadel, where they must have been relentlessly pestered, or taken to buy carpets, because Peter is unusually vitriolic: *The servants, the guides and the shop-keepers are fawning, dishonest, unattractive scum.*

The final port of call was Beirut, which at the time was enjoying its last peaceful period for several decades, then still the wealthy and sophisticated commercial hub of the whole region. They were met by Sheikh Gamayel, a Maronite Christian landowner from the Bekaa Valley, who drove them up through the oldest olive groves in the world, some trees more than two thousand years old, to his family home in the valley. On the portico terrace of the beautiful Venetian-style sixteenth-century villa, looking across to the snow-capped mountains, they sipped aniseed-flavoured raki until the sun set. The sheikh was extremely knowledgeable about winter sports both in the Lebanon and the Alps; however, he made it clear that his support would not be forthcoming unless a trip to Vancouver could be organized for him – and his brother – to try out the skiing at Whistler.

The whole expedition had been a great experience for Peter but he felt that, notwithstanding the cheap airline tickets and the lavish free hospitality, it had been a waste of GODA's resources, which, as treasurer, he felt were his responsibility: *Before you ever get involved in another project like this, subject it to the same kind of rigorous analysis you would apply to an accounting issue or an investment and ask the hard questions, like do we really want an Olympic event here yet and if we do could we possibly be ready in time.*

He ended the year with a poem of his own, tinged with prescience:

I think of death and yet I fear it not,
I walk in that valley and yet fear not,
Death does not touch me,
I am thirty-one
And fit and filled with life,
But faint and distant
Lurks the thought,
Beware, my boy, beware.

On New Year's Eve Yorkshire Trust Company had formally been appointed as the liquidator of Commonwealth Trust Company. The work was completely absorbing, even succeeding in anaesthetizing the painful end of yet another relationship that had potential for marriage. *Work is abstract and unbelievably hypnotic and lustful – no woman is a match for it.* The task involved a new dimension, which Peter found instructive – regular County Court appearances to deal with technical and procedural issues, as some of Commonwealth's previous executives, whose stewardship the RCMP were investigating, attempted to frustrate the process of "discovery" by withholding documents and protesting the jurisdiction. The situation later acquired an even more serious dimension with the launching of a criminal trial in which he was to be summoned as a prosecution witness. As the official liquidator, Peter needed a good lawyer to represent him and he turned to Gowan Guest, a Vancouver-based attorney who had a sound grasp of corporate law, although his tendency to address detail only as necessary was a constant irritation to Peter, who invariably preferred to be fully prepared in advance. From the outset it was a love-hate relationship with frequent disagreements and the occasional shouting match, but it matured very much to their mutual benefit.

With the Commonwealth situation still unfolding, Peter received an unexpected invitation to address the International Olympic Committee on GODA's behalf at its annual meeting in Amsterdam, at which the fate of Vancouver's first bid for the Winter Olympics would be decided. Although he entertained little hope of success, the opportunity to attend such a prestigious gathering and network on the international stage was more than he could resist. Nevertheless, having accepted, he raised the money to fund the trip himself.

The Netherlands gathering was conducted on a lavish scale that Peter had never before encountered. First up was a strategy meeting at the Canadian Embassy in The Hague where, over champagne and canapés, they discussed how best to use a letter from Prime Minister Pierre Trudeau that GODA had obtained through Premier Bennett. The next day brought an introduction to John Wayne, a visit to Rembrandt's house, a canal tour, and another splendid dinner – still no formal business. Then an excursion, to the Keukenhof Tulip Gardens, and a table at lunch presided over by King Constantine of Greece: *People are just people, there's nothing ethereal about them, even Kings still have to pee and it's not blue.* But Peter was impressed by the clubby atmosphere of the IOC and the relationship that clearly existed among the committee members, *all of whom are extremely influential in their home countries. It seems to be a forum at which much else of deep concern to the world can be discussed privately and informally within an international gathering of powerful men.*

Finally, on the third day, the formal proceedings opened with a ceremony attended by Queen Juliana. Peter duly made his presentation, but by the time he learned that Montreal had won the Summer Games he was pretty sure that Canada wouldn't get the Winter Games as well. The news that Denver had won was still disappointing, and Peter left at once to "get drunk" at Montreal's celebration reception. There he struck lucky with a girl from the Swedish Embassy who taught him to drink schnapps – just in case he didn't know how.

At the farewell reception Peter met Canada's minister of health, from whom he extracted a promise of fifty thousand dollars in federal funding for GODA. Armed with that, no one could suggest that the exercise had been a waste of money; and, in retrospect, what was learned in those early days about making a bid may have helped Vancouver's winning bid for the Winter Games forty years later.

Once Peter was back in Vancouver, a new love affair began to take shape. It began with a sailing adventure in a Lightning racing dinghy that Peter had borrowed in hopes of impressing his date with his nautical skills. As he navigated in the brisk 10-knot westerly all went well – until he tried to jibe with the spinnaker filled. In a fatal moment of over-confidence, he capsized the boat. Two hours later as the sun was setting Peter and his girlfriend made it back to shore, freezing cold but laughing and seemingly in love. *What women can find loveable is a never-ending, glorious, unpredictable surprise.*

The affair was as short-lived as it was passionate. She fixed him in her sights as a potential husband and no doubt failed adequately to conceal her intent. As soon as the reality dawned, Peter beat an instant retreat: *Oh God, she wants a statement of my intentions. There ought to be love and marriage contracts with break clauses and with children negotiated separately. I would require at least a 24-hour cooling off period and a due diligence clause, and agreement that either party could have a minimum of six months off every three years.*

The lady very soon realized that there was little chance of dragging Peter to the altar let alone molding him into an ideal husband. Peter was having to face the fact that, as he was now in his thirties, relationships with women were likely to be short-lived unless he showed signs of real commitment: *the loss is painful and yet I'm doing good professional work. I'm probably better off as a bachelor because my primary ambition is to be a great professional. I'm not sure if I really want children and I'm equally unsure whether I could ever live with just one woman. The thought of domesticity slightly repels me and given my strange set of routines how could anyone possibly live with me anyway?*

His aim of being a "great professional" appeared to be progressing satisfactorily. The Yorkshire Growth Fund having been ranked top in Canada in the previous quarter, Peter was featured in a *Financial Times* article and interviewed on TV for the first time. Yorkshire Trust's client and deposit base were growing steadily and, although he was uneasy about Trebell, especially his forays into real estate, Peter's focus was really elsewhere.

One of the institutions brought in to replace Power Corporation as a shareholder in the Yorkshire was Crédit Foncier Franco-Canadien. Curious as always, Peter scrutinized the annual reports of all the new shareholders, and when he came to the Crédit Foncier report, he read it twice and excitedly deconstructed the balance sheet – *a treasure trove of wonderful assets*. The bank had been formed in 1880 under Royal Charter to act as a mortgage and loan company throughout Canada and was backed by Paribas, a major French financial conglomerate. Paribas's interest was to secure broad participation in the economic growth of Canada, with the added advantage of the French-speaking element. So, as Canada grew westward, Crédit Foncier expanded with it as a pioneer financial partner in the agricultural conversion of the Prairies, and judiciously invested its profits in acquiring real estate in the country's growing cities. In the depression, instead of foreclosing and evicting struggling prairie farmers, it had offered generous lease-back options that many mortgagees accepted. As a result of this enlightened policy, it had become one of the largest landowners in Canada's western provinces. What was more, whenever it sold property, it had retained the underlying mineral rights, so that, as commodity prices, especially oil, began their dramatic upward trajectory in the early 1970s, Crédit Foncier was inadvertently possessed of highly valuable underground mineral wealth.

Throughout, the company's accounting practices had remained simplistically cautious. Peter realized at once that the whole real estate portfolio was carried at book cost not current market value and the mineral rights were accorded no value at all. He soon established that, while Paribas remained the controlling shareholder through a network of shareholdings within client accounts and in the hands of other friendly blue-blooded institutions, there was a float of 30% in the public domain, with the shares listed in Paris and Montreal. It was also evident that the Canadian board that ran Crédit Foncier on a day-to-day basis, in its concern for corporate governance, was becoming uneasy with the parent company's practice of using its Canadian offshoot to provide perquisites to French executives who were not remotely involved.

Peter's assessment of the market value of the assets less the negligible amount of debt far exceeded the company's market capitalization – and it was respectably and consistently profitable and dividend-paying. Furthermore, latent tension among the executives risked bubbling over into the public arena at some point, drawing investor attention to the company and probably to its unrecognized true value. Time was of the essence.

While working out a strategy for accumulating a significant position in Crédit Foncier, Peter had a five-hour lunch with Trebell, by the end of which, at least in Peter's mind, they had thrashed out a development plan

to propel the Yorkshire forward. Peter was to move to Toronto the following year to build up the trust company business in the east and then
return to Vancouver to take over as president, allowing Trebell to step
up to chairman and become more involved in public life. Meanwhile, he
obtained Trebell's approval for him to a make a three-week scouting visit
to Australia and New Zealand.

Aside from fuelling Peter's growing addiction to being on the move and
exploring the globe, the projected trip had a serious business objective. In
his short time in Vancouver he had observed at first hand the economic
impact of immigration and investment from Hong Kong in stimulating
economic growth, reinvigorating Vancouver's sluggish real estate market,
and adding cosmopolitan glamour to the city. Having been brought up to
appreciate the vitality of Montreal's multicultural society, he now watched
with satisfaction as his adoptive city emerged from its cocoon.

Peter had always regarded Australia and New Zealand as countries
with heritages comparable to Canada's. A glance at the map during his
recent visit to Japan had reminded him that the Japanese archipelago was
close to Northern Australia, and that Singapore and Hong Kong were
not much farther away. He was curious to see whether the presence of
the Japanese economic powerhouse on its doorstep might now be having
the same sort of influence on Australia that the United States had had on
Canada. Especially since Japan was so desperately short of exactly the
natural resources in which Australia is abundantly rich, the argument of
mutual self-interest seemed compelling.

Rather than taking a direct flight to Australia to begin his reconnais-
sance, he took time to acclimatize himself via Hawaii, Hong Kong,
Bangkok, Kuala Lumpur, and Singapore, before flying down to Melbourne
in the extreme south of Australia. As usual, when he arrived, he ran around
the city and through its magnificent botanical gardens. He derived a major
thrill from a chance to do some running in the company of John Bell, the
world's second four-minute miler. After enjoying the Christmas champagne
with his hostess Ros Roberts, Peter was quick to note that the Australians
made a variety of excellent wines and that, if they could produce them
in sufficient quantity to offset the costs of transport, it might become a
very successful export industry, perhaps especially in the direction of
Japan, which was just beginning to develop a taste for alcoholic drinks
other than sake and whisky.

As a city Canberra did not much impress him, except for the War

Memorial and the War Museum, which he felt was a monument to the birth of Australia as a nation rather than just a colony. Like Canada, Australia had shed its young blood unreservedly for the British Empire in the First World War, earning recognition of its nationhood. Ros drove him out to the Tidbinbilla Nature Reserve, where they saw cockatoos, emus, koala bears and kangaroos, some with "joeys" in their pockets, and enjoyed a romantic interlude, with more Aussie wine – *calm and comfortable together inhaling the rich smell of the gum trees ... It would not be hard to fall in love in Australia.*

Rather reluctantly, he continued to Sydney, where he sailed round Botany Bay on his own in a 12-foot catamaran, admiring the city's skyline and noticing what an inspired location Captain Cook had chosen for his famous landfall in 1770. On the flight to Auckland he recorded his overall impressions: *Australia could become the first "ethnically European" client state of Japan; for the country to continue just aping Europe must be self-defeating ... But I really like the way that Australians make a point of cultivating openness of manner. They seem to strive to find ways in which human relations can develop harmoniously, although I'm not quite sure whether they don't sacrifice true intimacy for the superficiality required in simply getting along.*

In Auckland Peter substituted an expedition in a Cessna 172 for his usual run, and flew in clear weather over sheep and cattle ranches and pine forests to Rotorua, about 120 miles southeast, right beside the renowned Blue Lake, which he could see was dotted with water skiers in the warm summer sunshine. He spent New Year's Day on his own, trying out the famous hot springs and in the evening went to an old Maori music hall to hear what he was led to believe was a concert – *colourful costumes but a lot of heavy-footed stomping in preparation for battle.*

His next landfall was Fiji, where he did his run around the capital, Suva, in the heat of the day. He stopped to watch a softball game between some Americans and Fijians and came away uneasy: *I felt menace in the air. I'm sure that there are going to be racial problems in this demiparadise. I see resentment in the faces of the natives. I think there is a real possibility of serious rioting at some stage. There may eventually be a power vacuum to be filled and the filling may not be too pretty.*

After an afternoon spent in awe of the stunning beauty of snorkelling amid the shoals of a coral reef, Peter stood out on the veranda of his hotel quietly puffing on an after-dinner cigar. His sensitivity to impressions of the natural world stirred up the poet in him – and a bit of self-examination: *I watched banks of cloud overwhelming the mountains about five miles away. The fuschia trees began to drip large rain drops like blood from their crimson blooms. As dusk gathered the purple morning glory climbing up the base of a palm tree began to close in the fading light, but I could still see the lush green grass sloping down toward a group of perfect white cottages and then the empty road to Labasa twisting along the coastline. I thought as I stood there, letting the melancholy peace of the scene envelop me, that the reason why I am still a bachelor is because I often yearn to escape all emotional conflict and just exist on my own; nor do I have any genetic ambition to reproduce.*

The last time Peter had returned from a trip, he had been faced with Trebell's erratic behaviour: *FDT yelled at me on grounds that I was flippant – didn't bother me at all any more – I don't know what he's been up to, but his nerves seem shot; I shall find out eventually.* This time, he was even more concerned about what his boss had been up to in his absence: *After eight years I am forced to question whether Trebell has reached the limit of his capacities. He now seems more emotional than rational, intellectually quite shallow and incapable of seeing the bigger picture. My own instincts are to make a success of the Trust company with investment counselling and mutual fund management as its natural corollary. I cannot see the rationale behind assuming additional risk, which may even be beyond our shareholder mandate. We are not real estate developers and I am not prepared to take corporate or personal financial risks like Trebell. I am now concerned that the Trustco will suffer from this policy by being starved of capital and exposed to potential loss of credibility and reputation should there be any bad investment decisions made in the Yorkshire Financial Corporation. The more I think about this the more I recognize that reputation and credibility are actually all that we have to sell.*

On voicing his great discomfort to Trebell, he allowed himself to be reassured that his reservations on strategy would be taken into account. But he was becoming engrossed by the Crédit Foncier investment. Within a few days he had begun to take a position first for the Yorkshire Growth Fund and then also as a personal investment, purchasing shares quietly in Paris at an average of $43 per share against his conservative estimate of a liquidation value in excess of $150.

A few days later Peter was invited to an investors' dinner at the Vancouver Club along with some of the city's wealthiest individuals and institutional fund managers. Unable to contain his enthusiasm, he regaled them with the essentials of the Crédit Foncier story, adding a review of changing corporate conditions in France for good measure. To his disappointment there seemed to be little reaction and he drove up to Whistler afterward – *feeling rather blue, but the stars were out and the black mood left me; I know in my bones that this is right.*

But his audience *had* listened. They had recalled that he had trumpeted the merits of Bethlehem Copper and it was well known that those who had listened on that occasion had done exceptionally well; he had already proven that claims he made were based on solid, painstaking homework. It was recognized that Peter Cundill was not the kind of speculative stock punter that was too common a feature of the Vancouver financial scene. The Crédit Foncier story gained currency by word of mouth, and over the succeeding quarter the shares crept up steadily from the low $40s into the mid $50s. Pleased though he was with this initial vindication, Peter was never a quick-flip trader. If the liquidation value was $150, as he had calculated, he intended, at the very least, to stick with it until it got there, using any dips to add to his positions.

It was several months before the full effect of Peter's Crédit Foncier exposé at the Vancouver Club became apparent. However, as the price continued to rise into the middle $60s, he learned that several heavy-weight institutions and investment funds had followed his lead. The Cundill-inspired group by then owned nearly 3 percent of the company's entire capital, making it second only to Paribas itself – and the buying continued.

Once again, though, friction with Trebell was mounting. After another bitter argument over strategy, Trebell dropped a bombshell – that the Yorkshire Trust Company should be sold 100 percent to Crédit Foncier. He implied he had already discussed the matter with his board and that the other underlying businesses should be the subject of "advantageous" management buyouts. Peter had kept Trebell in the picture about the Crédit Foncier story and the development of the buying program and had also bought shares for his own account. He was entirely aware that Peter would be extremely reluctant to become an executive within the

Crédit Foncier group. His position as quasi-promoter of his employer's stock would have been untenable and he would have been obliged to terminate all investment operations in respect of his Crédit Foncier shares and likely required to dispose of the position he had built up. Of course Trebell was a cunning negotiator, eminently capable of taking full advantage of any situation when he was confident of holding the better hand. He had Peter boxed into a corner. Consequently, a few days later he set off for Toronto and Montreal with a very reluctant agreement from Peter to sell the Yorkshire Trust company to anyone other than Crédit Foncier.

Trebell's machiavellian tactics shocked Peter out of any shred of complacency and forced him to review his options very seriously. He discussed his predicament with Warren Goldring, the head of AGF [American Growth Fund] Management, also a shareholder of Crédit Foncier, whom he rightly judged to be an ally. A few days later Peter received an invitation from AGF to set up an investment counselling business for them in Vancouver, where at that time they had no representation. As intended, the offer was extremely tempting. It would give Peter at least the same degree of independence as he had enjoyed at the Yorkshire, as well as the opportunity to develop his investment knowledge and skills. And it would help to define him as an investment professional rather than a jack of all trades.

Above all, it would enable him to cut the umbilical cord with Trebell.

PART · TWO ·

9

Taking the Plunge

TO CELEBRATE THE way Crédit Foncier was progressing Peter decided to throw a party – with no half measures. It was the start of a tradition of lavish and extremely generous Cundill entertainment that he maintained for the next forty years. On this occasion he was determined not just to play the good host but to feature as the undisputed star of the event, complete with image transformation. He appeared in figure-hugging white leather and blue winklepicker shoes, sporting a curly, long-haired, blond wig and dark glasses – the complete rock star. An instant success, the costume became legend, appearing with increasing frequency over the next few years – until the future Mrs Cundill decided she'd had her fill and it quietly disappeared from the wardrobe.

At a cocktail party in Whistler, where he betook himself, disconsolate, after the Vancouver Club revelation of his Crédit Foncier story, Peter had met a beautiful, impressively statuesque, raven-haired divorcee with two charming children, and a sportswoman to be reckoned with – an elegant skier and a runner. She made an immediate and favourable impression: *had a slight attack of the "shys" for the first time in years; it's a very strong attraction.* This was the woman who was destined to become Mrs Peter Cundill, but not before the relationship had been subjected to unprecedented levels of doubt and procrastination by the wary game-fish struggling at the end of her line, and her patience was tried to breaking point more than once in the process.

Joan Wiewel was the ex-wife of Peter's friend and tennis adversary Roger Wiewel. Their relationship developed quickly. She was a good listener and her home soon became a refuge where Peter could relax completely, sleep when he pleased and follow his eccentric exercise and work routines without a murmur of protest. She appealed to Peter in almost every respect, and to his surprise he found that he enjoyed doing things *en famille* with her and her children, Evelyn and Roger. *The sense of peace and ease is growing – not deep but pleasant and satisfying. Normally I get really irritated by mounting pressure. This time I find I quite like it, although I still crave independence. I'm not yet converted to monogamy.*

He had introduced her over dinner one evening to his friend Ian Watson, to sound out his opinion, but in the "post mortem" the men concluded that Joanie had little sense of humour. So, for the moment at least, there were still other girlfriends. Joanie's initial stance on marriage had been that it was of no particular advantage to her. She was financially independent – better off than Peter – and marriage would substantially reduce her alimony payments. On the face of it, nothing could have suited Peter better.

However, as the relationship matured, Joanie became increasingly suspicious that Peter had something of a roving eye and found the temptation to peek into his journal too much to resist. She was shocked by its revealing frankness and especially upset by an entry relating to a day when Peter had been "working late" at his own apartment: *On the spur of the moment I called Mary P. for dinner. In terms of a pleasant dinner, good conversation, grace and easy sensuality it was one of the best evenings of my life.*

This inside knowledge altered Joanie's view: locking Peter in by means of marriage would be worth the financial sacrifice – Peter's career was blossoming and the reduction in their joint incomes would be very short term. So began her deployment of her entire arsenal of feminine wiles to overcome Peter's reluctance to commit and take the drastic marital plunge. Journal accounts of the ups and downs in the process produced a number of memorable asides: *We had some tension all day because McDermott is marrying Giselle. I was soft with her – did the dishes and was generally soppy. Really got soppy at night; found myself saying "this is my true security" – Christ, what am I doing?*

The whole concept of everyday domesticity appalled Peter; it was one routine too far, even though he had begun to discover that it could be relaxing to play the family man as an escape from the pressures of work – but not all the time. Joanie was smart enough to understand this and not to push it too far.

Peter's first few months with AGF were generally positive, although he found it quite lonely to be isolated in Vancouver while the head office and the mainstream of the business were all in Toronto and he wrote rather plaintively: *I'll never do a deal again without having a partner to get me going in the morning, listen to my problems and to share experiences.*

However, what was really preying on his mind and causing him sleepless nights was his worry about Frank Trebell. By early 1972 the worldwide recession that had already precipitated a bear market in equities had begun to affect real estate values right across North America. Despite the continuing inflow of Hong Kong money, Vancouver had not been immune, and some of Trebell's real estate speculations were looking decidedly shaky. Trebell's continuing evasiveness about the mechanics of these operations gave Peter serious concern about what the real exposure might turn out to be. Judging from Trebell's general demeanour, Peter suspected that a serious crisis might be looming.

This unquantifiable uncertainty left Peter feeling insecure about his entire professional life, and he suffered what he called a *mini mental breakdown*. In his misery it was to Joanie that he turned: *I took J to dinner and told her of my nerves. She was understanding and put things into better perspective. In reality everything is going very well. I have nothing to fear but fear itself.*

Despite Joanie's acknowledged support, his vacillation over the question of marriage continued. When she gave him an ultimatum, his response was to take another girlfriend to Las Vegas for the weekend, only to find that he had missed Joanie much more than he had imagined possible. He rushed over to see her as soon as he got back to Vancouver, but ended up telling her it would be better if they stopped seeing each other. A week later they were back together again, and so it went. There were visits to London, where he tried hard to get her out of his system by spending his evenings engaging the talent at Annabel's nightclub, and also a trip to Paris: *Dined with some of the Paribas people at Chez Josephine – truffles in champagne sauce and a fine duck pâté. Then on to the "Pussy Cat" and $100 later at 3 am I wandered home. What a waste!*

He even tried setting out some impossible terms which he put to her on a weekend in Reno:

Marriage Conditions
– House her responsibility.
– Ceremony to be conducted in secret.
– One weekend per quarter is to be mine to go off by myself; no questions asked.
– No monetary responsibility for 3 years, afterwards escalating on my side but only gradually.
– For the moment my dough is to remain available for investment purposes and will be limited for anything else.

Not surprisingly she rejected these terms out of hand, and another stand-off period ensued: *Trying to puzzle through my relationship with J. Very tiring process.* A few days later he went to pick up his belongings from her house, but he failed – they ended up in bed. Then Joanie read the journal entry about the Vegas trip and it was off again. He tried making a shortlist of the girls who he thought would have potential as a semi-permanent replacement. With fourteen names, it was not short. But then: *Absolutely devastated by the loss of J. I had no idea how bad it would be. I must be really in love.*

Even after that there was still a final wriggle. Peter flew to Seattle for another weekend away from Joanie and invited an old flame to dinner. They partied and danced until four in the morning, but it was no good; he dropped his date home in a cab. Back in his hotel room on his own, clutching a corned beef sandwich and a glass of milk, he telephoned Joanie and found himself asking her to marry him. He called his parents in Montreal to announce the engagement, checked straight out of the hotel, and drove back to Joanie's house in Vancouver, where he slept for twelve hours.

Their wedding on November 9, 1973, was not large but was at least public. Peter played squash in the morning with his best man, Michael Meighen, lost miserably, and then went straight on to the church. As bride and groom kissed after the nuptial blessing, Joanie whispered into Peter's ear "You're going to go to ski school, my boy!"

The couple spent their wedding night in a hotel suite, the first of many, and hosted a cocktail party the next day at the Vancouver Lawn Tennis Club, of which Peter was by then treasurer. A more intimate dinner followed. Joanie was not entirely thrilled by the speeches. She learned a lot about Peter that she had not picked up from her perusal of his journal.

10

Epiphany and a Fallen Idol

IN A PROFESSIONAL as well as personal sense, 1973 was a watershed year for Peter. Ever since the success of his investments in Bethlehem Copper and Crédit Foncier he had been seeking a formula that would enable him to identify similar opportunities systematically rather than on an ad hoc basis. His quest led him down most of the alleyways of investment theory, which was then undergoing a periodical surge in theoretical exploration led by Harry Marcowitz's 1967 work on Modern Portfolio Theory. Peter had devoured it and found much of value, particularly its discussion of the mean and variance of a portfolio of assets and the adjustment of that portfolio to reflect individual investor preferences in relation to risk and reward.

Nevertheless, he found its conclusion unsatisfactory. Marcowitz argued the need to take account of the interaction between individual securities and classes of securities, calling it a mistake to select securities purely on their individual characteristics or merits. But, of course, that was precisely what Peter had done in the case of Bethlehem Copper and Crédit Foncier. He had ignored market considerations and made no attempt whatever to arrive at a "balanced" portfolio structure.

The section that treated estimations, inputs, and the construction of indices caught his attention too, and he followed its development in the market model formula developed by William Sharpe. He noted Sharpe's equation in his investment notebooks:[1]

$$Rit = \alpha i + \beta iRmt + \sum it$$

---

[1] R represents the return of a security i over a time period t, a is the anticipated return of a security i, βi is the degree of sensitivity the security manifests in relation to changes in the overall market, Rmt is the broad market return over period t and $\sum it$ is the actual risk return of the security i over period t and has a mean of zero with variance expressed as $O2ei$.

Would Sharpe's equation, he wondered, help simplify his own effort
to create a formula for regression analysis that could help identify
other Bethlehems and Crédit Fonciers? The equation he arrived at was:
$App\alpha = Jpp\alpha- (V_1+V_2+V_3...)$.[2] He tried to cover the waterfront with his
categories of variable, from simple factual items such as book value and
dividend growth to the seriously nebulous such as the "feel of the company" and the "general economic environment." But he soon recognized
that he would have to return to the drawing board. As one progresses
through Peter's investment notebooks, however, the lines of thought that
ultimately led to the construction of his famous "net-net" value investment sheets begin to emerge.[3] The ratios that he considered important
illustrate his natural tendency toward a value investment perspective.[4]

What also becomes obvious is Peter's growing skepticism about modelling as practised in the investment analysts' world. Increasingly his view
was that lessons from the grand sweep of economic history are entirely
unreliable for predicting future events. Market calls based on quantative
analysis had no more mathematical validity than roulette systems and
could not predict unexpected events that have material power to reverse
investor sentiment in either direction.

Peter's view of the forecasting capabilities of most corporate manage-
ments was equally cynical. However, he had begun to recognize that in
the management of a common stock portfolio it was important, especially
as an investor who favoured the bottom-up approach, to be conscious
of the time value of invested cash. He had been lucky with Bethlehem

---

2 $App\alpha$ was the actual percentage price appreciation, $Jpp\alpha$ the anticipated percentage
   price appreciation and V a variable to which Peter gave a weighting.
3 For an example of a net-net Work Sheet, see Appendix A.
4 Current assets to current debt, net profits as a percentage of net sales, net profits
   as a percentage of net tangible worth, net profits as a percentage of net working
   capital, net sales to tangible net worth, net sales to net working capital, average
   collection period, net sales to inventory, fixed assets as a percentage of tangible
   net worth, current debt as a percentage of tangible net worth, total debt as a
   percentage of tangible net worth, inventory as a percentage of working capital,
   current debt as a percentage of inventory, funded debt as a percentage of working
   capital, pre-tax profit as a percentage of revenue, pre-tax profit as a percentage
   of total assets, pre-tax profits as a percentage of net worth, inventory turnover,
   inventory as a percentage of sales, cost of sales as a percentage of sales, and
   total expense as a percentage of sales.

and Crédit Foncier but, given the low public profile of most of the stocks he tended to favour, the majority would probably be "slow burners" as both of those stocks would likely have been without his active promotion of them. This consideration initiated a continuing debate as to what extent a portfolio manager ought to engage in the role of catalyst, either by drawing investment professionals' attention to the opportunities or, at a corporate level, engineering events that would propel shares upward.

Peter gradually reached the view that national economic forecasting was scarcely more reliable than corporate. Troubled economies, he observed, normally provided rich pickings for vultures, although he conceded on the macro plane that industry analysis could be useful as an addendum to the detailed study of individual companies. And investors were entitled to be presented with a clear statement of the investment policy to be pursued by the manager. What that ought to be was still eluding him.

However, the breakthrough was not far off. When Peter had first joined AGF, Allan Manford, the chairman, had given him Charles Ellis's book *Institutional Investing*. Ellis had suggested that any money manager worth his salt ought to be able to achieve a 35% compound annual rate of return. This was clearly not being achieved by AGF itself, or indeed by any other money manager with whom Peter was familiar, but he was rivetted by the statement: Bethlehem and Crédit Foncier had each surpassed this benchmark.

With growing frustration, he clambered onto a flight from Toronto to Vancouver in December 1973, nursing a colossal hangover and clutching a copy of *Super Money* by George Goodman alias Adam Smith. It was his Eureka moment: *Goodman devotes chapter 3 to Benjamin Graham and the margin of safety. It struck me like a thunderbolt, there before me was the method, the solid theoretical back-up to selecting investments based on the principle of realizable underlying value. My years of apprenticeship are over. THIS IS WHAT I WANT TO DO FOR THE REST OF MY LIFE.*

Goodman was referring to Benjamin Graham and David Dodd's remarkable book *Security Analysis*, which Peter dove into as soon as he finished Goodman. His library contained all six editions, as originally published in

1934 and frequently updated. Every copy is heavily underlined and anno-
tated, showing that he was continually reminding himself of basic
principles and evaluating them in the light of contemporary circumstances.
The underlined passages and annotations in the pages headed "Stock
Selection Based on the Margin of Safety Principle" are seminal to understanding the techniques that Peter adopted for his investment approach.

> The third approach … is based on the margin of safety principle. If
> the analyst is convinced that a stock is *worth more* than he pays for
> it, and if he is reasonably optimistic as to the company's future, he
> would regard the issue as a suitable component of a group invest-
> ment in common stocks. This attack on the problem lends itself to
> two possible techniques. One is to buy *at times when the general
> market is low,* measured by quantitive standards of value.
> [Not strictly a technique, just common sense, though psychologically
> quite tough to do]
>
> The other technique would be … to discover undervalued individual
> common stocks, which presumably are available even when the
> general market is not particularly low. In either case the "margin of
> safety" resides in the discount at which the stock is selling below its
> minimum intrinsic value, as measured by the analyst.
> [I think it ought to be possible to practise this in other markets than
> U.S. and Can]
>
> Of more practical importance is the question of whether or not
> investment can be successfully carried on in common stocks that appear
> cheap from the quantitative angle and that – upon study – seem to
> have *only average* prospects for the future. Securities of this type can
> be found in reasonable abundance, as a result of the stock market's
> obsession with companies considered to have unusually good prospects
> for growth. Because of this emphasis on the growth factor, quite a
> number of enterprises that are long established, well financed, impor-
> tant in their industries and presumably destined to stay in business
> and make profits indefinitely in the future, but that have no speculative
> or growth appeal, tend to be discriminated against by the stock market
> – especially in years of subnormal profits – and to sell for considerably
> less than the business would be worth to a private owner.

[This is the stuff on which fortunes are built. Investors largely ignore the merits of compounded returns]

We strongly incline to the belief that this last criterion – a price far less than the value to a private owner – will constitute a sound touchstone for the discovery of true investment opportunities in common stocks. [This discount IS your "margin of safety"]

Before Peter could devote his full attention to putting his discovery of the principles of value investment into practice, he had to confront and overcome a major hurdle. His misgivings about Frank Trebell's real estate activities had been all too well founded. Although Trebell had clearly been rattled by the downturn in real estate values and Peter had suspected an uncomfortable degree of leverage in the financing of some of the deals, his former boss had seemed to survive the market decline unscathed. Peter had earlier concluded that Trebell's relationships with his lenders must have been strong enough for them to ignore "temporary" considerations of negative equity and be patient in respect of interest arrears.

The truth was quite different. Trebell had become involved in a real estate transaction with Robert Dolan, one of the Yorkshire Financial Corporation's most important clients. They had expected to finance the operation through the Toronto Dominion Bank, but the facility had been withdrawn as the market weakened, and they had "solved" the problem by borrowing from the cash reserves of a mutual fund managed by the Yorkshire group against Dolan's personal security. As the market picked up they had been able to sell the property and repay the borrowing. However, the unusual terms of the transaction had not gone unnoticed within the finance department of the Yorkshire's savings and loan subsidiary, and it had been reported to the Ontario Securities Commission (OSC) within whose jurisdiction the mutual fund lay. The Commission promptly initiated an investigation.

While the structure of the borrowing had clearly been fraudulent, the money had been repaid in full and no member of the public had suffered financial loss. In a different financial climate, the matter might have been allowed to drop. But the OSC was keen to demonstrate zero tolerance and the strength of its enforcement power. To make an example of

Trebell and Dolan, and, if need be the Yorkshire, would risk nothing by way of damage to the Canadian financial system. Neither of the culprits was of outstanding individual stature and the Yorkshire as an institution was of relatively small consequence; the principle could be hammered home without risk of collateral damage. Thus, the investigation went full-steam ahead. What subsequently emerged turned out to be even more unsavoury.

The Toronto team that managed the All-Canadian group of funds, for which the Yorkshire had the management contract, had practised "back pricing." If a client had made a commitment in advance to purchase or sell units in any of the funds, the administrators could exercise their "discretion" in timing the execution of the order, thereby permitting them to select a unit price that favoured the manager and not the client. They had also engaged in short-term trading activities in which the distinction between transactions for their personal accounts and transactions for the fund's account had become quite clearly skewed in favour of themselves. Because his own account had been a regular beneficiary of such operations for several years, Trebell was directly implicated.

As a result, all the Yorkshire executives, past and present, whether in Toronto or Vancouver, came under suspicion, including Peter himself. It was messy and potentially disastrous, and above all deeply disillusioning to discover that the honesty and integrity of several of his colleagues was so seriously flawed. And, of course, he risked being implicated by association, his reputation in tatters. Most hurtful of all was that Trebell, his erstwhile mentor and hero, had been equally dishonest and self-serving. His journal is to the point: *I will make no more Gods of other men.*

His response was energetic and unequivocal. He contacted the Commission at once to offer his full cooperation and flew straight to Toronto to meet with Ted Brown, the case officer at the OSC. Fortunately it had already been established through discreet enquiry at the highest levels that he had never participated, benefitted, or acquiesced in any part of what had taken place, and his personal reputation for integrity and square dealing was intact. Consequently, he and Brown quickly developed a working relationship of mutual respect and trust. Although Peter was no longer an employee of the Yorkshire, he was still an officer with an unrivalled knowledge of the company's internal systems – who was responsible for what, who was likely to be "in the know," and exactly where the relevant documentation might be found. Beyond disillusion-ment, he was extremely angry to have been subjected to deceptions and wasted no time digging out information to assist the investigation.

It was becoming clear that criminal indictments would come down and that the cases would go to trial. At Trebell's request, Peter met with him and was even further incensed: *He tried to get me to "remember" facts calculated to support his innocence and to cast the blame on his subordinates. He is constructing cover-up on top of cover-up. Whether or not the Commission will be able to demonstrate collusion legally and sufficiently convincingly to persuade a jury, Trebell is effectively destroyed. I told him that I was horrified by his attempt to "script" me and that, if called upon to do so, I would give a forthright account to the best of my recollection and that he could not expect me to bend the truth out of some misplaced concept of personal loyalty.*

At the same time, despite Peter's justifiable fury, his compassion and sensitivity to the personal tragedy are also on record: *Watching FDT disintegrate is a sad and painful spectacle. It is awesome how a single character flaw, in this case an overwhelming capacity to obliterate incon-venient facts, has led to complete self-destruction. The flaw is combined with many admirable qualities, but it has simply eaten away at a fine man. Shakespeare understood the destructiveness of the phenomenon bet-ter than anyone before or since and we find ourselves sympathising with his tragic heroes as I do in a way with FDT.*

In the end both Trebell and Dolan were convicted and sentenced, and an employee of the All-Canadian Fund Group took his own life. It was a searing experience. No hero would in future command Peter's blind trust to the point of naïveté. He developed a keen, although tolerant, eye for weaknesses of character in others, and a practice of rigorous personal examination that was not so tolerant. He had always appreciated the fundamental importance of nurturing a reputation based on the highest professional standards. Excellent administration and attention to detail, he now recognized as never before, were paramount. Never again would he tolerate any sloppiness in this regard.

Peter's underlying friendship for his fallen idol did not waver in adver-sity; he visited Trebell in prison and offered to help him after he was discharged. But Trebell found himself unable to accept the reversal of roles and he consistently rejected Peter's overtures.

11

The Cundill Value Fund

STRESSFUL AS THE whole episode about Frank Trebell had been, some of its fallout played directly into Peter's hands to provide him with a vehicle for putting his newly discovered principles of value investment into practice. Just before the scandal, All-Canadian Funds, which had been the victim of the Trebell group's illicit trading activities, had been bought by an entrepreneur named Phil Spicer. As the news gained currency and the scale of the misdemeanours was amplified and publicized, the level of redemptions in these funds grew from a trickle to a tidal wave. Spicer, who was watching helplessly as the value of his investment evaporated, suffered what amounted to a nervous breakdown, and the management contracts for the individual funds were put up for sale at bargain price levels.

Peter was already familiar with one of the funds – the All-Canadian Venture Fund, some units of which had been in the portfolio of an AGF client. This fund had been launched in 1967 with retail subscriptions of about $14 million. During the stock market boom of 1967–69 its assets had grown to about $50 million, and the unit price had risen from $4.30 to just over $6.00. At launch the fund's prospectus had proposed concentrating on investment in high-tech companies with the potential for rapid growth. However, with the bear market of 1969/70, investors shied away from capital-hungry stocks with few assets and no earnings in favour of more solid businesses that paid dividends. The fund was swamped with redemptions, and by the end of 1970 the assets had fallen below the level at launch and the unit price had collapsed. In desperation the manager had switched focus to energy, which was experiencing a boom. Initially this reorientation worked well but, as the elevated price of oil began to hurt developed economies and push them into recession, the stock market collapsed again. By the end of 1974, All-Canadian Venture Fund's price had tumbled to barely $2.00 and, in the aftermath of the scandal, the assets had again halved to little more than $7 million. There was no longer much pressure for redemptions, the remaining investors presumably feeling so beleaguered that they had abandoned all hope and were throwing the quarterly reports away unread.

Peter seized the moment. He resigned immediately from AGF and, with Gowan Guest as his partner, set up Peter Cundill and Associates, which then bought the management contract for the All-Canadian Venture Fund, changing its name to the Cundill Value Fund. He used the proceeds of the sale of his shares in the Yorkshire to fund the acquisition. The total consideration was $160,000, and it turned into the best investment he was ever to make. He celebrated the event in signature Cundill style; *Drinks with George and Anne MacLaren, dinner at La Cantina. On to Annabel's and Alexander's.*

In the meantime Peter had considerably progressed in his investment thinking. His reading of Graham and Dodd had convinced him that investors' and analysts' prevailing obsession with corporate income statements caused them to ignore more than half the picture and especially the part where the "margin of safety" could be expected to reside. Thinking back on his two most rewarding investments to date, it was now clear that in both instances his conviction had been based on balance sheet analysis. In the case of Bethlehem Copper the shares had been selling at less than the value of the company's cash and in the case of Crédit Foncier the company was awash with assets that were either accorded no value at all, or were carried at cost when it was obvious that the market value was vastly higher.

Prior to reading *Security Analysis* Peter's accountancy training had led him to regard book value per share[1] as a valuable measure of a company's relative investment attraction when compared with its actual stock price. In addition, book value calculation offered the analyst a marker for gauging the strength of a company's financial position as well as showing its capital structure and providing a cross-check on the reliability of the earnings figures being reported. However, Graham and Dodd went considerably further in focusing on current asset value[2] and cash asset value.[3] For Peter this was as near as he could get to the core value of a

1 The value of a company's assets as shown in the balance sheet less good will, franchises, patents, leaseholds etc., generally referred to as intangible assets, divided by the number of shares outstanding.
2 Only includes current assets less intangibles and fixed and miscellaneous assets.
3 Cash plus marketable securities marked to market, call loans and insurance policies less all liabilities.

company – the sum that the owner could absolutely rely upon receiving if he were to put the company into liquidation. As Graham and Dodd expressed it, when a company's shares were selling at below current asset value per share, the company was worth more "dead than alive," and the shareholders' risk at that point was virtually reduced to zero.

However, there were important caveats in the calculation and Peter wrote a note to himself about the need to assign value to assets according to their category, and on a case-by-case basis: *It is customary among investment analysts to apply standard percentages to all of these classes but I think that this is a dangerous over-simplification and I believe that it is essential to work through the minutiae because it is precisely by so doing that hidden assets or problems may be uncovered.*

Having clarified his strategy to himself, Peter immediately articulated it as a matter of policy in a letter that was sent out to the remaining, distinctly bruised unitholders of the All-Canadian Venture Fund. Even reduced to its essentials, it rings with newfound confidence and authority.

I would like to suggest a new concept that will offer shareholders an opportunity to realize significant and steady capital appreciation ... The essential concept is to buy under-valued, unrecognized, neglected, out of fashion or misunderstood situations where inherent value, a margin of safety and the possibility of sharply changing conditions create new and favourable investment opportunities ...

Based on my studies and experience, investments for the Venture Fund should only be made if most of the following criteria are met:
– The share price must be less than book value. Preferably it will be less than net working capital less long-term debt.
– The price must be less than one half of the former high and preferably at or near its all time low.
– The price earning multiple must be less than ten or the inverse of the long term corporate bond rate, whichever is the less.
– The company must be profitable. Preferably it will have increased its earnings for the past five years and there will have been no deficits over that period.
– The company must be paying dividends. Preferably the dividend will have been increasing and have been paid for some time.

– Long-term debt and bank debt (including off-balance sheet financing) must be judiciously employed. There must be room to expand the debt position if required.

In addition, studies should be made of past and expected future rates of profitability, the ability of the management and the various underlying factors and hypotheses that govern sales volume, costs and profit after taxes.

To the best of my knowledge, this investment philosophy would have outperformed every mutual fund in Canada.

In practical analytical terms, what resulted from Peter's reading of Graham and Dodd and his reflections on their concept was the development of the unique net-net sheet upon which all his company research was based from then on. He had redefined Graham and Dodd's terminology of current asset value per share as net-net working capital per share, and made it the *sine qua non* of his investment process.

Using the relatively simple methodology of the net-net work sheet, Peter and a small team at Peter Cundill and Associates were able to follow hundreds of companies on an international basis. The collection of net-net sheets was known as "the bible," and Peter took a copy of it with him wherever he travelled. His BMW in Vancouver even sported "NET NET" as its license plate.

Peter's journal is a mother lode of pithy examples of his thinking processes in his new situation as the sole manager of a mutual fund:

– *Value in an investment is like character in an individual; it stands up better in adversity and overcomes it more readily.*
– *I have the knowledge and the ability to be a great investor. Now is the moment to put it all into practice with absolute commitment. Keep seeking out people who see investment realities as I do. Start to build a network. Do the unappealing things first, never shirk the detail. Detail gives the grounding for strategy and keeps the mind clear. Intuition based on experience and instinct is what makes investment an art form.*
– *You must always be willing to discuss your failures frankly if you're going to learn from them. Patience needs to be combined with nerve and the determination to go to the brink time and time again. There will be humiliations.*

*– Once you've done your homework properly and are absolutely con-
vinced that an investment is right you should not hesitate or wait for
others to share the adventure. The price at which you start buying will
almost invariably be imperfect but that should never discourage you. The
initial price is only important in that it must incorporate your margin of
safety – beyond that it is of little consequence.*
*– You will inevitably have to take losses from time to time and then you must
do it decisively – no vacillation and no self-flagellation; just a sober assessment of what went wrong and why so that the mistake is never repeated.*
– If cash is King then net-nets are Queens!

Apart from investment procedures, the most important routines in Peter's
life were the fitness regimes that he had maintained with quasi-religious
fervour ever since the decision, taken while he was still at McGill, that
he would never be chubby again. The journal is full of quotations on the
subject drawn from his wide reading. However, he had long since
achieved his objective of sporting a lean, athletic body, and his motive
for exercise had gone through a subtle metamorphosis. For Peter bodily
fitness had become inextricably associated with the high levels of mental
agility and endurance, and the maintenance of that elevated pitch of
curiosity and awareness that he considered so vital in life. Excellence as
a goal in itself had been drummed into him from early boyhood, particularly by his mother, and he had spent a lot of time considering how it
might most effectively be pursued.

*Both Plato and Aristotle made useful observations about fitness and
the pursuit of excellence and I find myself more and more drawn to their
point of view:*
*"Lack of physical activity destroys the naturally good condition of
every human being, while movement and methodical physical exercise
save it and preserve it." (Plato)*
*"Excellence is an art won by training and habituation. We do not act
rightly because we have virtue or excellence, but we rather have those
because we have acted rightly. We are what we repeatedly do. Excellence,
then, is not an act but a habit." (Aristotle)*

A little while later Peter again wrote: *The more that I think about the way that the Greeks, especially the Spartans, regarded the subject of exercise and the necessity of maintaining peak levels of physical fitness, the more I am convinced that the health of the mind and the spirit are either bolstered or hampered by the condition of the body.*

Now aged thirty-eight, Peter was keeping himself supremely fit with at least two hours of daily exercise, which included running between three and five miles. He was familiar with ancient accounts of heroic runs, particularly Plutarch's story of Eucles' delivery of the news of the victory over the Persians at Marathon to the anxious Athenian Assembly. Having fought in the battle himself, and then run the twenty-six miles to Athens, Eucles gasped out, "We have won!" and then expired. What now fascinated Peter was the concept of the marathon as an endurance test or a measure of personal willpower: *I no longer run because I believe it is beneficial (though I have no doubt that it is) but because I love doing so and I find it supremely liberating physically and spiritually. We live in a world full of constraint and each of us needs to find the means of satisfying our desire for freedom. For me it is in running that I find it.*

The seed had been germinating for some time and with a little encouragement from his friend John Clark, who was both a marathon runner and an investment counsellor, Peter went into training to run the Buffalo to Niagara Falls marathon in the fall of 1976: *The first 21 miles were essentially easy. I ran in a kind of trance from mile 15 to mile 21 passing a number of people. Then I ran into the wall, my legs had no punch in them and I could only run 8 minute miles. At the end I fell into Anne Clark's arms; sugar depleted, eyes glazed and my balance shaky, but it was a glorious sense of achievement – well worth the pain. My time was 3 hours and 13 minutes and if I hadn't hit the wall ... Faded by 10 pm. and could hardly move in the morning. Had to walk downstairs to breakfast backwards - another new experience!*

It was the precursor to a further twenty-one races in the course of his running life.

––––––––––––––––––

Peter's letter to the shareholders of the All-Canadian Venture Fund did not elicit a single response. Fortunately, the unitholders' consent to his

radical change of investment policy was not necessary; but the approval
of the members of the board of the fund was. With this in mind, Peter
made a clean sweep, bringing in a group of colleagues – all friends with
whom he had discussed his investment ideas exhaustively over many
months and who fully endorsed them. Most of them had participated in
Peter's previous investment successes and all were convinced of the merits
of the value approach. Gowan Guest became chairman, and the other
board seats went to Peter's boyhood friend Michael Meighen; Peter
Webster, who had been at Lower Canada College with him and had
become Peter's client at the Yorkshire (both continue to serve today as
directors of The Peter Cundill Foundation); John McLernon, a Montreal
friend and co-founder of Macaulay Nicholls Maitland, Vancouver's most
successful real estate brokerage; and the president of Western Mines,
Hugh Snyder, who had watched Peter's development with great interest
as well as profiting from his investment advice.

Within three years the rechristened Cundill Value Fund was one of the
most talked of on the street and it is not hard to see why.

	Cundill Value Fund	DJII	TSEII
1975	+32%	+39%	+10%
1976	+32%	+17%	+6%
1977	+21%	-21%	+6%

Despite these results, the funds under management at the end of 1977
had grown only marginally. The stellar performance had simply made
the units an irresistible sell to the old shareholders. So redemptions more
or less offset the capital gains in the portfolio. It was a significant trial of
Peter's patience, as there were no resources to fund any real marketing –
and word of mouth takes time.

However, fortune was smiling on Peter. Yorkshire Trust was not the
Norton family's only Canadian investment. They also owned Norton
Investments, a private holding company with assets of about $10 million,
consisting of a portfolio of marketable securities and the freehold of a
Vancouver office building. The original purpose of the vehicle had been
to minimize the incidence of British taxation on the family shareholders
and it had worked very well in that way for three generations. However,
with the advent of a fourth generation, the number of shareholders had

proliferated and the fact that there was no mechanism for selling shares – and hence no liquidity – had become irksome. Simple liquidation would immediately have triggered a substantial capital gains tax liability for all the shareholders. The family was looking for a tax-efficient way to resolve the problem.

The chairman of Norton Investments was the same George Norton whom Peter had impressed when they had first met in Vancouver and had made a point of visiting in Huddersfield. As luck would have it, Peter's old friend Ian Watson had recently moved to London to manage the European branch of Burns Fry, the Canadian investment bank. I was then part of the institutional team in Burns's London office, and my wife was a Norton. Over lunch with Watson, I happened to mention the family's difficulty with their Canadian investment company. Watson immediately suggested that Peter's relaunched fund might be able offer the kind of solution that the family were seeking.

A few weeks later, I visited Peter in Vancouver. We took an instant liking to each other and had a productive discussion about the idea of a possible exchange of Norton Investment shares for units in the Cundill Value Fund. On my return, I went straight up to Huddersfield to see George Norton. Somewhat to my surprise, I discovered that he was considerably more familiar with Peter's investment track record than I was, and had been impressed by the way Peter had handled the difficult situation with Frank Trebell. I obtained Norton's agreement in principle to go ahead, and Peter then went to Manchester himself to meet the nominees of the four branches of the family with the tax partner of Armitage & Norton, who ratified the deal. Back in Vancouver Peter wasted no time in getting the assent of the Value Fund board.

Once the transaction had closed, at the end of the year, the Cundill Value Fund instantly more than doubled in size. Peter acquired a group of less volatile long-term unitholders – and I, privileged later to become Peter's biographer, joined the board as the Nortons' representative.

12

Tilting at Windmills

THE TIMING OF Peter's entry into the value investment arena in 1975 was fortuitous. That year heralded a decade of opportunity for stocks that matched his strict Grahamite criteria. The compound return of the Cundill Value Fund until 1985 was just over 30% per annum with no down years. This result naturally bolstered Peter's confidence in the validity of his value analysis approach to investment, and he stuck to it with enormous discipline and determination.

On one occasion, however, he received a striking demonstration that superior knowledge gives an investor the edge, no matter what the asset class. He had been responsible for persuading Peter Bentley, whose family controlled Canadian Forest Products (CFP), to make a significant investment in Crédit Foncier for its own account, and Ron Longstaffe, an executive vice-president of CFP, had been charged with overseeing this investment. Longstaffe was a man of many parts, *decisive without being authoritarian, balanced not fuzzy, confident but not conceited, hard-nosed, although never to the point of being unreasonable, an innovator rather than a radical, never unduly hasty, though expeditious when required to be – a good man with a keen dry sense of humour!*

They had discovered their mutual interest in the visual arts, although Peter's eye was as yet relatively untutored, and Longstaffe took pleasure in sharing his enthusiasm and discerning knowledge. He was already well known for generous philanthropy and Peter had attended a spectacular dinner in his honour at which they had got to know each other better on a social level: *We dined in the garden under a clear sky in the warmth of the lovely June evening, with the scent of the roses and a slight breeze off the sea shore. The menu was magnificent – caviar with ice cold vodka, real turtle soup, white asparagus with hollandaise sauce, smoked sturgeon, veal Holstein and bombe framboise, liberally washed down with Perrier-Jouët and magnums of Beaune '69. We were spoiled and sated.*

After dinner, the friends talked into the wee hours, first about art and investment, and then about art as an investment, with Peter maintaining vigorously that a well-researched value investment would, over the long term, outstrip any art investment that Longstaffe could propose.

Several months later when they were in Paris for the annual meeting of Crédit Foncier, Longstaffe took Peter on an expedition to buy a Matisse print. En route back to Vancouver, they came back to the question of art as an investment class. The upshot was a wager: they would each commit $5,000 to their prime investment picks – Peter's field was to be value securities and Longstaffe's, works of art. The winner, the one whose choice had appreciated the most after five years, would be treated by the loser to the finest dinner money could buy at any location in the world – and have the honour of choosing the wines.

Peter's chosen runner in these stakes was a single bet on Crédit Foncier and Longstaffe's was a small portfolio of artworks: a Picasso linocut, *Femme au Chapeau à Fleurs*; a Braque print, *L'Oiseau Bleu et Gris*; and an original landscape by Tony Onley, then an unknown Vancouver artist. To begin with, Crédit Foncier did relatively well; nevertheless, Longstaffe's thorough understanding of the art market was the trump card. With Picasso dead for more than a decade and Braque for nearly twice as long, the supply had gradually been drying up while demand had increased as the effects of the recession of the early 1970s wore off. Art connoisseurs' interest in Picasso and Braque was enhanced by major retrospective exhibitions, the Picasso Museum had just been founded in Paris, and public imagination was piqued by new revelations about Picasso's colourful and impressively long love-life.

At the closing date, the Picasso print alone was worth over $20,000, the Braque $15,000; and Tony Onley had been discovered. The little collection was worth nearly $50,000. Crédit Foncier, by contrast, had not quite doubled. Peter's Value Fund had itself of course done extremely well over the same period, notching up a five-year compound annual return of just over 30%. However, he did reflect on the fact that the art collection had beaten even that enviable record with a staggering compound return of nearly 60%. Albeit somewhat tongue in cheek, he posed some questions:

Could I be in the wrong investment area? What are my skills really worth when someone with a hobby, admittedly a serious one, succeeds instinctively in picking out a portfolio that knocks my professional choice, based on many months of hard work, into a cocked hat? Could I develop an "eye" with similar acuity, or is it only a matter of timing; a combination of circumstance which serves as a catalyst to draw attention to any fundamentally undervalued item? But still, in the final analysis, what I identify is the ignored value of hard tangible assets and I can be certain that over time, independent of taste and fashion, their value will eventually be recognized ... I am going to look harder at paintings and sculpture and try to learn more but I shall stick to my numbers!

Peter did indeed learn to look more carefully: *I am beginning to understand that looking at a painting is not just a one-dimensional experience. You can factor in your knowledge of the artist's life, the mores and the social and political temper of the period, the materials that were available, the creative tension and what the painting expresses emotionally, sensually and philosophically. It can be a rich contemplative experience as well as a feast for the senses.*

He eventually developed an informed appreciation of art but, realizing that his eye was unlikely to become as acute as Longstaffe's and that the general quality of "professional" investment advice on art is even less reliable than in securities markets, he never became a serious collector. However, when the Montreal City and District Savings Bank bought Crédit Foncier a few months later, he perhaps took some comfort. The premium was handsome enough that, had the sale occurred just a little earlier, the bet with Longstaffe would have been far closer run.

For most people the ups and downs of a career as an investment manager, combined with marathons and the occasional life-changing event, would have satisfied any yearnings for adventure; not so for Peter. Some years earlier he had made a trip to Hawaii with his friend Brian McDermott, who eventually became president of the Cundill Value Fund. One evening, McDermott recounted his experience of being shipwrecked in the Caribbean as a young man, a tale of high adventure and endurance that was a good part of the night in the telling.

McDermott had been crewing on the racing yacht *Morning Star* on its voyage from San Francisco to Newport, Rhode Island, to participate in a transatlantic race. In heavy weather they were carried off course into a narrow channel in the middle of an ink-black night. The yacht was pitched onto a coral reef, its mainmast lost, its back broken, and two of the five-man crew swept overboard. The story of how they pulled their shipmates to safety, urinated on their lacerations to counteract the coral poisons, and rowed for fifteen hours, bailing continuously until they were picked up by a fishing boat had gripped Peter so strongly that almost forty years later, despite their subsequent friction when McDermott retired, Peter's gift to him was to commission a perfect scale model of the *Morning Star.* But he had meanwhile been hooked on adventure. A few days after returning from Hawaii, he was moved to write: *I think now that for me only by occasionally brushing with death, or feeling that I may have done, will it be possible fully to grasp the ineffable joy and splendour of life.*

He had a short-lived flirtation with ballooning in the hope that it might stimulate the adrenalin, but it turned out to be just a "bit of fun." *Went ballooning, drifting over Scotsdale airport up to 3,000 feet. It was silent except for the flaring which is noisy and hot. It only frightened the horses and dogs underneath. The landing was a little bit rough, but I've had a far worse time in a sea-plane in an unexpected storm; then I really thought I was going to die. We drank some champagne in the setting sun.*

The newly developed and ultra-dangerous sport of hang gliding had caught Peter's attention in the early 1970s when Bill Moyes, a pioneering American enthusiast, successfully hang glided down from the peak of Mount Kilimanjaro. Intrigued, Peter had done some research, and read chilling historical reports of crashes and fatalities as far back as 850 AD and into recent years. The foot-launched hang glider that had been developed in the early 1970s seemed to work better than previous models, however, and caught the imagination of the daredevil community – and Peter. He set off with an instructor to a beach near Los Angeles for some lessons: *It was physically extremely difficult and exhausting even though I'm fit and I was very tense at first. Klaus got me to visualize ahead and I flew a lot of times for two or three seconds, cutting and bruising myself on landing. But my final flight lasted about ten seconds. It was extraordinarily exhilarating as well as terrifying. I felt so vulnerable and so little in control.*

Peter had not shared the dangerous history of hang gliding with Joanie, but his battered condition was so alarming that he was forbidden to continue. Nevertheless, two years later, on a skiing holiday in Val d'Isère, he couldn't resist trying again: *I embarked on an adventure without telling Joanie. I flew on a hang glider … with a pilot. You wear skis and a harness and hold onto the pilot for dear life. You go for about two seconds straight down the piste and then you're off. It feels like parachuting except that you're actually flying – unfortunately there are no thermals in the winter. The landing was really gentle, not at all like my earlier experiences. I had absolutely no fear after push off.*

For a year he waited for another chance, and then he played his cards adroitly. One evening, in the glow of several after-dinner drinks, Joanie agreed to join Peter's friend Budge Collins on an expensive and dangerous course in advanced Formula 1 driving techniques. This was his moment. Having acquiesced in the driving project for Joanie and agreed to pay for it, he casually mentioned that while they were taking the course, he might take a few more lessons in hang gliding. There was no protest at all. This time he flew down to Mexico for the adventure: *I had six flights … none of them as good as on the beach in LA. The problem was not running hard enough at the launch and overcompensating on the bar, but I had a bit more control than before. This is even more tiring than I expected. I was relieved when the wind died again. In bed by 8.15 shattered.*

And then the next day: *Arms black and blue this morning and knees completely skinned. I managed some longer flights as I began to get it. I learnt to adjust my legs and hips for the cross wind. In the end I managed to fly from the top of the hill to the bottom three times. It was an extraordinary sensation; exhilarating, terrifying and liberating all at the same time. Afterwards I could hardly walk. My injuries are very painful. I left a lot of skin out there. Lucky not to break anything, especially my neck, but it was thoroughly rewarding. I had a delayed rush of sheer excitement as I went to bed.*

It was to be the last time. The spectacle of her hobbling husband, bruised and torn on his return, gave Joanie a severe shock. Assuming her "steely-eyed look," she extracted a solemn promise from Peter: "Never, ever again under any circumstances."

Peter and Joanie's marriage was gradually assuming its unique pattern. It was a relationship where an extraordinary degree of independence and freedom of action was paramount, but at the same time, no matter how much time they spent apart, they were deeply dependent on each other emotionally. After their first five years of matrimony, Peter wrote: *I owe an enormous debt to J. – she calms me down, stands up for me and is my great friend and companion and she's also a hell of a runner!*

Peter was far more of an intellectual than Joanie, but she possessed a solid common sense and a calmly pragmatic approach to life which he came to rely on; and she combined these qualities with intense family loyalty and a strong will. In a way she became the ultimate driving force behind Peter, always there to support his ambition and bolster his confidence in moments of crisis and self-doubt. The fact that she understood little about value investment was probably an advantage. She was a superb athlete, a far better skier than Peter, and enjoyed arduous sporting adventures as well as the glamour of the social round. She also had a contrasting taste for simplicity and solitude, especially in the "great outdoors," and made sure he had chances to enjoy peaceful interludes in an otherwise frenetic existence.

Their first expedition of this kind was near Baker Lake in Washington State, a short distance south of Vancouver. With Evelyn, Joanie's daughter then aged nine, they hiked – with camping gear – from 8,000 to 9,000 feet, as far as the lake: *The smell in the cool air reminded me of Murray Bay … We set up our tent and then swam, still hot from the climb, although surprisingly enough the water wasn't too cold. We ate grilled chicken and canned potatoes – not too bad in the final analysis. It got pretty cool when the sun went down. J and Lyn slept in the tent – me outside in a cosy sleeping bag with the West wind blowing. I woke in the night to see the moon framed by the pines and then just the clear prickly starlight after the moon had set … The dawn transformed the sky from indigo to a flamingo pink that tinged the mountains until bright sunshine hit the summits in a breathtaking eruption of light …*

There has been some tension recently between J and me; probably just the usual thing of knowing each other too well; a certain frustration with routines and a kind of general "ennui," but this has broken the spell and we've recovered that sense of deep involvement in each other.

Naturally, accommodations had to be made at home for Peter's eccentric habits. Joanie revelled in home building and acquiring possessions that make a home personal. She had a hard time accepting Peter's almost complete indifference to such matters. The unpalatable truth was that most of the time he actually preferred living in a hotel suite. *I was tired at home. J was talking incessantly about the design of the new house. I just can't get interested. I really have no sense of possession.*

When it came to moving house, Joanie had to swallow hard and face being on her own in the process; it was actually a smarter idea not to have Peter involved. He remained somewhat undomesticated, in his forties still committing the sort of faux pas – polishing his shoes and walking over a new white carpet – that most men have learned to avoid by that age. But their reunions and reconciliations were made sweeter by Peter's willingness to repent tangibly, with well-considered gifts and *dîners à deux* and, despite his innate antipathy to conventional home-life, he gradually found that homes, as created and organized by Joanie, became something of a haven: *Home at last to read and think in the warm sunshine. Biked down to fetch fish and chips and then walked with J in a lovely sunset.*

Nevertheless, even as they approached their tenth wedding anniversary Peter's latent yearning for the complete independence of his old bachelor life could still engender bursts of impatience and frustration: *On the drive home from Sun Valley I almost killed us all. J told me that I drove like a suicidal maniac – an exaggeration, but the dangers of my impatience with the claustrophobic aspects of wedded bliss and family life are real enough. I must never let that happen again: there are other lives at stake and far too many people relying on me.*

But the marriage worked, largely because Joanie was another independent, free spirit and not given to being clingy. She had her own needs for solitude and adventure and didn't hesitate to make plans and put them into action, a characteristic Peter admired and encouraged. She organized an expedition for herself to climb Mount Kilimanjaro and hike in Kenya and Tanzania, and was away and out of touch for almost a month: *J arrived back at 7.30 this morning. Wonderful to see her, I have missed her, I really do love her. I read her diary of the trip. The pages were dirty both from the volcanic ash on Kilimanjaro and from the hotels she stayed in, where there was very little water and often no electricity. I think what most characterizes the happy couples that I know is their ability to remain self-reliant on occasion and thereby to de-escalate the grounds for conflict. This implies equality in the relationship and strict adherence to few maxims: don't lie, don't make promises you can't keep and above all don't quit.*

Of course, with his analytical, balance-sheet–oriented way of assessing "value" in every sphere, Peter found it impossible not to subject their relationship to a similarly pragmatic summing up on their tenth anniversary: *It has been a superb relationship over all – friendship, love, shared interests, respect for independence. The weaknesses are a lack of "magic" – but can one really expect this after 10 years? – and perhaps too much independence for us to have developed a really deep relationship, but we have served each other well on balance and I cannot think of a replacement. If the next ten years are even 75% as good it will have been an excellent marriage and if it were to come unstuck for any reason I would stay a bachelor.*

This might appear unattractively clinical and devoid of romance, but it actually expresses only one side of Peter's character, and not the side that most endeared him to women. He gave Joanie a magnificent pearl necklace from Tiffany's as a tribute to their first ten years, remarking, *it is a truly beautiful thing on its own, but even more beautiful when it is on her.* The tender side of his nature, always just beneath the surface, came out when he visited Joanie after a minor operation:

I drove to see J. at the hospital in Morristown and read poetry to her. We both cried after I read the Bertrand Russell:

Through the long years
I sought peace.
I found ecstasy, I found anguish,
I found madness,
I found loneliness.
I found solitary pain that gnaws the heart,
But peace I did not find.
Now old and near my end,
I have known you,
And, knowing you,
I have found both ecstasy and peace,
I know rest.
After so many lonely years
I know what life and love may be,
Now if I sleep,
I shall sleep fulfilled.

13

European Experiments and Expeditions

BY THE MID-1980s, as Peter's investment orientation became increasingly international, he was feeling less and less comfortable with Vancouver as his centre of gravity. Much as he loved the city and its way of life, the time zone was not ideal either for the Eastern seaboard of North America or for Europe, whereas the major financial centres on the continent were all no more than a two-hour flight from each other. Also, Peter had watched the evolution of the first Thatcher government in Britain and was fully aware of pending major changes to the governance of the City of London which eventually led to the deregulation known as the "Big Bang" in 1986. He was just too far from the action. But Joanie was unabashedly reluctant to abandon the life she enjoyed out West with all her favourite outdoor activities at her doorstep, as well as her pleasant social life among friends who gladly included her when Peter was travelling.

Peter felt completely at ease in the clubbable male-oriented society of London, which overlay a vibrant cultural and intellectual life. Big breakfasts and nursery-style cuisine suited him, and Annabel's in Berkeley Square was still in its heyday. Nevertheless, he knew he couldn't impose this on Joanie, but she agreed to go to Paris for a three-month trial, taking a charming apartment in the fashionable seizième arrondissement. Peter imagined that the European experience would appeal to her, but that her lack of language skills would eventually sway her in favour of London. The plan was only partly successful.

Joanie enjoyed the European experience, loved Paris, and was indifferent to the language problem – most Parisians in their milieu spoke excellent English – and she liked French manners. Englishmen, she said, had very bad teeth and were generally intimidated by North American women; and the fitness vogue had not yet crossed the Atlantic so her enthusiasm for exercise regimes was not shared. Peter, on the other hand found the Parisian experience far less satisfying than expected. He had realized that Paris was insignificant as a financial centre compared with London, which was the hub of the growing Eurobond and foreign exchange markets, and was closely related with major trading centres. And Paris's rainy spring hadn't helped. Worst of all, his French hadn't improved much and in any case was largely superfluous. However, he recognized that converting Joanie would likely be an uphill struggle.

In the meantime they sought out some much-needed sunshine, and flew to Rhodes for a holiday with Bryan Reynolds and his Greek girl-friend. They joined a group on a 30-metre yacht named *Moonbeam*, a sleek craft built in 1919 to race in the Americas Cup and subsequently bought (and sold) by Prince Rainier of Monaco. For Peter and Joanie it was ideal – old-fashioned yachting décor, without glitz; and slightly cramped so that it felt like a working sailing boat, and yet with wonderful food and impeccable service. They sailed across to Marmaris on the Turkish coast in a snappy breeze and lunched in the late afternoon on crayfish bought from the local fishermen off the side of the boat and char-grilled on a barbecue that hung over the water attached to the yacht rail.

Always curious about the history of the places he visited, Peter had brought along his usual bag of books. This time it must have been quite heavy since it contained Gibbon's *Decline and Fall of the Roman Empire* which, even though an abridgement, was still a solid tome. That evening he sat on deck, in moonlight that was clear enough to read by, looking up at a sheer, eerily illuminated cliff face on top of which he could see some of the ancient Lycian royal tombs silhouetted against the sky. On the other side he could peer down through the clear, moonlit water and see the ruins of a Byzantine monastery, submerged over a thousand years before, and he jotted down a line from Gibbon: *"Conversation enriches the understanding but solitude is the school of genius."*

Peter never travelled anywhere without considering the location's potential from an investment standpoint. It is fascinating to read how prescient his comparison of Greece and Turkey has turned out to be. *The population of Greece is 9 million and Turkey 46 million. Greece has fewer resources and its only real industries are tourism and shipping. The shipping magnates pay very little tax, in fact almost no-one does, and the work force are mostly lazy and self-satisfied with an inflated idea of their own connection to the cultural heritage of the Golden Age. These chick-ens are bound to come home to roost some day.*

Meanwhile I think that Turkey will eventually do very well. It appears to be an orderly, courteous and hard working society with some sense of civic responsibility, with a legal system that functions moderately well and so it is largely without the flaws that bedevil other Muslim countries. But, of course, thanks to Ataturk it is a secular society ... The country is filled with Graeco-Roman archaeological sites that are every bit as exciting as Greece itself and not nearly as crowded or regimented and the girls are much prettier ... Turkish real estate is cheap by comparison with Greece, as are most other things, including the Wall Street Journal!

The holiday had crystallized Peter's thinking, and he decided he was going to relocate to London come what may, but that his head office and its staff would remain in Vancouver. So London was presented to Joanie not as a *fait accompli* but as another trial run after which the final decision would be made.

In the meantime Peter went into training for the Portland, Oregon, marathon, determined to break the treasured three-hour barrier, which separates serious marathon runners from the "also rans." He was about to turn forty-five, so time was not on his side. As well as building up his stamina and speed, he turned the training into a kind of *valete* to all his old running routes in Canada, in anticipation of his runs in Hyde Park, Green Park, and Kensington Gardens. With profound nostalgia he ran the sea wall around Stanley Park in Vancouver and his Montreal route up Sherbrooke, around the grounds of Lower Canada College, through Westmount and then back to the Ritz.

There were a great many farewell lunches and dinners as Peter's intentions percolated through the financial community, but the training took precedence and it paid off. He did the Portland run in 2.59: *I ran a consistently strong race speeding up on occasion and then settling back. I had real strength in the wall running miles 20–25 in 34 minutes. The weather was ideal, 54 degrees and overcast with a spritzer of rain towards the end. I was so high I couldn't sleep – lots of hot baths, a jacuzzi and a walk, then well-wishers for champagne at 6.00 pm followed by dinner at the Couch Street Fishhouse. I faded by 10.30 p.m., but WHAT A DAY!*

The move to London, trial or otherwise, began in the spring of 1984. With the help of Jenny Bingham, who was later to become a vital member of the Cundill team, Joanie had secured an apartment on Walton Street, within five minutes of the famous Harrods department store, and close enough to the parks for Peter's purposes: *I know I'm going to like living in London. I like the taxis and I enjoy talking to the drivers even though I don't always get everything they say. I love running through Hyde Park at dusk when it's a little misty and the lights begin to prick out along Park Lane. The climate is just fine for everyday living. Hot sun in the Med is only two hours away and the mountains are even closer. I ran to Battersea Park today and back past Chelsea barracks. Stopped to watch the guards parading before marching out to the Trooping the Colour ceremony for the Queen's birthday – very stirring.*

Peter's run around Hyde Park one morning had a unique destination. He jogged on toward Berkeley Square and presented himself, in his running shorts, at the immaculate Mayfair premises of Holland and Holland, to hire a pair of shotguns. He was preparing for a once-in-a-lifetime expedition to Hungary that I had organized early in the New Year, to shoot wild pheasants in deep winter conditions. The urbane sales staff at Holland's never even blinked at Peter's rather strange attire, and he emerged kitted out with the necessary paraphernalia – shooting breeches, long socks with garters, shooting mittens, a quilted Barbour jacket, leather-lined French Wellington boots, and a splendid pair of Holland "Royal" twelve-bore shotguns.

The shooting group departed in late January, determined that a good time would be had in more than just the shooting field. Malev, the Hungarian state airline, flew Russian-built Tupolev Tu-154s, and the team had the economy section almost to themselves. The first-class compartment was crammed with what we took to be Communist Party members returning in high spirits from a London excursion and expressing lively appreciation of the stewardesses.

We were met at the airport by Erica, an attractive woman in her early thirties who was to be our guide and interpreter. Peter was impressed that she spoke impeccable English, despite spending a mere two weeks in England as a student. She lived with her parents, had no car, and seemed far from being a dedicated Communist. She had a decidedly pragmatic attitude to capitalism and was fully prepared to party with her guests and enjoy its fruits to the full. We lodged at the new and very contemporary Hyatt, which sported a huge atrium with a bi-plane suspended from the roof.

Before dinner Peter went out for his customary run: *Went along the Danube in the dusk over the Chain Bridge, a fine old suspension bridge, over to the Buda side, not too cold and very attractive with street lights on the snow and the impressive grandeur of the buildings; still very imperial looking. The city has an aura of permanence and stability. The people are well dressed and look contented. On my way through the shopping district I saw a washing machine for $160.00, an electric razor for $33 and a nice looking ladies' sweater for $7. I noticed a Pan Am advertisement for direct flights to Cleveland, which struck me as odd until I found out from Erica that Cleveland has the largest Hungarian population in North America.*

We crossed the Danube to dine at the famous Fortuna restaurant in a handsome fifteenth-century mansion in the heart of medieval Buda. To our astonishment we were surrounded by portraits of old Hapsburg royalty, rather than photographs of Lenin or members of the current Politburo, and the clientele had an air of well-established *haute bourgeoisie*. David Norton, of the eponymous Huddersfield family, had hired a gypsy band of six fiddlers to get the team into the right mood – Erica ordered up Hungarian specialties, wine and brandy flowed, and the evening was an unqualified success.

The next morning Peter set out for another run *to clear the cobwebs*. He found surprisingly little evidence of the Communist regime en route to Buda Castle – only a couple of small busts of Marx and Engels and a monument with a red star commemorating the Red Army's "liberation" of the city in 1945. The exhibition in the castle itself was completely apolitical, even displaying a 1930s painting of a white hand grasping a white cross beating up on a cringing hammer and sickle. There was no reference to Admiral Horthy, the Nazi's Hungarian quisling, but the interminable series of foreign invasions suffered by Hungary over the centuries, from the Turks and the Hapsburgs to the Germans and finally the Russians, were well illustrated.

After lunch we boarded our mini-bus, into which the carefully labelled luggage and guns had already been meticulously loaded, and began the 150-kilometre journey to the shooting estate, now state-owned but maintained, as it always had been, for sporting pleasure. No longer the playground of the princely Esterhazy family, the whole 25,000 acres was today the pride and joy of the new aristocracy of the Communist party, President János Kádár in particular. And in fact our group had had to spend an extra night in Budapest because Kádár suddenly decided he wanted to shoot wild boar on the estate on Sunday, and he definitely took precedence over a few Western capitalists, fee-paying or not.

We travelled southwest to the summer resort area of Lake Balaton, Europe's largest lake, nearly a hundred kilometres long, and then on to the small town of Balatonfenyes, from which the vast estate runs inland for about fifteen kilometres. The farming was principally maize and barley, and Peter noted at once that the machinery was Deere and Massey Ferguson, with no concessions to equipment of Communist bloc manufacture. The woods were manicured to hold the birds, and the entire crop-farming enterprise was organized into "game strips" to shelter and feed the wild birds, and huge fields of stubble were left standing for the game to pick over.

Our quarters were in the presidential lodge consisting of extremely comfortable cottages, with three bedrooms apiece, each with its en suite bathroom, surrounding a larger central building that housed the kitchens and a magnificent beamed and raftered hall with crackling open fires. The walls were hung with every imaginable kind of game trophy, from little pointed roe deer antlers to magnificent red deer stag heads sporting well over twenty points and one record-breaking head with fifty points – a count unheard of either in Scotland or North America. Nearly all the food came from the estate; boar, venison, pheasant and partridge were presented with a splendour that might not have disappointed the Esterhazys themselves.

Breakfast was an enormous spread of sausages, cheeses, smoked fish and caviar, eggs, sizzling bacon, devilled kidneys and game hash accompanied by red wine, beer and schnapps so that our party should emerge proof against the frigid cold. We drove to a small railway station on the estate where a miniature-gauge steam engine, another Esterhazy relic pulling four small carriages, was waiting for us. We disembarked into horse-drawn sleighs covered in bear skin rugs and were driven, to the sound of tinkling sleigh bells, across open fields right up to our shooting pegs for the first game drive of the day:

There was a sense of formality about the hunting expedition which

*presumably goes back to the Esterhazy era, when the Hapsburg emperors
hunted here. We all had a loader, an assistant loader and at least one dog
... The dogs were incredibly well behaved and did a wonderful job picking up the birds. There were about forty beaters in uniform, also with
dogs, and the usual procedure was for five or six guns to be placed forward, generally in front of a line of trees, poplars and larches about thirty
feet high, with one or two guns following behind the beaters to shoot the
birds going back. We used Hungarian cartridges, which all the English
members of the group thought were excellent, especially at long range,
but they do give a powerful kick.*

Lunch was another extraordinary meal. In a sheltered clearing in the
snow a long table had been fully laid, complete with linen napkins.
Surrounding the table at the four corners, huge flaming bonfires gave the
effect of central heating inside the circle while we ate borscht laced with
vodka, and goose stew with foie gras dumplings. It was a splendidly
surreal moment and the light was already beginning to fail by the time
we were ready for the next game drive, the last of the day. We had fired
well over a thousand cartridges for a bag of 300 head – and Peter's shoulder was suffering the consequences.

The following day we decided that breakfast and lunch were going to
be shorter and more abstemious and the bag higher, and so it was. There
was quite a stiff wind and it was even colder so that the birds flew high
and fast, and the guns warmed up quickly, swinging hard and loosening
their shoulders. By the afternoon Peter's shooting had immeasurably
improved: *The last drive was in the larches. Randall missed a cock as it
rose over the tops of the trees, I swung and fired, the bird dropped like a
stone. It was purely animal – a reflex action and it felt beautiful. There
was a drift of smoke across the sky and a hint of dusk in the air.*

At the end of the day the bag was an astounding 470 pheasants, 35
partridges, 6 woodcock, 7 duck, 22 rabbits, 12 pigeons, and 6 hares, with
another 40 pheasants picked up by the dogs out of the hedgerows the
following morning. About 1,800 cartridges had been fired for a ratio of
3:1, compared with nearly 5:1 the previous day. Peter's own score had
more than doubled to 30 birds in what were extremely challenging shooting conditions. What really captured his imagination, though, were the
formal proceedings of the closing ceremony:

*A series of fir boughs were placed in a square at each end of which
there was a bonfire. The birds were placed in line from one corner to the*

next; first of all the miscellaneous bag, the rabbits and partridges etc; then the cock birds in groups of ten, with their colourful plumage glistening in the firelight and then the hens arranged behind. On one side of this fire-lit array stood the keepers, the loaders and the beaters and the guns stood opposite. There was a fanfare of hunting horns which sent a shiver down my back and then the Head Keeper stepped forward, doffed his hat to the dead game and made a speech about the nobility of the wild animals and the respect due to them, followed by a eulogy addressed to the guns. CR-G responded on our behalf, speaking of the wonderful professionalism of all the shoot servants, the quality and presentation of the birds and the disciplined efficiency of the dogs. After this we gave "three cheers" and a "hoorah," tossing our caps in the air and at once glasses appeared with bottles of bison vodka and apricot brandy and the gypsy fiddlers broke into frenzied action, jigging for all they were worth to prevent their fingers turning blue. It was an unforgettable spectacle. As the jingling sleighs arrived spraying the powdery snow behind them, I thought of Dr Zhivago.

As the twilight deepened we headed back to the Hyatt where, of course, a splendid dinner, ordered by Erica, was waiting, with magnums of very passable Georgian champagne. Toward the end of the meal, Erica boasted that she could dance from one end of the table to the other without breaking a single glass. She surveyed the terrain, took off her shoes, leapt onto the table, and danced its length faultlessly, swirling her skirt as she went. Not a single breakage. Cheers and gypsy strains raised the roof.

After closing out the evening hobnobbing with the international community at the Hyatt bar, Peter still managed his run in the morning, assessing potential as ever: *I was amazed at the amount of traffic; there are some three million cars among eleven million inhabitants, also every house appeared to have a television antenna. I didn't see a single queue; the shops seemed to be filled with goods, especially the grocery stores which had plenty of fresh fruit. I am not in the least surprised that Hungary enjoys the reputation of being the freest economy within the Iron Curtain. I think it may have a great future.*

14

A Tale of Two Cities

PETER CUNDILL AND ASSOCIATES was incorporated on April Fool's Day 1977. Although not a deliberate choice, it gave Peter much amusement over the years. The company was funded by way of $160,000 of Preferred Shares and eight common shares, of which Peter owned five and Gowan Guest three. The original capital was used to purchase the rights to manage the All-Canadian Venture Fund, which subsequently became the Cundill Value Fund. In 1979 Peter bought one more common share from Guest for $25,000, which left him owning 75% and Guest 25%. During the first decade of operation the net annual return on average shareholders' equity was just over 40% (after tax and bonuses). Peter reflected with satisfaction on the company's success:

It was fortunate that I started to manage the fund at a time of generally improving markets but we remain to be tested under dramatically bad markets. Whether by design or luck ... we have developed a business where the relatively steady cash flow from the fund side ought to be able to maintain the integrity of the business in years where the fees from performance/counselling are limited. In 1979 we also began to take our agency income and invest this in our own vehicles and we have incurred some leverage in order to support this activity. I am satisfied with this strategy provided that the element of leverage remains modest.

Rather than add internal staff for marketing and administration he had, as far as practical, subcontracted these functions. He used his lawyers and accountants to undertake basic research such as in the area of distressed debt and in the initial exploration of new markets where he relied on their economic work and their introductions. Trust companies and banks took care of the custodian and registrar functions. The research activity he retained for himself: *By keeping the primary research function (essentially me) in-house, I am trying to ensure that my main focus – no less than 80% of my time – is based on identifying investment opportunities for the fund and our other clients. The danger in any investment counselling firm is that*

the principal officer who develops a reputation for sound investment deci-
sions becomes an administrator and is taken away from his primary role.

Although Peter continued to favour outsourcing of administrative
functions, it was becoming clear that the fund's size now demanded that
more resources should be devoted to ensuring that the technical functions
operated efficiently. It was also apparent that the fund's marketing was
suffering because Peter was unwilling to dedicate enough time and effort
to it, preferring to rely on good press, third-party endorsements, and
superior investment performance to do the job. However, this reliance
would eventually hamper growth.

Two key employees had been with the company virtually since its
inception: Ursula Kummel, whom Peter regarded as his confidential PA,
and Margaret Vrabel, a chartered accountant who acted as his book-
keeper. His initial solution to the administration problem was to give each
of them additional responsibility, with the incentive of offering 5 percent
of the business to them on highly favourable terms. But unfortunately,
the two women could not get along, to the extent of outright hostility.
And the division of the incentive, three percent to Kummel and two to
Vrabel, only encouraged Kummel to regard herself as the "office manager."

Peter's efforts to calm the waters had simply brought forth streams of
accusation and vituperation, as each portrayed the other as incompetent.
Matters were further complicated by the fact that Kummel, unlike Vrabel,
was not happily married and had taken a more than maternal interest in
Peter. While this was not in any way reciprocated, Peter had allowed her
more license in organizing his life than was probably wise, and she had
perhaps imagined there might be a possibility. He had also taken mischievous delight in teasing her for her streak of Germanic prudery: he
once gave her some valuable but highly erotic Japanese prints – at which
she had almost swooned, murmuring "Oooh, Peter!"

Unsuccessful in achieving a reconciliation, Peter high-tailed it back to
Europe. It was time, he had decided, to devolve his least favourite responsibilities by engaging a president for Peter Cundill and Associates – an
executive permanently located in Vancouver who could oversee administrative functions and spearhead a marketing strategy. Serendipitously,
shortly after arriving in London he got a call from his friend Brian
McDermott, whose story of his adventures at sea had so influenced him.
McDermott was then based in Paris, having spent a decade working for

Kaiser Resources, successfully selling coal around the world. He was not happy. The recent acquisition of Kaiser Resources by the British Columbia Investment Corporation had left him with options within the Kaiser empire that he found unappealing – not to mention that cobblestones were already flying in Paris at the start of the 1986 student riots.

The following day McDermott flew to London and within a few hours the deal was struck. McDermott would move with his family to Vancouver as president of Peter Cundill and Associates and within a reasonable period would be offered an equity stake in the business. The specific brief was simple in concept if not in execution – to keep the administration and especially personnel issues out of Peter's hair and to assume responsibility for marketing the fund. In principle, McDermott's authority was to be absolute, except over the research department, which was Peter's bailiwick. But the research team were quick to perceive that they could ignore McDermott, and keeping the peace between the two ladies was a thankless task – as Peter had already discovered.

———————

London was more than a convenient time zone for global fund management. It offered an array of new experiences of the kind that Peter relished, in a way that Paris, although physically so beautiful, hadn't. One of the first was a luncheon at the Mayfair residence of the Canadian high commissioner in honour of Pierre Trudeau.

Roy Heenan, a friend from McGill days, was now a distinguished practising and academic lawyer, as well as the founder of his own firm, Heenan Blaikie. After Trudeau retired as prime minister in 1984, Heenan, a long-standing friend and legal colleague of Trudeau, had persuaded him to accept a role as legal counsel for Heenan Blaikie. They were on a tour of Europe to introduce the firm's prestigious new member. In spite of Peter's well-known Tory affiliations, he was equally reputed to be a strong supporter of Trudeau's efforts in resisting the aspirations of the Québec Libre movement, which had been defeated in the 1980 referendum. Heenan invited him to the lunch:

Trudeau was a much smaller man than I had expected, but frankly captivating. We had a good chat about Quebec and I went on with him to look at a painting which I had been admiring out of the corner of my eye.

"Group of Seven, but I don't know which," I ventured.

"No, I think perhaps not," replied Trudeau. "Maybe Alex Colville, he's a Nova Scotia artist and a very good one."

He was right.

Sir Peter Walters, the chairman and CEO *of British Petroleum was also at lunch and we talked of the privatization process [at the time Mrs Thatcher's new Tory government was selling off a number of British state-controlled entities including a majority stake in* BP] *and where he thought it might lead his company – "to an exciting future," was my conclusion. He surprised me ... not at all stuffy, a good communicator, youngish looking and rather informal, wearing a button-down collar!*

Peter also found London's culture more varied and more adapted to his personal taste than the highly intellectualized and centrifugal French version. He was captivated by the annual Chelsea Flower show: *The attention to detail and the extraordinary combinations [of flowers] were frankly stupendous – all of them in flower or bloom and an unimaginable show of different roses. But this was not all ... the human display ... was just as enthralling; well-built tweedy ladies from the shires with hearty voices, the soft burr of country accents, women in the height of fashion, like elegant thoroughbreds, cooing gently on the arms of impeccably tailored gentlemen with rolled umbrellas and the old-fashioned courtliness of lifted hat brims to others that they recognized. It was not only a show, it was a pageant.*

And there was the English countryside with its unique concept of the country-house weekend. He spent a Saturday night with the Williamses, who had welcomed him fresh off the *Homeric* for his London work experience years earlier. *[Gerry] took me to Scotney Castle to run – the* PM *has an apartment there for personal use. I ran past Finchcock's, a pretty mainly 18th century house named after the family who owned it in the 13th century! The present owner has a collection of musical instruments which is open to the public. It was a fine day with lambs frolicking on the hillside, extremely dumb, sluggish pheasants sauntering about. The horse chestnuts were in bloom, some with pink candles and some with white, the hawthorns were in deep pink flower in the hedge-rows and the bluebells were scenting the woods. The hills looked lush and green and rolled away into the distance in the clear air, under a hazy blue sky. All in all it was enchanting.*

And he was invited to watch the polo at Smith's Lawn in Windsor Great Park: *Prince Charles was playing, obviously enjoying himself and not on duty ... The teams lined up for the ladies, including Princess Diana, like medieval knights, but without the bestowal of garlands or handkerchiefs. Princess D. rather taller than I had expected ... and beautifully dressed in white linen, showing a very fine figure to perfect advantage. It is a dangerous and violent game and I am going to do it. The announcer amused me by suggesting that "restrained applause would be appreciated as an encouragement to the players."*

And play he did. He had a lesson two weeks later – first, standing on a chair learning to swing the polo mallet, and then a half an hour on the wooden horse, hitting a ball backward and forward, then the real thing: *We started to play, three-a-side and I forgot that I couldn't ride and just pressed on, cantering willingly after the ball and sometimes galloping involuntarily – the pony didn't really care for cantering when it saw the ball in front. After an hour my inside thighs were stiff and raw, BUT I HAD SURVIVED. As I was standing around, Galen Weston came riding by and we had a nice chat, me leaning on the polo mallet, sweaty and dusty and looking quite the pro, or so I thought!*

The following week he scored his first goal: *Hang gliding was described to me as the most fun you'll ever have with your pants on. Now I'm not so sure!*

But Peter did not buy a string of polo ponies. Rather in the vein of the hang gliding, Joanie had assessed the risks of serious or fatal injury and gave him another ultimatum, which would be far more difficult to circumvent. He compensated by buying a two-year-old mare aptly named "Defiantly," in partnership with his friend Nathan Avery, the founder of Galveston Houston, and gave Joanie his share on her birthday.

With the Averys they drove out to Arundel in Sussex to visit their mare and meet her trainers, John and Susan Dunlop: *A very pretty drive. The strength and beauty of England is in the countryside ... Defiantly is "high in the haunch," but very friendly. We had drinks at the Dunlops' – trainers here can be of significant social as well as professional standing. We lunched at Bailiffscourt, formerly the home of Lord Moyne of the Guinness family and now a luxurious country hotel – a genre which is something of a new development and becoming a runaway success, perhaps catering to the growing prosperity of the middle class here who do not necessarily own, or have access to country houses. I think that to understand the English countryside is to understand much of the English character.*

Another countryside event was shooting, part of England's social fabric like fox-hunting or the King James Bible. Peter was invited to a day's pheasant-shooting in December in Northamptonshire, about sixty miles outside London: *Drove through dark and rain to Wakefield Lodge a 4,000 acre estate which originally belonged to the Dukes of Grafton, the first of whom was an illegitimate son of King Charles II, but now owned by the Richmond-Watsons, whose money was made more conventionally and more recently in real estate … I knew most of the other members of the party and there was a great feeling of "bonhomie." The whole organization was extremely efficient, though not at all formal. [After hot drinks, marmite sandwiches and homemade sausage rolls], the shooting began promptly at 9.30 … We shot for four drives until 1.30 with a break for "bull shots" – hot consommé laced with vodka – or sloe gin … and more sausage rolls. The pheasants flew well in spite of the drizzle … the bag was nearly 250, of which I must have accounted for about 20 …*

Lunch was a proper sit-down affair with Mrs Richmond-Watson senior presiding over a long mahogany table, gleaming with crystal and silver, and overlooked by portraits of sporting gentlemen and fine ladies with powdered hair. There was champagne and first rate red Bordeaux with a world class steak and kidney pie … As we sipped the port, we could see … that the rain was really setting in. But Julian Richmond-Watson called out "boots and spurs" and we set off again to brave the elements. It was in fact a wash-out, as the rain turned to sleet, nothing much would fly and we gave up after one drive and went back to the house for tea and/or malt whisky "to banish the cold" …. Tea continued into the evening and the party was definitely well warmed up before it broke up. CR-G forgot his dog and didn't remember him until he was back in London so he had to drive all the way back to pick him up!

Keen that his board members appreciate the commercial case for his London residency, Peter planned a quarterly meeting at the Savoy Hotel right next to the City. He had arranged visits to the Stock Exchange and a number of the merchant banks and brokerage houses, including some continental and Japanese institutions. As anticipated, they were suitably impressed by the unconstrained global perspectives that were demonstrated – people were as at home discussing markets in Tokyo and Hong Kong,

New York or Paris as they were with their domestic market. Wanting to offer them some amusement in British country fashion, he organized a day's partridge shooting in Wiltshire close to Salisbury plain so as to include a visit to Stonehenge, Salisbury Cathedral, and Winchester.

Despite speculation among some of the English contingent about how "the Canadians" would manage, they thoroughly distinguished themselves, behaving with "perfect propriety" in the field. But there was a moment of some confusion when Michael Meighen asked his loader how long they usually left the partridges to hang before cooking them. The laconic reply was distinctly mystifying: "We don't eat Frenchmen in Wiltshire, Sir!" Unbeknownst to Michael, they had been shooting red-legged partridges known as "Frenchmen" (or "Spaniards" depending on which English county you are shooting in), and the locals eschew the "red-leg" variety for the pot.

At the time the Concorde was still in its heyday, crossing the Atlantic in a mere three and a half hours at twice the speed of sound, with the passengers being treated to the civilized norms of pre-war first-class shipboard travel – endless vintage Dom Perignon, an unlimited supply of caviar, and impeccable service. Adding to the Concorde's hedonistic appeal, as in any decent club, there was no lack of kindred spirits offering interesting and sometimes highly informative conversation. The environment suited Peter perfectly and he soon became a regular, taking a seat in front of the bulkhead which offered a little more leg-room for a tall fellow. The mere possibility of making the journey from London to downtown Manhattan for a meeting and an early lunch and back to London for a late dinner had the appeal of fantasy – and was of occasional practical value.

15

Cycles and Sashimi

PETER AND JOANIE'S most compelling European discovery was the joy of the bicycle as a touring vehicle, under the auspices of the highly innovative Canadian travel company Butterfield and Robinson. Combining the smooth efficiency of a military operation, the spirit of adventure, and the finest of personal service, B&R had refined the sweaty bicycle trip into state-of-the-art luxury travel. No lugging of cumbrous machines through railway stations and cheap hostels. Best-of-the-breed bikes were provided and serviced "sur place," and luggage transported from one superb accommodation to the next. Culture vultures could enjoy lectures on local history, architecture, and archaeology and plenty of agreeable wine-tastings – a formula perfectly calculated to appeal to the Cundills.

The first of their many B&R trips was in 1986, a fairly leisurely tour of Burgundy. Each day's itinerary offered alternative routes for those who simply wanted to potter along viewing the sights as well as those who, like Peter and Joanie, were intensely competitive and wanted challenges. Peter and Joanie managed to intensify the exertions to their complete satisfaction – Joanie would always insist on taking the toughest route possible and Peter even supplemented by running several miles a day before setting out.

But Peter began the vacation in a slightly bleak mood: *I did some numbers while waiting for the flight to Lyon. We are making money in absolute terms, which is fine, but in relative terms it's awful. We manage $333 million of which 34% is in cash, but we have far too many holdings. I am tense because of the lack of performance, insecure and off form, which tends to make me aggressive and adopt a tone that jars.*

He was taking a hyper-critical attitude. The Value Fund had actually appreciated by 22% in 1985, and 1986 was just proving a little more difficult. Few securities around the world qualified under his strict value criteria, and markets were decidedly frothy. Although he had occasionally been tempted, he rarely compromised, with the result that cash had piled up as markets rose to dizzying heights, with the positions he held in the fund becoming statistically "overvalued" and therefore automatically subject to pruning. The high number of holdings worried him, because concentration was almost invariably important in achieving good performance. In this instance the self-criticism was not entirely justified because the Value Fund's top ten holdings actually represented 30% of assets and cash a little more than 30%. But the positions he intended to build had run away in price before he could accumulate normal-sized holdings, and a number of small holdings had been introduced by way of having an initial "look and see."

Only by getting the big decisions right can investment performance be maintained, so small positions ... have virtually no impact on the portfolio as a whole and consume a great deal of research time. Nevertheless, as a value investor it is unavoidable to have a certain quantity of small positions either because one remains unconvinced for the present of the share's intrinsic worth or because ... it is very attractive but difficult to buy. To my mind the second reason is perfectly in accordance with strict value practice. The first, however, seems to me to be more awkward to rationalize since it is often the result of insufficiently profound research or of a tendency to compromise ... We should be very wary of such a drift and nip it in the bud by imposing even stricter disciplines on ourselves during overvalued market conditions.

The fund had suffered few losses of any consequence; nevertheless, Peter had continued to assess his principles of value investment and reached conclusions slightly at odds with purist Benjamin Graham theory. At the outset he had declared that he would buy any share that met strict value criteria. He now added two small but important corollaries: *One must have a clear understanding of what a company does and how it actually makes money out of doing it, or even sometimes how it could make money out of doing it. I don't believe that this understanding is achieved just by looking at a company's own statements; it is essential to read around its industry. For instance, it is well to know what its market share is in its main cash-generating business. We have occasionally overlooked the fact that a company's management was extremely mediocre. We should in fact be under no illusions about the fact that our precious "margin of safety" is under the custodianship of the management.*

The Burgundy vacation was obviously needed to give him time to consider such questions away from the daily cut and thrust, and Peter's outlook became brighter as the trip progressed. On the first day: *We took the train to Beaune in 90 degrees of heat and the air conditioning was totally inadequate. We lodged at the Hotel Le Cep – but it's the wrong season for mushrooms – I ran three very slow miles in the hills above the town – no gas.* But on the next: *Had a really fine sleep and woke to thunder and lightning. I ran in the fresh rain from Beaune to Pommard and Meursault and back. It felt good.*

Although Peter fell off his bike while demonstrating how to ride with no hands, skinning his elbows and calves, and then had trouble with a constantly-slipping bicycle chain, he was soon ecstatic. The eighty-kilometre ride through countryside that resembled a Sisley landscape was "glorious," and a visit to a ninth-century abbey founded by Charlemagne's grandson "Charles the also Bald" allowed him to bask in the peace of its honey-coloured stone and sniff the surrounding meadows. The day ended with *wonderful garlicky frogs' legs* from the local ponds and comfortable chats with the other members of the party, lolling in the soft night air and sipping very cold champagne. However, the highlight of the journey was another triumph of athletic endurance:

We set out in the early morning, leaving the magnificent, fortified Château de Rochegude behind us, perched up on its hill overlooking the Rhone. We rode towards Orange, passing a perfectly preserved Roman amphitheatre, which just seemed to be waiting for the crowds to arrive for the blood and guts that evening ... J and I got separated, but I had told her that I would take the detour up to Les Baux de Provence and so, about 3 kilometres outside St Remy, I turned off for the 5-kilometre climb straight up to the medieval town, which sits, clinging to the top of a rocky gorge, like an eagle's nest. I said I would do it and I did and it was worth it. The view down onto the plain below is incomparable. I coasted back down to the main road in a euphoric state expecting an easy ride from there to St Remy. No such luck, with my muscles still juddering slightly after the effort up to Les Baux, I was confronted by another very steep hill. I was psychologically, as well as physically unprepared, but I didn't flinch – just gritted my teeth – and I didn't once get off my bike ... Arriving at the Hôtel Vallon de Valrugues was like entering Paradise. I just hugged J and plunged into the pool.

In Peter's end-of-year summing up, that first cycling expedition enjoys pride of place: *In many ways it was a disappointing year with mixed investment results and no marathons or hang gliding. On the other hand there was the biking trip, which was every bit as physically testing as a marathon and really good fun. All in all, in spite of the disappointing numbers (+7%), we had a good conference, there was a useful trip to Japan and we had a few good parties. It was a building year.*

The Japan trip deserves mention because it was the precursor to a long and successful investment involvement there. The entire Cundill Value Fund board and their wives were invited, and it is important to understand why. The road of a value investor is a lonely one, inevitably contrarian and often placing the practitioner in the uncomfortable position of being stubbornly wrong in the view of the majority of the investment community. Self-doubt easily creeps in, and from time to time – even for Peter – clinging to numbers and his well-tuned intuition was not enough. He needed to feel the confidence of his board. They were admirers of Peter to a man but by no means yes men; a case always had to be made, sometimes repeatedly. It was a reinforcing and comforting process in moments of adversity, and Peter relied on it. Board visits were well organized to the business purpose, and Peter regarded the social and cultural aspects as vital to the immersion process.

As I sat stark naked on my stool in the sauna/massage cubicle at the hotel being washed and brushed with sloppy soap by a hideous old hag wearing white overalls and wellington boots I wondered, "Will they get it, the extraordinary character of this economic power house which in so many cultural and sociological ways remains entrenched in a pre-industrial world?"

[At] a cocktail party at the Canadian Embassy for our party and a group of important businessmen, there were the usual canapés, some held together by small wooden cocktail sticks whose presence was not always immediately obvious. One of our Japanese guests ... helped himself from the tray and slipped the canapé into his mouth without removing the stick. I was mesmerised. He did not spit out the stick but manfully chewed his way though it and swallowed it with his eyes watering. He was absolutely not going to lose face by doing something inelegant. Momentarily I had been severely tested to restrain an outright burst of

laughter but then I thought, this is the kind of self-discipline that we would be investing in.

Some of us got up very early to pay a visit to the fish market – a remarkable experience – the fish so absolutely fresh and the place so clean that it didn't even smell of fish. Hundreds of workers were going about their business in such an orderly, organized way, all dressed in spotless white plastic coats and white rubber boots, their hair completely covered with white cotton hats. We watched the tuna auction – hundreds of enormous, beautiful beasts to be eaten raw for Tokyo's lunch, an industry in itself. The auction was nothing like the screamed gesticulations on a stock exchange floor – fast and efficient but not noisy. We had breakfast there – okayu (rice porridge), tamagoyaki (rolled omelette) and, because of where we were, the most amazing selection of sashimi ... We were energized for the day ahead.

The board left Japan convinced, although ironically, Peter's first investment move subsequent to this visit was to go short on the Japanese index – the Nikkei 500 – a position that cost him many sleepless nights and a good deal of unease among the directors of the Value Fund. He gritted his teeth for over three years before the Japanese market collapsed, making him a substantial return. Not until the mid-1990s did he buy Japanese equities in any considerable way.

16

Crisis and Opportunity

No hangover! Oil price strong, stock market up, bond market robust but JK Galbraith says we're heading for a crash. I'm with him but God knows what the catalyst will be. What I do know is that wherever I look my kind of buys are scarcer than gold-dust.

Peter felt it in his bones – a tumble was in the works. But for the moment it seemed nothing could be done. His opening diary entry of 1987 was somewhat pensive: *There have been thousands of different representations made of our globe and numberless accounts of what purports to constitute reality, every one of which places gods ... in a different orientation. Clearly not all of them can be correct ... and yet society after society has fulfilled its destiny for transitory greatness, or doom and obscurity by following ... these fictions that humanity has projected upon our innocent planet. As though from a giant television screen they get beamed out unedited, lit solely by the illusions of passion, dogma, fanaticism, or over-weaning pride and ambition, until they fade or are deliberately expunged and become a note of history, a joke of time.*

Peter's first crash of the year was not the stock market. He rented a mountain bike to ride up Sabino Canyon near Tucson. On the final uphill stretch he was doing his imitation of Pedro Delgado, the renowned Tour de France rider, standing out of the seat with his full weight on the pedals in high gear. It was more than the rental bike could take; the chain broke, hurling Peter off onto his right elbow. New Year's Eve in the Eldorado Emergency Ward getting the gash in his arm stitched up was less than ideal – and Joanie was less than sympathetic. Show-offs, she said, nearly always get their come-uppance but have usually reached the age of discretion well before they reach forty, let alone fifty. Perhaps, he mused, quoting Benjamin Franklin, a special gift might be in order: "There are three faithful friends: an old wife, an old dog and ready money."

I ran for three hours under the Tour Eiffel and round the Champs-de-Mars ... Then on to Cartier to do penance in diamonds. In the evening the Cundills and McDermotts went to Lasserre for dinner where we ate macaroni (admittedly with foie gras and truffles) and crêpes suzette washed down with vintage Dom Perignon. J's froideur after the New Year debacle finally melted with some dancing at Regine's.

In the early spring, Peter touched base in Montreal to see his aging parents and revisit his roots: *Ran up the side of Mount Royal in arctic blue sky, just above freezing, sleigh bells tinkling and a wonderful view of the city ... The apartment in Gleneagles exudes warmth and comfort. It was all very nice – except my tough Mother almost burst into tears with her aches and pains. I rather love my Mummy. I was devastated and it brought them both back into focus.*

As summer approached, the bullish markets continued to roar. Peter was troubled by the danger signals, with money being "recklessly printed," risking the inevitable consequence of higher inflation, higher interest rates, a credit crunch, and a burst of the market bubble. He was frustrated that sticking to his principles had left him holding over 40% cash. For the moment this was hurting his comparative performance.

Alan Turing [the British cryptologist who broke the German High Command's Codes during the Second World War] said, "What do you do after you've broken the codes?" So how by analogy do I go on after developing the logic of successful investing. The best professionals feed on each other not just out of fellow feeling but out of the need for nurture, for argument, for support and for the insight to unlock the next door. At the moment I almost wish that I could change my investment skin to meet each variant moment. Only George Soros seems to have been able to develop a global strategy that can successfully adapt to all kinds of market conditions and it is implemented vigorously and forcefully with appropriate and well thought out action.

Waiting for the storm to break, he could only travel and listen. He went to Los Angeles to visit Tom Spiegel, head of Columbia Savings and Loan, and heard that the Security and Exchange Commission's prosecution of Drexel Burnham and Michael Milken for violating U.S. securities laws was proceeding, with no settlement negotiations being explored. The high-yield bond market was thus extremely fragile.

In Bermuda he met with his friend John Talbot, whom he invited to operate Peter Cundill Holdings Bermuda as his holding company. He offered Talbot $28,000 a year and was astonished to be negotiated down to $18,000 – the first time such a thing had happened to him.

He called on Asher Edelman in Lausanne, impressed as ever with his

sophistication and the enviable art collection he had assembled personally, including not only Braque and Picasso – owned too by Peter thanks
to Ron Longstaffe – but also the much more avant-garde Rauschenberg,
de Kooning, Warhol, and even Basquiat. He ended the trip at Templeton
College, Oxford, to see the eponymous Sir John receive his Honorary Degree.

*After these visits I was struck again by how important humility and
the elimination of ego are in the learning process. One must have the
capacity to turn oneself into an empty receptacle in order to assimilate
new things.*

In the end, the anticipated breaking of the storm found Peter in Hong
Kong on a Jardine Fleming pleasure cruise with a party of bankers and
investment managers. They had swum, water-skied, and enjoyed a splendid lunch: *No stock market nerves exposed here, I thought.*

But as they returned to the Star Ferry Terminal, the news came through
that the Dow Jones Index had dropped by 108 points, or 6%, that day,
with no suggestion of a rally at the closing bell. The carefree holiday
atmosphere was extinguished as the men migrated to their offices to
assess the damage. Peter, on the other hand, slipped quietly home to his
suite at The Peak and opened a bottle of champagne.

Two days later the Dow dropped a further 500 points in a single day,
the Nikkei by 600 points, and the Hong Kong exchange by 400. These
were unprecedented collapses, comparable only to the Wall Street crash
of 1929, and investors, professional and retail alike, were running truly
scared. On a conference call with his team in Vancouver after Black
Monday, Peter was asked how he felt about the outlook. "You can't see
my forefinger and thumb, but they're practically touching and I'm just
that far from euphoria. However, I'm staying low profile with the former
optimists. I see distress and pain in faces all around me and I haven't the
heart to gloat. We don't need to blow our own trumpets. The word that
we have been prescient is already on the street."

The window of opportunity was short-lived in the end, as markets
quickly rebounded in response to the rapid stimulation and easing of
credit undertaken by the financial authorities on a global basis. It was
the first time such a co-ordinated international response had ever been
witnessed, and it worked. *At such junctures bolstering confidence and
stimulating growth are of paramount importance and the continuing
obsession with inflation is entirely inappropriate.*

17

A Farewell and a Promise

FALL-OUT FROM cataclysmic events such as the October crash of 1987 can take many forms. It is well known that elderly people worry inordinately about their finances, and Peter's father, Frank, now well into his eighties, was no exception. He became unshakeably, although unjustifiably, convinced that the stock market collapse spelled penury for himself and Ruth. Until then Frank had remained supremely unaffected by his advancing age, continuing to hunt and fish, and even competing honourably in cross country skiing events. However, the fear inspired by the meltdown raised spectres from the past – memories of 1929 and his father's bankruptcy. Peter's efforts to reassure him were to no avail, and his health soon began to suffer seriously: *I have spent all week on the phone with my parents, Father is very clearly getting senile, focused on one thing only – the stock market. For the first time ever I told him today that I loved him.*

On learning that Frank had tried to commit suicide by jumping out of a window, Peter cut short a business trip to fly back to Montreal. He found his father sitting at his desk, his hands shaking, looking unseeingly at his papers in complete despair. He got him into hospital straight away and then returned to the apartment to look after his distraught mother:

I went through Father's records – simple, tidy and effective. He has managed his affairs very well as I was certain would be the case. When I returned to the hospital he was very low, shuffling, dispirited and confused. I left the room for a moment to speak to the doctor and he tried to follow me; then, as I came back in I found him trying to climb out of the window again. I picked him up gently, noticing how extraordinarily light he was. I was shaken.

The next morning I went back. The weather was well below zero – a real Montreal winter's day. McGill kids were playing a new kind of ball hockey with girls! When the snow lies dirty on the edge of the road and the greyness sits heavily there is no great charm, just the dampness and penetrating cold. BUT it is my roots.

When I got to the hospital I had a huge surprise. Father was wonderful, lucid, cheery and curious. He'd even done a few push-ups. Boy, was I glad to see it. It means that there's hope which I didn't have. As I headed for Mirabel there was a wonderful orange and red winter sunset. My mood was lighter but I know that Father's illness is profoundly on my heart.

Within two weeks Peter was rushing back to Montreal: *He was very, very weak and now seemed unbelievably old, wearing an oxygen mask, muttering and waving his hands around feebly. I held his hand and told him I was there. He revived slightly and started to talk of going to the bar and how long it had been since he had had a gin and tonic. Funnily enough, it felt nice just being there with him.*

By the time I got back to the hotel Mother had called to say that the hospital had telephoned her to ask permission not to put Father back onto the support system. I agreed. His poor brain and body are shot. Good-bye Daddy.

How do I feel about FHC's death? I am calm, numb, curious about the process; relieved he had no real pain and the mental anguish quickly converted itself into pneumonia and then coma. I wonder, did the fighting parts just stop functioning? At the moment I feel no grief, but a nagging sense of loss and even more strongly a feeling that the cycle of life simply played itself out, without a ripple on the harmony and order of the universe.

Peter's mother, thoroughly organized as always, had the obituary ready and made all the arrangements within twenty-four hours. On the morning of the cremation Peter went for a run, taking a route that passed most of the old locations with family memories: *Just as I turned from Atwater into Côte des Neiges I felt FHC's presence beside me. We chatted – he suggested that I learn to fish properly if I wanted him to hang around – maybe silly, but very comforting! The cremation was mercifully brief. Mother held Grier's hand and mine tightly but otherwise kept perfect control.*

The service at St James the Apostle Anglican Church was attended – surprisingly, given the short notice – by over two hundred people; old Montreal had turned out in force to say farewell to one of its most endearing members, a gentleman and a sportsman to his fingertips. The swelling chorus of "Onward Christian Soldiers" that concluded the ceremony left

Peter holding back tears, not wanting to look around him in case he broke down, still holding his mother's hand tightly.

Since the Cundill plot and gravestones in the Mount Royal Cemetery were dilapidated and vandalized, it was decided to bury Frank's ashes at Cap à l'Aigle. Peter was unable to be present, but a few months later he made his own pilgrimage to the tiny church of St Peter on the Rock, perched on the cliffs above the village in peaceful isolation, with a sweeping view across the St Lawrence. It was run-down and lacked a minister, but the familiar scent of pine, wet rocks and sand lingered, although the tang of creosote was long gone.

Peter stayed for the weekend, basking in nostalgia. He visited his cousin Robert Cundill, whom he found watching the Wimbledon tennis, called on Anne Cabot, receiving an invitation to visit her gardens, and had a *chien chaud* for lunch. He found the Manoir Richelieu, the grandest hotel in La Malbaie, "bustling and almost as stylish as in the past," and took a post-prandial stroll along the Boulevard smoking a cigar. On Sunday he attended Morning Prayer at St Peter's in the company of about a dozen, mostly elderly, ladies. Before heading back to Quebec City along the coast road, with its spectacular views, he promised the verger he would take care of the roof repair.

PART · THREE ·

18

Vintages '48 and '38

IN THE AUTUMN of 1988 Peter was to turn fifty and was determined to celebrate in style with a party in New York as the culmination of the Cundill Value Fund conference. But first, there was a fortieth birthday in Venice to attend.

Peter and Joanie flew in with the other Canadian guests. The most spectacular views of "La Serenissima" greeted them as they crossed the lagoon from Marco Polo airport in a high-speed motorboat and then made a slow progress along the Grand Canal to the water entrance of the Gritti Palace Hotel. *We went for tea at Harry's Bar to see Patti and CR-G, where they were meeting up with the leader of the band that is to play at the party. Patti was saying that she wanted a string quartet as well, to welcome the guests at the top of the stairs as they arrived. Too late for that, I thought ...*

In the evening we changed into our "glad rags," me into white-tie, and took a leisurely gondola ride through narrow canals ... to the Palazzo Pisani-Moretta, on the opposite side of the Grand Canal, not far from the Rialto bridge. We landed at the water entrance and climbed the great staircase, garlanded with white, richly scented gardenias, to the strains of Vivaldi played by the quartet I'd said would be impossible [but found at the eleventh hour through the good offices of CR-G's friend Nabil Chartouni]. The huge reception rooms of the palace known as the "piano nobile" don't boast electricity, so the entire floor was lit with candles burning in chandeliers and wall brackets. It was a magical sight with the ladies in all their finery, wearing their most precious jewels, showing off a generous amount of cleavage, and the men in full evening dress. It was like being transported back to the "belle époque."

We started with flagons of the famous bellini (fresh white peach juice mixed with ... "prosecco") made by Harry's Bar, who were doing the catering, and then moved into the reception room which overlooked the Grand Canal ... Buffet dinner had been laid out on huge sideboards like

*an Italian renaissance still-life painting, exotically festooned with fruit
and flowers. I sat beside Wendy, Countess of Caledon, a handsome 32-
year-old divorcee with plenty of spark. We had a good conversation and
a nice dance. Later I joined the Guests and the McLernons and danced,
among others, with Valerie Black, a cousin of CR-G's, bright and
extremely attractive – makes jewellery in London and I shall visit her studio. We headed home to the Gritti, footsore at about 4:00 am by water
taxi unfortunately missing the later antics with CR-G's brother-in-law
hijacking a motor boat and driving it at high speed down the Grand
Canal and plump young Bowen's seduction of Georgina, Patti's very
skinny secretary.*

For his New York conference, Peter arrived in the city a day early to
dine with Sir Crispin Tickell, UK ambassador to the United Nations, and
Lord Jenkins of Hillhead, who was to be his introductory speaker at the
Metropolitan Club. Jenkins was quite a catch; recently elected as chancellor of Oxford University, he had served as Chancellor of the Exchequer
and deputy leader of the British Labour Party. As the first president of
the European Commission, he was supremely well qualified to address
Peter's audience on the subject of the European Union and its political
and economic significance. A press reference to his being the son of a
miner from South Wales had drawn a trenchant comment from Frank
Johnson, the famed political sketch writer: "True, certainly; but only in
the sense that it is true to describe Mrs Jacqueline Onassis as the widow
of a Greek merchant seaman. It simply does not do justice to Jenkins'
position in cafe society."

The conversation that evening went in a direction entirely to Peter's
taste. There was a discussion of *War and Remembrance*, a TV production
serializing Herman Wouk's novel *The Winds of War*, starring Robert
Mitchum. Its sweeping canvas prompted entertaining reminiscences from
Jenkins, who was a great raconteur and had served in the Royal Artillery
during the Second World War and was one of the code breakers at
Bletchley Park. Jenkins had a reputation as a *bon vivant* as well as an
intellectual, and Sir Crispin brought out the best the ambassadorial cellar
could offer – Château Lafleur 1961 claret and Taylor's 1945 port.

Jenkins was in fine form the next morning, in spite of the previous
evening's port and cigars. He delivered a brilliant and witty *tour d'horizon*, in which he acutely observed that if the planned common currency

was to be successful, EU members would have to move rapidly toward fiscal union, with a European Central Bank eventually assuming a role akin to that of the Federal Reserve.

As chairman of the Cundill Value Fund, Gowan Guest took the floor at the end of lunch on the final day to present Peter with a silver plaque signed by all the board members, with a voucher for an expedition for two on Mount Everest under the guidance of Sir Edmund Hillary – Peter's fiftieth-birthday gift from his grateful directors.

The party was held at the Rainbow Room, overlooking Rockefeller Centre. The theme was blue, Peter's favourite colour, and the whole effect, with the flowers, the lighting and the table settings, was stunning: *It was a magical evening. My old flames Patricia Lorsch [née Welbourn] and Janet Blatchford were there, my family, my patrons, my friends and business associates. The band led by Bob Hardwick was magnificent, and at about one o'clock Ursula [Kummel] had arranged for Betty Brinkley to come on to sing "Embraceable You," "Memories," and "You Make Me Love You." At about 2 a.m. about 30 of us went on to Doubles and carried on dancing until 4.*

Joanie was not as ecstatic. She had been seated at a table remote from Peter's with Patricia's and Janet's husbands, who were also less than amused that their wives had been placed on either side of their host. The last straw was the spectacle of Ursula mooning over Peter to the strains of "Embraceable You." Joanie did not go on to Doubles.

19

The Everest Trek

IN ALL HIS TRAVELS, Peter had never been out of touch with markets or his Vancouver office for longer than the duration of a plane flight. For his trip to Mount Everest, he would be incommunicado for almost two weeks and, while the thought did cause him slight disquiet, his two deputies, Brian McDermott, president of Peter Cundill and Associates, and Gowan Guest, chairman of the Cundill Value Fund, were in a state of near total panic. The imponderable "what ifs" became frankly ludicrous:

We had a board meeting ... prior to which I spoke to Gowan and Brian. I was both anxious and extremely irritated. I cannot pretend that I am completely unconcerned as to what course events may take in my absence ... But I had supposed it to be the role of these two grown-up and experienced men to be reassuring me that all would be well and not the other way round ... Should I be more worried than I am? I suppose that in a way I have to regard their discomfort as flattering, but it under-lines for me the absolute necessity of building an in-depth investment team to whom my investment precepts are like second nature and who are, therefore, competent to take the helm with confidence, whenever or if ever it may be necessary ... Should anything happen to me I have asked Mike Price [of Mutual Shares] to take charge of the investment manage-ment of the fund and he has agreed.

The first view of the great mountain range from the air was so sensa-tional and otherworldly that the gloom instantly lifted, all motion seemed suspended at the roof of the world, and the recent squabbles, personality clashes, and investment concerns faded into insignificance. When they landed, the air was a draught of champagne.

The battered taxi that struggled up to the Yak and Yeti Hotel in Kathmandu was a vintage 1940s Buick, and the scene right out of a film set. Peter was half expecting to see Gary Cooper lunching outside, instead of his fellow trekker, Woody Maclaren. They were both slightly appre-hensive about whether they would be up to the physical challenges of the adventure ahead. They spent that afternoon soaking in the atmosphere of the town, wandering though crowded markets still unused to tourists, rich with animal and human smells and the fragrance of spices and street food. The people were evidently poor but not downtrodden or hangdog; just full of earthy humour and with a touch of arrogance.

After icy pre-dawn showers the next morning, they boarded a single-engine Cessna for their base camp, landing on a grassy airstrip that reminded Peter of Courchevel in the French Alps. They were greeted by Sir Edmund Hillary with an assembly of Sherpas – small mountain-tanned men with peaceful, smiling eyes, dauntingly fit and clearly more than able to shoulder their allotted forty kilos of baggage.

The first day, as a warm-up, they crossed and re-crossed the Dudh Kosi River up to Lukla at 9,000 feet. The suspension bridges were quite sufficient challenge without the climb. With nothing but a single handrail, they stretched perilously over the river gorges, swaying in the wind. Mid-afternoon, the group pitched camp on a small hillside over-looking the river and settled down to a "happy-hour"as the sun faded and the temperature dropped. They were all in their sleeping bags in pitch black by seven o'clock, but when Peter woke in the middle of the night, the stars were poking out from the indigo sky, lighting up the peak of Everest itself in brilliant white. He felt he was staring straight up into an abode of the gods.

When he rolled out of his sleeping bag again at five the next morning, the Sherpas were ready with steaming hot tea, biscuits, and bowls of hot water for shaving. The day's march went up and down along the river to the village of Jorsale, where the local lama, anticipating their arrival, was prepared with a petition for help to rebuild his monastery after a recent fire and to repair the school roof, which had blown off in the win-ter gales. However, he made the mistake of trying to charge Peter and Woody for a blessing – and the Sherpas revealed that he was not above feathering his own nest. Peter decided that donations through the Sir Edmund Hillary Foundation would be more effective.

After a hurried snack, the party pressed on for another couple of hours, at which point, to Peter's surprise, the Sherpas pitched camp again just before lunch. The campsite was truly lovely, on the banks of the river just above a rock pool where Peter and Woody washed and "dunked" in the glacial water. The rest of the day was spent leisurely

reading and lazing about in the sunshine, but Peter wished the hike had
been more physically testing.

The following day they again had energy to spare: *Tea and cookies at
dawn. Woody and I led the trek up to Namche Bazaar where we got our
first close-up view of Everest. Everyone is telling us that this is world-
class trekking, but I found it like a medium/hard half day's hike with
Joanie in the Alps. After a tour of a forest nursery sponsored by EH, we
climbed gently up into a small valley near Tesho where we camped.
Woody and I were still full of energy so we hiked upwards on our own
through a landscape that reminded me of the Dorset Downs, except dotted
with yaks not sheep. We had a great view of Khumbu, the sacred mountain, and we got hot enough to splash in a mountain stream and drink the
bitingly cold water .... It was EH's last night with us, so the Woodchuck
brought out the Sockeye Salmon jerky and the vodka, and that really
stimulated the conversation. EH relaxed thoroughly and there was lots
of laughter, in between serious discussion of the projects closest to his
heart ... He is articulate, charming, and quite erudite when he gets going.*

In reference to the element of luck that affects any venture, including
conquering Everest, Hillary quoted a remark apparently made by Field
Marshal von Blücher, who arrived at the battle of Waterloo in the nick
of time to support Wellington: *"All skills are in vain when the angels piss
on your flintlocks."*

Peter was up again at dawn, nursing a splitting headache for which
the altitude was not altogether to blame, but a run along the river bank
and a "head splash" had cured it before they said goodbye to Hillary.
Their new leader was Zeke O'Connor, head of the Sir Edmund Hillary
Foundation of Canada, which had provided funding for Hillary's most
important projects, including the Khunde Hospital and the Khunying
High School, which were on their itinerary that day. As they skirted the
lower slopes, they spotted herds of mountain goats – *thars* – grazing in
the lush vegetation and, what especially caught Peter's eye, indigenous
pheasants, the original stock from which the species had been introduced
into Europe and then North America.

The visit to the high school, the first in the district, was delightful. The
younger children sang English songs for them, and they were impressed
that the school was now teaching children for miles around up to tenth
grade. After gratefully quaffing draughts of the local beer, they went on

to the hospital, where Peter had the "peak experience" of his day: *Changed at the hospital in Dr. McLauren's quarters and had my first decent crap of the week and then the joy of a hot shower – such simple carnal pleasures – while looking out onto Amai Dablang, the "turquoise goddess" up at 15,000 feet, Kangtega, the "saddle" at 17,000, and Thamserku at 16,500 ... unforgettable.*

Peter woke before sunrise to visit the open "privy" where he could gaze on the snowy peaks in silhouette against the black sky. Walking back, he caught the first light as it touched the summits, sending shivers down his spine. It being a "rest" day, Peter and Woody explored, gambled in a tearoom, rolling dice with forest wardens, and chatted to a young woman doctor, recognizable from her t-shirt as a McGill graduate. When they joined Zeke for drinks at their camp downriver, Peter took the opportunity to announce his pledge of $5,000 a year to the Hillary Foundation. And out came the Crown Royal Canadian whiskey.

Under a cloudless sky the next day, they made their final outward trek, to the Tengboche Monastery at 13,000 feet. There on the plateau beside the monastery, with a hen pheasant fluffing herself contentedly in the dust in front of them and Everest rising in all its magnificence as a backdrop, Woody unfurled his red and white umbrella, prominently decorated with Canadian maple leaves, and the companions posed for a triumphant photo. Their celebratory dinner featured the chicken that had travelled alive with them, dangling from a Sherpa's belt. The conversation focused mainly on mountaineering, and they toasted Picard, the French climber who had left at dawn, preparing to climb to the summit of Everest by moonlight, without oxygen. And there were snippets of gossip; the supposedly celibate abbot of Tengboche, who also blessed heads for money, was in disgrace, having got a young girl pregnant. His fall from grace was ascribed, by locals at least, to the corrupting influence of a recent visit to the United States. Peter was somewhat skeptical, recalling Chaucer's description of the friar in *The Canterbury Tales* as "a wanton and a merry."

They said farewell to Zeke at first light and started their descent in the charge of Sherpa Kensa, with the prospect of seven bridges ahead – five of the swaying suspension variety and two rickety wooden ones. Peter had been extremely wary of them to begin with, but concentrated on a vision of Hillary striding nonchalantly across deep gorges without even holding a handrail, and by the end of the second day was managing to do the same. The most serious challenge, however, was to come:

We had breakfast outside, beside the Everest Lodge ... As we were finishing, we began to see plumes of smoke rising from further down the valley and I had a premonition that this did not bode well. While we waited for the porters, black and white cinders floated past, more and more thickly, on a stiff breeze and we could even hear the crackle of flames, which we thought were coming from the West side of the ravine. In fact the fire was on our side, started by two woodcutters preparing their lunch. There was a strong southerly wind which was ... whipping up the flames so that they were leaping a couple of hundred yards at a time. As we began feverishly to criss-cross the gorge, we managed, more by chance than design, to keep to the opposite side of the main blaze.

I was anxious from the beginning; Woody and Kensa unconcerned, but as we continued the arduous business of traversing, Kensa began to be a little nervous as well, and Woody, by now exhausted and suffering from thirst and heat burn, simply gave up caring what would happen. At one point he stopped dead with the flames only about 250 yards from us. Kensa was urging us to press on as fast as we could, but Woody just murmured, "I'm not moving and I don't give a fuck if I die." But Kensa and I managed to get him moving again.

I was keen to push on towards Lukla, to put as much distance as possible between us and the flames, but Woody probably couldn't have made it. Miraculously the wind now shifted and Kensa was then certain that if we crossed the gorge again, via the suspension bridge, we could camp safely on the other side, putting the ravine between us and the fire. We climbed up to a knoll about half a mile further away from the flames and sank onto the grass completely shattered after the longest trek of the trip – nearly 9 hours practically without a break. I slept like a log, waking only once in the night to peer across and check that the fire was no closer.

We woke before dawn in the glow of the flames and wasted no time getting moving on to Lukla, making it there in about four hours ... Woody was still played out when we arrived, but my adrenalin was racing and so I hiked around Lukla for a couple of hours. The "King of Lukla," the Mountain Trail guy, got us onto the first flight out at 8 a.m. and as I watched the breathtaking spectacle of the light hitting the high peaks for the last time there were tears in my eyes.

We reached Bangkok before we knew it, checking in at the Oriental,
me in my dirty khakis, smelling of fire and wearing a black baseball cap.
I must have looked like a refugee from the Vietnam War. I tried to sleep
after a wonderful hot bath but was still too keyed up, my mind filled with
the images of an extraordinary trip, so ... W. and I set out once more,
now resplendent in suits and ties, for champagne and a magnificent sea
bass in butter sauce at the Shangri-La and finally on to Diana's to chat
up air-hostesses.

In his absence, there had been no panics or disasters in the investment
world, and Peter went straight on to Hong Kong, where the Cundill
Conference was to take place that year, and where he planned to spend
three months. While dining one evening with Winnie Wong (a well-known
Hong Kong notable) at the American Club in Repulse Bay, she began to
talk about the Japanese occupation of the colony which she had experienced as a child. Time had not moderated the hatred that she, a Chinese
woman, felt about the atrocities perpetrated, especially in mainland
China. Peter could only speculate on what impact such antipathy might
eventually have on Japan once China emerged as a rival global economic
force, although he was inclined to think that justifiable Chinese distaste
for the Japanese would be tempered by pragmatism. Winnie recounted an
incident that stuck with him – she had once peeped through a keyhole to
watch a Japanese executioner who was billeted in her family home, as
he was praying in his permanently darkened room: *that image makes it*
even harder to imagine at what point ethics and civilization succumb to
primitive brutality.

Peter travelled on to Tokyo with this vignette in mind. He spent an
evening with his friend Yuge-San, who took him, for the first time, to his
geisha house in Koa. Was this privilege perhaps even more significant
than his introduction to Yuge-San's family twenty years earlier? he wondered. Mukowzima, Yuge-San's favourite lady, was in her mid-forties,
officially under the "protection" of a wealthy elder statesman; Peter was
in the care of two much younger ladies. They all drank beer and sake, and
the girls sang and danced while Mukowzima accompanied. During one
of the games organized by Mukowzima, one young lady leaned against

Peter very subtly, but suggestively, fully intending that it be noticed. Notwithstanding, the evening was all over by nine o'clock and Peter left, musing on what might have happened if he had responded. It was difficult to fathom, given the elegance and formality of the occasion, but he knew that the bill for the evening would have been eye-watering either way and he turned to Oscar Wilde for a rather enigmatic reflection: *"Saints always have a past and sinners always have a future."*

The International High Life

CASUALTIES FROM THE 1987 crash surfaced for some time after the initial shock waves. In early 1988 Prudential-Bache closed down the London end of its "risk arbitrage" activities, which I had directed since 1982. I decided to launch the Petrus Fund, a "fund of funds" invested primarily in hedge funds, in partnership with Count Hadelin de Liedekerke-Beaufort, who had been a close colleague at Pru-Bache, and Peter readily agreed to join our board.

In July of the following year Peter found himself flying to Brussels for the first Petrus board meeting, at the home of Count Roland de Kergorlay, its chairman and largest investor. A distinguished graduate of the Sorbonne and McGill, with a doctorate in economics from Harvard, Kergolay had led the team that negotiated the entry of the United Kingdom into the European Union, during which he had got to know Roy Jenkins well. When Jenkins became president of the European Commission, he appointed Kergorlay as its ambassador to Washington. Kergorlay was also a gifted and original investor, particularly as a venture capitalist and as a real estate investor in less well known corners of Europe, notably Portugal. With his love of shooting, old master drawings, and "haute cuisine," he was just the sort of character that appealed to Peter.

Kergorlay's home was at Hougoumont outside Brussels, very close to the site of the Battle of Waterloo. After a lunch accompanied by the "incomparable" Château Petrus, and a tour of Kergorlay's collection of drawings, there was a visit to the nearby Cyclorama of the famous battle. Then on to the Ardennes to the Liedekerke family estate:

I ran about five miles around the estate ... and then to the little town of Celles, where I went into the church, dedicated in 900 AD to St Hadelin and full of Liedekerke-Beaufort family monuments. On the outskirts of the town I came across the shell of a German Tiger tank from World War II. It had been left there as a monument, marking the limit of the German panzer breakout during the Battle of the Bulge in 1944. As I ran back I

passed the Liedekerkes' huge Victorian pile of a castle built in the high
Gothic manner and now serving as a boarding school. Further on I saw
their original medieval castle above the village of Veves ... dominating
the whole area like a mini kingdom.

We had tea in the library of the newest family home. The room had
been dismantled from the old castle piece by piece and re-erected inside
the shell of a huge barn attached to the ancient farmhouse complex that
now formed the third residence occupied by the Liedekerkes over the
last thousand years. We dined ... by candlelight from branched silver
candlesticks, joined by Hadelin's very charming wife, Angele, and we
repaired, for coffee, liqueurs and excellent cigars, to the library again, in
which the enormous open fireplace, about five yards wide, had been lit
and was crackling with great logs off the estate. The firelight threw shad-
ows up onto the rows of leather-bound books lining two stories, with a
balcony walkway in between, emphasising the rich colours of the book
bindings and the warm reds and russets of the rugs and furniture. It was
truly a room to be loved and lived in – no wonder they didn't want to
leave it behind.

Peter's involvement with United World Colleges, and his generous gifts
to Pearson College, its school in British Columbia, had led to two invi-
tations to visit the original Atlantic College at St Donat's Castle in
Wales. There he had met several trustees, including the young Duke of
Westminster, and former prime minister Sir Alec Douglas-Home, with
both of whom he had struck a chord, admiring them for their dedicated
work and practical approach. It was therefore no surprise to receive an invitation to the silver jubilee celebrations of the United World Colleges
foundation. What did astonish him was the lavish scale of the affair, even
though UWC was close to Prince Charles's heart because of the support it
had enjoyed from Lord Mountbatten. And so at the beginning of August,
Peter and Joanie flew to London on a specially chartered Concorde, with a
hundred other guests, including Jeanne Sauvé, Canada's governor general.

At Highgrove, Prince Charles's country house in the Cotswolds, they
were welcomed personally by Charles and Princess Diana, and escorted
on a tour of the celebrated organic gardens. At the splendid lunch in a

spectacularly decorated marquee on the lawn in front of the house, Peter was seated beside a rather supercilious ten-year-old girl, the daughter of a Florida mall developer. She had been on Concorde plenty of times, she said, but was a little cross that her dress for the ball at Blenheim Palace was not new – she had already worn it once before.

At the dinner at the Royal Academy of Arts in London, Peter was more fortunate in his companion – *very rich, very LA, a little overpowering but actually very nice with it.* The speeches designed to open cheque books failed to impress: the last speaker was a *patronising dandy who considered himself to be the last letter in superiority and thoroughly enjoyed the sound of his own voice prattling on.* But the highlight of the three days was a grand ball at Blenheim Palace, hosted by the Duke and Duchess of Marlborough, as well as the Prince and Princess of Wales:

We entered the gates just as the sun was setting. What can one say except to repeat Prince Charles's line, "As palaces go, it's OK." There were cocktails in the Great Hall and the guests were received by our two hosts and hostesses, and [philanthropist] Armand Hammer and the Westons.

By contrast with yesterday the speeches were excellent, focusing on the achievements and goals of UWC. Prince Charles was especially good and he paid a warm and charming tribute to the work that Lord Mountbatten had put in before his death. After dinner we made our way out to the terrace to watch a floodlit display by the trumpeters and drummers of the Life Guards and the band of the Coldstream Guards who performed a tattoo. For some strange reason I thought of Nuremberg, but it was a spine-tingling, rather than spine-chilling, experience by any standard. There was a wonderful finale when all the Atlantic College students marched out carrying seventy different national flags ...

We danced to Lord Colwyn's band, which played jazz numbers, the Charleston and Dixie. Galen [Weston] danced with Princess Diana, who looked stunning, with a slight air of mystery and detachment about her. She has a stunning figure – finely toned as well as elegant – but with a distinct provocative allure. I danced the Charleston with J, rubber-legged as always, and then with Hilary Weston ... I was very proud to be Canadian. The Yanks and the Brits came to Blenheim to party after a two-day skirmish. The Yanks were flaky, vapid and ignorant, the Brits aloof above the fray. The Canadians were refined, never rowdy and only let themselves go when they were dancing, which is just as it should be! We won the party.

With scarcely a pause for breath, Peter and Joanie flew to Zurich for a
hiking expedition in the Alps around Interlaken. Peter loved it for the
physical challenge and the breathtaking mountain scenery. Although not
as awe-inspiring as the Himalayas, it provided much tougher exercise
than the Everest expedition. Peter described a typical hike:

*We got up to about 7,000 feet and lunched at the Hotel Obersteinberg.
It has no electricity and the delicious food is all cooked on wood fires
with the produce being carried up 4,000 feet on mules. The sound of
rushing water is everywhere and the spray too, glistening in the sunshine.
After a lunch of spit-roasted veal with wild mushrooms and rösti, we
climbed down almost precipitously back as far as Stechelberg and then,
without stopping, straight back up again to Murren, which may have the
most spectacular views of all across to the Eiger and the Jungfrau. We
took the little cog railway train back. We had walked and climbed for
nearly five hours and were deliciously tired, with protesting muscles, after
a truly magnificent day.*

Protesting muscles notwithstanding, Peter rose at dawn to do his
favourite run, winding along the paths at the bottom of the river valley
to the little town of Lauterbrunnen: *It is perhaps the prettiest of all the
runs I do anywhere and I delight in it. It is about 16 miles and I was
pleased with my strength after yesterday's strenuous efforts. Later on we
moved to the Palace Hotel in Gstaad; it is much grander but I love the
gentle Victoria-Jungfrau more – probably as much as anywhere I have
ever been. After dinner ... I watched a breathtakingly magnificent elec-
trical storm flashing great bolts of lightning across the sky and lighting
up the mountains in a way which reminded me of one of my favourite
paintings, John Martin's "Plains of Heaven" in the Tate Gallery.*

In Dante's Dark Wood

THE 1980S HAD been Peter's decade. With fifteen years of unbroken performance in the Cundill Value Fund under his belt, he was seen as no obscure maverick who got lucky but as a "contrarian magician" with a genius for stock picking and an unerring instinct for avoiding trouble. His energy was undiminished and his curiosity boundless.

In early February 1989 Peter's curiosity extended to joining me for a day and a half visiting a new venison-farming venture being developed by a friend of mine on an estate in Hertfordshire. Here is a sample from the detailed report in his journal.

[Kit Hughes] is an old friend of CR-G's and already known to me from our shooting expedition to Hungary, where he was very good company. With the help of some City friends, including CR-G, Kit raised about £300,000 to found Pelham Venison Ltd.

The 17th-century manor house is occupied by Kit's mother and sits in a fine garden populated by peacocks. The interior was quite a surprise, crammed with the most amazing art collection ranging from Canaletto and Reynolds, through the impressionists and post-impressionists and on to artists like Buffet and Dubuffet. Mrs Hughes, whose wealth comes from South Africa (her father was Oppenheimer's partner), has a great eye. She owns a lot of British artists including Ben Nicholson, Epstein and Matthew Smith and there is one room almost entirely hung with Rowlandson's caricatures – quite raunchy and very amusing ...

In the morning we toured the estate to see the deer. Not at all like cattle – one can see that they are in no sense domesticated – quite edgy in fact and I imagine difficult to handle. The deer share some of their paddocks with long-haired, long-horned pedigree Highland cattle – also pretty wild I believe but old Mrs H. likes to see them. Kit has very ingeniously converted a large listed medieval barn into his venison "factory" by erecting another structure inside the frame of the barn ... The factory also has a plucking line where pheasants and partridges off this estate

*and others are prepared in season for game dealers and the supermarkets
… The tour was followed by the AGM, the presentation of the report and
accounts and a very jolly lunch – rather like a shooting party really. The
company is not yet profitable but it may become so if venison really
catches on … CR-G drove me back and got caught speeding at 99 mph,
which means he escapes with a hefty fine rather than the automatic loss
of his licence for six months for doing 100 mph or more. I thoroughly
enjoyed the whole experience, including the drive!*

Despite a good start to the year, problems in the Vancouver office
were beginning to stack up. Issues with Ursula Kummel were proving
intractable, and Brian McDermott, as president, was clearly unable to deal
with them – indeed, she was really Peter's burden, largely self-inflicted.
McDermott had tried to improve matters by taking on another staff
member to help with Peter's non-stop travelling schedules, but Kummel
had taken umbrage at this invasion of her jealously guarded control of
anything related to Peter personally, even interfering with arrangements
and then blaming the new girl for the subsequent confusions. McDermott
recommended dismissing her for gross misconduct but Peter, in denial,
was incapable of disciplining her.

Kummel knew exactly how to play on his sense of obligation and
tribal loyalty: *Took Ursula to lunch where we demolished two bottles of
champagne and discussed the universe and her future. The time passed
very pleasantly – she seemed to be ahead of me, but there are still omis-
sions and commissions which would never have happened before. I
scolded her a little, she is taking up a lot of management time; but she is
the former heart of the business.*

Peter's relationship with Joanie was also at a difficult pass that may
have stemmed from a deeper malaise than the affront at Peter's birthday
party. She had finally decided Europe was not for her – certainly not
London – and had persuaded Peter to allow her to set up home in San
Francisco. The apartment in Chelsea had been sold and Peter had moved
into the Grosvenor House Hotel on Park Lane. By any other name it was
a separation. Peter did visit Joanie's home in Hillsborough but infre-
quently, and Joanie occasionally visited him in London, where she was
heard to remark that she didn't mind what he did when she was not
around but wished he would put the photographs away before she
arrived. Coincident with the two moves, Peter had insisted on their signing

a "post-nuptial" agreement, witnessed by Joanie's daughter, Evelyn. The terms were not ungenerous but the principle rankled.

No diary from Joanie has survived, so one can only speculate how she felt, although it seems likely that she had sensed that the marriage was under external threat of a kind that it had not previously confronted. The journal is revealing of a struggle on Peter's part: *Last night I experienced this feeling of active dislike of J, quite disturbing. It was a quick wave of feeling which then disappeared. Disquieting – you must try to combat it. I think it may be easier to see solutions if you can distinguish between context and content. If you can place a problem within the framework of the larger universe its dimensions are put into perspective and automatically diminished.*

When Peter had visited Templeton College for Sir John Templeton's investiture, he had travelled with a financial journalist who was working on yet another article about him, to which he had only reluctantly agreed. But one thing had led to another: *Took the train to Oxford with my journalist. Tape recorder both ways. We chatted with the students at the college after lectures. Later I took her to the High Commission for a Canada Day celebration and then to The Étoile and Annabel's, which she was keen to see. I wonder how this is going to turn out. There's the danger of exposing oneself unduly and that she will overcompensate by writing too sympathetically. I now, of course, regret having agreed to do this.*

Peter's dalliances thus far had been relationships of convenience involving decorative public companionship, social skills, and sex of a fairly casual kind. This time it was different – by the time the article appeared, a full-throttle love affair was underway: *She says the front page photo makes me look like an axe-murderer and the one on the inside like a Machiavellian courtier ... The piece itself will be gentle – she says the photos are really brooding, even wistful – just transformed by the glow I expect! All that out of ten minutes of camera work. I sat down with a glass of wine to read it. The article is quite flattering and well crafted. I could hear her voice.*

This, for him, was a new experience and fraught with danger. The journalist was a mature, intelligent woman, single and unattached, with a mind of her own and a successful career. For once his emotions were seriously engaged, and the pair mused about a trip to Vienna together. When he left to spend the Easter weekend in Yorkshire with David Craig, the senior partner of IFM Trading and a Far East investment expert, he was beset by doubts. However, he was immediately transported into a world about as far from the pressures of management, investment and romantic attachment as one could imagine:

David met me and we drove to Oswaldskirk to his wonderful old rectory, inhabited by his wife Sarah, children Emma and Josh, two dogs and a cat. I ran past Ampleforth College, David's old school, the Eton for Roman Catholic boys ... a Benedictine Abbey perched high on the edge of the Yorkshire dales – pretty bleak I thought. In the village I saw an old-fashioned wooden sign-post which read Wells – Cundall – a surprising and rather satisfying link with my Yorkshire origins ... There is something pleasant about being welcomed as a foreigner – one is not regarded as an outsider or an interloper, just accepted as "different," which isn't so bad.

We went to Easter service in the private chapel at Castle Howard and I took communion. No-one seemed to mind even though I'm not Catholic. God must have had to look me up on the list. It's been ten years at least. I had a tour afterwards, read for a while in the private quarters, and then Simon Howard led us off to the local pub in Morton for a pint of beer before lunch. I drank "bitter" for the first time – not too bad. Lunch was a [three-generation] family affair ... In the afternoon we went over to the Worsleys at Hovingham for a children's Easter egg hunt with huge excitement and high spirits, followed by "high tea."

This was his last completely carefree interlude for some time. The emotionally charged intensity of the affair was troubling him. It was clear that she wanted nothing less than marriage. Although Peter's relationship with Joanie might have had all the marks of an "open partnership" – and sexually-speaking this was true – the reality was not so simple. While they were mutually willing to tolerate frequent and lengthy periods apart and to cast a blind eye in the other's direction, they remained closer in other ways than many couples with far more conventional relationships. They were actually heavily reliant on each other and their intimacy remained real on a number of levels. But Joanie was not prepared to tolerate being made to look foolish, and Peter's occasional lapses of judgment in that regard had hardened her attitude.

However, she was a pragmatist at heart, and enjoyed what life as

Peter's spouse offered – many shared enthusiasms on the social and athletic front, as well as independence and an absence of financial constraint. For Peter she still represented a centre of gravity. The only home he had that was not associated with a hotel was wherever Joanie was, and she provided a place he could return to at any time for domestic comfort, tranquillity, support, and common-sense advice. The more he considered the alternative the less willing he felt to allow all this to unravel. He certainly recognized that the lady to whom he was presently so deeply attached would require fidelity, a more traditional measure of domesticity, and probably children – a change in lifestyle that would represent a wrenching about-face. Nevertheless, he was feeling the pressure.

On the professional front, his confidence and self-belief were being eroded by the performance of the Value Fund. He sensed a slippage of morale within Peter Cundill and Associates, suspecting that some among them felt that preaching patience was not enough and that he had perhaps lost his touch. The fact that he was so rarely physically present in Vancouver did little to redress the incipient malaise – he was shocked to be greeted one morning by the receptionist asking him, as if he were a client, who he was there to see.

The Viennese excursion went ahead and, with both parties studiously avoiding the subject of the future, it was an unqualified success. *We flew to Vienna to stay at the Palais Schwarzenberg … Our lovemaking was impassioned and abandoned with added spice from the gorgeously romantic background – wonderful food, wine, warmth and intellectual companionship such as I have never enjoyed before … we went to the Hofburg to visit the Imperial Library and the Crown Jewels … And finally the Belvedere … We came for the Klimts but were completely captivated by the entire experience and it has to be admitted that for lovers there is no more romantic painting than "The Kiss." Clichéd though it may seem, seen in the flesh it is heart-stopping. We held hands and melted before it.*

Peter's sense of well-being quickly evaporated. While in Bermuda for a board meeting of his offshore investment fund, the Cundill International Company, which had two new board members, Peter's old friend Ian

Steers of Wood Gundy and Peter Ackerman of Drexel, he received some
unwelcome news. Although the meeting was a success, as soon as he got
back to the hotel he received a call from a profoundly shaken Ackerman.
He found him in the lobby, ashen-faced, with his wife in tears. It transpired that a former Drexel employee, who had been "cooperating" with
the SEC, had named him as having manipulated a stock in 1986, which
meant that Ackerman was now firmly back in the frame right beside
Michael Milken. Peter could offer little comfort other than his unwavering friendship and a belief in his innocence, but he could see that he
would shortly have to ask Ackerman to step down from the CIC board
onto which he had so recently been invited.

World stock markets were choppy during 1990, but the fact that Peter
was beset by indecision for the first time since the start of the Value Fund
was probably more a symptom of his personal loss of confidence. He
seemed reluctant to confront the demons and sought escape whenever
possible and not just from markets. *You have to remember in any romantic
crisis that passion and love are not the same, any more than fire constitutes the source of light.*

In this frame of mind Peter embarked on a round-the-world trip, with
perhaps unrecognized escapist undertones, a trip that was exceptionally
long, even by his standards. Whether in South America, Africa, Australia,
Hong Kong, Japan or Hawaii, his journal documents few exceptions to
an uncharacteristic flatness and lack of enthusiasm. He had an engrossing
safari experience, renewed some old acquaintances, and explored some
new places and possibilities – and in Tokyo received a heart-warming
note from his "friend." But on returning to Canada he discovered that
the trip had resolved nothing and he was back to square one – with a
further complication. His skin had broken out in welts and he had no
idea why, although he feared the worst and dreaded the obvious necessity
of telling both Joanie and the girlfriend. While he waited for the results
of the blood test he reflected:

*I really know nothing about these diseases. Can they be cured? I know
that Aids cannot … The major issue is, of course, my two partners. It
seems to me that I shall have to tell them, unless I could be certain that
they would not be infected. Where J is concerned there is another argument for telling her, which is that our marriage is drifting apart. Either
she'll say get lost and that might be some sort of a solution. Alternatively*

I should feel obliged to recommit myself to her alone, but could I really do it? We would have to speak very candidly about how to enrich the relationship. If we ended up divorced or separated, my life would be transformed. With the other it might possibly be healthier, maybe less self-centred, or maybe not. But my relationships with all women would be different – I'm not sure I want to find out. I called J – she had a car accident last night – another reason to be in or out.

Four days later the results came through: the Aids test was negative – it was just an attack of herpes. Nevertheless, the whole episode highlighted the dilemma of having two female relationships. As he expressed it, Joanie represented a sort of peace, a certain stability, sometimes good comradeship, and the steadying sense of an inescapable obligation. However, at that moment it was tempting to feel this was not enough. In the throes of romantic love, his other lady was in his thoughts night and day like an incessant craving.

In another display of uncharacteristic behaviour, Peter took a decision to aim for 30% cash in the Value Fund, began selling aggressively and then stopped. But this uncharacteristic wavering was a symptom of a more fundamental problem which Joanie picked up on over the telephone. Peter called her one evening for a chat, and she called back again the next day to ask him why he was so depressed: *I was surprised. It is true that I am concerned at the moment about any number of issues. We could be in for a very difficult time in the world – politically and financially – but I'm puzzled by the "depressed" suggestion; tired yes. I believe one can actually thrive on anxiety, at least I think I can. Confidence is the issue and how to re-establish it when it wavers.*

Back in London again, Peter busied himself with arranging speakers for the November conference, including Barbara Amiel. *She came to the apartment for a drink – she is very attractive and highly intelligent: funnily enough though, I think a little uncertain of herself. I think we may have been trying to detect each other's "rhythms." She will be a good speaker.*

By now the Berlin Wall had fallen and, with reunification the topic of the day, Peter headed off to sniff the breeze. He began with a twenty-mile run, crossing into East Berlin at the Brandenburg Gate past the Russian War Memorial with its Red Army sentries on duty outside. He ran on through the Marx-Engels Platz as far as the Ostseestrasse and back through the infamous Checkpoint Charlie, whose buildings were still intact. At the Potsdamer Platz he picked up a souvenir lump of the rubble.

It was like time-travelling through the history of Europe from 1870, when the Prussians defeated France and took Paris for the first time, to the present day, with streets and buildings to remind the traveller of all the momentous and catastrophic events that comprise it ... After lunch I walked in the Kurfurstendam – expecting a message – no luck and I restrained myself from calling. In the evening I did the fair and caught the midnight show at La Vie en Rose. I won the male Can-Can show – marathon runner's legs!

But he was still in denial mode.

22

Confidence Regained

AT THE 1990 CONFERENCE in New York, Peter had an opportunity to chat about his mental state with his friend Bryan Reynolds, taking comfort that Reynolds had been through a similar experience. Nevertheless, as year-end approached he was still beset by indecisiveness and facing the prospect of the first negative result in the Value Fund's sixteen-year history. In the end it closed down 9% for the year, very much in line with the Dow and not nearly as low as he had at one stage feared. But his New Year resolutions reflected the still unresolved problems of the year.

Objectives for the coming year:
- *Help others – financially and emotionally. You have much to be thankful for.*
- *Maintain the disciplines, both physical and mental. They are vital to achieving a better year.*
- *Work on your spiritual progress. Don't let your curiosity flag and make sure you laugh a lot. Life is a game – a series of connected experiences. If you can teach yourself to see the good and the bad just as episodes in the pageant it becomes more bearable.*
- *No formula works forever. It has to be under continuous review and development. Always be receptive to new ideas. Keep searching for the spark. Think about how you communicate – how to set about sparking off others and how to make it easier for them to strike sparks off you.*

Peter's fragile state persisted and he continued seeing the game of life in fairly dark colours. He jotted down a quotation from Jean-Paul Sartre's play *Huis Clos [No Exit]*: "L'enfer, c'est les autres" – "Hell is other people" – and perhaps most telling, the inscription over the gates of Hell in Dante's *Inferno*: "Lasciate ogni speranza voi chi entrate" – "Abandon all hope, ye who enter here."

Unfortunately, recovering from depression requires more than the recognition that one is suffering from it. It would take Peter enormous courage, determination, and discipline to struggle with it and keep on top of the professional side of his life at the same time. Above all, he needed to rediscover belief in his own abilities – a difficult task because he had to live with the less-popular decisions he had taken in the previous two years: *Markets are booming and our shorts are still costing us dear. I must focus on the short Nikkei position as well as the S&P shorts. I feel in my bones that the Japanese stance is the right one and that if I had not (painfully thus far) already been committed to it I would be itching to do it now.*

The remedies Peter sought for his psychological health were, like the man, in no sense conventional. There was no rush to medicate or seek counselling beyond his family and closest friends, but his natural mindset led him to explore self-help methods, the first of which was Cognitive Therapy.

What we consciously think determines how we feel about ourselves, so it makes sense to try to identify what automatic thoughts flit through the mind when one is at a low ebb. It then becomes possible to control such thoughts, suppressing the negative ones and refocusing on the positive. The term for this is reattribution ...

Attribution theory argues against concepts of permanence in ourselves, the world around us and indeed in the universe itself. It challenges any tendency to assume that things will always continue on a given course. It persuades one to regard all situations as temporary and to deflect oneself from any temptation to see the development of events as inevitable ...

We often try to personalize our misfortunes, occasionally blaming ourselves but more often blaming others, or circumstances supposedly out of our control, or even God, which is particularly facile. What one should be doing is accepting one's own responsibility fairly and squarely and facing up to whatever correctives may be necessary.

His established routines were a help. The running was more; it was a therapy and physical health regime combined, with the added bonus of boosting his self-esteem. Looking toned and fit helped him "walk tall," metaphorically peering down at a sea of troubles rather than being engulfed by them. His old Parisian running route along the *quais*, up to Place Vendôme past his first office, and back to the Hotel Georges V helped him appreciate how far he had come and what he had achieved. The impressionist paintings, now in the Musée d'Orsay not the Jeu de Paume, were a solace too – as was a secret glade he had discovered among the pines near Courchevel. Sitting on a fallen tree beside a tiny stream of tinkling water on a sunny day in the sparkling snow, he felt a complete sense of peace and spiritual well-being.

Perhaps more than anything, it was the unlooked-for positive surprise that was most effective in dispersing the hopelessness characteristic of depression. A journey to York to visit David Mathews of Plaxtons was an instance, though it did not start well.

King's Cross to York and stupidly I got off without my overnight bag and the train had left before I remembered it ... rather than chase the bag, or do the boring replacement shopping, I walked in light rain without an umbrella to the Minster – huge and yet so delicate. A fleck of sunshine broke through and lit the rose window like magic as I walked in, and then I noticed a statue towards the east end. It was of Sir George Savile, "inter alia" an ancestor of Lord Savile, CR-G's godfather. What arrested me was the inscription:

"January 9th 1764. To the memory of Sir GEORGE SAVILE *Bart., who in five successive parliaments represented the County of York, the public love and esteem of his fellow citizens, have decreed this monument. In private life he was benevolent and sincere, his charities were extensive and secret, his whole heart was formed on principles of generosity, mildness, justice and universal candour. In the Senate incorruptible, in his commerce with the world disinterested, by genius enlightened, in the means of doing good he was unwearied doing it. His life was an ornament and blessing to the age in which he lived and after death his memory will long be beneficial to mankind."*

I felt uplifted and encouraged. The meeting with David was a great success. We ... bought me some kit and ran together above the beach, below Scarborough Castle, looking out onto the grey, frothy North Sea ... I enjoyed D's company – attractive, charismatic, not trusting, but wanting to. We will I believe do business together. On my own later I sat thinking good thoughts. In 1977 Peter Cundill and Associates opened its doors and it has been a remarkable run. Now it needs to be revitalized. Hopes and expectations will be converted to no particular hopes or expectations – just a determination to do an exceptional job. On that note I had a glass of champagne and a cigar and then went to bed and slept like a baby.

Peter did at this stage recover some of his energy, and a reorganization of Peter Cundill and Associates began. First, he bought his partner, Gowan Guest, out of the last 10% of his cash flow entitlement, ending an arrangement that, although convenient at the outset, had been cumbersome and ultimately expensive.

Next, he had to address the concerns of McDermott, who was pressing for economies in Peter's travel expenses and large cuts in office overheads, with the intention of grooming the Cundill organization for sale to a larger entity. This was far from Peter's dream, but his preoccupation with getting back on track with the fund's performance made him reluctant to resist McDermott – and he felt personally responsible for McDermott's all-too-evident lack of confidence in the future of the fund as an independent entity. He needed only to have pointed to the fact that the Safeway pension fund had opened a $26 million account for Peter to manage on value investment principles.

McDermott invited Peter to lunch to pass along what he considered great news: the Royal Bank of Canada was interested in buying out Peter Cundill and Associates, the management company, for between $4.5 and $6 million. Peter was decidedly unenthusiastic, but reluctant – and almost certainly not yet strong enough – to prick the bubble. The fund and the company were his creation and his life, and if he had any inclination to sell, which he did not, he would have wished it to be on the crest of a wave, not while performance was languishing and his reputation as a great investor was under scrutiny – apart from which the mooted price was derisory. However, he was concerned that a flat refusal would appear selfish.

In early 1991 the investment climate was buoyant; in fact in April the Dow broke through 3,000 for the first time in its history, although it deteriorated in the second half after the coup in the Soviet Union which ousted Gorbachev. As the annual conference approached, McDermott had realized that no deal was to be done now and that they would have to continue to go it alone. This would have been music to Peter's ears, except that the uncertainty had taken its toll on his condition, which was still parlous. There had been bruising exchanges in the interim on the subjects of the investment in Westar and the Nikkei put options.

The upshot was that on the day of "Pete's Morning" at the conference, his self-assurance was again at rock bottom. On waking he could not imagine what he might say – nothing he had prepared seemed relevant or capable of delivery with conviction. He felt like curling into a ball rather than running, but Central Park on a clear crisp day helped him recover some balance. He threw away his notes and addressed his audience with passion about the investment principles he believed in and the opportunities they presented. The effect was electrifying. It was perhaps his best performance ever, and the audience lapped it up.

It was a make-or-break day which showed me that the spirit can always triumph, although you have to quash the negativity and fatalism with absolute determination and just cling to the positive. When we reached Windows on the 32nd floor that evening I set about drinking and chatting as though I hadn't a care in the world, too much perhaps. But, Hey, the market was off 150 points and we were up!! I may be feeling better for some of the wrong reasons. The gloom is now pretty much universal, so I'm no longer unique. I feel ready to be creative again.

After, Peter flew down to Canyon Ranch, where Joannie now had a home. The newspapers were full of the release of Terry Waite, the Archbishop of Canterbury's special envoy, who had been sent to Lebanon to secure the release of four hostages and had been captured himself and held for five years. Waite's plight made him see his own situation in a different light: *He was held in a single room, in solitary confinement, without books or writing materials and under the daily threat of execution and he passed the test with flying colours. What a perspective for me. Whatever the duress I have been under recently, I have mostly had a fine time of it in those five years. We all have to pass through the fire if we are to progress and for some it is worse than others. When I arrived I looked at my fax traffic and found that the funds were up for the week, bucking the market. I went for a long run under a clear blue sky. My chemistry has changed. I think I'm ready to face the world again. Either this business will be taken away from me, voluntarily or involuntarily, or I shall rebuild it.*

What drove me to the verge of suicide was not really the ebb and flow of the investment business with its daily measurement. That I can cope with, but I had begun to see myself as the "burnt out kid" and I felt the waning of support and confidence right at the top of my organization, with an atmosphere of every-man-for-himself beginning to rear its ugly head and pollute the culture of service I have tried to create.

However, Peter was not quite out of Dante's dark wood yet. On his way back to London, he spent two days in Vancouver, making time for an inconclusive five-hour meeting with McDermott. Peter told him he could offer no definitive solutions for his disappointments, could not wave a magic wand, but would do his best to accommodate him. The following morning, while out running, he decided he would have to grasp the nettle and confront McDermott, or risk reverting to the semi-catatonic state from which he had so recently emerged. His approach was bold. He arrived unexpectedly early in the Vancouver office and went straight in to see the president.

He had decided to withdraw from all administrative and personnel responsibilities for six months, he announced. It was McDermott's job, as president of the company and on the spot in Vancouver, to take full control of these and to sort out whatever internal problems there might be. The company was profitable and would continue to be so. To that end, he said, he wished to suspend all negotiations for selling or merging the business and expected to receive McDermott's agreement to this course of action at the latest straight after Christmas.

Peter settled back into his London life, actually finding plenty of bargains, which was encouraging. He attended the christening of the Watsons' adopted baby, Lucinda, at St Michael's, Chester Square, and the party that followed, after which he went home to change out of his new and "extremely painful" Gucci shoes and went off to see Derek Jacobi in Jean-Paul Sartre's play about Edmund Kean, the early nineteenth-century actor. Curiosity, observation, and humour were on the menu: *Sartre postulates a universe devoid of inherent meaning or purpose – a cosmic system without any objectives or values. He suggests that the very fact of existence is presumptive of individual responsibility for one's actions ... No wonder the road to hell is paved with good intentions! I listened to a Saturday evening chat show "Inter alia" discussing Charles and Di's sleeping arrangements. PC appears to be interested at intimate moments in the kind of things that I think of when I'm trying not to orgasm – architecture and the environment.*

He socialized quite a bit – went to a *Daily Mail* cocktail party, after which he took Soraya Kashoggi, ex-wife of the billionaire Saudi arms dealer, out to supper and on to Annabel's, where they ran into a sensationally beautiful Ashanti princess from Ghana who watched Peter dancing and asked if he was a professional. "Just an accountant," he responded, but he was pleased. And the edge was returning to his sense of humour – *I prepared my intellectual loins, so to speak, for lunch at Harry's Bar with Barbara Amiel.*

McDermott's response came sooner than expected. He flew over to London and asked to be bought out of his PCA stock because he was concerned about Peter's emotional state and what it might augur for the future, and had to consider his family. After an afternoon of thinking, he told McDermott over dinner that he was in no position to buy him out, and that, despite any appearance to the contrary, he had never lost his grip on the investment portfolio. He did concede that timing had sometimes been an issue, but pointed out that it had required immense patience and a good deal of nail biting before the Nikkei put options had proved their worth. He felt completely comfortable with the portfolio as it stood, having checked and rechecked the numbers in every case.

While the air was cleared for the moment, the relationship had suffered permanent damage; nonetheless, the confrontation heralded Peter's recovery. He had survived, not unscathed, but having learned a lot about himself and the value of the support he had received from so many quarters, not least from Joanie. Any tendency toward hubris was checked, and the desire for recognition as a star was sublimated into the more serious ambition of continuing to be an exceptional fund manager and honing the skills and the creativity through which this could be achieved and sustained. Before making his way to spend Christmas with Joanie in Sun Valley, he broke off his liaison and began the process of turning that relationship into an enduring friendship – a piece of awkward acrobatics at which he was unusually gifted.

Just before leaving London he went to see Steven Berkhoff's play *Kvetch: It is a comedy of manners examining people's capacity to worry endlessly and needlessly. How timely! In the morning I went to the Royal Academy to see the Hokusai exhibition. The "Wave at Kanagawa" depicting a tsunami was on display. It is dramatic and I had the impression that it is what I have just narrowly escaped, but I moved on quickly, without dwelling on it, to enjoy the work of his later years, rich with autumnal colours and so confidently realized.*

23

Reclaiming the Initiative

PETER'S PROLONGED DEPRESSION had prompted a profound re-examination of his life in all its dimensions. From the business standpoint his conviction that the Graham and Dodd value approach to investment was the right one emerged stronger. Method and organization were another matter. The series of episodes with Brian McDermott had terminated with an interview on the subject of his bonus.

He insisted on having a bonus of $200,000. In his view he held the business together. I think that a rather extravagant claim and his support for the business's owner and founder at an extremely difficult juncture left something to be desired – still I have been derelict in some respects, especially in failing to deal firmly with personnel issues or alternatively backing him unreservedly to do so. To that extent he may have a point but he conceded nothing to me. I detected a note of fear, even hysteria on the issue. Pay – but remember for future reference.

Peter's determination to be much more hands-on led to the formation of Cundill Investment Research Limited, which, with Peter himself at the helm, would henceforth be exclusively responsible for all the portfolio managers and analysts. He also bit the bullet with Ursula Kummel. She was summoned to his Vancouver hotel to receive the news that Maureen Crocker had been appointed his sole personal assistant – an inspired choice, as she proved supremely efficient, reliable, and intelligently supportive until her death in 2003. *UK came at 5pm. It was a brief interview. She was shocked. I'm not sure she is balanced at all. In any case I needed a dry martini afterwards.*

These new arrangements were in part intended to leave McDermott freer to focus on marketing. In portfolio terms a spring clean was put in motion – the number of holdings in the Value Fund reduced by a third, and the size of the average position increased by a fifth. Peter used a shooting analogy. When confronted with a large covey of birds it is a poor strategy simply to shoot into the middle and hope to bring something down: better to select a single target and focus on that, and then move on to the next. In consequence, the research work acquired sharper momentum within the whole team and especially from Peter. This change was to bear spectacular fruit in the following year's performance.

In my endeavours to get my mind back working in top gear I believe that I have needed to improve in the following ways; reducing procrastination; concentrating with absolute clarity on one thing at a time, i.e. avoiding the temptation to flit. However, it is essential to be aware that procrastination and indecision are not the same things as measuring one's response and allowing sufficient time to elapse for a good decision to emerge. As to flitting, certainly dilettantism is not desirable, but the insatiable curiosity of the Renaissance man is.

In my dealings with my research team I have found that the desire to be fair sometimes dampens criticism and this is not always a good thing. Firm constructive criticism is a powerful incentiviser. Muted approval just inspires a gorgon-like paralysis. I am sure that sacred self-images and slavish adherence to routines, including my own, can both benefit from a dose of healthy iconoclasm from time to time.

A new team member also was invited on board. Tim McElvaine, a young Canadian accountant and Chartered Financial Analyst, arrived via Peter's typically unorthodox hiring procedures. While working as an analyst at the Bank of Butterfield in Bermuda, McElvaine had become a convert to the value investment approach and desperately wanted to find a position at a fund management outfit that specialized in the field and would employ him in Canada. Diligent enquiry produced a shortlist of possibilities of which the Cundill Group was probably the best known. So he flew to Vancouver to meet the company president. McDermott was sympathetic and fully appreciated McElvaine's abilities. but made it clear that Cundill was not hiring at the time, and that Peter Cundill was unfortunately not in Vancouver – and was in any case under present circumstances too busy to see him.

McElvaine returned to Bermuda clutching a copy of the Cundill portfolio – the rather over-extended one prior to the spring clean. Undeterred by McDermott's verdict, he proceeded to conduct a thorough analysis of the Canadian portion of the portfolio with recommendations, putting forward some buy candidates of his own, and sent the package to McDermott. There being no immediate response, McElvaine persevered with a similar analysis of the U.S. portfolio. McDermott eventually sent both reports to Peter in London as a "curiosity." He read them through with increasing interest and was so impressed that he arranged to meet up with McElvaine on his next visit to Bermuda: *Tim McElvaine and I met at last. We talked in detail. He is a first-rate analyst and absolutely understands all the principles of value, not at this stage a successor but I believe I need him. If he and Geoffrey Scott get on it will be terrific.*

They did and it was.

Peter was not a natural technocrat; he was a natural and inveterate note-taker and scribbler. However, despite his own technological ineptitude, he well understood the growing power of the computer as an investment tool. As part of the process of rationalizing the portfolios and reducing the need to take small "look see" positions, he initiated the construction of a computer system that could track more than five hundred securities through a proprietary monitoring system. It was designed to identify every equity in the world that was trading below liquidation value and to rank each of them in order of attractiveness. The project was even more sophisticated in that it was intended to encompass markets outside North America, including the UK, Japan, France, Germany, and Switzerland, countries in which there were at the time anomalies in accounting standards by comparison with the United States.

The final component of this reinvigorated investment brew relates to Peter's notebooks. From the 1960s onward, they had recorded all his research and analytical work in painstaking detail, invariably in McGill or UBC A4 student notebooks. However, they now acquired an added dimension. As well as being a voracious reader Peter was also a compulsive clipper, extracting everything that caught his eye from an astounding breadth of sources. The clippings, carefully pasted into his notebooks, illustrate the natural instinct for lateral thinking and unexpected connections that he called into play: *I think very often the best decisions are made on the basis of what your tummy tells you – always assuming you have covered the bases thoroughly. The Jesuits argue for reason before passion. I would argue for reason and passion, intellect and intuition. It's a balance, one that requires cultivation and it is very relevant to the direction I have chosen to follow in my profession.*

Putting the business side of life back on course was a complex process needing careful strategic planning, a lot of energy, and a little luck. However, the personal side of Peter's life was probably the greater challenge. Whatever his protestations, the emotional ties of the intense liaison had not simply evaporated, as is evident from a series of journal entries for a full year after he had finished the affair:

I called her – she was unknown at the Wyndham. Felt blue. She called. Felt better. We met ... under the clock on 50th and 6th, had a sandwich together at a deli on 6th and 58th – then on to the New York Public Library, my first visit although well known to me from its appearance in "Breakfast at Tiffany's." It was more than well maintained and an active hush prevailed. I watched her using the computer to search for info on Edith Wharton. She was impressive and endearing, exploiting the power of the internet that is a closed book to me.

Later: *Dinner with her at a local bistro. Wonderful conversations and intimacy.* Some months later: *No dinner with her – this is rubbish – forget it, we are neither friends nor lovers. It is a mid-way position which is completely unsatisfactory.* And finally: *Supper with her. She has a new love, but at least there is happiness for her. How emotions can change but we shall remain friends!*

Nor was Joanie entirely convinced that all was unthreateningly back to normal. She had supported Peter with real devotion during the worst periods of his depression but she was now weighing up the relationship and might well have decided that she had had enough. They attended the wedding of one of Peter's cousins in Montreal, at which Peter committed a major faux pas: *At the reception ... I danced with Sarah Scott and the bride but not Joanie – an omission which meant that I had to write a note of abject apology later.*

This time Peter was acutely aware that the relationship was at a crossroads and needed special measures – uninterrupted time together doing things they enjoyed. At the last minute, he secured three places for Joanie, himself, and daughter Evelyn, on a two-week biking tour around Tuscany and presented it to Joanie as a *fait accompli*. She was delighted by the unaccustomed spontaneity. Although she had fallen in love with Florence as a student, she had never returned, and longed to share its romance with Peter on his first visit.

Before joining the biking party they spent three days at the magnificent Grand Hotel Villa Cora overlooking the city from beyond the Boboli

Gardens. Its acres of marble, parquet floors and frescoed ceilings set the right tone. The contrast with her student days was not lost on Joanie – most of the inconveniences of tourism were smoothed over by the limousine with its impressively knowledgeable chauffeur. As a tourist Peter never did things by halves.

The majesty of the *David*, not to mention its athletic build, so deeply impressed Peter that he carefully transcribed Michelangelo's personal comment on his work: *"What spirit is so empty that it cannot recognize the fact that the foot is nobler than the shoe and the skin more lovely than the garment that it clothes. My David's eyes are watchful, he has the neck of a bull, the hands of a killer, his body is a reservoir of energy, a symbol of the unquenchable human spirit as he stands poised to strike. He represents the precise moment between reflection and action and yet he is but a shadow of divine perfection."*

They also took in many of the other Florentine "must sees," ending up one morning at the Uffizi, especially impressed by Botticelli's splendid *Birth of Venus*. Of course there was the obligatory shopping for the "girls," a run along the Arno and across the Ponte Vecchio, and a legendary *bistecca fiorentina* at the iconic Sabatini restaurant. Peter was content: *Reality always turns out to be more or less than what we are expecting of it. Today was more.*

The biking part of the trip was no let-down either, as physically challenging as Peter and Joanie could possibly have wished, up and down the steep Tuscan hills. Peter was thrilled to discover that a competitive marathoner, Karl Egg from Boston, was in the group. The contest was immediately engaged! It began with the ride up to the famous Vallombrosa monastery high in the Florentine hills, normally snow-capped until the summer. It was tough going with no stops and no quarter given; fit though he was, the sweat poured. On the way down, in the crisp fall air, he froze, but was elated to have "beaten Egg." Peter was in his element that evening surrounded by admiring ladies, including Joanie and Evelyn.

The race continued the following day, a marathon by any other name, all the way up into the heart of the Chianti to Gaiole: *I hung in there with Karl Egg and levelled it with him at the top. E and J had dropped out – not enough fuel in the quick sandwich lunch – but I felt increasingly strong ... The autumn sunshine that afternoon was glorious, enriching the yellow and russet colours of the vines and the pale green olives.*

We had another gourmet dinner, cooked by a chef who rejoices in the name of Seamus de Pentheney O'Kelly, an Irish South African married to a Roman. The menu bears recording – poached quail breasts with shaved white truffles, salad of marinated funghi porcini (huge mountain mushrooms – like the truffles only found at this time of year), spaghetti al cinghiale (local wild boar), salmone al cartoccio con acetosa (salmon with sorrel in puff pastry), a mulberry sorbet, fillet of veal with pancetta (Italian bacon) and a sensational chocolate dessert.

By this time the magic was evidently working on Joanie, dispelling any remaining sense of looming disaster. Being with Peter was fun again: *The beauty of life has cast its spell again and we are at ease with each other. We lunched in Castello di Broglio ... like Watteau's paintings, except that we weren't wearing the exquisite silks. After lunch I went back to the hotel to collect a dictionary and a phrasebook and set off on an adventure to the barber shop. Got the message across with "corto," short and "rasoio," razor. Some local lads came in for a gossip with the barber. I recognized the word "caccia" (hunting) – an expedition must be afoot. What a delight that would be!*

The last day was a final massive work-out of forty kilometres, which Joanie and Peter more than doubled on their own. *We did the steep climb to the ancient, walled Etruscan city of Volterra, perched on the top of a hill looking down to the sea 20 kilometres away ... The day was mixed and cool so J and I decided we'd go for it and ride to San Gimignano. No other takers, so we set off together on another 50 km or so. What a work-out! San Gimignano was a lovely sight. We saw it first from a bluff, with sun and cloud interplaying between its towers – well worth the effort and on my birthday! At the trattoria in the evening the whole group sang happy birthday for me, which sounded rather good, and a little girl gave me a birthday card.*

The last night of the trip was in Rome, without the group, in a magnificent suite at the top of the Hotel Hassler Villa Medici at the top of the Spanish Steps, with a panorama view of the entire city and the Vatican. There was no question but that Peter had convinced Joanie that it was worth sticking together, if only for the companionship in the good times. *I slipped out to buy the papers and have a snoop. When I got back I received lovely cards and ties from both my girls. There ought to be a law about ties. This has been a resounding success and yet ... "Things sweet to taste prove in digestion sour." (Richard II) Let's hope not.*

Peter did his customary city tour on a run in the Roman dawn. After breakfast on the terrace they set off for Joanie's treat – a visit to St Peter's and the workshops of the Vatican museums; he was particularly impressed that a staff of seven was required to maintain the mosaics alone. *After the Vatican we went to the church of San Pietro in Vincoli (St Peter in Chains) to see Michelangelo's Moses. I remembered it as being more forceful. I was just astonished by the horns on his head such as are usually associated with cuckolds which, presumably, Moses was not!*

The horns, as Peter was later to learn, have a curious history. The original Greek translation from Hebrew reads more correctly that "Moses knew not that the appearance of his skin was glorified from his conversation with the Lord." However, St Jerome, who was responsible for its translation into Latin, produced an unfortunate version rendering the glorification effect as Moses having a pair of horns sticking out of his head. Even after the scholars of the early Renaissance had put the text right, this image stuck. So there the old "cuckold" sits in scowling majesty with goat-like sprouts coming out of the top of his head instead of a halo.

The trip worked its restorative effect. On their last day, sitting in the warm sunshine on the Spanish Steps *outside the house where Keats died*, he mused: *There's been a lot recently about James Boswell, Sam Johnson's biographer, including a quotation from his London journal – the naughty one in which he gets a dose of the clap: "Joy has its rights – not just hedonism but the feeling of delight in all that being alive provides."*

He had recovered his *joie de vivre*. The convalescence was over.

24

Travelling with Purpose

BY THE END OF 1992, Peter had completely recovered his mental acuity and was able to focus on what he had learned and what he needed. He had decided that the time was ripe to recruit another person to his research team, and the search had been going on since October. None of the candidates had so far been satisfactory and Peter was becoming impatient. He had lunch with Andy Massie, who had been with the firm for some time, doing an excellent job in the back office. *In a moment of wine-inspired creativity I offered Andy the job in the investment department.* It was an inspired choice, since Peter was able to mold Massie from scratch, first as an analyst and later as a portfolio manager. It was Massie who eventually emerged as Peter's successor in managing the Value Fund.

And he could now more objectively contemplate the new streamlined portfolio of the Value Fund and renew his inveterate exploration of new possibilities worldwide. *I watched the 1992 numbers come in – not distinguished but the portfolio is thoroughly well ordered (almost pretty) and loaded with potential. If this was the year of recovery I suppose that 1991 was the year of self-inflicted torture. So what did I do, or learn? I relearned my craft by honing my existing skills and acquiring some new ones, especially in relation to investment in Europe. My awareness, curiosity and intuition revived and I recovered my sensuality, which had almost deserted me. So, on with the game with renewed passion.*

At the invitation of his cousin Michael Alexander, he set off refreshed for Bruges to attend a Council of Europe session and give a presentation on global accountancy. It was a receptive and sophisticated audience that asked the right questions and Peter thoroughly enjoyed delivering his exposé. And, as always for him, the visit had its cultural aspect as well. He did a private tour of the works of Hans Memling, one of the great masters of early Renaissance. A reliquary of St Ursula caught his attention. His eye for art was gaining acuity as well. *The shrine of St Ursula will stay with me. In vibrant colours it depicts the saint's story which goes like this. When the Huns sacked Cologne in the 4th century they really beat up on the ladies. They decapitated St Ursula, who went to the block proclaiming her Christianity, along with eleven thousand more unfortunate virgins – what a waste – they couldn't all have been hideous; in fact in the Memling panels they are decidedly attractive.*

After Bruges, Peter set off on another whirlwind tour of Europe, meeting up with Paul Desmarais in Paris and taking in the Fragonard exhibition at the Petit Palais – attracted especially by the girl on the swing with her skirts billowing up to show off a fine pair of legs – then on to Geneva and Lausanne to discuss mutual investments with Asher Edelman and see the Roy Lichtenstein Exhibition. He continued to Zurich where he sensed that, if he could only gain access to the club, there were opportunities within that idiosyncratic, secretive and tightly held market. There, he was seen dining at the Kronenhalle, a bastion of the financial and commercial establishment that boasted one of the world's great private art collections. It was the perfect place to see and be seen, and an excellent launch pad for the networking initiatives at which he was so adept. By the time he left he had established a good confidential relationship with the people at Vontobel, one of Zurich's most prestigious private banks, which had its finger directly on the financial pulse.

The peak athletic experience of this trip was the Cresta Run at St Moritz, a three-quarter-mile ice slide with a long tradition. It begins from just below St Moritz's twelfth-century leaning tower and twists its way down a steep gully through ten extremely difficult corners. The runners position themselves head first on their toboggans and reach speeds of over 80 mph. The only way to slow down is to use the rakes attached to the rider's boots. It was a speed sensation like no other, with enough time to savour the peril. In the afternoon, as a complete contrast, Peter skied the cross-country trail to Val Rosen via Pontresina: *The whiteness of the snow seemed to blend with the swish of the tracks, the sound of my breath and the song of the blackbirds. The backdrop was peaceful, greeny brown spruce and local village sights. I dined alone reflecting on my day and, armed with a martini … I was in heaven.*

Of course, the calm was momentary. The following month, after brief trips to London, Vancouver, and San Francisco, where he gave a lecture on value investment principles to the second year MBA class at Berkeley, Peter went back to Paris to see Paul Desmarais again: *Walked from the*

Plaza Athenée up the Rue Montaigne to lunch with Paul Desmarais at the Traveller's Club. He is not the fastest financial quick study but he understands global relationships better than anyone else I know.

From Paris he went on to Madrid to visit his new discovery, the Corporación Financiera Alba, a conglomerate with stakes in some of the most attractive companies in Spain – San Miguel Breweries, the Banco Urquijo and the supermarket chain Carrefour, as well as an intriguing position in Airtel (eventually Vodafone), the dominant mobile telephony provider in a market that was really taking off. Most important of all, it was trading at a substantial discount to asset value. True to form, he settled in at the Ritz and headed straight for the Prado. This time, it was not the virgins that caught his eye.

Goya's nude "La Maja" is an enigma. The pose is not convincing and her breasts seem unnaturally wide apart. The subject apparently was the very aristocratic Duchess of Alba with whom G is said to have had an affair ... It is erotic – the first ever realistic representation of female pubic hair. The inquisition thought it was so indecent that they confiscated both pictures [there were two versions], the clothed and the unclothed, and interrogated – perhaps even tortured – Goya, in an attempt to make him divulge who had commissioned the nude version ... I can imagine the Grand Inquisitor drooling over the naked Duchess in private. A Playboy spread would have nothing on this huge lush canvas.

Peter was also looking into Lusutor-Sociedade de Financia y de Turismo, another deep-discount conglomerate involved in transport, cargo handling, real estate, and resort development. It being his first visit to Portugal, due process had to be followed to get below the surface. He began in Oporto with a call on Dr Pinto de Luso, an industrialist and entrepreneur whom he described as *a little walnut grove of wisdom and, I suspect, dogged tenacity – illuminating.*

He went on to Lisbon. *I still get a vibrant sense of empire, maritime greatness and mission from this city as I do not from Vienna's grandeur. I have the feeling that for the moment the economy is relatively robust. I dined at Severa, a famous old eatery in the upper town, the Barrio Alto ... the recommended squid in ink seemed unlikely but was excellent, still the magic was the "fado" ... There are two kinds, Lisbon "fado," which has a tendency to be gloomier and Coimbra "fado," just the opposite. So we had haunting and romantic as well as provocative and flirtatious. The*

Portuguese are certainly different from the Spanish, not so much of the gravitas and self-importance, more light-hearted if you will ... I am going to buy some Lusotur.

He did, and by the end of the year it was up by 50 percent.

In the aftermath of the 1989 U.S. invasion of Panama, "Operation Just Cause," which had removed the criminal Noriega regime, Peter had made a considerable killing by purchasing the country's deeply discounted debt. He had established that the entire outstanding foreign debt was covered by dollar deposits frozen for the moment in U.S. banks and was convinced that the ownership, administration, and resulting revenue from the canal would eventually be returned to Panama under the terms of the suspended treaty. However, the effects of the invasion, and the dislocation of over twenty thousand people, had exacerbated the country's economic woes. Peter had taken his profit on the debt investment quite early and, in the absence of a spirited economic revival, the bonds had sunk again to a very steep discount. He suspected it might be time to have another look and went to nose around. His account of his investigations in Panama and Ecuador reveals much about his decision-making processes.

There's a good view of the Pacific from the Marriott and of the new apartment blocks which are now going up to replace the rubble of the destruction of the invasion (plenty of cranes, on this occasion a good sign). Peter used "the crane test" – too many were normally indicative of an overheated real estate market, perhaps an altogether overheated economy with interest rates likely to rise, occasioning the usual negative stock market reaction.

I went to [a real estate company] office to chat with Arturo Tapia and then to call on Pepe Castanedas, General Manager of Bladex [The Foreign Trade Bank of Latin America] in Panama, both of whom I had got to know and value last time round. Lunched with David Norland at the U.S. Embassy and visited with Rob Braines, the head of the BOLSA [Stock Exchange]. All of them were mildly ... positive on the direction of the economy. I am inclined to concur ... The U.S. presence here is still both large and visible. Finally back to Arturo's office to meet Roberto Motta, who turned out to be an outstanding "godfather," filled with humour, insight, real ability and determination. I think we should re-establish our position in Panamanian debt.

He was also contemplating getting back into Ecuador, where he had made an earlier successful foray into bankrupt bonds. *Quito: [We] walked over to see Rod Carreas, the Vice Minister of Finance. The Ministry is really run down. We went on to visit Roberto Bamquenzo, Head of the Monetary Authority. We lunched at a so-called French restaurant, the Rincon de Francia. All the heavies were there; ministers and ex-ministers.*

After "nosing" around Guayaquil, Ecuador's largest city and its economic powerhouse, he made up his mind: *The dilapidated Union Club contrasted sharply with the hectic open air market – bananas, fish and sweet potatoes, all looking very fresh, but such limited vibrancy is not enough. The country is poorly governed and I have decided not to push this one.*

A week later, with no relaxation of pace, he was in Chicago to visit the chief executive of Evans Furs, which was becoming a problematic investment in an international climate increasingly hostile to the use of real animal fur in *haute couture*. He took in the Magritte retrospective exhibition while he was there: *Such a strange but compelling ability to juxtapose unlikely images that are impossible in the natural world. Surrealism seems to me to be the mystical end of lateral thinking, of making connections that are far beyond convention but lie at the extremes of imagination and intuition – so good for me professionally.*

Then back to London to visit Dan Coulson at the *Daily Telegraph*, where a buy-back offer from Conrad Black seemed imminent, before recrossing the Atlantic to address the Jay Lorsch [Louis Kirstein Professor of Human Relations at the Harvard Business School] conference on corporate governance at Harvard: *I am more than a little interested in the refreshed corporate spirit and the shake-up of shareholder apathy. Should we be becoming more interventionist? Should we be seeking an active catalytic role? If so should this just be in North America? In any event if the trend continues it will create new prospects.*

The culmination of this North American odyssey was the celebration of Peter's step-daughter Evelyn's wedding to Mark Updegrove, a promising young writer and journalist who later became the director of the LBJ Presidential Library in Austin, Texas. All went well with the speeches, including Peter's own, until Doug Campbell, an eccentric and fairly disreputable friend of Peter's, *disgraced himself by drunkenly con-fusing and mixing up his speech, grossly offending most of the audience. Evelyn burst into tears. Joanie became hysterical, both then and later in private! It will become folklore. There was nothing for it but to carry on chatting and dancing and that's just what I did.*

Campbell had apparently intended to flatter his highly cosmopolitan audience with a short catalogue of the strong-points for which their respec-tive countries were internationally known. The list was supposed to run as follows – a Swiss engineer, an Italian lover, a French cook, and an English bobby – not very original but harmless. However, it came out as – a Swiss lover, an Italian engineer, a French policeman, and an English cook. Naturally the audience assumed that they were deliberately being parodied.

Peter escaped back to London having agreed, in the aftermath, to allow Joanie to bid on a very expensive house in Aspen.

As summer turned to autumn it seemed increasingly necessary to pam-per Joanie a bit more. Peter flew to Perugia to meet her for another of their favourite biking expeditions, through Umbria on this occasion. Being seasoned participants, they were quite at home with the group for the 28-kilometre warm-up ride around the walls of Torgiano along the valley and up the steep bluffs. Nor were they surprised by the seven-course dinner. Peter merely remarked that the Grappa was essential after it. In Assisi on the anniversary of the death of St Francis, among crowds of pilgrims in medieval costume, Peter picked up a copy of *La Nazionale* and read of the recent upheavals in Moscow. He promptly phoned Vancouver and learned to his surprise that financially no one seemed to care, so he settled down with a glass of wine to bond with Harold Goldsmith, who controlled the Aspen Institute's axis in Baltimore.

One morning, the Cundills were late for the 56-kilometre trek to Todi, a route of major hills, but by noon, to his intense satisfaction, Peter was back in the lead: *I ran again into Todi in the early morning up to the Duomo right at the top of the hill, my running legs were a little unhappy. Todi is supposed to have been built by Hercules, in which case it ought to have qualified as one of his twelve labours – certainly well up there with cleansing the Augean stables.*

At the Hotel Badia, previously a monastery just outside Orvieto, Peter secured the best suite, once the abbot's private quarters. It was the last evening of the trip and cocktails were served on the terrace looking over the valley, across the vineyards and olive groves in the manicured Umbrian landscape to the breathtaking Duomo of Orvieto, with its white and pink marble facade glowing in the sunset. By the time they got to Rome the next day, Peter had the impression that Joanie had once more been mollified – and that his investment methods shared something with the ancients.

I ran [through the Forum] on a dewy, slightly misty day, with the sunlight creating sparkles on the ancient paving. I get a thrill down my back when I think that this was once the centre of the western world; the empire extending from Britain to the Middle East, from Germany and Hungary to Egypt and all of North Africa … As I stood in front of the Curia where the Senate used to meet, I thought of the amazing concept of drawing senators from every corner of that world and emperors too, not just from Rome, or even Italy but Spain, Libya, Greece, Turkey and Iraq. In a strange way my concept of global investment is in this same tradition of universality.

Later that fall, Peter went to visit his mother, now obliged to live in a seniors' residence – Place Kensington – in Montreal. His brother, Grier, had taken care of the move and Peter acknowledged that he had done an excellent job of it. Nevertheless, their relationship was strained, and Peter was uncomfortable speaking about it: *Grier drove me to the airport. He made an attempt to get into an intimate discussion. He said he was hurt that I had not confided in him about my bad time. He feels I insulted him. I was silent … It may be my fault not his. On a lighter note I heard a French Canadian phrase in the street that made me chuckle, "Le clutch de mon char est fucké," I remember the feeling.*

The annual Cundill conference at the end of November was exceptional even by Peter's standards. Lord Rees-Mogg, former editor of the *London Times*, spoke about globalism, the Arctic explorer Sir Ranulph Fiennes talked about pain and how hatred could be a useful tool in stiffening one's determination to overcome adversity. There was a panel to discuss the developing multi-manager industry and its focus on hedge funds. Sir John Templeton spoke about his early ventures into Japan, and Lord Gowrie, chairman of Sotheby's, discussed art as investment. Then it was "Pete's Morning." His talk on the outlook for the silver market got off to a lively start. Peter had planned a dramatic opening gambit – to sprinkle an ounce of silver dust out onto the table in front of him.

However by the time he poured, the silver had inadvertently become mixed up with his bran muffin. The audience roared with laughter. Peter held them enthralled for the next three hours in confident, punchy style.

The Russian crisis that Peter had seen reported in the Italian press in October was no false alarm. Frustrated by the attempts of the Communist party within the Congress to thwart his economic reforms, President Yeltsin had dissolved parliament and disbanded the Supreme Soviet. Violence had then erupted, and Yeltsin had called in the army. Yeltsin ultimately regained control, but it had been a close-run thing. Peter had been monitoring developments in Russia ever since the entrenched Marxist oligarchy had collapsed in May 1989, paving the way for the democratic process that saw Boris Yeltsin become Russia's first freely elected president. The world watched developments closely as Yeltsin announced that Russia would immediately initiate radical market-oriented reform that would include massive privatization of state-owned industries. What emerged was a program colloquially known as "shock therapy." Price controls would be lifted immediately, and state subsidies to both industry and agriculture would be phased out – all accompanied by liberalization of foreign trade and the free float of the ruble.

By the autumn of 1993 the inflation rate had climbed to 1,000% per annum, hyperinflation was in full spate, and the economy in chaos. (The phenomenon was not lost upon the Chinese, who later chose to follow a more measured approach to the introduction of a freer market.) To Peter, chaos almost invariably spelled opportunity, so he decided to visit both Moscow and St Petersburg.

I was charged with energy at the prospect of visiting Moscow at this juncture. Like everyone else I have been bombarded by the propagandist media accounts and there is plenty of residual mythology, so I need to clear my mind a bit although I have the distinct sense that we are at a crucial turning point and that events in Russia will reverberate far beyond its own frontiers ... I checked into the Kempinsky – a new womb. My room was a good size with a direct view onto the Kremlin and Red Square. In the morning as I ran across the Moscow River to Red Square, the coal smoke from the power station partially obscured the orange of the rising sun.

My guide for the day [took me] to see GUM, *Lenin's tomb, Swallow Hills and the Moscow State University campus ... I bought a rabbit hat there for $15 to save the tips of my ears. We continued to Tolstoy's house and the Arbat Pedestrian Mall, which appeared well stocked and quite busy. I had a light lunch serenaded by a private violinist and a pianist followed by a lecture on Pushkin, a visit to the Lubyanka, the infamous erstwhile headquarters of the* KGB, *the broken statue of Stalin and finally Gorky Park ... We finished up with a ride on the metro to Revolution Square and the Lenin Museum. After a quick and thankfully very hot bath I took a cab to the Bolshoi [where] we watched "The Sleeping Beauty" – the seats were desperately uncomfortable and I wasn't feeling my best. The theatre was very plush and the costumes and the set lavish but I noticed that there was still a huge hammer and sickle above the curtain.*

His conclusions? *Far, far too early – even for me. The institutional and legal structures are rudimentary, and accounting in any comprehensible – let alone honest and transparent – manner does not exist at all. I foresee a situation reminiscent of the "Wild West" – robber barons and gun-slinging ... It remains possible that with a strong leader and a titanic effort (accompanied by massive foreign investment) a new order could be forged. In any event the vastness of its natural resource base, its size and population are such that it cannot possibly be ignored. There may come a moment for us.*

As it turned out that moment never really came. Peter visited several times over the next few years and always came back with the impression that the country could erupt into chaos again at any moment. Events proved him right on more than one occasion.

As the numbers for the Cundill Value Fund came in at the end of 1993, they were a triumphant vindication of the restructuring of 1992 and the investments added as a result of Peter's tireless international quest for value. The fund had appreciated 43% by the end of the year.

25

Alarums and Excursions

IF PETER HAD expected that exceptional performance to bring an influx of new money, he was quickly disabused. The 43% rise of 1993 occasioned a wave of redemptions that eliminated much of the increase in funds under management, resulting from capital gains. At the end of 1992 net assets in the Value Fund had amounted to $256 million. By the end of 1993 they had only risen to $319 million, which meant that redemptions had totalled nearly $50 million. It was a serious disappointment, compounded by the fact that the overheads at Peter Cundill and Associates had been climbing steadily since 1990. But Peter never indulged in "blame games." His answer to a problem was to seek a rational solution divorced as far as possible from emotion.

The Vancouver team was not quite so immune. Fingers were pointed at Brian McDermott, as the man who wore the marketing hat. He in turn cited three factors: the investor base of the value fund being heavily weighted toward retail rather than institutional unit holders; the difficulty of getting Peter in front of audiences and the institutional community, given his travel commitments; and the failure of the Value Fund to follow the industry in increasing the commission payout to independent distributors. He had a point, but solutions were less obvious. Creating a proper in-house marketing team would have added considerably to fixed overheads and Peter doubted it would produce the scale of result that would make it viable. As for his travelling, he saw it as indispensable to the investment process, as the results of the investigative journeying of the previous eighteen months attested. McDermott's final point was less easily defensible.

While Peter was an icon of generosity, and his lavish entertainment was already legendary, in some areas he could be parsimonious to the point of meanness and irrationally inflexible. One of these blind spots was sales commissions. Given that there was no obvious corrective panacea to McDermott's concerns, Peter Cundill and Associates would either soldier

on, accepting the constraints while perhaps making some modest miti-
gation attempts, or it would have to merge with a larger organization. A
merger was at that point of no interest to Peter. However, mainly in order
to still the rumbling, he agreed to explore the possibilities.

Meanwhile, Joanie had not let the grass grow under her feet. Having pres-
sured Peter into agreeing to buy a house in Aspen, she made sure there
was no chance for him to change his mind. By the spring she had spent
$1.5 million acquiring a fine property. Peter provided the money, but the
house went firmly into her name. He was delighted with the house, and
had his own "den" with fine mountain views, where he could comfort-
ably hide himself away to read and think and write. But, he had, as he
put it, begun to experience "the creeping onslaught of indifference" as
far as she was concerned and it was likely mutual.

And he had social and investment concerns to attend to back in
London. In 1989, as he was coming out of his depression, he had entered
into a personal investment adventure in the London fashion arena with
Merryn Corcoran, a New Zealand friend, an attractive statuesque lady
and a regular dancing partner at Annabel's. Whether it was the opportunity of learning about the retail operation and development of a virgin
enterprise or the prospect of a steady stream of long-legged models is
open to question. He had agreed to join her and a couple of her cronies
as a partner in MOA, rather ominously named for the flightless New
Zealand bird, and they duly opened a shop on London's fashionable
King's Road in Chelsea, "to sell frocks to the aristocracy."

To celebrate, Merryn had suggested that Peter visit her and her family
in New Zealand where she would act as his guide. He accepted enthusiastically and early December found him on the way to Wellington. The
highlight of the visit was an expedition to Queenstown where he and
Merryn signed up for rafting on the Shotover River: *We had some dry
land instruction on how to go down rapids. Thank God we did ... as we
got into the real rapids we were bumped solidly against a large rock. The
raft folded in half and I thought "bye bye baby." I swallowed a lot of
water – still I managed to come up holding onto the raft. A guide shouted
to me from the bank to go downriver and I went looking for Merryn ...*

By sheer luck, the current whirled us into the bank just before the curve of the river, after which we would have faced a great expanse of white water and would probably have drowned.

They had both survived, if only barely. But far from abandoning the attempt, they clambered straight back into a new raft, rode through the rapids and the tunnels at the end, and then went on to brave another set as well.

Later, Merryn had been keen to expand MOA and persuaded Peter to take a trip to Bath with her to look at possibilities there. By that stage, he was not sure the original venture could do more than survive, but he enjoyed the excursion nevertheless: *We toured the city on the top of an open air bus – an excellent way to get a feel, though not as good as a run – the city is a real jewel of Georgian streets and squares, one after another, all perfectly proportioned neo-classical architecture, rather like Dublin only smaller and less spoilt ... I can see that the city could easily turn into an up-market, shoppers' paradise, but MOA ...?*

Peter enjoyed being a fashion mogul and playing the patron at charity functions, and through Merryn he had met a completely new echelon of English society – upper class and devoted to pleasure. But by 1994 MOA's finances were in complete disarray. He had come to see the company as an open maw that gobbled cash, and he was the only shareholder with the real means to support it. His every instinct told him to shut it down, write it off to experience, and rationalize it as an expensive toy he had grown out of. However, Merryn was very attached to MOA, and Peter was fond of Merryn – and highly susceptible to her tears and pleas. Besides which, he found that he had become socially dependent on her. So, the cheques continued to be drawn. Strictly speaking, money was not the issue – in his terms it was only a bagatelle. What grated was that parting with it ran against all his deeply ingrained business principles and he had the uncomfortable feeling that those in the know had begun to regard him as a bit of dupe. Nothing was more precious to him than his reputation for shrewd and disciplined investment, and MOA was perhaps beginning to expose an Achilles heel.

Nevertheless, the social whirl continued and Peter celebrated his fifty-seventh birthday at a grand house party weekend organized by Jenny, Lady Chelsea, a good friend of Merryn's. They drove up to Macclesfield in Cheshire on the Friday afternoon to the Rotunda, a superb replica of Palladio's Rotunda inspired by the artist Felix Kelly and built for the inventor and engineer Sebastian de Ferranti:

No one should imagine that the aristocratic wealth of England has been decimated. Scrambled into my dinner jacket to meet the crowd ... To my surprise dry martinis were served – premier grand cru claret with dinner. There was a savoury after the sweet. It was called "Scotch Woodcock" – of course nothing to do with woodcock at all – I'm told it was a piece of fried bread spread with anchovy paste, topped with hollandaise sauce – sounds disgusting and heavy, but not at all. The ladies retired before the port and the cigars came. When we rejoined them, we played vingt et un. Light-hearted stuff, not bridge, thank God. I'd never have remembered the cards ... In the early hours [someone] sprang the alarm. Fun and games all round. Who emerged out of what bedroom?

In the morning I joined Merryn and Jenny. Birthday presents. I am now 57 and I think it will be a grand year.

While MOA may have been floundering, the Portuguese investment in Lusotur had by now doubled, although it remained statistically cheap. One of the company's major projects was an enormous tourist development at Villamoura in the Algarve on Portugal's Southern Atlantic coast. The general practice in the Value Fund was to sell half of a position when it had doubled. Before doing that in this instance, Peter flew down to Faro to take a look at the Vilamoura development, and checked in at the Lusotur hotel on the property. He hired a bicycle and toured the estate, explored the marina and the raw golf courses, and tried out the restaurants. He saw that the development was being carefully tailored to appeal to increasingly affluent middle-class families from Britain who were tiring of the ugly, concrete resorts of Spain's Costa Brava and Costa del Sol and were ready for something a little more appealing but not vastly more expensive. In Peter's view Vilamoura might fill that gap. The Lusotur position remained and he was subsequently proven right about the development. During British half term and school holidays, Portuguese becomes the second language in this resort.

Peter returned to London in time to participate in the ceremonies marking the fiftieth anniversary of the D-Day landings in 1944 and on June 2 there was a very special celebration of the enormous contribution of Canadian troops and especially their sacrifice in the battle for Normandy. For Peter it was especially nostalgic because of his father's important role in training the raw volunteers who so distinguished them-selves and he was riveted by the account given by the high commissioner:

Got there just in time to sit down to dinner ... The 1st Canadian Parachute Battalion had the job of destroying the bridge over the river Dives and the German HQ *and radio station at Varaville. They were dropped before dawn and had secured all their objectives by midday – but at what a cost. Out of 27 officers and 516 men, 24 officers and 343 men were dead. Apparently there is a fine memorial to the battalion at Varaville. In the battle for Normandy, which broke the back of the Wehrmacht, the Canadian 2nd and 3rd divisions were in action through-out. Out of 18,000 men over 5,000 were killed. I was prouder than ever to be Canadian. The highlight of the tribute to this effort and its cost was Dame Vera Lynn singing "We'll Meet Again." We were all in tears.*

The following day Peter attended the ceremony in Green Park where the Queen inaugurated the Canadian War Memorial. *She spoke most warmly of meeting "some of those gallant young men" during her time as a driver in the Territorial Service. Later in the day I ran over to the memorial and put a maple leaf on it in memory of Dad.*

Another important anniversary in the same month found Peter in Zurich. His bag had been lost en route, so he had no kit to use in the gym – the morning's exercise was dancing on the spot in the suite in his underwear. With no suit or tie, he had to rearrange his eleven o'clock meeting so that Matthew Gonzalez, a private banker with an interest in value investment, called on him rather than the other way round. Peter greeted his fellow investment guru, champagne bottle in hand. They had to drink a toast, he explained, to Luca Pacioli, the scholar and Franciscan monk who in 1494 had published *Summa de Arithmetica*, his mathematics textbook, which had expounded for the first time the principles of double-entry accounting. They raised a glass to "the father of our profession, the *sine qua non* for accountants and especially for value investors."

Peter had been eyeing Turkey for some time. In the 1980s it had come to be regarded as something of an export-led miracle economy and exem-plary in the region, the darling of the U.S. credit-rating agencies. But with deteriorating conditions in the Middle East, this golden period had come to an abrupt end, and the Turkish economy plunged into crisis. By mid-1993 inflation had hit 73% and Turkey's international credit rating was dropped to below investment grade. But after the elections of early 1994 the new government instituted an immediate austerity and privatization program that persuaded the IMF to advance $740 million to fund public works designed to stimulate growth. With the stock market still on its knees, Peter felt it was time to pay his first visit to Istanbul.

He elected to stay at the most opulent hotel in the city, the Kempinski-run Ciragan Palace, built by an Ottoman prince in the 1860s right on the Bosphorus. Peter did twenty laps in its spectacular "infinity pool" on arrival and then dined in his suite watching the sun set over the sea and the lights twinkling on the Asian shore. After running to the Galata Bridge and back the next morning, he set off with two guides to explore the city starting with Hagia Sophia, the Church of the Holy Wisdom, originally a church, then a mosque and now a museum.

The vast dome is one of the marvels of Byzantine architectural engineering. It is the mother of every mosque in the Islamic world including Istanbul's enormous and beautiful Blue Mosque. Inside it the mosaics still glow with Christian fervour and the images look fresh; Christ in Majesty; Justinian and his notorious, nymphomaniac Empress, Theodora, making offerings to the Virgin and Child, not humble, not penitent, boasting the full magnificence of their imperial regalia. Islam is, of course, in evidence, but in here it pales before the sheer glory of its Christian antecedents.

We went on to visit what was for me the most exciting experience of the tour ... the Byzantine cistern was also built by Justinian, or to be more exact by 7,000 of his slaves. One of its three hundred columns has tears carved onto it, said to be for the hundreds of slaves who died in its construction. I suspect that is apocryphal. The cistern is like a vast floodlit cathedral. I was rowed through it in a small boat to the strains of Beethoven's Choral Symphony. Thinking of it now the prickles run down my back. Every column is individually carved; mostly Doric and Ionic capitols ... The greatest thrill was suddenly to encounter a column whose base was supported by a gigantic and superbly carved head of the Medusa, its eyes wide and staring and its head wreathed with wriggling serpents – truly awe-inspiring and still slightly sinister. It was almost instinctive to avert one's gaze.

The next port of call was the Grand Bazaar, the biggest and oldest covered market in the world. On a first visit a guide is essential, but guides inevitably press-gang their charges to "special" shops where they enjoy a comfortable commission deal. It was the carpets that got to Peter. I now have one of them in my office – a true work of art and a daily pleasure for which I have little doubt that Peter failed to drive a hard enough bargain.

Mehmet Kutman, the founder and CEO of Global Securities, the largest and most important investment house and dealmaker in Turkey's capital markets, with seats on Nasdaq and the NYSE, recommended in their visit that afternoon that Peter look at the Koch Group. As Turkey's largest and most successful conglomerate engaged in energy, automotive, consumer durables, finance, and banking, it was in effect a proxy for the most dynamic sectors of the Turkish economy – and was then selling at a substantial discount to break-up value. Peter laughed, confessing that he already had an appointment with Rahmi Koch, the chairman, the following day.

At the Koch compound on the Asian side of the Bosphorus bridge, he was greeted by Rahmi, a graduate of Johns Hopkins, and his son Mustafa, who had been at Millfield School in England and then Columbia. The far-reaching conversation over lunch on the terrace look-ing back onto the city eventually touched on the subject of Bartholomew, the Patriarch of Constantinople, who interested Peter immensely because of his work fostering the revival of the long-repressed Orthodox Churches throughout the territories of the old Soviet Union. Rahmi, also an admirer, as well as a friend of the Patriarch, arranged a meeting:

I am excited to be meeting the Patriarch; he is a scholar and a humanist in the great tradition of churchmen. I'm told that he speaks eight lan-guages including fluent Latin and classical Greek. He was awarded the Congressional Gold Medal for his work on Human Rights. The Orthodox Church had a fairly comfortable accommodation with the Ottomans but has been subjected to persecution, confiscation and much indignity under a succession of secular Turkish governments. This man may be a saint – the first I will ever have met!

The Patriarchy is hidden away in the Phanar, a little-known corner of old Constantinople overlooking the mouth of the Golden Horn. It is a beautiful wooden palace dating from the sixteenth century. With the nearby Church of St George it is practically the only property left to an institution that was once more richly endowed than the Vatican and still has a communion of over 250 million. Bartholomew received Peter without ceremony, simply dressed in a black cassock and black hat, and with just a handshake. They talked and walked together for over an hour:

I have now met a saint. Despite the indignities and the persecution visited on him, the Patriarch remains warmly supportive of Turkey and all of its peoples. He is an international peacemaker and a striver for human rights in the same league as Mandela and Martin Luther King, yet in a global sense. We discussed an invitation for him to speak at the Aspen Forum and he expressed great willingness to do so. He has a deep sense of mission, of history, of tragedy and a great love of humanity with all its frailties. He might be the only man capable of bridging the gulf between Islam and the predominantly Christian West. He said to me that "war in the name of religion is the same as war against that religion and all religion."

At the Patriarch's suggestion, Peter went to the Porphyrogenitus Palace, the only remaining part of the huge Blachernae Imperial palace complex: *It is an eerie place. There were no visitors and not a great deal to see, but the atmosphere is extraordinary – laden with doom ... I went on, also at the Patriarch's suggestion, to visit the Church of the Holy Saviour in Chora (in the fields) ... It is perhaps the most beautiful church I have ever seen, not vast but still with a perfectly proportioned dome ... I went inside to be flabbergasted. The interior is covered with the most brilliant, powerful, glowing mosaics, the whole of it dominated by a mosaic bust of Christ covering the entire dome. It is a noble face and he has his hand slightly raised. The inscription in Greek is Ἐγὼ τό ἐιμι τό λύχ κόσμόσ – "I am the light of the world." The whole impression would encourage the worshipper to believe so.*

Topkapi, once the palace of the Sultans, now houses the Archaelogical Museum among others. Peter traipsed through the now deserted harem with little interest, and quickly made his way to the archaeological complex: *For me there were two highlights. There is a small fragment of the sarcophagus of Constantine the Great, the Emperor who is supposed to have had a vision before the decisive battle of the Milvian Bridge in which he succeeded in destroying his rival for the imperial throne. The vision was of a crucifix and a voice said "In hoc signum vincit," meaning roughly, if your boys wear this sign you'll win. Whatever the truth there is no doubt that he made Christianity the official religion of the entire Roman Empire, consigning the old pantheon to oblivion ...*

*My other favourite was the Alexander sarcophagus, which is a thing
of great beauty. It was not made for Alexander himself but it must have
been for someone very close to him. What it has is two exquisite relief
figures of Alexander. One is him throwing a spear from his chariot at the
Battle of Issus and the other hunting lions with his Macedonian mates,
of whom his favourite Hephaestion is also recognizable. The figures are
so perfectly lifelike that one has the impression of witnessing the actual
event and seeing Alexander in action in the flesh with full facial expression. It is a weird and wonderful experience.*

As Joanie's sixtieth birthday approached, she exuded a considerable
"froideur." When Joanie and Peter arrived from Aspen at the apartment
in the Grosvenor House she found that her portrait photograph had been
relegated to a drawer in favour of a large picture of his friend Paul
Lévesque's (the Canadian luge Olympian) favourite bulldog, Napoleon.
She was not amused. Peter vigorously maintained that he had lent the
apartment to Lévesque to thank him for having organized the Cresta run
and had no idea about the joke. Privately he thought it very funny,
although he promised to have serious words with Lévesque. Joanie was
not convinced. Perhaps the bottle of scent in the bathroom of a variety
that she did not use and seemed unlikely to belong to Lévesque was part
of the reason.

The "special measures" needed this time consisted of a hiking party
with friends in the Swiss Alps which Joanie had requested. They stayed
in the delightful Schlosshotel Chasté, styled like a Swiss chalet.
Unfortunately Peter found the whole thing rather wearisome – *too many
interminable, boring dinners and Joanie only wants me to be there to be
social. I just want to get on with training for my marathon.* Wisely, he
confided his frustration only to the pages of the journal, which now was
kept under lock and key. On the day there was plenty of jewellery among
the presents. The party hiked up into Heidi country, the Bernese
Oberland, to lunch beside a spring-fed lake. As they arrived Peter dove
into the icy lake and came up clutching a bottle of Dom Perignon. The
applause was universal.

For the following evening Peter had made special arrangements for

a party in a private room at the Palace Hotel in St Moritz. At Joanie's
place at the table, Peter had placed charming little toy dog that barked.
It was risky but it worked. Joanie was enchanted and the dog was
christened "Schatzi." The next morning she wrote Peter a note: "Dear
Peter, Thank you for the best birthday ever. You have done so much planning, plus your generous gifts and sentiments. I recommend turning
60 to everyone. xxx J." It was not overly effusive, but that was not her
style and Peter understood.

On his return to London Peter had a long-planned engagement to
keep. Some months earlier he had met Michael, the Earl of St Aldwyn,
and their friendship had led to an invitation to join St Aldwyn's cricket
team to play the St Aldwyn village team and spend the weekend at the
family home Williamstrip in the Cotswolds. Peter was a complete novice:
he knew little more than what a short briefing and one team practice
could convey. However, he was impeccably turned out in spanking new
white flannel trousers, white flannel shirt, and cricket boots. Most of the
players on his team were sporting colourfully striped school or university
cricketing caps and Peter's one concession to North America drew a good
deal of amusement from both teams. He wore a baseball cap boldly
marked "Boogies Diner." Certainly nothing quite like it had ever been
seen in Gloucestershire before.

The opposing team began batting, and Peter was placed at mid-wicket.
The significance of the term "silly mid-off" quickly became apparent; the
fielder in that position is placed ten feet or so in front of the batsman,
who frequently wallops the very hard cricket ball straight at him. When
it came to the batting, it transpired that despite his briefing, Peter had
not heard about a vital piece of equipment – the "box" – which protects
a gentleman's most tender parts. That deficiency corrected, Peter waddled
out as fourth batsman, wearing leg pads and gloves and brandishing his
bat aggressively.

*The fast bowler had been told about me so he only started his run up
from about a quarter of a mile off. I got my bat in the way and scored a
run. It was the last ball of the over so I ended up facing the bowling again
from the other end. The next bowler made no concessions, hurling his
missile at me with incredible speed. I managed to block it but nemesis
struck with the next ball and I was bowled out, earning myself the soubri-
quet of "one run Pete," of which I am very proud. There was great*

exultation and applause as I made my way back to the pavilion, doffing my baseball cap.

Peter was definitely becoming more immersed in English life than ever before, and most of it was not to Joanie's taste. She had become deeply involved in Aspen society and was less and less willing to leave it just to put in an appearance as Peter's spouse. However, she did fly over with Peter to attend a society wedding in the country. From the outset, things did not go well:

John met us at the airport. The fan belt went on the M25. There were several hours of waiting including an interlude at the motorway Little Chef and a snooze on the couches of the Automobile Association. Finally another car drove us to Huntingdon and the glories of the George Hotel – not an auspicious start – J fractious.

Donned my morning-coat next day and with the Binghams, we went to St Mary's Church for the ceremony. Reception at Hinchingbrooke House – former home of the Earls of Sandwich, [one of whom] was a great gambler. He is said to have ordered his valet to feed him with meat tucked between two slices of bread so he wouldn't need to interrupt his card playing … to take sustenance.

And so it continued with Joanie. They attended a "War and Peace" Ball held at the Dorchester Hotel in London in support of White Russian charities and chaired by Count Nikolai Tolstoy. Joanie knew practically no one, but Peter was in his element, dressed as a Russian grand duke, wearing a magnificent collection of orders, and dancing mazurkas in his own inimitable fashion. Unfortunately, a photo of the *War and Peace* Ball appeared in *Tatler* and *Hello!* magazine shortly afterward of Peter staring down the ample cleavage of a very attractive blonde lady. Joanie was incensed, convinced that Peter was having an affair with her. This he vigorously denied, asserting that he had never met the lady in his life before and did not even know her name – which in this instance was perfectly true.

Arriving for the Atlantic Colleges Ball at Bleinhem Palace

Peter surreptitiously reading the *Wall Street Journal* while on holiday

White-water rafting in New Zealand

The *War and Peace* Ball

An encounter at the *War and Peace* Ball

Canyoning in Switzerland

Performing *Macbeth* in Kyoto

Something's caught his eye

A toast

Peter in bed with a rose

Peter's favourite Miró at the Maeght Foundation

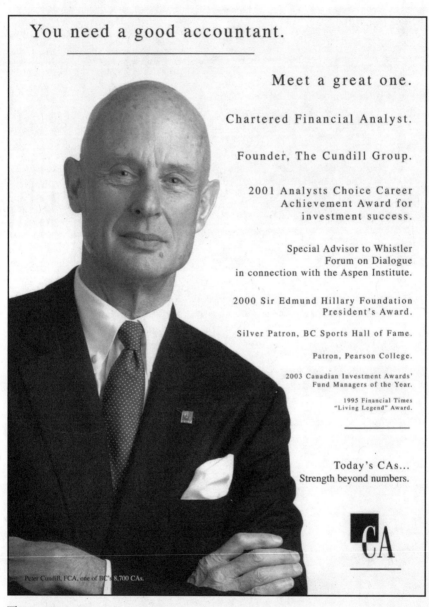
The accountant

Celebrating the New Year in Hong Kong with Jane Dobson

Dancing with Phyllis Ellis

The brothers, Peter and Grier, in Montreal, October 1996

Dining with Chantale Joseph (CJ)

Peter jogging in Kensington
Gardens, 2010

Peter's father's plaque at Cap à l'Aigle, surrounded by Peter's ashes

Grier scattering Peter's ashes into the St Lawrence from Granny's Beach

The world at his fingertips

PART · FOUR ·

Reality Checks

THE FLOW OF REDEMPTIONS from CVF that had come as such an unwelcome surprise after its stellar performance in 1994 eventually ceased. The following year had produced another respectable gain of 15.4%, bringing the size of the fund to $371 million. To Peter this seemed satisfactory. However, the senior members of his team, especially Brian McDermott and Tim McElvaine, were increasingly dissatisfied. Peter personally owned 80% of Cundill Investment Research, the stock of the management company, so that his personal net worth was appreciating substantially through the predominantly organic growth being generated.

To the smaller shareholders, it seemed that the record of 19.2% compound return over twenty years was being squandered by the failure to market the fund aggressively. They could see that the constraints on size, which were perhaps valid in running a pure value Fund confined to North American markets alone, no longer applied to CVF, with its global investment strategy. Indeed, they could see no difficulty in running a fund with assets in the billions of dollars. Nevertheless, it was quite clear by now that Peter would never sanction a meaningful in-house marketing team. Getting him to agree to spend money on the essential upgrading of the firm's computer systems had been difficult enough, even though the business case for doing so was irrefutable.

Peter was not unaware of this undercurrent, but the business was his creation and he liked it the way it was. It allowed him complete independence and supported his chosen lifestyle – change in the status quo might constrain his personal freedom to operate in his inimitable freewheeling fashion. Shortly after Tim McElvaine became a shareholder, he had written Peter a memo about his exorbitant travel and entertainment expenditures, including trips on the Concorde, suites in the world's most luxurious hotels, and streams of bills from Annabel's night club. Peter had barely contained himself from writing an extremely terse response. In the event, he decided to play it "cool," and confined himself to reiterating that any future discussion of the founder's expenses by the minority shareholders was completely off limits. McElvaine had taken the point, but it had undoubtedly registered negatively with Peter.

Nonetheless, it was becoming evident to him that in the mutual fund business, as in any other, economies of scale are vital to bottom-line profitability. Running a $20 million fund, as he had done in the '70s, with just himself and two employees, had worked very well, but growth had necessitated additional staff. Now, with nearly $400 million under management, he had in place a team that could perfectly well handle substantially more with little additional personnel cost. It was time to bend a little to internal pressure. Peter was still adamant that he would not countenance any attempt to make more than a marginal increase in the firm's marketing budgets – which left as the only options either an alliance with a much larger organization with real marketing clout, or an outright takeover.

At this point Peter sanctioned an "exploration of the possibilities," although privately he felt that the chances of eliciting an offer that would come anywhere close to reflecting the fair value of the whole company were remote. The prospect of some kind of marketing deal did seem more likely, but even this was not obvious since CVF occupied a niche space in the mutual fund world. Notwithstanding, his team wasted no time. After some confidential discussions with Prem Watsa of Fairfax, a preliminary meeting was arranged with Peter's old boss, Warren Goldring of AGF. Peter noted rather flatly: *We called on Warren Goldring. I did about 40 minutes of relationship stuff and then left the others to do hard numbers. Warren wants to do a deal. We'll see.*

Goldring did in fact make an offer that predictably was nowhere near the mark from Peter's perspective: *We met with Warren again. He cajoled and threatened by saying that I wouldn't grow the business if I didn't do the deal. Tant pis, but I'm not giving my business away.* For the time being that was that, but the idea that a suitable deal might be possible with the right entity and could potentially be advantageous was now firmly lodged in Peter's mind.

Meanwhile, he was more preoccupied by what he perceived as overvalued stock markets, since he was finding it tougher than usual to come up with investments that met the value criteria. He gave an interview to Patrick Bloomfield of the *Financial Post* in which he explained some of the nuances.

I suffer from the tedious habit of reading annual reports and prospectuses from cover to cover. It's my bedtime reading and I enjoy it ... In the current crop I find plenty of warning signals. Asian-orientated funds are all the rage these days. Now, we don't buy IPO's ever, but I happened to look at some prospectuses coming out of China. One of them concerned a historic hotel in which shares were being issued at what was represented as below asset value. This intrigued me, so I read on and indeed with the hotel as a freehold belonging to the corporation the claim would have been fair enough. However, in the notes to the prospectus, but still large as life, it states that the hotel is leased from the government and has been valued for purposes of the prospectus on the assumption that it will be renewed in six years time on exactly the same basis as now. In practical terms, the thing has no asset value at all other than whatever value you place on the six years. On top of this, in a country where inflation is rampant, how in the world can you expect that this lease will be renewed at the current level?

There was another prospectus where the auditors expressed some doubt as to whether the business could continue ... and then I read a U.S. prospectus of a company controlled by a semi-retired football player. Its most recent revenue statement showed a turnover of $36,000 but it was planning two new divisions in virtual reality games and products related to professional sport. On that promise of future greatness the stock immediately climbed from an issue price of $5.00 to $16. It wasn't remotely worth $5.00!

We used to look for what we called magic sixes – stocks with a dividend yield of 6% or more, a price earnings multiple of 6 or less and selling at less than 60% of book value. In today's markets there are none, but we have been exploring what I term "the antithesis of value" with a view to shorting some indices. We started with this test which we christened "the twinkling twos." We had the computer search for stocks with a dividend of less than 2%, a price earnings multiple of over 20, and selling at more than twice book value. We found 8,700. We tried again on a yield of 1.5%, a P/E of 50 plus and selling at five times book. There were 593. Finally we really went for it – no dividend, making a loss, negative book value. We found 94, of which quite a few had a market capitalization of over $1 billion and were household names.

We don't ever try to predict when reality will resurface either on a micro or macro basis, but there comes a point when it is no longer a question of if, and that is the time to act before it's too late.

I should emphasize that while the task of finding value is made immeasurably easier by the computer age, it is not a substitute for on the ground investigation and a global approach. This is why I regularly travel over 100,000 miles a year.

And he continued to do so.

Peter was for a time a shareholder of GEC, the huge electronics and defence conglomerate created by the late Lord Weinstock, a somewhat controversial figure. His logic and deep intelligence were universally acknowledged, and his supporters praised the way his drive and ambition had, against the odds, created one of Britain's biggest businesses. His detractors argued that, having constructed the company, he was content to run it as an adding machine. Peter visited Weinstock on several occasions, became a strong supporter, and was diametrically opposed to the conventional City of London view that the shareholders would be better served by Weinstock going on an acquisition splurge and putting the company's £5 billion cash pile to work.

Peter held his position in GEC until Weinstock himself was forced to retire at the age of seventy-two, and then sold the shares at a substantial profit. Subsequently he watched in dismay as Weinstock's successor, Lord Simpson of Dunkeld, embarked on the spending spree that the City institutions had been lobbying for. Simpson piled into telecommunications, selling off GEC's profitable defence and electronics businesses, squandering the entire cash pile and borrowing hugely on top to acquire what turned out to be worthless businesses. Renamed Marconi plc, the company was destroyed within two years. Lord Rees-Mogg, who had been a speaker at one of Peter's conferences and was a past director of GEC, wrote an article in the *London Times* describing this catastrophe and the devastating impact that it had had on Lord Weinstock personally and financially.

Peter commented: *It makes sad reading and is a sobering reminder that brilliance and hard work are simply not enough. You have to be lucky as well. Arnold Weinstock was probably Britain's greatest contemporary industrialist, a man of many parts with huge creative energy and charm. He could also be a perceptive observer and commentator on British Society and I specifically remember some remarks of his that I thought really hit the mark. He said, "You will occasionally hear the view expressed that Britain is not class-ridden and I think that I agree with that. The problem is more that it is clique-ridden. There have been union cliques and capitalist cliques, political cliques and Masonic cliques. I think all of that has damaged the UK."*

As for Marconi, what a lesson in how poor management is capable of eliminating the margin of safety in the blink of an eye, no matter how large the numbers are. Lord Simpson undoubtedly thought he was doing the right thing in following the herd in pursuit of the telecoms chimera. His was not an attempt at fraudulent deception of the market or his shareholders, unlike some others. His problem was that he was simply not grounded by concepts of value.

Unexpected encounters always piqued Peter's curiosity and reinforced his conviction that life is dull without surprises to leaven the routines. He relished recording the best of them:

I attended a Deltec board meeting at the Lyford Cay Club in Nassau … After lunch I wanted to get away from it all and went for a run on the beach where I found another solitary figure. It was John Templeton. We power-walked together more or less in silence for a while and then we slowed down and chatted. John has been an icon to me. His pristine personal conduct has been a sort of beacon, although in many ways unattainable by me. Now at 83, he has had a facelift, he has a 50-year-old girlfriend, never says no to a party, and may take a drink or three. Holy Moly. I am in shock!

And trips on the Concorde often provided journal-worthy material:

In the Concorde lounge I ran into Barbara Amiel and Conrad Black. They said that they were making a very quick visit to London to attend some gallery opening and returning to New York the following day.

Behind them one of the other passengers remarked of Barbara in not so "sotto voce" tones, "She'd go to the opening of an envelope." I thought that Conrad winced slightly but not Barbara, though she must have heard. I admire her; she has real "sang froid" and a man's balls and brass ...

I watched the UK election results through the night before taking the Concorde to New York in the morning. Labour destroyed the Tories. We have an unknown quantity of a Prime Minister in Tony Blair and John Major who unseated the Iron Lady is out. Geoffrey Howe was two seats up from me on the plane [Chancellor of the Exchequer, Foreign Secretary and Deputy Prime Minister under Margaret Thatcher]. I went up to him and said, "Lord Howe. I guess you must be the first of the Tory émigrés." He roared with laughter.

Using the journal as a commonplace book meant that Peter could go a good deal further than simply recording events on a daily basis. He used the notebooks as a means of gradually enunciating his own quirky philosophy, which was a unique amalgam of the stoic and the epicurean. The result was a framework that he wrote on a single A4 page and distributed to select friends and colleagues. Clearly it would never achieve cult status or attract faithful disciples, although viewed dispassionately there is something in it for most people. Its slightly tongue-in-cheek style makes it entertaining and instructive, but never messianic. The contradictions and juxtaposition of opposites can seem quite barmy at first glance, but in its fashion it is thought-provoking. Perhaps it is more revealing about the contradictions in Peter's own personality than anything else. It sometimes comes fairly close to being an *apologia*:

PETE'S TIPS FOR A GOOD LIFE
- Exercise between half an hour and two hours every day. Do more on Saturdays. Take one day off every two months. Keep your body fat at less than 10%.
- Don't be afraid of eating junk food but eat lots of fruit as well. If you choose to eat fat-free yoghurt, make sure you complement this with plenty of hot-dogs, hamburgers and French fries.
- Sleep a lot.
- Read even more.
- Drink alcohol two days a week; once in a while to excess.
- Cigarettes are bad. Cigars after a meal are good.
- Be curious. Never stop learning.

- Once a year run a marathon. Once a year do something that scares the shit out of you: a bungie jump, the Cresta run, white-water rafting.
- Laugh a lot but be reflective.
- Strive for balance through contradictions.
- Be a warrior. Be a priest. Be a monk. Be a hedonist.
- Reason and passion go together but not reason before passion.
- Rotate between day-dreaming and acute awareness. Do reality checks and focus on detail.
- Think positive thoughts even when you're lying to yourself. The brain doesn't know the difference.
- Seek balance through harmonizing the different aspects of life: physical, spiritual, emotional, sexual.
- The physical world is illusion but deal with it as if it were real. At every moment in all societies contradictions are developing and these inevitably lead to discontinuities. In his book "Beyond the Mexique Bay," Aldous Huxley wrote, "Life is a series of routines punctuated by orgies." It is and it should be, and neither Huxley nor I mean it in the purely conventional sense.
- The Roman stoic philosopher Seneca said a lot of useful things. Here are a few: "Happiness is balance; to teach is also to learn; knowing is better than remembering; we are born unequal, we die equal; to govern is to serve, not to rule."
- Be passionate but avoid zealotry.
- Be politically correct. Be a Bubba. Use Bill Clinton as a role model. Wear sackcloth and enjoy pain. Lead an opulent lifestyle.
- Own a house. Enjoy hotel rooms.
- Travel to extremes. Consider each resting place a sanctuary and a home.
- Strive for high levels of awareness. Enjoy brain moments.
- Be responsible but remember that the ultimate freedom is the utter absence of obligation.
- Be highly principled, but be flexible and above all fair.
- Be optimistic, or be pessimistic but above all be realistic.
- Seek order, confront chaos, retreat from the maelstrom.
- Be open, but you can keep a few dark secrets.
- Be a historian, be a prophet.
- Be deductive. Be inductive.
- The stock market is almost always wrong; once in a while it is right.

- God is infinity. Don't question any further. This is an absolute truth.
- Don't own a car. Ride a bike. Use the subway. Hire limos.
- Remember that in life one is both a participant and an observer.
- Study systems and financial statements. Remember, though, that the beauty of numbers can delude. Be intuitive, warm and fuzzy in your analysis.
- Understanding relationships is as important in investment matters as financial analysis.
- Be humble but believe in yourself.

As Peter's personal wealth grew, he felt increasingly obliged to "give something back." It was a matter that he discussed with Archbishop Bartholomew of Constantinople when he visited him in Istanbul. The Patriarch's advice had been quite singular: "Follow your heart and give where it leads you. It is often better to give to people rather than causes. Disproportionate good can result from quite insignificant amounts through the intermediation of passionate and committed individuals. Think of the parable of the sower. Do not try to reason too much in your giving, take joy in it and remember that our hope always resides in the youth of this world."

The counsel, particularly in relation to youth and individuals, clearly influenced the pattern of Peter's philanthropy from then on, and he registered his gratitude to Bartholomew in a tangible way by sending him $5,000 to support his own charitable work. In his letter to the archbishop's treasurer, Peter wrote: "I was overwhelmed by my visit with the Patriarch, both in his capacity as a man and as a representative of God. I also recognize that you work within a difficult environment." Shortly afterward Peter received a personal letter from Bartholomew in Greek under the Archiepiscopal seal. When translated it read:

The Esteemed Mr Peter Cundill, Chairman of the Advisory Board of the Cundill Foundation, our Modesty's beloved in the Lord: Grace and Peace from God.

With paternal love we acknowledge your gift and through our Patriarchal letter express our warmest thanks. Thus, we bestow upon you, your family and your co-workers, our wholehearted paternal and patriarchal blessing. We further pray that this Holy and Great Lenten Season will be one of spiritual contriteness and that you will joyfully welcome and venerate the Resurrection of our Lord from the dead. We invoke upon you His grace and infinite mercy.

Your fervent suppliant before God
B

One suspects that Peter kept the letter among his private papers more out of admiration for the man than out of adherence to any formal religion.

The previously mooted invitation to Bartholomew to address a forum at the Aspen Institute never materialized because, as Peter learned, the institute avoided giving a platform to religious leaders. However, his own involvement with the institute increased substantially and during his lifetime it became the largest recipient of Peter's charitable funds, leading to his appointment as a trustee in 1998.

On another occasion at Aspen, he brought along a book by Toyohiko Kagawa that was to be an important influence on his thinking about philanthropy. Born in 1888 of a philandering business man and a concubine, Kagawa broke with all tradition by becoming a Christian, a pacifist, and a social reformer. His first book, *The Psychology of the Poor*, published in 1916 and based on his experiences living among the poorest elements, stunned middle-class Japan with its revelations of illicit prostitution, child prostitution, incest, bigamy, and the acceptance of capital sums for the care of children who were subsequently murdered.

What struck Peter was that Kagawa's approach to social reform had much in common with that of Bartholomew. He too believed that, in addressing the general problem of poverty, institutional charities were of little value, recommending instead targeted individual giving and education. But what appealed to Peter particularly about Kagawa was the Eastern quality of his philosophy, and he quotes from Kagawa's biography *Before the Dawn*: *Living as already dead. In this state a man eliminates all self-watchfulness and thus all fear and circumspection. It is a supreme release from conflict. Nothing remains but the goal and the act that accomplishes it. The observing self is eliminated.*

Continuing briefly on the philosophical tack, Peter had dinner with his friend Katherine Bain of the Aspen Institute. Katherine was probing him on a subject close to his heart – the vital statistics of a great investor. Curiosity was always Peter's number one choice, which Katherine challenged. If curiosity were such a good thing, she asked, why did God punish Eve for eating the apple. Peter paused and thought for a moment before responding: "Because she violated a clear instruction, and if curiosity isn't allied with discipline, it is a bit like trespass. It's what killed the cat and got Eve chucked out of the garden wearing a fig leaf." This brought the philosophical part of the evening to a close.

The Aspen Summer Festival every July became a highlight of the Cundill calendar. He enjoyed it on several counts. Obviously it was a great opportunity for networking, since the attendee list included everyone who mattered in U.S. political and financial circles; from the U.S. president and the chairman of the Federal Reserve on through the ranks of power brokers, financial wizards, major philanthropists and the aristocracy of global arts: *I was standing behind President George H. Bush as he waited to speak. We chatted about Nathan Avery. He spoke well and he's very fit. He was introduced by his son Marvin, who is a Hedge Fund manager and smart, unlike his older brother. Afterwards there was an emerging-markets panel chaired by Jamie Rosenwald and Peter Gruber – stimulating. I met Jamie later and we hit it off really well.*

Peter enjoyed the cultural side as well, loyally supporting Joanie's musical events with the Aspen choir and even commissioning some music for her. One of his personal contributions was an appearance in a starring role as Creon in Sophocles' tragedy *Antigone*. The story is a very dark one. In Creon's kingdom of Thebes a civil war has just concluded with the death of his son, a leader on the opposing side. Creon damns his son forever by forbidding his burial and ordering that he be left exposed as carrion. Antigone pleads with her father to spare her brother such eternal punishment, is abruptly refused, and conducts the interment herself in secret. Of course, she is found out and Creon orders her to be buried alive. The result is a welter of deaths on the scale of *Hamlet*. Creon relents, but too late, and breaks down as the messengers arrive one by one with the awful tidings.

Peter relished the role – not only was it a fine opportunity for showing off, but he was fully attuned to its moral of complete responsibility for one's actions and their often-unforeseen consequences: *I was asked to play Creon because I read nicely. I agreed and then I read through the play from the viewpoint of establishing the character. A couple of days later we had a dress rehearsal and then ... outside in the hollow that is known as the sculpture garden we did the play. I threw myself into it feeling real emotion. My final gesture as a broken old man was to drop my crown as I left the arena for the last time. It was well received. I might have an alternative career if only I could remember my lines!*

Peter's memory could falter in other directions as well. On a wet and windy evening he and Joanie dined with friends at the Caribou Club, where they had congregated after the day's events. After dinner Joanie said to Peter that she hoped he had parked the Toyota nearby: *I was in trouble for not bringing the wretched Toyota – great embarrassment on Joanie's part, we were supposed to drive the Lerners home. The problem was that I didn't even remember that we had a Toyota. What an awful sense of possession I have!*

27

Now We Begin Again

AFTER ONE THOUGHT-provoking session at the Aspen Institute, Peter put pen to paper to write the most defining statement of his investment philosophy since the letter he had written to unit-holders of the All-Canadian Venture Fund following its acquisition in 1976. He called it "Notes from a Battle-Scarred Warrior" (see Appendix B).

It would be hard to overstate the significance of this document. It restated Peter's entire investment process, incorporating all the innovations in value investing that he had developed from the basics of Benjamin Graham over twenty years. There are marked departures from the original formula. The weight he attached to balance sheet analysis was still paramount, but he introduced other important considerations in the business of stock selection: operating and profit margins, management compensation, the corporation's relative position in its industry, and brand recognition. Peter went much further – way beyond anything envisaged in Graham's *Security Analysis*.

He introduced the concept of risk arbitrage as a tool for enhancing returns on cash reserves, explaining that such operations have little correlation to the overall direction of stock markets. Workout situations were given room (this would include the purchases of Latin American Brady bonds and the debt of corporations in Chapter XI bankruptcy). And he discussed hedging strategies. This was no longer the blunt and relatively inflexible instrument of the mid-1970s but a highly sophisticated tool box which, when combined with Peter's global approach, offered the real possibility of providing superior long-term returns under all economic and stock market conditions. It set the scene for the next stage in Peter's career.

In the early 1990s Peter had taken the view that the high-technology stocks in the United States were overvalued. Following the same strategy that he had applied to the Nikkei 225 a decade earlier, he began to go short the S&P 500 as being the index that best represented the sector.

Once again it was painful to watch as the fad for growth stocks gained ever more numerous adherents and shares rose inexorably. The short positions hurt the performance of the Cundill Value Fund and led to his having to endure much criticism from investors as well as some redemptions, most notably that of Sir John Templeton.

His desire to be understood prompted Peter to write a memo entitled "The Patient Value Hedger," which he addressed to his critics and his own investment department. He began with an instructive and timely chart analysis of his Nikkei short trades from 1987 to 1995, detailing the initial pain and the subsequent rolling profits, and continued with some additional thoughts:

- The Nikkei shorts were an experiment and initially they hurt our performance, but in the end it was really worthwhile. Hopefully this experience will give us the confidence to go for it whenever circumstances dictate. Unless one replaces options as they expire, assuming that one has a serious view, one loses money and momentum. You just have to grit your teeth and do it. With futures, you can stay in the game on a seamless basis.
- We increased our short option positions in the Nikkei as valuations became obscene. This was wisdom in hindsight!! It was hairy at the time. We must be ready to keep going in the same way now in the U.S. high techs. The s&p is nowhere near as overvalued as the Nikkei was in 1989. But the Nikkei came off from 38,000 to 15,000. The s&p could easily come off 20% as the Nikkei did in the first quarter of 1990; this would just be a normal correction.
- We have always had plenty of cash with which to meet margin calls. Keep focused. Let's concentrate on getting better at this game, not bottling out.
- If nothing else, experience has demonstrated that the dictum of "patience, patience and more patience" holds true as long as we have done the work thoroughly, are continuing to review it, and we remain convinced that we are right on the fundamental analysis. Anxiety can be fun.
- Finally here's one to ponder: "You can teach a donkey to climb a tree but it's easier to hire a squirrel."

An additional pressure on Peter at this time was that his relationship with Joanie was becoming increasingly distant. She had become entirely acclimatized to leading her own life in every way, and making room for Peter was not necessarily convenient or welcome any longer. His assumption that he could do whatever he liked *in absentia* and that Joanie would always be available when he needed her had grown precarious, and he recorded plaintively in Aspen: *I slept upstairs. Joanie says she's not used to me. Is this a marriage?*

And a few weeks later, as he was getting ready to leave Canyon Ranch: *Joanie didn't come back for a hug. I think that's symbolic. On balance it sort of works with no touching from her and very few endearments, but that is her. If we were together all the time I would be bored out of my skull. Although when I'm in a Joanie place I think I like her and at the same time in some respects I can't think of a better companion. We have a range of common interests and neither of us would really care to give up the other. It is convenient.*

Convenience aside, the range of common interests was getting narrower, now more than ever confined to hiking and biking. Accordingly, Peter persuaded Joanie to go biking with him in Corsica. They arrived after an extraordinarily bumpy flight from Nice during which Joanie kept cool and calmed Peter down. The hotel Le Maquis was exquisite, set in the wild countryside after which it is named and looking down onto a deserted sandy beach: *I now see why the French Resistance was code named the "maquis." The vegetation is dense and virtually impenetrable although so fragrant. The smell of the sea and the wild flowers reminded me of Cap à l'Aigle. I still want to be buried there.*

They rode to the famous megalithic site at Filitosa, which dates back to 3500 BC. Peter was interested in the history; Joanie was not, except in the athletic aspect: *There were many free-standing columns called "menhirs" which I remembered from the Asterix comic books. You approach through a glorious ancient olive grove – hot and scented. The columns have stern faces carved in relief at the top. They are thought to have been made to frighten invaders away but they aren't frightening – just old. Joanie sat in the shade and took no interest. She perked up on the long up hill and down dale ride to Propriano. We dined "en groupe." For once I did not find it too long – better than being on our own.* For the first time ever, they had not recovered their intimacy.

In the background, the search for a suitable home for the Cundill funds was continuing. It was not a promising environment. The prevailing fashion was all for growth stocks, in particular high-tech and telecoms, where prices were rising to dizzying heights on the basis of hugely optimistic forecasts that focused mainly on exponential revenue growth and almost never on the balance sheet or bottom line profitability: *The markets are listening to the tunes of yesteryear, only the orchestra differs. Then it was either oil or mining. I feel sad for the gullible and vulnerable who are being sucked in and will inevitably come to grief.*

Peter's was a primarily retail clientele, albeit quite sophisticated, and it was not immune to fashion – on top of which the performance of CVF appeared pedestrian when compared with the top-quartile growth funds. There was also the issue of trailer fees, which provided little annual incentive for the independent financial advisors, who constituted the principal sales force, to keep their clients invested. To Brian McDermott's dismay, Peter had categorically refused to introduce trailer fees for CVF.

Consequently, funds under management stagnated, and no improvement on the offer from Warren Goldring was in sight. A potential merger with John Clark of Connor Clark came to nothing, since it was difficult to see what the real benefits would be on either side. The prospects looked bleak, but Peter was in a buoyant mood in early 1998. *Our U.S. shorts worked for us this week, Japan began the long road back, Singapore buckled and values abound there. Great lunch with Prem Watsa. He too is very negative on the U.S. share market and encouraging on Japan. Now for more money.*

Peter's axiom that "luck is the necessary final ingredient to business success" was about to be validated. Enter Mackenzie Financial Corporation, one of the largest retail fund managers in Canada. It was run by Jim Hunter with a particularly innovative and forward-looking team. Hunter was quite close to Prem Watsa, as was Peter, so it was not unnatural that Watsa should mention to Hunter that CVF was looking to do a deal. One of Hunter's primary ambitions was to expand Mackenzie's product offering to encompass the broadest possible range of investment styles. By 1998 most of that ambition had been achieved, with one significant exception – they had no "value" manager in their stable.

There were not many true value managers out there, and those that existed were either too big, like Warren Buffett, Mason Hawkins, or Charles Brandes, or too parochial. Peter, by contrast, was small enough and at the same time unarguably global. Hunter discussed the possibility with two of his closest senior executives, Phil Cunningham and David Feather. Peter's reputation for integrity and discipline was unimpeachable, his track record, if a little tarnished in recent years, was nonetheless compelling, and Mackenzie possessed the marketing muscle that would have the capacity to turn Cundill into a powerful brand. They decided to proceed.

The approach followed almost immediately, and Hunter and Peter met in Toronto. There was an instant mental accord and, equally important, considerable personal respect and liking between the two. Hunter recognized Peter's acute intellect and the element of the maverick in him, so essential to success as a value investor. Peter in turn saw Hunter as *a very straight shooter with considerable insight and the imagination to think outside humdrum conventionality*.

A second meeting came fast on the heels of the first. This time, Hunter brought in Cunningham and Feather, and Peter took along his corporate advisor, Doug Klassen of Cambridge Associates. Peter instantly recognized kindred spirits in Cunningham and Feather, who possessed *an ethic of hard work tempered by a keen appetite for a party*. The meeting lasted several hours, toward the end of which Hunter and Klassen were monopolizing the discussion, horse-trading over numbers. After about half an hour of this, Peter suddenly stood up, walked to the opposite side of the table, put his hand on Feather's and Cunningham's shoulders, and said, "I think I'm going to have a better time over here." They retired to the bar of the Hotel Four Seasons in Yorkville, conveniently situated opposite what were then the Mackenzie offices.

Feather met with Peter in his suite the next morning to discuss the two main areas for which he had primary responsibility – product development and marketing. The two were destined to become great friends, embarking on a journey that would see funds under Mackenzie Cundill management grow from around $600 million to a staggering $20 billion in the space of about six years. As Feather later described it, he found Peter very direct and refreshingly open to new ideas and initiatives. He felt instinctively that Peter needed to be handled like a thoroughbred racehorse and that, if given full rein at the right moments, he would be the perfect incarnation of a successful brand. And so it proved.

In the role of Peter's trainer, as it were, Feather was ideal. With an engaging personality and a great sense of humour, he was able to persuade Peter to do things and go in directions that others could not. The trailer fees that Peter had so stubbornly resisted were quickly introduced, and in due course Peter was launched on an intensive cycle of marketing trips and presentations such as not even McDermott had envisaged. The key was that Feather made them fun and Peter was never burdened with the rigorous planning that went into their success. Peter's style was eccentric and his delivery could be uneven, but there was something enthralling about his piercing blue eyes and his lithe figure, restlessly pacing back and forth across the platform. And he was likely to pull a trenchant comment, a pithy aphorism, or an unexpected lateral thought out of the hat at any moment. This is one example: *When the U.S. capital markets go through a place, they are like General Sherman marching through Georgia. They only leave a few blades of black grass, so you'd better get there first.*

Together Hunter, Cundill, Cunningham, and Feather launched a number of winning new funds: the Mackenzie Cundill Recovery Fund managed by James Morton, and the dazzlingly successful Select Managers Fund, in which the Value Fund's share grew from a few hundred thousand dollars to over $2 billion.

The deal with Mackenzie proceeded to closure with remarkable speed. From the first meeting toward the end of January, it took only six weeks to reach the point at which Peter signed the letter of intent, and by July the deal was done. It was a surprising structure, especially as there was no capital consideration. What Mackenzie bought was the mutual fund assets under management, but not Cundill Investment Research, the management company, which Peter would still lead and control as before. The consideration for the funds was a monthly payment to CIR of between 15 and 25 basis points on the money actually in the mutual funds at the end of the month, and a personal payment of between 5 and 7 basis points to Peter himself. Mackenzie took control of the marketing from the outset, and over the next couple of years Peter was able to outsource all the administration to Mackenzie as well, leaving CIR with just the investment process, which he regarded as an ideal result.

However, not all of Peter's minority shareholders greeted the deal with

enthusiasm. The absence of capital consideration was a real disappointment, and it led ultimately to the departure of Tim McElvaine. In
hindsight it turned out to be a wonderful transaction for both parties,
but the reality was that it was likely the only kind of deal that would
then have been possible, apart from a relatively paltry capital payment
for the group, such as had been on the table from AGF. What Peter saw
more clearly than anyone else in CIR was that the key to the deal's success
lay not in the agreed number of basis points but in having the right partner on the other side. Jim Hunter and the Mackenzie team had convinced
Peter that they had what it took, and his concurrence was endorsed by
those whose judgment he most respected on the matter: Prem Watsa,
Peter Ackerman, and James Morton.

Peter was in a more than usually serious mood after the deal with
Mackenzie was completed, and he was fully aware that, given the way
in which it was structured financially, the model would only work if he
could produce the performance. He was fortunate that there was a strong
caucus of the management at the top of Mackenzie who were real believ-
ers in "deep value" principles and understood that in its pursuit patience
was an absolute necessity. They were prepared to stake a measure of their
credibility on persuading the sales force to present clients with this
unfashionable, but relatively safer, alternative to the growth funds that
were then the rage. To their credit, they managed to carry the team with
them through the trough of an 11% loss in the Value Fund in 1998 and
reap the rewards of the sparkling years that followed. At the same time
Peter's own group, including Andy Massie, David Briggs, and James
Morton, overcame any doubts they may have had, and threw themselves
wholeheartedly into making a success of the newly branded Mackenzie
Cundill Funds.

Peter wrote a cautionary note to self: *You now have all the elements
that it takes to reach the very top. You have what it takes to be rich and
famous. You have what it takes to be a leader of men. You have what it
takes, full stop. Just remember to balance all this taking with some giving
too. You have what it takes to be exceedingly generous.*

*As an antidote to the negative thoughts which still occasionally
obtrude from that old Pete Cundill, I have created an optimistic character
in the form of Frank Cundill. He takes over most of the time, except in
the early morning when Pete is too strong. Pete and Frank debate from*

time to time, with the realist acting as arbitrator. I wonder whether the superimposing of a "good healthy" persona over a flawed one is a psychiatric trick that is known and in use.

In any event this is rebirth time. I am being pushed to do new things. It is a time of high adventure that will probably be accompanied by some turbulence. Twenty-one years ago I founded the business on a hope and a prayer. Now we begin again.

28

A Year of Anniversaries

HAVING SUCCESSFULLY HOSTED the first Mackenzie Cundill Annual General Meeting and established the new Board of Governors, Peter was feeling in need of a sunshine holiday incorporating some culture. On his latest visit to Aspen, he had found Joanie in particularly good humour, and they now met in Nice at the Negresco, the world-renowned, grand hotel that fronts the Promenade des Anglais, before heading for St Paul de Vence, a gem-like medieval town that nestles high up on the mountain-side of the Alpes Maritimes, variously the home of Chagall and the haunt of Yves Montand and Brigitte Bardot among many other celebrities.

Their destination was the Maeght Foundation, an art museum designed in the early 1960s by the Catalan architect Josep Sert to present modern art in a new and more accessible way, and it became the inspira-tion for the reinvented Getty Museum in California. Sert was able to realize a truly inspirational concept by integrating the works of art into the building and the gardens. It features a Giacometti courtyard, a Miró labyrinth filled with his sculpture and ceramics, a complete mural in mosaic by Chagall, and a pool and a stained glass window by Braque, as well as the sculptural building itself, which houses a broad collection of the work of other twentieth-century artists of exceptional quality. Peter was bowled over by the way the sculptures were displayed in an intimate way that was completely unlike any other museum of its time. *We enjoyed the scent of the pine trees not the ubiquitous sun tan lotion!*

That evening they enjoyed a celebration dinner *à deux* at Boccaccio, then one of the best restaurants in town. As he often did, Peter recorded the menu: roasted scallops with cèpes mushrooms, sea bass in a salt crust served with sauce verte, a lobster salad with shaved artichoke and passion fruit dressing, a magnificent piece of ripe Roquefort cheese, and finally a selection of chocolate desserts presented like a work of art, washed down with no less than two bottles of Montrachet, possibly the best and cer-tainly the most expensive dry white wine in the world – *perhaps it was a little elaborate – read over the top – but by God it was good! One should never regret a bit of proper excess!*

The following morning Peter and Joanie left for Naples and their first experience of southern Italy. The limousine failed to turn up so they had to resort to a Neapolitan taxi. The driver tore through the city's steep and narrow medieval streets at breakneck speed, by-passing traffic by mounting pavements and going down one way streets the wrong way. *Although a woman endowed with plenty of courage, Joanie was shaken to the core by the experience. For me it was different. The hard driving made me feel like a passenger in the Montecarlo rally and I loved the whole atmosphere, the rattling of the Vespas, the fumes, the beaten up cars, the swearing and gesticulating, even the whiffs of the driver's garlicky breath. It was the real vin ordinaire of life.*

The next day they were driven much more sedately along the coast past Sorrento to rendez-vous with a speed boat that was to whisk them across to Capri. Peter's love of history was sated: *We passed by the Villa Sessa … the former residence of Sir William and Lady Hamilton and the setting where Nelson was so comprehensively captivated by the voluptuous Emma.*

Having at last found and destroyed the French fleet at Aboukir Bay in Egypt, Nelson hot-footed it back to Naples to the embraces of the libidinous Emma where he became caught up in the French-inspired revolutionary uprising against King Ferdinand. Without the Admiralty's sanction, he used the British fleet to transport the king, and perhaps more importantly the queen, who was very friendly with Lady H, with their entire entourage to the safety of Sicily, for which he was elevated to the Dukedom of Bronté.

Scarcely drawing breath, what had now become the "ménage à trois" of Nelson and the Hamiltons took advantage of a temporary peace with France and set off on a very public land progress back to England. This left nothing in the relationship to the imagination and scandalized what was left of aristocratic Europe after the guillotine had cut a swathe through it – not to speak of stuffy old George III and his rather prim Queen, Charlotte. I am in awe of the sheer bravado of the whole thing.

The speed-boat trip from Sorrento across to the island of Capri was luxurious in that informal style that is peculiarly Italian. The moustachioed captain had something of the swashbuckling style of a Venetian gondolier with a fine build to match and a mildly flirtatious manner that instantly appealed to Joanie. Their guide, Emilia, was equally attractive, with a figure that reminded Peter of Romney's portrait of Lady Hamilton dancing. However, she was more than decorative – a trained archaeologist with a degree in the history of Imperial Rome.

With the motor at full throttle they roared across the Tyrrhenian Sea, skipping over the waves with Joanie at the wheel and the captain in close attendance, peering through the spray and the sunlight as they approached the legendary cliffs and crags of Capri. Fortunately it was calm enough to get inside the Blue Grotto in a rowboat, although they had to lie flat in the bottom to avoid bumping their heads. Once inside they could marvel at the intense turquoise blue of the water while Emilia explained that the emperors had turned the whole grotto into a "nymphaeum" with naked sculpted beauties in the niches and marble sea monsters in the water. However, she really startled them with a story about the Emperor Tiberius recounted by the Roman historian Suetonius in his book *The Twelve Caesars*. Suetonius says that one of Tiberius' favourite sexual pleasures was swimming in the blue grotto with his "minnows" – beautiful slave boys from all over the empire who had the task of diving between the old man's legs, nibbling his genitals, and tickling him.

They motored on round to the Green Grotto, where the water glitters like liquid emeralds. There they swam, sunbathing on the rocks to dry off before going on to the charming Marina Piccola. They drank a delicious Capresi Bianco Riserva made from the "falanghina" grapes that have been grown on Capri since Etruscan times and were the main variety that was used in making the great Falernian wines of antiquity. It was as close as one could get to drinking what Tiberius would have quaffed.

Their Canadian travel agent had booked them into the best suite at the smartest and most palatial hotel on the island, the Grand Hotel Quisisana. "Very nice, lovely views," commented Emilia with a mischievous smile. "You'll probably see quite a few well-fed, elderly Roman uncles entertaining their beautiful nieces there for the weekend. *Come niente si cambia* [nothing ever really changes], but Peter your version of the male figure should get favourable notice round the pool." She was not wrong on either count, as Peter discovered. Before leaving the Cundills to enjoy the evening on their own, she suggested that they should take a stroll along the Via Krupp to catch the sunset and the evening breeze. The evening stroll was a great romantic success, mingling the scents of jasmine and honeysuckle with the smell of the sea from below. *Snuggled in with J. We had a swell time. I would be "bouleversé" without her.*

The morning project was a hike to the Villa Jovis, Tiberius's enormous palace whose ruins occupy most of the eastern tip of the island: *As we hiked along the Via Tiberio we passed some of the most stylish villas ... Ruined though it is, the Villa Jovis is immensely impressive. It's perched at the top of cliffs where peregrine falcons nest and the view stretches right across the Bay of Naples with Vesuvius looming, thank heaven peacefully at present, behind. Tiberius ran the whole Empire from here for the last eleven years of his reign, so in part it must have had to house his secretariat ... Stories abound about what the old man got up to, but "inviting" those about whom he had suspicions to visit him here, entertaining them lavishly and then having them pitched off the cliff top seems highly likely ... For me the most atmospheric bit was a long pillared loggia with niches at either end, which enjoyed the whole sweep of the view out towards Naples. I could easily imagine the old emperor dictating letters as he strolled here, watching the huge imperial fleet on manoeuvres in and out of its base at Misenum, or simply looking out for packet boats bringing messengers, "guests" and mail from Rome.*

After a swim in the pool at the Quisisana and a good look around at the selection of spread-eagled "nieces," most of whom were sunbathing topless, Peter and Joanie joined Emilia and the speed boat captain for the passage to Amalfi. They zipped along at the same break-neck speed, only slowing down to pass through the three islands of the Sirens so that Emilia could recount the myth.

I was in two minds about whether Emilia was a Siren in disguise. She certainly has a mellifluous voice to go with her looks. Those dangerously beautiful "femmes fatales" lured sailors to a grizzly doom on the rocks with their enchanting singing ... Canny old Odysseus – a hero after my own heart – was determined to have it both ways. He had his sailors stuff their ears with bees' wax and then tie him securely to the mast so that he couldn't leap into the water – the only human being ever to listen to the song of the Sirens and survive. As Homer said, Odysseus was "a man of many devices"!

They continued around the coast to Amalfi, where they especially admired the cathedral, and to Positano, the picturesque village set into the steep cliff-side, and the hotel Le Sirenuse. *Chatting with the barman before Joanie came down to join me, we got onto the subject of Italian lovers. He told me that Casanova had made love to 132 women in his life. I said I didn't think it was all that impressive. He looked at me rather strangely so I said, "What about Don Giovanni with 1003 conquests in Spain alone?" He was still chuckling when Joanie arrived.*

It was an early start in the morning; back in the speedboat and round the peninsula of Sorrento to reach the port of Torre Annunziata by seven a.m. in order to beat the crowds for their visit to Pompeii: *It was awe-inspiring, especially with the menace of Vesuvius constantly in our vision, almost as though we could touch it … It cannot be other than moving under any circumstances but there we were virtually alone among the plaster castes of the real bodies of those who died in the cataclysm: the children; the tiny baby; the crouching man with his head bowed in final despair; the couple clinging to each other as they died; the looter finally overcome, although still desperately clutching his bag of money; the chained dog, twisting frantically in its efforts to escape and the little pig with the missing leg. Eventually we could take no more. I came out with tears in my eyes and the thought that no photographic images could ever express the desperation and agony of a natural disaster in all its dimensions as this does.*

The last night of the holiday was to be spent in Ravello, perhaps the most beautiful town on the Italian Riviera. *Before we took our leave … Emilia treated me to an illuminating five minutes on the subject of Ravello and our last hotel, the Villa Cimbrone. It was like a short "tour d'horizon" of a century of the kings (and queens!) of culture and intellectual brilliance. To begin with Ravello hosts an annual Wagner festival because the Villa Cimbrone inspired the stage that Wagner eventually designed for his opera "Parsifal"… I'm not sure I can remember the names of all the visitors Emilia mentioned but here goes: Virginia Woolf, E.M. Forster, Maynard Keynes, D.H. Lawrence, Henry Moore, T.S. Eliot (apparently wrote most of "Murder in the Cathedral" here), Churchill, arriving armed with his paint box, found that the cellar had been specially stocked with his favourite Pol Roger champagne, and there was a box of Romeo and Juliet cigars in his bedroom … The best was the last touch of colour – Lord Grimthorpe died in England but, under the terms of his will, his body was embalmed and shipped back to the Villa Cimbrone where it was buried in the garden beside the little temple of Bacchus. I went to see and there I found a small memorial stone with a short quotation from Catullus, my favourite Latin lyric poet:*

Oh what is more blessed than when the mind,
Of cares relieved, lays down its burden
And we return home, weary of journeying,
To rest upon the bed for which we have yearned.

What lovelier epitaph could he have chosen? This has been a voyage filled with riches of all kinds, a feast for the senses and the palate, for the intellect and the imagination, all seasoned with laughter. It will remain with me.

Peter and Joanie returned together to Aspen in time for the Aspen Music Festival and for Peter to attend his first Institute board meeting. As one of the ancillary activities there was a seminar on communication and public speaking. Peter was aware that the new relationship with Mackenzie would require him to make much more frequent appearances on the podium, addressing less sophisticated audiences than he was used to doing. This was the perfect opportunity to hone his speaking skills. A characteristic of his style in addressing the conferences was to involve members of his audience. He liked to think of "Pete's Morning" as a dialogue rather than a monologue. Clearly this tactic would not work on a "road show." Peter's performance at the seminar earned him some useful comments from the instructor: "Be careful not to slouch; modulate with care; keep the hands and arms loose. You use the investment mantra of 'patience, patience and more patience'; when you're speaking make it 'pause, pause and pause.' The success of a speech is only about 7% dependent on its content; 38% is voice modulation, and an astonishing 55% is body language. When you are talking to an audience that is not expert in your topic, make sure you illustrate what you are saying with examples and stories." *I was shown a film of myself in action so I was*

*better able to appreciate the comments. There's work to be done. I do
find the Institute events are of an incredibly high standard.*

He also attended a workshop on meditation. *I want to try to summa-
rize the thrust of it: To reach a plane where the mind is at one with the
whole universe is the ultimate goal. At that point one's vision becomes
clear and untroubled, still, like the reflection of the stars in a calm lake
untouched by the fury of the storms beyond. This sublime point of immo-
bility is the ultimate achievement. Death, which is inevitably approaching,
joking and smiling, is just an adventurous journey into the vastness of
the universe. Suicide is never an option. In life producing wealth is necessary and distributing it generously even more so. This is even truer in
matters of the spirit.*

This was a year of anniversaries; 1998 signalled twenty-five years of marriage, twenty-one years since the founding of the Cundill Value Fund,
and Peter's sixtieth birthday. The celebrations were to be held in Europe,
and at Joanie's request in Paris rather than London: *The UK is still a
charmed oligarchy and I love it like that, but I suppose that Paris has
more glamour. It may be a more exciting venue for a party and more
appealing to our Canadian and American guests.*

For this occasion he had chosen the most aristocratic hotel of all that
Paris offers, the Crillon, which occupies a third of what is arguably the
most perfect example of eighteenth-century city architecture in the world.
Overlooking the Place de la Concorde at the top of the Champs Elysées
it has views across to the Grand Palais and the Tour Eiffel on one side and
the Jeu de Paume, where Peter discovered the Impressionists, and the
Tuileries Gardens, on the other. However, what makes the Crillon unique is
that it has kept the atmosphere of the private residence that it once was.

*Twenty-five years ago, Joanie and I were at the West Vancouver reg-
istry office and I stood in the rain waiting for the AA to come and help
me get back into the car. I had locked the key inside. A lot has happened
since then, "mais plus ça change"! Joanie and I eurostarred it to Paris ...
and so to the Crillon for the first time. Madonna in residence, but no
extraordinary fuss being made – just perfect old-world courtesy and consideration.*

For the first Mackenzie Cundill conference, Peter had secured the use of the premises of the Aspen Insitute in Paris. It was an excellent choice – comfortable and tasteful as well as superbly equipped with the latest technology. *I was up at 4 a.m. to prepare my speech and to psych myself into putting into practice what I learned at the Aspen seminar. My session was fine: I skipped over the bad numbers, touching on a lot of other useful stuff. Should maybe have done more share stories. Stories do work well even with this highly qualified audience. Lunch was Jacques Perot on museums – frankly rather dull but there was one good quote: "We pay too much attention to museums; sometimes a sunrise or a sunset are enough."*

The sixtieth birthday party was at the Cercle de l'Union Interalliée, one of Paris's most exclusive gentlemen's clubs right next door to the Crillon: *"113 of my closest friends in a lovely room, black ties, pretty frocks and sparkling jewellery. CR-G now quite slim in a red velvet smoking jacket and back with Patti. Cocktails, great food, Bob Hardwicke played his piano. Patricia Cook wonderful, doing Cole Porter and Gershwin. I didn't make the mistakes of my 50th. I spoke about friendship from the heart, and Joanie as my best friend ... I was close to tears. I danced with her, and so was she.*

There was a postscript to the party. The Mackenzie contingent included Jim Hunter, Phil Cunningham, and David Feather. Hunter had balked at the price of staying at the Crillon and decided to set a good corporate example by taking a room at the more modestly priced Meurice. Cunningham and Feather were having none of this, and insisted on booking into the Crillon anyway. Toward the end of the evening, Hunter having departed for his modest abode, Cunningham and Feather decided to hit the town together. They arrived back in time for breakfast, and not alone. With them were two very attractive young ladies who had not been at the party and who were wearing the boys' bow ties.

As they strolled through the lobby toward the breakfast room, they were somewhat discomfited to find a number of the other guests from the previous evening at the reception desk engaged in paying their bills. Naturally the foursome was politely ignored, but within five minutes Peter was regaled with the story. He was so delighted that he immediately rang the cashier and personally picked up the bills for the two truants. History does not relate what Hunter had to say when he heard.

29

The Perfect Balance

AT THE END OF 1998 the rechristened Mackenzie Cundill Value Fund had closed down on the year for only the second time in its twenty-five-year history. Unlike the fall of 1990, this 11% loss did not dent Peter's confidence in the slightest. His reaction was more of irritation that value was still being ignored in favour of the hot-shot growth stocks, particularly those like Nortel in the telecommunications sector, which he viewed as a disaster waiting to happen. He was content with the structure and positioning of the fund's portfolio and fully prepared to argue the case on a macro or a micro level. Equally important, he was supported by the key executive team at Mackenzie who were preparing to back their judgment with a major marketing campaign in which Peter was to play the starring role. They wasted no time. By mid-January Peter was on the road through Ontario in the company of David Feather and Phil Cunningham:

Feather and Cunningham picked me up and drove me to my first major engagement on the road show – the Royal York and 400 people. The Mackenzie team sure can whistle up an audience when they put their minds to it. I spoke with confidence and passion. I remembered the pausing techniques I learned in Aspen and I told stories. It worked ... Back to the Four Seasons for 45 minutes' exercise and on to the King Eddy for a client/analyst dinner. Long day but good.

The following day it was Kitchener and Waterloo. Before speaking at Waterloo, Peter was sitting in the wings with David Feather, waiting to go on stage. At the time he and Feather knew each on a professional level but were not yet the intimate friends they became. If anything, Feather was still a little in awe. Peter suddenly looked up, fixed Feather with his piercing blue eyes, and said, "You know David, when I was a fat boy I didn't get laid that often." Feather was taken completely off balance, unsure whether he had heard quite right. After a moment or two he mumbled rather lamely, "Oh, I do all right." There was a pause and then Peter added dismissively, "Purely on personality." As with most things that

Peter thought needed addressing, he was not one to give up easily, and there was to be a sequel to that exchange.

The road show continued all week – London, Windsor, Scarborough. *I'm listening a lot, bonding with marketers and analysts. Before the Windsor Casino I was up at 4.20 a.m. to run outside for an hour – dry crisp and bitter cold, looking at the Detroit skyline – lovely feeling before my breakfast speech. By Friday I began to feel tired – sort of lost a little focus – but good overall, not nearly as dire as I'd feared.*

As a result of raising Peter's profile on his home ground in Canada, the cash began to roll in. He found himself spending more time in Toronto, becoming something of a fixture at the Four Seasons. His usual suite looked straight across to the Mackenzie office. Consequently, some of Peter's more eccentric routines became the stuff of legend – the scantily clad dance aerobics and especially his habit of talking on the phone by the window while stark naked. There was intense speculation among the secretaries as to whether Peter was aware that he could be seen, as well as much admiration of his tall, athletic build. No one mentioned a thing, and his visits were most popular.

Nor was there much let-up with his travel program. Early that year he visited Moscow again and went on to Khanty-Mansiysk, a centre of the oil industry about 1,500 miles northeast of the capital. It reminded him of northern Quebec at the end of winter. The river Ob was beginning to break up, but it was cold and clear enough for the stars to appear in high relief, and the moon seemed close enough to touch. Heavy investment was obviously going into industry and infrastructure. There were plenty of cars around, and a number of very attractive young women wearing expensive furs. He could see that there were investment opportunities. However, notwithstanding the numbers, for Peter the margin of safety was insufficient because the politics still remained too murky.

But the trip yielded one gem that he clipped from the English language *Moscow Times*:

"Fun Spanish couple visiting Moscow seek attractive bisexual girl for company, fun and more. He is a mature business man and she a 28-year-old ex-model." *Boy, the Spanish sure have embraced the sexual revolution.*

Two weeks later he was in Kyoto for the International Forum sessions on social change in Japan organized by his cousin Michael Alexander: *The grip that corporate Japan has had on the work force is loosening;*

50% now own their own homes as opposed to living in the company accommodation that used to be the norm. Women have careers and marry later, putting pressure on the birth rate but providing additional support for the aging population. I remain comfortable with our Nikkei commitment. What we own is just too cheap to ignore and, slow as corporate change may be in Japan, it is in the wind. As employee centricity diminishes, the shareholder may even get a look in!!

It was Mother's Day. I called and she quoted Lewis Carroll to me, "And hast thou slain the Jabberwock? Come to my arms, my beamish boy." I'm not sure the character quite fits but not bad for a "dying" woman in her nineties. She's still so witty; she said, "I've been dying for so long it's getting boring."

He went on to Tokyo and met up with his friend Yuge-San, to whose home he had been invited on his first visit to Japan. They walked in the Ginza on a cool day, pleasantly chatting and strolling through the crowds and then dined on *Kushiage*, a variety of fried foods; fish, minced meats and vegetables served on sticks in wicker baskets. *There was a buzz of prosperity in the air – where, oh where is this much vaunted recession?*

Peter was back in Aspen for the summer festival. The sessions once again prompted some interesting reflections: *I am even more convinced that the secret of success in business is no different from winning in sport – control is everything. The only thing that gives you control is time and the only thing that buys you time is success. McDermott almost tried a coup and it was not prescience that headed it off but investment performance. I will do a deal to buy him out but it will be on my terms and in my time. I solved a cracker of a clue in the New York Times crossword today. "If a pig loses his voice, what do you call him?" "Disgruntled." I think that my success may have been inspired by thoughts of McDermott!*

There were also some revealing comments about Peter's private spiritual credo: *Joanie went to church. I went to the music tent instead … Music gets closer to "infinity" than any religious ceremony or Church and I regard choral music in the same light. Christianity has been sustained by music, not by either doctrine or practice. Remove the music and the cracks in the logic are laid bare at once. Prayer remains a powerful tool, not because it's going up to heaven but because it is cathartic and concentrates the mind.*

During the festival, Aspen was more than usually abrim with the talented and successful with whom Peter loved to associate, but he was always on the look-out for the frankly unusual. On this occasion he bumped into a U.S. attorney who had been involved in the defence of Martin Frankel, the biggest Ponzi fraudster prior to Madoff, and the conversation turned to the characteristics most frequently exhibited by serious financial criminals.

He maintains that all these villains exhibit the same group of character flaws; greed, hubris, ruthless selfishness, and they are sociopaths. The greed ... can be for power, status, admiration, and respect, or a combination of all. I suspect he knows what he's talking about. The one that interests me most is the Ponzi guy because I imagine that such schemes are not born of original intent but out of failure and the loss of status and admiration that admitting to failure would occasion. So the first instinct would be for concealment, and the grand larceny would follow with a sort of shrug of the shoulders. Of course such crimes are facilitated by sloppiness on the part of the regulators and indeed of the investors themselves. All the more reason to be rigorous in every analysis one undertakes.

In August the Cundills relocated as usual to Interlaken to their favourite hotel, the Victoria-Jungfrau Grand Hotel and Spa. Their regular program was tough hiking in the mountains, but on this occasion Peter had something more extreme in mind – "canyoning." Canyoning involves the descent of a river gorge through the water using ropes for rappelling, jumping, climbing techniques and swimming. Peter had chosen to do the Grimsel Pass which makes its precipitous way down from 6,000 feet. Joanie resisted almost to the point of ultimatum, having heard about the recent deaths of a student and three guides when a freak rainstorm washed them into the canyon. Peter's argument was that lightning never strikes in the same place twice, at which point Joanie threw up her arms in resignation.

I must have been the oldest by 35 years. We changed into wet suits and donned our helmets. Wet socks are important. The first stage was a 40-metre rappel (abseil) in which I was tentative and then I got it. At the bottom of this steep ravine was the white water ... We walked along on uncertain footing knee deep with a strong pressure of water pushing us along. Then we had to jump, or slide, interspersed with rope-assisted descents. The final bit was a long slide attached to a master line with a slip knot. Near the bottom you have to undo the knot with the right hand and drop into a mirror like pool below. There was a lot of rope work. We were at it for an hour and a half and then climbed back part of the way to do some extra jumps and then back up again to the grassy meadow where we had changed into our wet suits.

This is not a riskless sport but there was no pre-clearing or discussion of the uncertainties ... I felt fulfilled. Why – a contact with youth? In touch with death and the muted sense of relief when it was over? A sense of being extremely alive? Leadership qualities? Was I frightened? Yes, a little; more in anticipation than anything else.

Meanwhile, in the investment world Peter's value stocks were having a good time, but not nearly as good as the growth and high technology crowd. However a spin-off effect was that money was pouring in to the Select Manager's Fund, so that the Mackenzie Cundill Value Fund was an indirect beneficiary of the boom that Peter so deeply distrusted.

The business community is insanely excited about the Internet. We are into "extraordinary popular delusions." The "madness of crowds" is upon us. Internet company flotations are reproducing like randy rabbits, hoping to emulate (or at least cash in on) the relatively rare success stories like Amazon, which is itself still losing millions of dollars a year with no end in sight to the red ink. It would seem that the more money an Internet company is losing the more appealing investors find it. The only rational explanation is that they have grapefruits where their brains ought to be. At the moment you could start a company called "Good Money After Bad" or simply "Your Money Down the Drain" and they would still go for it like a pack of hyenas. Will the Select Fund growth managers be immune on the day of reckoning? I doubt it. But we shall see.

Prompted by his value vulture habits, Peter surmised that there might be some worthwhile pickings once the inevitable massacre was over. Instinctively, he felt that the richest of these pickings with the greatest future potential lay in software development for Internet Service Providers; online billing systems, for example. He was not inimical to the Internet – he had sufficient imagination to be well able to conceive that the harnessing of its immense power was merely in its infancy. His concerns were that current analysis placed absurd valuations not even on earnings, or on cash flow, but on future revenues that were themselves in the stratosphere of optimism, and there appeared to be no strategies for converting such revenues, even if realized, into bottom-line profit.

Nevertheless, Labour Day saw him on his way for the first time to Israel, an emerging crucible of software development for the Internet and high-tech industries. At Tel Aviv he was surprised that Israeli customs and immigration were swift and uncomplicated. In fact, the officer at passport control was even pragmatic enough to ask whether he preferred not to have an Israeli stamp on his document.

Up with the lark ... Wonderful orange juice fresh from Jaffa and then a cab to see Tischak Shrem of SKF, *the brokerage that underwrites most of the issues for this new high-tech stuff. Great insights – he is a realist if not a value guy. On to see Scott Stein – who is developing intellectual property risk management as a speciality – not so foolish I surmise. Lunch with Tom Rose, publisher of the Jerusalem Post – a highly erudite and succinct survey of the political and economic scene. Volatile as the Middle East may be, there is a tenacity of purpose about everything the Israelis do. I believe the economy will continue to thrive within a political climate that is basically stable and has practically infinite U.S. support.*

Peter had taken a shine to Chaim Nimron, his 83-year old cab driver, and retained him for the drive from Tel Aviv to Jerusalem. The old man had served in the British Army, not with the Jewish Brigade but with the Black Watch, which of course recommended him to Peter. He had fought in the Six-Day War of 1967 as a tank commander, drove and guided David Frost when he was reporting and touring the battlefields with Moshe Dayan, and spoke an astonishing eight languages. He drove the cab because he hated the idea of retirement. He took Peter to the Mount of Olives first of all to see the famous view of the city with the golden Dome of the Rock glowing in the sunshine.

I was surprised to see Robert Maxwell's grave there. The old fraudster may be an object of vilification to the thousands of destitute pensioners of the Mirror Group in the UK but I suppose that he was a huge bene-

factor of all sorts of Israeli causes. Did he jump from his yacht or was he pushed? I doubt we'll ever know. There is a little restaurant at the top of the Mount. I was amazed to see that it refuses to serve Jews!

On for the Jerusalem tour led by the indefatigable Himy (as he is affectionately known to the Archbishop of Bethlehem) who walked my ass off ... Off again to the Knesset. Impressive buildings and grounds set behind bullet proof glass. It was a historic evening. They were debating the Sharm Accord.

Peter and his guide were forced to turn back on their drive to Bethlehem on account of hordes of young Palestinians hurling stones indiscriminately, in their fury that only some detainees – and not the worst offenders – were being released by the Israelis under the Sharm Accord.

A purpose of a different nature took him to the south of France to join a very high-powered group that included Canada's minister of finance – to watch the France versus Canada rugby match to be played at Béziers. The rugby match was an excuse for a group excursion in style. On arrival there was a dinner at the famous restaurant L'Oustau de Beaumanière in Les Baux de Provence. *L'Oustau was once reckoned to be the best restaurant in France, by implication therefore the best in the world. I can believe it. Raymond Thullier the chef owner is now dead but his traditions are clearly still very much alive. The Queen and the Duke of Edinburgh stayed here while Thullier was running the show.*

The drive to Béziers the next day took the party through the famous Camargue region with its wild white horses and huge colonies of flamingos living on the salt marshes. They broke the journey for a visit to Aigues-Mortes – another treat for the historian in him. *I was delighted to be able to visit Aigues-Mortes. I had read of the town in Runciman's "History of the Crusades." In the thirteenth century it was the Kingdom of France's only port on the Mediterranean, so it was from there that St Louis sailed for the 7th crusade. It is very ancient, founded by Marius the great Roman general in about 100 BC. We walked the walls – just over a mile – and climbed the famous tower that looks out to the sea, now several miles away, hence its name – Dead Waters.*

France won the game but we didn't disgrace ourselves 32–20. It was fast and open and good to watch. I yelled my head off at our two tries. We made our way back to Avignon with a stop at another ancient mon-

*ument that I've long wanted to see – the Pont du Gard. The great Roman
aqueduct is every bit as impressive as I'd imagined … It's a miracle of
engineering achieved with minimal resource.*

The next day Peter made his way to the château of his old friend and
carousing companion Phil Bieler at Bras in the Var, a little above Aix-en-
Provence. They talked grapes, vintages, and vineyards and how to get the
best out of the rich, rust-red soil. Bieler's knowledge and enthusiasm were
absolutely convincing, and Peter was confident that his investment in the
vineyard would prove sound and, in any case, he thoroughly enjoyed por-
traying himself as a "châtelain" with his own wine and no responsibility
for producing it.

After a few days at home in London, Peter flew to New York to
address the NMS Management family wealth conference on the topic of
investment in Japan. It was the type of highly sophisticated audience he
was most at ease with because it allowed him to discuss in depth without
the necessity of technical explanation. What he said makes interesting
reading in the context of today, bearing in mind that history has a tendency to repeat itself, even if not in precisely the same fashion:

Today we are finding values in Japan that have not been seen since
the mid-1970s in U.S. markets and in some ways they are even better
in Japan now. As you know nearly all Japanese companies have
share portfolios. If you adjust for the value of these, about 35% of
the 3,000 listed companies on the Nikkei trade at below book value
and roughly 10% are trading below net cash and at BIG discounts to
their intrinsic value, assuming that their businesses are worth six
times earnings before interest, depreciation and tax. There is more,
because about 150 companies with market caps of $125 million or
more are trading at below net-net working capital. That is approximately the same number as there were in the US in 1975 and some
of these are very big businesses indeed.

In over a hundred instances you can end up paying less than
nothing. Some of them have net cash almost equal to their market
value. In our calculations we assume that they sell their share
portfolios and that they are then taxed on this at 50%. I'm not even
sure that we should be deducting the tax to establish our margin of
safety, but we do it anyway. Then we net out the short and the long

term debt. We don't include receivables or inventories in the compu-
tation and when we have done all that we can still find over a hundred
securities trading below our punitive definition of net cash. In those
cases you are in effect paying a *negative* price for the business.

I should add that *all* the companies that we are looking at, or
that we own, are making money. In many cases they have no debt
and in about 80% of cases, they are not spending their cash flow so
they are generating free cash. That's because they're frozen in the
headlights like mesmerized rabbits because of the huge fall in the
Nikkei from 40,000 to well below 20,000.

Peter's address, of which this is a much abbreviated version, received
prolonged and thoughtful applause.

The other object of the visit to New York was to attend an Aspen
Institute board meeting at the Harvard Club, which was to be followed
by a Lifetime Leadership awards dinner honouring General Colin Powell,
Senator Dianne Feinstein, and Sidney Harman. General Powell, at whose
table Peter and Joanie sat, drew a particularly appreciative laugh from
the elite audience when he confessed to having felt initially a little unde-
serving of an honour that was customarily reserved for leadership in the
business world. "But then I got to thinking. I *was* CEO of a very large
organization with 4 million people working for me, with a $300 million
operating budget and a trillion-dollar book value and the nastiest board
of directors you ever saw." Peter's comment: *War is big business – often
the biggest. Leadership and strategy are the most important parts of the
turf just as they are for the CEO of a major corporation.*

The second Mackenzie Cundill conference was a very high-powered
affair riding on the excellent performance being anticipated for the year
and was to be held at the Beverly Hills Hotel in Los Angeles. The speakers
were more than usually distinguished. They included Charlie Firestone,
a former director of the Aspen Institute's Communications and Society
program, a distinguished lawyer in the United States Supreme Court and
advisor to the U.S. government on communications policy, speaking on
"Elections in Cyberspace."

The afternoon session featured the renowned author and sociologist
Peter Drucker. *I was seriously intrigued by what Drucker had to say. He
maintains that the 21st century will see the demise of corporations as we
know them. While people will still work for a living, their lives will not*

be spent working for a company. What Drucker refers to as the "knowl-edge workers" ... of today will save their best efforts for non-profit social service organizations where they can make a bigger contribution – a real difference. He terms the twentieth century "the century of business" and the next will be "the century of the social sector." I fervently hope that he may be right but there's a long way to go; selfishness and naked greed persist in U.S. corporate culture, especially in banking and finance. There are problems everywhere.

There was a private evening visit to the new Getty Museum, which was opened in the hills above Bel Air in 1997. It was Peter's first visit and he was greatly impressed by Richard Meier's architecture, with its feeling of space and intimacy, by the gardens and the sculpture, but he was disappointed that the paintings appeared to be lost in their surround-ings. *Sensational as this is, I prefer its inspiration, the Maeght Foundation in St Paul de Vence, where the less monumental space of the galleries accommodates small drawings and large canvases without incongruity. I think that I also prefer the more natural, less contrived landscaping. Nevertheless, the Getty Centre is an experience not to be missed.*

Before "Pete's Morning" began, there was a sequel to his "locker room" conversation with David Feather at the beginning of the year. Under extreme pressure from Peter, Feather had been persuaded to com-pete for the annual Cundill Fitness Award. Not only had he competed but he had actually won the $10,000 prize and the cup. The presentation, choreographed by Peter, had Feather seated on the platform in front of the entire conference audience while a nubile young woman performed an erotic, although not naked, dance around him extolling the irresistible attractions of his newly minted, svelte body to the strains of Gershwin's "Porgy, I Is Your Woman Now." Feather was pale with embarrassment, but the audience rocked and roared its approval.

After the conference, Peter flew to Tokyo to do his usual round of calls, in particular to speak to John Ehara, who was quietly building up stakes in some of Peter's favourite Japanese names, including Fuji Electric. The highlight of this visit was his stay at a very traditional *ryokan* in Hakone National Park close to Mount Fuji. Determined to do it in unadulterated Japanese style, he arrived just before lunch and donned his *yukato* (robe) and *geta* (wooden clogs) and headed for a communal tatami room, where a six-course meal was served, including a wild boar hot pot. After a run and a massage he made his way to the bath house. Peter already knew the routine of sitting on a stool and washing very thoroughly before venturing into the plunge pool, while keeping the genitals carefully shielded with a special small towel until the very last minute, at which point the towel must be placed strategically on one's head while one soaks in the opaque water.

Dinner, served quite early, was a Kaiseki, a multi-course meal, so named after the hot stones that Zen priests used to tuck into the folds of their kimonos during the long evening prayers before dinner, a procedure that was believed to stave off pangs of hunger. From Peter's account there was little danger of any pang remaining after the *shikana* haute cuisine fare they enjoyed. After the meal the attendants rolled out the futon mattresses on the floor and the guests settled down for the night. There was no possibility of carousing into the early hours.

Peter's last port of call before Christmas in Aspen was Hong Kong and his favourite suite at the Mandarin. Fortunately, he was lean and fit and full of energy. He dined at the American Club with his old friend Ed Rubin, a successful Canadian corporate lawyer and long-time resident with excellent connections in mainland China. After dinner they repaired to one of Peter's favourite haunts, the Captain's Bar at the Mandarin, to smoke a cigar. The following day he was booked for lunch – *thank heaven for being fit. I lunched intelligently with Vijay Sheth of Great Eastern Shipping, Stewart Patterson of Credit Lyonnais, and some of the Lloyd-George boys. The debate between growth and value erupted. We are ever closer to the tipping point and it will be in my favour.*

Peter heralded the evening of the Millennium itself at Conundrum, the "happening" restaurant of the day in Aspen, whose name appealed to him, and followed this with a cigar and gin daiquiris at the Jerome. He had found the local celebrations distinctly below par. *I went home to watch the <u>real</u> millennium from London – Big Ben chiming, splendid stuff. The rest was "bupkus"!*

Peter telephoned Ruth to wish her a happy beginning to the Millennium. His mother had been in hospital with a sore foot but was back at home again. *Another weakening, but she's a tough old bird, hook-nosed with chaotic, luxuriant, white hair and rosy cheeks – still attractive. All in all she's had a good life and has been a fine mother. Touchingly she told me that she loved me – not a common occurrence but the more to be treasured for that. Then, amazingly, she recited the perfect lines from a Shakespeare sonnet:*

> *That time of year thou mayst in me behold*
> *When yellow leaves, or none, or few do hang*
> *Upon those boughs which shake against the cold,*
> *Bare ruin'd choirs, where late the sweet birds sang.*

30

The Turn of the Tide

PETER USHERED in the new Millennium with a two-hour medical at the Canyon Ranch Clinic. Not surprisingly, he was pronounced to be in A1 condition, with the physique and the healthy organs of a man in his early thirties. He might have celebrated the medical report with Joanie but tension was in the air once more. She had been talking about buying one of the *casitas* at Canyon Ranch, which he considered a downright waste of money. He had been forthright in saying so and Joanie had not taken it kindly. Peter knew from experience that it was a battle he was bound to lose, but he had been at the ranch for ten days and was getting irritated by Joanie's relentless reprise of the theme. Their parting, as he set off for another Mackenzie road show, was the frostiest for some time.

Still early in the new year, he was back in London in intense negotiations with James Morton, with whom he wanted to establish a permanent relationship. He'd had a high regard for Morton since the fund manager and author had interviewed him for his book *The Financial Times Global Guide to Investing*. In the chapter entitled "Learning from Living Legends," Peter was featured as "The Patient Purist." Morton had earned Peter's highest accolade: *He's the fastest I've ever known in evaluating a balance sheet* AND *he has instinct with natural intuition. Can we afford him? I think rather, can we afford not to?*

Ever since making money on Brazil's distressed debt, Peter had maintained a watching brief on the country. He had visited several times and come away feeling that it was a sleeping giant of economic power not about to awaken in the near future. Now, after talking to Arthur Byrnes at Deltec and deepening his own research, he was not so sure that the tag about Brazil "having an infinite capacity to squander its obvious potential and a consequent growth rate as skimpy as the swimsuits" still fitted. He also had an in-depth chat with the emerging market specialists at Goldman Sachs, from which he intuited that they were about to put the finger on Brazil, as indeed they did a year later, with their famous coining of the BRIC acronym for the four countries – Brazil, Russia, India and China – whose economies they claimed would dominate the world in the twenty-first century. It was time for another visit.

In Sao Paolo, he visited the Banco Itau, one of the largest banks in Latin America and reputedly the most dynamic. The executive team, he wrote, was highly motivated with bold ideas but thorough realism. He also called on the Central Bank and was impressed with their determination to keep inflation under control and hack away at the stifling bureaucracy. *Sao Paolo reminds me of Tokyo in the late '70s. It is undoubtedly set to become the power house of the Brazilian economy as it is already its financial centre. The problem is that securities that meet my criteria are virtually non-existent. We will need to wait for a major market crack before we pounce.*

With that pronouncement he made his way to the domestic airport and flew to enjoy the magnificent Iguazu Falls. *I took the walkway along the canyon on the Brazilian side up to the Devil's Throat, where the river Parana cascades down for three hundred feet into the gorge ... There were huge brilliantly coloured butterflies everywhere, some as large as a giant maple leaf, especially the yellows. One kind had wings glowing like lapis lazuli and another was patterned like a Miro painting. There were literally clouds of them. I saw giant Macaws with yellow breasts and bright blue wings and a wonderful scarlet, blue and green variety and, to complete the magic, a toucan. There were lots of monkeys around and fantastic ferns with their fronds, dew-dropped with spray, shining like diamonds. It was unimaginably beautiful and the stuff of legend, which indeed it is ... Hemingway's journalist wife, Martha Gellhorn, wrote that "the fountain of youth is not a spurt of water but a spurt of travel." I think it's both.*

As negotiations with James Morton continued, Peter changed tack. He had contemplated a merger between Morton's company, Chelverton Investments, and Cundill Investment Research but concluded that the investment styles were incompatible. He now began to explore the possibility of engaging Morton to manage the Cundill Recovery Fund as the best way to entice him without paying a fortune. He continued thinking on the move, as he walked over to pay his first visit to the newly opened Tate Modern.

The gallery is a cross between the Pompidou Centre and the Musée d'Orsay. It is highly stimulating. One could spend a lot of time in it. There's a view of St Paul's Cathedral across the river which, when looked

at in an artistic sense, is a very moving tableau. It is unquestionably the
ideal vantage point from which to admire Wren's magnificent architecture
... With the strollers and the Millennium Bridge as a contrasting modern
design, it had the feeling of a painting by Canaletto. Walked back still
thinking. Not a single cab to be had.

Peter had been thinking in other directions as well. The last few months had included several discussions with Prem Watsa of Fairfax on the subject of the exponential growth of the derivatives markets and what the implications of this previously unknown phenomenon might be. Neither of them was comfortable about it, distrusting the supposedly perfect mathematical models upon which the trading was increasingly based. They felt that the latest fad of packaging mortgages of variable quality together as bonds and persuading rating agencies to grade them on the basis of the highest quality content in the package was dangerous, bordering on fraudulent, and encouraged financial institutions to lend recklessly. Neither could understand why the regulators did not step in. They could only conclude that the administration was tacitly encouraging the practice – an extremely disquieting notion. During the Bush presidency tacit encouragement would be transformed into active promotion.

We are in danger of an explosion of leverage due to the derivatives
markets – beyond imagination or comprehension. There is currently $290
billion or so of market credit but this is only the tip of the iceberg. It
doesn't include mortgages and mortgage top-ups, which are partly being
used by the borrowers to engage in chasing "growth stocks" in the stock
market – not value for sure. Above all it does not include the leverage-
friendly stock index futures that Congress placed under the Fed's
margin-setting grouping. None of this bodes well.

Further explorations of London's cultural treasures included a party at Old Battersea House, a beautiful late-seventeenth-century mansion that was bought as a near derelict and then lovingly restored by the American publisher Malcolm Forbes. It was a real home, perhaps the family's favourite, but at the same time it housed one of the world's great collections of Victorian art, accumulated by Forbes under the advice of his son Christopher. The occasion was a private party. However, Peter easily persuaded Christopher to give him a personal tour.

This is a stunning house and no museum. It is truly lived in and con-
sequently has the kind of warm atmosphere that you just don't get at the
Frick or the Wallace. The English often fall short in looking after their

treasures – just too many of them perhaps and not enough cash – but this is an example of what can be achieved when great taste is combined with limitless money … It is filled with fine ornaments of all sorts but the pictures are the thing and are evidently Christopher's first love. There were too many to absorb at one go, but there are some that will stick in my mind; a very fine J.J. Tissot of an elegant lady in a grey coat … waving a white handkerchief towards a liner with red funnels that is steaming out of Liverpool harbour – presumably in the direction of New York … The Pre-Raphaelites are particularly well represented: I noticed Holman-Hunt, Burne-Jones, Rossetti and Lord Leighton among many. I had a good chat with Bob Forbes too."

In Vancouver on his way back to Aspen, Peter received the news that Ruth had died. He knew it would have been a welcome release for his mother, and that as a non-believer she had no fear. Although he could not have been surprised by the event, he was surprised by the void opened up by her passing.

I couldn't sleep, remembering the early years when it was just the two of us before Father came back and Grier arrived. She was so intelligent and stimulating for a child. Although not unfeminine, she had more of a man's mind and fundamentally preferred the company of men. This was not a sexual thing. It was purely intellectual. In fact I suspect that she was not very taken with the physical side of male/female relationships. She was not a touchy feely mother but she really cared, and one knew she would always be there. I think that my withdrawal from her – deliberately going it alone after Dad came back and keeping her at a distance – must have caused her pain, which I now regret.

She was witty and funny when she chose to be. I thought of doing the dishes after supper with her reciting the witches' speeches from Macbeth as she bent over the sink, with Grier and me waiting to do the drying up. "When shall we three meet again …" And then the recipe for the cauldron, which we loved:

> *Eye of newt and toe of frog,*
> *Wool of bat and tongue of dog,*
> *Adder's fork and blind-worm's sting,*

Lizard's leg, and howlet's wing,
For a charm of powerful trouble
Like a hell-broth boil and bubble.

Salve atque vale, Mother!

After a nostalgic few days in Montreal for Ruth's funeral, Peter was back in London full of energy. Markets had at last begun to go his way, and the long-awaited collapse of the overblown telecoms sector was triggered by the first stages in the demise of Nortel, Peter's *bête noire*. Within two years the company's share price was to drop from $134.50 per share to just $0.47 amid a welter of scandal, including accounting fraud. It was the biggest corporate collapse in Canada's history. At its peak Nortel's capitalization had represented more than a third of the total value of the Toronto share index. Peter had often and publicly pointed to Nortel as a prime example of "the antithesis of value" and had circulated a memorandum of numbers comparing Nortel with Brascan. Very few had listened. Now they increasingly began to do so. Triumphalism was something Peter studiously avoided in public, if not in private, but his open and well-publicized hostility toward Nortel had an extremely positive effect on the subscription flow into the Value Fund; the assets rose for the first time to above a billion dollars. The performance of the fund was excellent in absolute terms and even more spectacularly so in comparative terms. The faith of the Mackenzie executives was fully vindicated, and the sales team now had a value product that they could get their teeth into with real conviction. It was the start of another "golden era" for value investors.

Peter's journal at the time exudes confidence as well as whimsy. He fantasized about a new London Club in the heart of the City: *The Walbrook is in a new Queen Anne style house ... just a stone's throw from the Mansion House. It's lavishly appointed and has Albert Roux of Le Gavroche as the food and wine consultant so the scoff is excellent. The speciality is "truffle cuisine" and they've bought a terrier called Charlotte who is a champion truffle sniffer. So members can enjoy their breakfast of scrambled eggs and truffles in the safe knowledge that the fungus has been unearthed by one of their own! It's almost irresistible. I do love a little decadence, and the Brits are the past masters because it's done with dry humour. They're going to do power breakfasts with "captains of industry" as speakers. Of course, when the participants eventually arrive at their usual place of business everyone will know where they've been as the none-too-subtle aroma of truffle pervades the atmosphere – possibly, but not certainly, better than burping kipper.*

A few days later he bumped into Henry Catto, erstwhile U.S. ambassador to the Court of St James, while dining at the Connaught Hotel: *Nice conversation with Henry C ... I reminded him of his speech in Northern Ireland when he excoriated "the misguided and ignorant people in the U.S. that support the* IRA *who are just terrorists getting their arms from the loonies of Libya and their inspiration from Don Corleone and the Mafia." He was host to Margaret Thatcher and Bush at his ranch near Aspen when they took the decision to confront Saddam Hussein over the invasion of Kuwait. There's a great description of the moment in Henry's autobiography [Low Adventures of a Diplomat, 1998]. He recounts that Thatcher sat "bolt upright, spine straight as a Queen's, bolstering the President's backbone with the interjection, 'This is no time to go wobbly, George!'"*

The extreme adventure for the Millennium year was to be in Australia, swimming with sharks in the Coral Sea off Queensland. Joanie had not protested – being under the impression that he was just going diving to admire the aquatic life. As a preliminary, although rather late in the day, Peter had to take a diving test and write an exam on decompression tables. The dive in the pool got off to an inauspicious start when a frayed rubber gasket broke and the air blew. An hour's wait ensued, giving Peter the time to write a terse entry in his journal. *Jesus Christ, I would have thought reliable equipment was pretty key to this operation!*

The expedition of fifteen passengers and four crew set off on the 20-metre *Rum Runner* into a stiff breeze, with white caps that made the boat roll and pitch uncomfortably. Peter made it to his cabin feeling quite queasy, and was pitched out of his bunk during the night. Several other adventurers spent the night on deck being sick. Finally, after a slow 120-mile journey to Holme Reef, *Rum Runner* anchored off the reef and the pitching stopped. On his first dive, "The Matterhorn," they immediately got among the sharks, several white tips and then a group of the larger and much more aggressive grey whalers, six to seven feet long – fast, agile and known to attack divers. Fortunately they were not hungry and the guide made certain that nothing was done to provoke an attack. The afternoon dive called "Nonki" ("easy going" in Japanese) got them into a group of smooth hammerheads fourteen or fifteen feet long, dangerous to humans but generally solitary night hunters.

The trouble began the following day when the crew were unable to start the engine. They hoisted the jib and limped the boat along through the Coral Sea toward the Great Barrier Reef. Peter read Kafka's short stories, listened to the wind, and watched the white caps on a dark sea barely lit by a crescent moon. By dawn the toilet batteries were on their last legs, the radio telephone unable to make contact, and the water system inoperable. All attempts to restart the engine failed, but one of the crew managed to get through to Cairns on a cell-phone and arrange for a plane to rendez-vous and drop a replacement battery when they reached the Barrier Reef fifty miles ahead. By afternoon neither the lights nor the stove were working. Finally a seaplane hove into view and, after several passes, dropped a package – a battery charger that was of no use. The coast guard tried to raise them, but they could not reply. To top it off, the captain confessed that they had no flares on board.

Now this is really passing muster as a scary adventure! Our Captain, Gavin, won't admit that we're in distress. Question of salvage? The thought of negligence raises its head. This is a unique chain of things going wrong. I said that one has to surrender to the fates before the luck will change. I don't think Gavin thought that was very helpful! Che sera, sera. There is bilge water now as the pumps don't work. We'd better pray the weather doesn't break. At least someone knows our rough position. We have to pass through the gap in the great coral reef sans navigation lights and some of us are to be posted in the bows with flashlights. I watched as we tapped into our water supply manually. Dusk is falling – no lights. Ate the smallest of salads. Didn't like the look of the remnants of a beef stew two days old – no fruit left. Retired to my cabin with the flashlight and a pee bag to await the call to man the bows.

Woken at 2.30 am by rattles and shaking, and a conversation being conducted by megaphone. The coast guard had arrived with batteries and an engineer – not, mark you, anyone from the expedition operators. I'd had enough of the dangerous incompetence, so the Swedish couple

*and I jumped aboard the cutter. Two hours later we were docked in
Cairns harbour. In bare feet, with no shirt and toting my briefcase, I
found the Hilton. My duffle bag is on board Rum Runner. Watched the
dawn break over Cairns – bright orange – reminded me of the Hilton in
Athens and dawn light over the Acropolis. Coffee, bath and CNN, bliss
and relief!*

There was a humorous sequel to the adventure. Peter's account was
circulated within Cundill Investment Research and it caught people's
imagination. His personal assistant, Maureen Crocker, invited members
of the team to write their own alternative accounts of the *Rum Runner*
affair. Some of their tales of water-borne sharks, as opposed to his tales
of derring-do in the world of finance, are worth relating.

(To be sung to the theme tune of *Gilligan's Island*).
'Twere a sunny morn when they set sail,
Cundill, the babes and crew.
'Twas only the beginning when
The trouble began to brew,
The trouble began to brew.

The weather was warm
The bubbles in flow
And sharks forgotten then
As the clothes began to go,
The clothes began to go.

Well our hero was in a hurry,
His trousers they went aft
And sank beneath the ocean waves
Stuck on the propeller shaft,
Stuck on the propeller shaft.

Things went from bad to worse,
Our hero's luck hit low
When he found that his would-be fling
Was really a man named Joe,
Was really a man named Joe.

'Twas lucky the sun was bright
And our hero's head was bare,
The coast guard spotted the light
Bounced off a head with no hair,
Bounced off a head with no hair.

The rescue was swift and sure,
Though the trousers were still adrift,
Our hero regained dry land
Wearing nought but his shorts as a shift,
Wearing nought but his shorts as a shift.

Nary a shark had he seen,
Nor tempted their slavering jaws
But escape nonetheless it had been
As narrow as narrow can be,
As narrow as narrow can be. (Tim McElvaine)

There were an unusually large number of sharks swimming around
in the best spot. The crew busied themselves preparing the protective
cage but Cundill waved it aside. Fixing the scantily clad supervisor
with his brilliant blue eyes, he insisted that he wanted "the real
experience." She was mesmerized and the two of them plunged into
the darkening depths of the pool. As they went down, the sharks
seemed to follow for no apparent reason. The supervisor didn't like
the look of this and signalled that they should go back. As they
started to ascend, the sharks began circling to corral the pair.
Suddenly one shark made a dart at the girl. Cundill swam straight at
it causing it to swerve and then took off his mouthpiece and gave it
a blast of air. Grabbing his shocked companion, they rose quickly to
the surface while the sharks regrouped. As they surfaced they saw
that their boat was on fire and sinking. There was an explosion that
catapulted the crew into the water, diverting the attention of the
sharks. There was nothing for it but to swim for the nearest spit of
land. From the beach they watched the boat disappear beneath the
waves and listened, horrified, to the screams of the crew as the
sharks went in. Cundill put his arms round the distressed supervisor.

Using the skills he'd learned trekking in the Himalayas, he lit a fire with driftwood and comforted his companion, who clung to him hungrily. An hour or so later the coast guard, alerted by the explosion, rescued the pair, who appeared uncommonly relaxed. Of the rest of the crew nothing was to be found. Safely ashore, the lovely supervisor embraced Cundill fondly and then fainted.

Later, as Cundill strolled back to the hotel, he wondered what he was going to do for fun that evening. (ACP)

Rogue pirates boarded *Rum Runner* while everyone was in the water swimming with the sharks. They stole the engine, along with Peter's trousers, hoping to find a wallet full of cash and endless credit. Instead they only found microfilmed versions of the Mitsui and Kmart annual reports. Disgusted, the pirates threw the wallet into the water, and the sharks, who'd been determining to eat Peter, decided that the wallet had more body fat and would make less of a fuss. This gave our leader the chance to swim to the mother ship and safety. However, when he realized that the engine had gone and that the only attractive woman aboard believed in discounted cash flows, Peter was utterly confounded and immediately called the Coast Guard. (Wade Burton)

From these vignettes the esteem and affection in which Peter was held is evident. At the same time, there appear to be few illusions about the direction in which any *faiblesse* of his might lie. It is interesting that there is no ring of sycophancy, because the flattery, such as it is, is thoroughly dressed down with irony.

Over Christmas at Canyon Ranch, which was celebrated in the new *casita*, the truth about Peter's diving expedition gradually leaked. Joanie was obviously displeased but Peter was wise enough to be very conciliatory about her purchase of the *casita*, and she quickly thawed. He was also complimentary about her cooking – which required a certain imaginative effort: *Joanie made chicken for dinner (pre-frozen). Turned out to be fish. I said it was a very tasty mistake. While Joanie was in the kitchen I gave some of mine to Emily, the new cat, who then purred dangerously loudly! Anyway it's been a great year. Very good numbers, good running, great adventure and travel – especially the shark experience, lots of good nights out and great reading.*

The Seeds of a Troubled Decade

Boy, good health is important! Aged sixty-two, with the physique and toning of a fit man in his thirties and parents who had both lived full, independent lives into their late eighties, Peter had every expectation of vigorous longevity. Sadly, this hope was to prove vain. Nevertheless, with the new Millennium still young, his Canyon Ranch health check showed him to be in the peak of shape: *Very satisfying! You can do anything you want with discipline, focus and patience.* Over the next few years, that maxim was to be severely tested.

Peter's next visit to London was so brief that he didn't even bother to change his answering machine message. But it exemplified a typical day for him – an ideal mix of work, culture, and pleasure. A conversation with Mark Coombs of Ashmore about sovereign debt convinced him that Coombs and his team were now the cutting edge of the world of distressed debt and were working with modelling that related very closely to the kind of value-based balance sheet analysis at which he excelled. The afternoon and evening were spent with Maddie Jenner, one of his London girlfriends, with whom he went to see the exhibition of Turner watercolours at the Royal Academy – *a glorious panorama of liquid light – if this is not impressionism in action three decades before Monet I don't know what is.* After a champagne supper and a little dancing, Peter reflected: *God, the intellectual companionship is refreshing.*

The next day, he was back on the plane for another Mackenzie road show, this time to the Maritime Provinces. The first stop was Halifax. At the Bank of Nova Scotia, Peter played his "Haligonian card" – his great, great grandfather William Lawson, the bank's first president. He was immediately invited to the boardroom to see the portrait of his ancestor. *Moving – almost overwhelming, such a young man and good looking too!*

Part of the allure of a trip to the Maritimes was the promise of a visit to Prince Edward Island, the only Canadian province where Peter had never set foot. Lying in the Gulf of St Lawrence about 150 miles off

Halifax, it is the sort of remote and unspoiled spot, reminiscent of Cap
à l'Aigle, that Peter always enjoyed. A last-minute cancellation was a huge
disappointment, and David Feather was deeply apologetic. However
Peter waved his hand airily – it was no matter and could not be helped.
The next venue was therefore to be St John's, Newfoundland, via Air
Canada from Fredericton, New Brunswick. But in the morning Peter told
Feather to forget the scheduled flight because he had hired a private helicopter to transport the party. Feather needed no persuasion; it would be
a lot more fun than hanging around commercial airports.

They headed out for St John's, flying over the Confederation Bridge,
which connects PEI with the mainland, and then, as expected, toward the
capital, Charlottetown. Suddenly, to the surprise of everyone except Peter,
the pilot doubled back toward the beaches beside the bridge and touched
down. Peter shot out of the cockpit, where he had been seated beside the
pilot, knelt down, kissed the ground, and seized a handful of sand. *We
ended up back in Halifax. Four provinces in a day! And especially* PEI,
*without which my life would not be complete – the birthplace of
Confederation, which made our nation in the 1860s, and the inspiration
for Anne of Green Gables. I've put the lovely pinkish white sand in a jar.
That night we did George St and the local bars. It was a Celtic romp!*

———————

The carefree interlude came to an abrupt end with a call from Brian
McDermott to inform Peter that his colleague Leslie Ferris had committed suicide. Peter had hired Ferris in CIR about eighteen months earlier.
Highly qualified, she had become a superb, intuitive value analyst with
whom he had found it a pleasure to work. In fact she had been a serious
candidate as his possible successor as Chief Investment Officer. Distressed
and angry, he called Joanie. As always, she gave rock-solid support and
excellent advice in a crisis. Unknown to Peter, Ferris had a history of
depression and had been on long-term medication. Joanie at once surmised that it was the fact of Leslie's depression that was most rattling
Peter, and counselled a visit to Leslie's husband and family in Miami to
offer comfort and closure. This he arranged at once, and spent an afternoon in West Palm Beach listening and sympathizing, and establishing
that Brian Ferris was surrounded by a fine support group of family and
friends:

I'm barely able to comprehend the shock, but he is at least cocooned by wonderful people. I almost got teary and it was hard to be restrained ... I understand why Leslie did it but I'm also very angry with her – she lied to me (understandably so), but she let me down by not trusting me. She had been in hospital several times and on medication for years. Why is depression such a taboo topic? It is just an illness. Maybe together we could have nipped it and I know better than most that the little demon doesn't let up and you have to have allies who understand. Such a waste. I ran along the beach for an hour and a half after visiting.

He wrote a note to everyone at CIR in Vancouver: "As I write this, Leslie Ferris was going to pick me up in twelve minutes. We were going to spend the day together. It is a sad moment for all of us. Depression is an illness that can strike hardest when one feels the wall has been climbed. It is almost as if a little demon waits to pounce. We shall miss her. She was of great energy, intellect, practicality and good humour. Life is fragile. Live it to the utmost."

Still feeling the after effects, Peter doubly welcomed his planned trip to Filao Beach on St Maarten. Joanie was waiting for him. *She was there, so lovely to see her.* After dinner, he unburdened himself about the tragedy, breaking into tears. Joanie was sympathetic and comforting, and it was a cathartic moment. Then, *a barefoot walk on the beach with a cigar and the moon with lazy clouds above the lapping waves. I did some damage to the bottle and fell into bed.*

By the morning, Peter had recovered his equilibrium: *Ran over the hill by the salt lake to the beach. Discovered it was a nudist beach. One runs to learn. Good breasts and plenty of them. My physique was comprehensively checked out!* His spirits lifted further when he received news that Nortel's share price had been decimated on markets around the world following a revenue growth warning. *How sweet it is to be vindicated.*

Nortel's freefall prompted a pithy memorandum to the team at CIR:

WHAT MAKES A GREAT SHORTING POLICY?
Not so long ago Peter Ackerman wrote an insightful piece asking rhetorically "What Makes a Great Buy?" In the wake of Nortel this is an attempt at the flip side.
· You must have overvaluation to start with. High book values and

price earnings ratios with non-existent or very low dividend yields are a good starting point.

BUT OVERVALUATION IS NOT ENOUGH. Some thought should be given to the general market and the characteristics of the moment ...

· The shares should be close to an all time high and beginning to drift down. The drifting down is probably a better working model as an all time high can keep on trucking.
· There should be the potential for an earnings disappointment. For example in the U.S., when the dollar is strong there is an automatic negative effect on U.S. internationals. This, of course, applies to all currencies wherever there are businesses that are export led.
· Lots of debt makes a short seller's job easier.
· Look out for aggressive accounting, i.e., lots of capitalized expenses.
· A whiff of fraud is useful. Check the backgrounds of the board and the management.

Our policy has been to use indices as our choice of instrument. It has not been effective because the very large companies dominate the indices. However, we have no background in borrowing securities to facilitate a short, and no relationships.

One of the alternatives is to develop relationships with specialists in creating baskets of securities. There are several such in New York. In each of the indices where we are short I have individual net-net sheets for the top ten to fifteen companies. I would welcome debate, nay die for it, on the composition of the individual securities. Here are some thoughts:

· Trailing P/E ratios are very high and seem to be more than the underlying growth rates. There seems to be increasing analyst attention to operating earnings which allows "restructuring charges" to pass unremarked. Some companies restructure every year. This is the current U.S. accounting abuse.
· I think, but don't know, that current earnings estimates are very optimistic. Can we confirm or deny? Do the estimates conform to our sense of reality?
· There must be some industries where expectations are very high. This would include the North American money management

industry. How should one play this?
- If you were designing a basket what would you include? Those with hefty recent acquisitions must be good candidates potentially.

I await your thoughts.

Having put the trauma of Leslie Ferris's death at least temporarily behind him, Peter set off on an expedition around northern Europe, first to Copenhagen. He was charmed by the city, its snow crisp and fresh in the sunshine, and pleased with his meetings with SAS Airlines and A.P. Moeller. However, the highlight was a meeting of minds with Ole Nielsen of Sparinvest, a fellow value enthusiast.

Helsinki was not as productive, though he liked the Finns. He struck up a friendship with a Finnish student, who introduced him to the philosophical works of Schopenhauer and earned a place in his journal. *I got lost on my run and a very pretty girl called Aina helped me out, leading me all the way back to the hotel. She joined me for a drink and then for lunch. I have been reading Schopenhauer at her suggestion – rather compelling. He says that the important differences in the human condition of individuals can be pared down to three clear distinctions:*
- *What a man is – his personality in the broadest sense, including his looks, health, strength, intelligence, moral character, education and temperament.*
- *His possessions of every kind.*
- *How he is seen by others, both the wide public perception and the more intimate perception of friends and family.*
It appears simplistic until you think about it, but in essence it is a pretty accurate assessment.

In the spring Peter and Joanie set out on another biking holiday, this time in Basque country. It may not be the Tour de France, but cycling over the Pyrenees is no mean challenge. Peter was fascinated by the Basque culture, which is quite distinct from any other part of France or Spain, and by Euskara, the unique and ancient Basque language, which predates both Latin and Greek. Surprisingly, given his antipathy to the cause of Québec Libre, he was sympathetic to Basque ambitions to achieve independence, although he deplored the terrorist tactics of the Basque separatist organization, ETA.

The ride began from the resort town of Biarritz, its grandeur much diminished since its heyday as a favourite of Queen Victoria and Edward VII – *clearly a drug centre, with syringes lying around in the untended parks.* They climbed up into the Basque heartland approaching the Pyrenees and crossed the River Nive into the pretty village of Itxassou, whose pronunciation gave Peter a little trouble. Then it was on past the town of Espelette, famous for its production of tingling hot red pepper powder. In the evening they made an excursion to Saint-Jean-Pied-de-Port, where Peter especially was keen to watch a game of jai alai:

It's the fastest ball game in the world. The little ball (steel strands wrapped in goatskin) can travel at up to 200 mph and it requires feats of unbelievable athleticism to play well ... The game is played between eight teams of two, of which two teams are on court at any time, and they rotate until one team reaches nine points and wins. Then there are play-offs for second and third place. It's a wonderful spectator sport – lots of betting and cheering. Players get badly injured and even killed every year, and as a spectator you'd be wise not to doze off!

Following the ancient pilgrim route, the Camino de Santiago de Compostela, they passed groups of pilgrims walking along with their distinctive staffs topped with the scallop shell badge of St James, and climbed all the way to the Pass of Roncesvalles, the scene of the Emperor Charlemagne's great victory over the Saracens and the death of his heroic nephew Roland: *As I stopped to catch my breath at the top of the pass and looked down into Spain across the magnificent sweep of lush green forest, I could almost hear the desperate blast of Roland's horn echoing through the valley. I remember mother reading to me when I was a boy from an old leather-bound translation of the "Chanson," as we sat huddled together in front of the stove in the cottage at Saint-Sauveur and I felt the thrill of the epic language.*

After an overnight in Pamplona – unfortunately, *sans* bulls – they went to Vitoria, a stop that Peter was eagerly anticipating because of its history. He had recently read Bernard Cornwell's *Sharpe's Honour*, a historical novel that gives a vivid account of Wellington's victory at the bridge there in 1813. Again he found a vindication of his own investment and leadership methods: *Talk about patience, endurance and sheer grit – Wellington had it all. Having taken Madrid the previous year, he had to abandon it due to lack of reinforcements and ... trudged his exhausted army back through Salamanca all the way to the Portuguese border, abandoning everything they had won. With almost any other commander morale would have plummeted, but the ordinary soldiers trusted "Old Nosey" and he had great subordinate officers. By the spring he was ready again and ... he crushed the French army of 80,000 ... Those kinds of virtues are indispensable in any enterprise – not least in my own profession – in short it's known as leadership.*

In Bilbao, they made their way to the new Guggenheim Museum inspiringly designed by the Canadian architect Frank Gehry. Clad in shining titanium and sitting like a great liner on the waterfront with the sea in front, the mountains behind, and the city in between, it has been a significant factor in the whole city's recovery after the ETA terrorist campaign brought it to its knees. Peter's verdict was succinct. *It needs no art works, it is a work of art in itself. Collection disappointing. I would not have missed seeing the building.*

Shortly after getting back to London, Peter had a visit from David Feather. When their business was concluded, they set off for a night on the town. It was a tried and tested formula – a good dinner at a humming new brasserie and bar called Hush in Mayfair, followed by cigars at Annabel's. However there was one small variation: *We ended the evening at Trader Vic's bar at the Hilton where we watched the "girls" working their cell phones – strange atmosphere.*

A few days later he spent a similar evening. Dinner with a lady friend at Hakkasan, followed by the cigar at Annabel's, dropped the lady home in Eaton Square and then walked back to the Grosvenor House. Bored by the lack of an amusing conclusion to the evening he decided, on the spur of the moment, to go out again. More by chance than design he found himself back at Trader Vic's: *I made two new friends, Chantale Joseph and Zee Brinan – a very full day!*

Harking back to the passages read to him by his mother from the *Chanson de Roland* seems to have planted the kernel of another scheme: *It would be a really fun thing to put together an anthology of poetry and*

*publish it privately as George Norton did with the account of his
American and Canadian travels in the 1880s. The idea has a satisfyingly
unconventional aspect to it, especially being collected by a chartered
accountant – an ode to the balance sheet?! It could be illustrated with
some of my favourite works of art. Hey!*

Although the project was never realized, some of his initial thoughts
are interesting. He mused about what would determine his choices: each
would need to express thoughts, or paint pictures, that could be recognized as universally true. The expression would have to be neat, whether
in rhyme or rhythm, and the words deft enough to reverberate and make
one want to learn the passage by heart: *it should create a "sursum corda"
(lift up your hearts) and make the reader wish he had written the piece
himself.*

He offered two poems he would include, examples that leave one
regretting that what would have been a highly unusual and stimulating
anthology never materialized:

*The world stands out on either side
No wider than the heart is wide,
Above the world is stretched the sky
No higher than the soul is high
And so I looked and after all
The sky is not so very tall.
The sky I said must somewhere stop
And sure enough – I see the top
The sky, I thought, is not so grand
I 'most could touch it with my hand
And reaching up my hand to try
I screamed to feel it touch the sky.[1]*

*Edna Millay is another legacy from mother. I believe mother knew her
– she was quite a gal intellectually and also beautiful. Many affairs –
openly and unashamedly bisexual too, with the courage to be indifferent
to censorious opinion. So was Catullus – though not I'm sure bisexual:*

[1] Edna St. Vincent Millay, "Renascence" (1912), stanza 3, *Renascence and Other
Poems* (New York: Harper, 1917).

Let us live my Lesbia, and let us love,
And let us judge all of the rumours of old men
To be worth just one penny!
The suns are able to fall and rise
When that brief light has fallen for us
And we must sleep a never ending night.
Give me a thousand kisses, then a second hundred,
Then yet another thousand more, then another hundred,
Then, when we have made many thousands
We'll mix them all up so that we don't know
And no one can be jealous of us when he finds out
How many kisses we have shared.[2]

Peter had developed an unusual sensitivity to certain historical anniversaries – although quite prone to forget the wedding variety. He remembered Queen Victoria's birthday nearly every year, and if he was in London would sometimes send a wreath to her statue outside Kensington Palace. He knew she had been born and brought up there in straitened circumstances after her father, the Duke of Kent, had died leaving a mountain of debt and few assets, and that it was there that she had received the news of the death of her uncle King William IV, thereby ascending to the throne at the age of eighteen. Peter was an aficionado of the National Portrait Gallery in Trafalgar Square, and often went to view the canvases of the youthful monarch, admiring her large doe-like eyes and especially her slim but full-busted figure.

The anniversary of Casanova's death on June 14 attracted his notice several times, and one gets the impression that he regarded the Italian adventurer as somewhat of a rival: *Casanova died 203 years ago today –* *one of the world's most renowned lovers, although his final tally of wom-* *anizing is paltry by today's standards – during 35 years of sexual activity* *he only had between 132 and 343 different women (I haven't got to the* *bottom of the enormous spread in this estimate) ... I believe that Peter*

---

2 Tr. Rudy Negenborn, copyright 1997.

Stringfellow's [the owner of a number of hostess clubs in Britain] tally runs into several thousand.

Peter's one-time white-water-rafting and investing partner, Merryn Corcoran, brought him good news – she had finally sold MOA, the fashion shop he had helped her develop, to the designer Beatrice von Tresckow. She came carrying a cheque – a fraction of his actual investment – but in light of his frequent statements that the fun he had out of it had been worth the money, she was taken aback when he accepted it. She had misread her man. However, he invited Merryn and Jenny Bingham, who had kept track of the investment in MOA for him, to a celebratory dinner at Harry's Bar.

London's hot new night club at the time was China White, just off Oxford Street, and Merryn was keen to visit, so it was decided that the obligatory cigar, champagne, and dancing would take place there for a change. When they arrived they found a queue stretched way up the street. Peter was all for abandoning the attempt, but Merryn was not to be gainsaid. Jumping out of the limousine, she dashed up to the bouncers to announce that she had a Russian oligarch in the car who wished to go into the club *at once.* With shaven head, startling blue eyes, and puffing at a truly enormous cigar, Peter fit the bill, and the three of them were whisked inside without a second's hesitation. It was such moments that had made MOA worth it.

Another new relationship was blossoming in Peter's life, on the opposite side of the Atlantic. He had attended the second wedding of his cousin Geoffrey Scott in Vancouver and was seated for the nuptial dinner beside the bride's friend Stephanie Nicolls, an attractive, intelligent, vivacious, and single Canadian lady in her early thirties who was also an excellent tennis player. She matched him glass for glass over the champagne, more than kept up with him on the dance floor, and challenged him to a game the following morning at the Vancouver Lawn Tennis Club, where she trounced him. She was clever enough to allow him to win on the return match, however, and he was smitten. She became his regular item out west.

———————

Whenever Leslie Ferris's suicide returned to Peter's mind, the issue of depression, its causes, and its relief again found its way into his journal.

Although he was not on regular anti-depressants and had never been hospitalized like Leslie, it was a spectre lurking over his shoulder. He had come across an article about music being commonly used in healing in nearly all cultures – even Martin Luther had successfully recommended the communal singing of psalms as a cure for women suffering from depression. For him, the most difficult time of day was waking up. He discovered that listening to a Bach cantata before going to bed was usually an effective preventive, as well as swallowing a litre of water when he'd had a lot to drink. He noted down two pertinent verses from a hymn by Thomas Troeger, a musician and pastor who often visited Aspen:

Articulate with measured sound
The song that fills all things,
For even atoms dance around
And solid matter sings

Let healing harmonies release
The hurts the heart compiles
That God through music may increase
The grace that reconciles.[3]

I believe that suffering from depression from time to time may make one a more loving and understanding human being and that it may possibly have a sort of redemptive power. However, once experienced you always live in its shadow. You win battles but can never be completely victorious in the conflict. Your own "margin of safety" will always remain quite fragile. I know that I am at the top of my game and yet I still suffer from a vague feeling of apprehension, particularly in the early morning. It goes away.

Peter was not the only one to recognize that he was "at the top of his game." In early December he travelled to Toronto for the Canadian Mutual Fund Gala Awards dinner where, at a formal black-tie gathering of six hundred of his fellow investment professionals, he received the Career Achievement Award as the Greatest Mutual Fund Manager of All

---

3   Thomas Troeger, *Borrowed Light: Hymn Texts, Prayers and Poems* (New York: Oxford University Press, 1994).

Time. His twenty-five-year record of a 17% compound return was ahead of both Charles Brandes and John Templeton. In fact, Peter was the only mutual fund manager in the world who could boast such a record over that length of time. His only rivals were Warren Buffett and George Soros – neither of whom had ever run a mutual fund. He received a standing ovation.

An Aspen Institute reception and dinner at the St Regis Hotel took him to New York for a few days. As a consequence of the 9/11 disaster, the speaker was Sandy Regis, who had been President Clinton's security advisor. His view was the antithesis of the belligerent approach of the Bush administration. He could see no short-term solution, especially not military, to Islamic extremism and believed that the only real solution was universal liberal education and an end to the repression of women in the Muslim world. On that sombre note, the dancing began, with Peter and former defence secretary Robert McNamara leading the charge. The two were almost the last to leave, and Peter buttonholed McNamara in the lobby: *I told him that notwithstanding his many accomplishments, his real contribution was as a dancer. He purred like the Cheshire cat and got me to repeat this to his lady when she appeared.*

Peter was back in London when Nortel reported a $91 million loss for the quarter that stemmed from writing off some "goodwill." Goodwill was one of Peter's special detestations on any balance sheet: *I have seen many businesses destroyed by vanity in the thin disguise of innovation and enterprise, and the certain way to kill any business is to run it out of cash. It seems that this lesson needs to be learnt time and time again. These markets now hate anything to do with telecoms or the internet. This is a unique moment and there will come an opportunity for us to fill our boots with the best of the fallen angels.*

Determined to have a celebration that evening, he met Chantale Joseph and her friend Zee for drinks at the Red Bar in the Grosvenor House before joining them at Chantale's flat for "Chinese takeaway and fun." At the same time he also saw his friend Louise Somers, a young Scottish lady he had met in Paris, and took her to see *The King and I* at the Palladium in London. *I cried like a baby in the second half – unusual magic.* They dined at the Connaught and then went to the Red Bar, which was humming with a group from a large Muslim wedding. In the morning Peter ran into two men from this party in the health club: *I chatted with the two Arabs. I was interested because I believe that the world has changed for their race forever after the Twin Towers and I wanted to get a sense of whether they were aware that this is so. One of them told me that working out and sex go together. As if I didn't know! We over-whelmed each other with courtesy but I suspect that the pictures running through their minds were the same as mine – two smoking towers and tiny figures plunging to their deaths below. Of course, the world HAS changed and not only for Muslims but for us all right across this globe of ours.*

32

Confronting Mortality

THE FACT THAT the 9/11 attack had fundamentally changed conditions for the developed Western world had struck Peter forcibly. No longer would it be possible to regard even North America as a safe haven; one would have to cope with a new environment where the soft underbelly of the West was uncomfortably exposed. He prefaced his first journal entry of 2002 with a stark quotation from T.S. Eliot's *Four Quartets*

> Go, go, go, *said the bird: human kind*
> *Cannot bear very much reality.*[1]

He was also prescient in his concern about the new European currency. *Euro banknotes and coins went into circulation today. It is now two years since the Euro began to stake a claim to a role as an important rival reserve currency to the U.S. dollar. How do I view it? I have talked to numerous wise men whose opinions I value, notably Mark Coombs of Ashmore, Peter Ackerman, Ole Nielsen, Prem Watsa, Mike Price and Michael Alexander. My sense is that a time bomb has been created because this Euro is flawed in concept. I don't believe it's possible to have a workable single currency for Europe without a unified cross-border tax regime and a fully functional central bank controlling monetary policy … Do I think that these will be implemented before it is too late? – I doubt it.*

Having got those two issues, as it were, off his chest and onto paper Peter proceeded to undertake a new adventure – snowboarding, which had just been adopted as an Olympic sport in 1998. However, it was generally regarded as the parish of the youthful, rather than sixty-four-year old swingers like Peter. *Off to my snowboarding lesson at Buttermilk … The initial learning process is done in a chair to pick up the lift procedure.*

---

1 T.S. Eliot, "Burnt Norton," 1935.

I fell continually and had a tendency to go right. After three and a half hours of teaching on the hill in the sunshine I got it, lost it, fell and got up again. After another two and half hours I began to lose my concentration. Tried to relax but it was hard. Supper in, after a wonderful hot shower. I do feel I achieved something ... I was still wired as I went to bed.

Peter's first voyage of the year was to Japan, on this occasion to attend a conference organized by Michael Alexander as part of a program for the International Forum. Michael and Peter were more than cousins; they were both accountants and kindred spirits in innovative thinking and athleticism. After thirty years in business as executive partner for international services at Touche Ross, Michael had an unrivalled appreciation of the challenges to international companies of doing business in a global environment without an understanding of cultural and social differences, and had launched the Forum in 1989. Along with its associated program, the Wharton Global Leadership Series, it brought participants face to face with people they might not otherwise encounter, seeking to integrate business with the arts, history, sociology, science and technology and music of other cultures. Michael was a frequent and valued speaker at Peter's conferences and Peter reciprocated at Forum events.

This conference venue was typical of the Forum style; uniquely different. The participants gathered in the 250-year-old Horai Ryokan, with views across to Sagami Bay and Mount Fuji. Although mostly strangers to each other, the guests slept four to a room, unavoidably pitched into a melting pot. After bathing in the traditional Japanese manner, they dressed in traditional garb and assembled for dinner in the softly lit tatami-floored banqueting hall. Dinner was served in feudal style as a long series of different small dishes, each a work of art. Music followed, played on the *shakuhachi* (bamboo flute) and the *shamisen* (three-stringed lute), and the guests were invited to perform something themselves. The Asians, used to karaoke, were not at all shy – the North Americans reluctant – but Peter provided the highlight of the evening with a solo performance of the witches' scene from *Macbeth*, delivered with a gusto that reduced the audience to helpless laughter and elicited an encore.

Later, Peter sent a summary of the conference conclusions to the CIR team in Vancouver:

The consensus ... was that the key to the future of the Asian region over the next twenty years is the Japan/China relationship. Japanese industry is rapidly switching its flag to the Pacific Rim countries. The cost advantages ... are just too compelling. This is a major factor in the decline in real estate prices in Japan. Make no mistake, China still has massive structural problems but it has energy and Japan has money. Combine the two and you have a potential world power to challenge America. I tried this idea out on Tom Friedman, the foreign correspondent of the New York Times, who threw up his hands in horror. Contemporary history between China and Japan, he said, had been too disruptive for a national reconciliation. But this has only been the case for a century or so. The shared writing system means that the two countries can communicate even if they can't actually talk to each other. Self-interest will prevail.

Joanie was four years older than Peter and, in spite of a fitness regime that would have been the envy of most women in their thirties, was experiencing a lack of energy. She wanted to sell the house in Aspen and relocate to Canyon Ranch, and he did not discourage her. Unlike his reaction to the purchase of the *casita*, this time he was supportive. Health had always been a topic of intimate discussion for them; however, it now seemed to have added meaning. While Peter had noticed changes in Joanie, she was becoming aware that he was experiencing shaking in his left arm and problems with his balance.

Joanie showed no lack of energy in executing the move, and within weeks Peter found himself long three houses, including a new one at Canyon Ranch for $3 million. He took it stoically enough: *I don't like the exposure but it's easy to handle.* He also noted that in addition to the Aspen house, which he thought ought to fetch $5 million, Joanie was selling the despised *casita* for a million. The net cash realization that this would mean might account for his equability – three weeks later the Aspen house went for a satisfying $5.2 million.

Unfortunately, he now had other preoccupations as well. His London friend Maddie Jenner was succumbing to cancer, and his faithful and most trusted personal assistant, Maureen Crocker, had relapsed from a reprieve. *My life is now going through change. The house sales, Maureen*

sick again, Maddie probably dying. Add on my unsought move from the
Grosvenor House to the Savoy and you have it. The last may not be so
unwelcome. Adopt a crisis mode and deal with all this at a slightly higher
level of intensity. Add on some system changes. Be aware of every
moment of good health.

Not all was gloom. Peter's relationship with Stephanie Nicolls had
moved up several gears and he invited her to visit him in London, where
he treated her to dining at Langan's Brasserie, a stalwart of the London
restaurant scene that is partly owned by the actor Michael Caine. He was
thoroughly enjoying "Steph"; she, unhappily, was falling in love with him.

In addition, his name was now in "the book" for election at White's
Club, the most exclusive and aristocratic of all such establishments. Peter
had been hankering after membership for years, ever since learning that
his fellow Canadian, David Graham, had been elected. Peter was envious
of the independently wealthy Graham, a successful entrepreneur in the
oil business, who played a handy game of polo and was master of the
Cattistock Hunt in Dorset, as well as being gregarious and extremely hos-
pitable – all desirable credentials for White's. Graham was naturally
clubbable in a way that Peter was not – perhaps because he tried a little
too hard and was too evidently impressed by a title. The truth was that
Graham had moved effortlessly into English society in a way that Peter
aspired to but never quite achieved.

Peter's investment commitment to Japan was unfaltering and he finally
opened an office there under the direction of Tadamichi Furuta, a shrewd
man with impeccable credentials and excellent connections in corporate
Japan. He had worked for years at Nikko Securities in Europe and Canada
as well as in Japan, where he had risen to be deputy general manager. He
was a Chartered Financial Analyst with a thorough understanding of
value-investment principles. From 2002 Tad was the face of the Cundill
Group in Japan and with David Briggs in Vancouver they made up the
team that, with Peter, oversaw all the Cundill Japanese investments,
which were growing both in percentage terms and in absolute value as
new money continued to pour in.

Markets, however, were drifting rather aimlessly at this juncture and
Peter treated this as an opportunity to pen one of his most effective
memos to the team at CIR. It summarized his most recent investment principles in his best punchy style:

It seems to me that a major difference between a value investor and the growth constituency is the former's focus on the balance sheet and the latter's preoccupation with the statement of profit and loss. Predicting earnings at any time is a mug's game. No one gets it right. In good times analysts are too optimistic; in economic downturns the reverse occurs.

Let's assume that globally earnings will be in a downturn and growth rates are broken. How does one make one's bones? One searches for the margin of safety in the balance sheet with cash-like instruments, extra hard assets, and little debt. I reiterate – the price should be at a low. One should pay only for low earnings multiples and free cash flow. One searches for catalysts. DIVIDEND YIELD IS REALLY IMPORTANT.

I strongly urge that more attention be paid to balance sheet items such as inventories, pension funds, and extra assets as well as questionable accounting techniques. I would prefer that Discounted Cash Flow Analysis be used only in an analyst's private working papers.

The link between the balance sheet and the profit and loss statement is the source and use of funds. We have done good work in analyzing this part of the business equation. We should do more.

I think there is an extraordinary opportunity to build an outstanding business on the old-style value principles as modified by our recent experience and knowledge.

The creative flow continued, percipient and even prophetic: *On the research side, I think we are relying too much on the seeming precision of mathematical models in our work. We seem to be ignoring such qualitative factors as relationships, the composition of boards of directors, etc. This sort of work is not just the prerogative of the old guys! I would refer the research department to the work of James Morton, which is a splendid combination of qualitative and quantitative analysis; and I share, with complete conviction, Tim McElvaine's caution on Discounted Cash Flow analysis. We underweight either side of the analytical equation at our peril.*

The then-current rage for mathematical modelling did indeed lead to nemesis. It was upon such supposedly sophisticated modelling that the whole case for packaging sub-prime mortgages was based. Discounted

Cash Flow analysis was another costly fad powered by imagination and wishful thinking, and led to the financial crisis of 2008 that continues to haunt world economies. The process relied on the estimation of what a corporation's cash flow – itself mostly a highly speculative variable – would be up to a given date in the future. A notional interest rate at that date was then also estimated (again a highly undependable variable) and applied as a discount rate to arrive at what was termed a share's "Real Present Value" – clearly a misnomer since "real" was the one thing it was not. But such "analysis" was nonetheless used to justify the ludicrous valuations ascribed to many growth stocks at the time. As true reality reasserted itself, investors experienced extreme pain.

"Patience" was still Peter's ultimate watchword, and he argued that it was preferable to be exposed to the Value Trap than what he termed the Growth Stock Trap. In a value trap one can afford to be patient as long as one has correctly assessed the margin of safety and it was not being eroded by incompetent management. In a growth stock trap, by contrast, the investor is unavoidably exposed to negative changes in the overall perception of the prospects for a particular industry or company, as well as to the vagaries of the stock market in general. Peter had found that in challenging economic climates, the shares that have experienced the extremes of speculative fever are the ones that get hammered and not the forgotten darlings of the value community. He went on to reassure his younger portfolio managers on the issue of market turbulence:

> Suffice it to say that we have generally prospered in difficult markets and that without such periods we should lack opportunity and our business would be far more difficult. To those of my colleagues who have never seen turbulence in the financial system; this will be the first of many. Don't fuss it. Be disciplined and focused within your appointed tasks. We shall survive and prosper.

Sir John Templeton had not only been a mentor and friend to Peter but had been the largest investor in the Cundill Value Fund in the mid-1980s. But he had become disheartened and redeemed his position after the fund's down year in 1990, and its failure to post much of a recovery the year after. Consequently, he missed out on the 43% bonanza of 1993. Nonetheless, the friendship had been maintained, and he and Peter met from time to time in London or Nassau. Now, out of the blue, a letter arrived from Templeton congratulating Peter on his "brilliant twenty-year performance" and asking some detailed questions. Clearly he was considering reinvestment. In the end the approach came to nothing, but no endorsement could have delighted Peter more – except perhaps one from Warren Buffett, for which he had to wait.

By April, again in Japan, he was steadily building the kind of mean-ingful corporate relationships that beget trust and eventually friendship. He spent considerable time with the people at Nipponkoa Insurance and Mitsui Marine, which between them represented over 12% of the overall investments of the Value Fund. At the same time he was fostering his con-tacts with Descente, a manufacturer of up-market sporting equipment, where he was building a significant position. He was thrilled to become a "test pilot" for the new range of super light-weight running shoes that they presented to him. Most unusually for Japan, the company's marketing manager was not only a foreigner but a woman. Peter liked and respected her, as well as having a soft spot for Iida-San, Descente's highly effective chief executive, and he enjoyed entertaining them at some fairly liquid din-ners. *I learn more when the cup is flowing than at any other time.*

From Japan he went on to India, where he now had one investment, although at $20 million a considerable one. Through all the chaos of Mumbai, the crazy tuk-tuk drivers and suicidal pedestrians, the sacred cows of many kinds and the endemic corruption, Peter had discerned an emerging market economy gathering pace. The difficulty was to find qualifying value-investment candidates. He was interested particularly in VSNL, India's dominant telecommunications company, which had also become the country's leading internet service provider: *By all the valua-tion metrics most commonly used for telecommunications companies, VSNL stands out as one of the least expensive. In addition there are a num-ber of embedded catalysts that could easily propel the share price upward; one is the impending sale of a 15% stake held by the Indian government, the second is the major domestic growth opportunity, as only 2.2% of the Indian populace presently has a regular phone service. At the current price the shares represent a good balance between the mar-gin of safety and capital appreciation.*

The Value Fund's largest holding, at nearly 10%, was Prem Watsa's Fairfax Holdings, which had a joint venture with ICICI, one of India's biggest banks. Peter felt it incumbent upon him to pay a visit. He met with Gopal Krishnan, the head of investments for the joint venture:

Gopal is knowledgeable and bright, and a true value man, as one might expect coming from Prem ... I met with K.V. Kamath, the CEO, *and Kalpan Morparia, who has been spearheading the merger.*

Kamath has an engineering background. ICICI *was founded in 1955 as a project finance arm of the Indian government. He is an impressive figure of a man. The culture of the bank has changed from a project lender to the financial service institution that it is about to become. It will be the second largest bank in India. Kamath has passion and facts; his presentation is just a shade too pat.*

I would suggest that the bank will sell at a discount to book value after taking a RS33 billion write-down of their industrial portfolio. The P/E ratio will be less than 10. A certain number of shares residing in treasury will be sold to strategic buyers – ourselves for example. It will help capital ratios. The life and mutual fund business and the joint venture with Fairfax are nascent but growing.

In theory this would appear to be a no-brainer. There are, however, questions that need answering:

- *Are the pro forma numbers that I have seen correct?*
- *The bank is expanding its consumer loan portfolio at a high rate. I accept that India has a fast growing middle class, but will there be marginal borrowers?*
- *Management is optimistic on spreads. How realistic is this?*
- *There are questions relating to the reconciliation of US and Indian* GAAP. *The answers, no doubt, are in the merger documents which I do not have. Oh, Hhu [Hhu Ng, one of the analysts at* CIR] *you will have such fun devouring them. I am so jealous ...*

ICICI *is worthy of more research. Let's hope it has legs.*

It did not. However, the memo is an excellent illustration of what Peter meant by qualitative analysis. His observation of the slightly glib presentation and his doubts about the company's assumptions on margins and risk sound a quiet note of caution, while not ruling out the possibility of making the investment if warranted by a very careful examination of the numbers.

As soon as Peter got back to Europe, he and Joanie set off for what was to be almost their last holiday together. They joined a party for a cruise in the Aegean on the yacht *Callisto*, the last word in luxury. Even meals on deck were served with linen, crystal, and fine china, and the gourmet cuisine was worthy of a grand Parisian restaurant. Joanie loved it all but Peter, not so sure, escaped another "dining experience" to eat lamb cutlets in a *taverna* on shore. The lectures on Homer and the fall of the Mycenaean Empire especially interested Peter, particularly when given on deck looking up at the sheer cliffs of Santorini, most of which had disappeared into the sea in the eruptions that destroyed the Aegean civilization, the cradle of the heroes of the *Iliad*.

Eschewing the state-of-the-art equipment on board *Callisto*, Peter took most of his exercise ashore. *We moored off Fira on the volcanic island of Santorini whose huge crater defines the place. I climbed up to Fira in eighteen minutes, dodging mule shit, meeting mules with singing minders on their way down ... J joined me for a simple but delicious lunch ashore looking out onto a tiny bay, then back to Callisto for a lovely swim off the back of the ship.*

Back briefly in London before returning to Canyon Ranch, Joanie spoke to Peter about his trembling left hand and urged him to see a specialist. So far, the physicians had simply diagnosed the problem as "benign tremor." To Joanie it did not appear at all benign and she thought it perhaps the onset of Parkinson's disease. David Feather too had broached the subject some weeks earlier, revealing that his concern was shared by Jim Hunter, the CEO of Mackenzie. Although Peter was inclined to rely on the existing diagnosis, privately he was worrying to the extent of resorting occasionally to an anxiety medication.

Not satisfied to count his snowboarding lesson in Aspen as his annual dangerous adventure, he was delighted to receive a call from his friend Joshua Ramo in New York agreeing to facilitate an experience of something scarier – an aerobatic flight:

On Saturday, July 6, 2002, I duly appeared at Westchester County Airport ... Joshua is a journalist and author, TV commentator, linguist and athlete. He had flown down from Middlebury where he is in the midst of a Mandarin immersion course ...

The plane was an Extra 200 ... a two-person aircraft: the passenger in front and the pilot behind. There is not much space when one is wearing a parachute and one's head almost touches the plexi-glass. It was not comfortable; my legs were always on the verge of cramping up ...

We set off due north to a practice zone. Security has been tightened recently. One must stay five miles away from such things as nuclear facilities. I took the controls for about ten minutes as we reached 5,500 feet. Below us lay some of the most opulent estates in the world, with many small lakes. The Hudson River was to the west.

Then the fun began. Lots of rolls and loops. Two hammer-heads. This is when you are climbing perpendicular to the ground, then you flip and head straight for earth. We had some moments flying upside down. We did a stall and spin. It was like my pilot training days except faster. We did a short outside loop, which was at a negative 5G force level. At higher levels, eyeballs are stretched and severe headaches can result ...

I really enjoyed the experience. My need for being at physical risk is now assuaged for the year.

A few days after the flying adventure, the WorldCom Telecoms accounting scandal broke. While Peter was not surprised, what most concerned him was the obvious implication that Arthur Andersen, one of the "big five" accountancy firms, was either incompetent or had colluded in the giant $3.3 billion fraud. The company had sought to conceal its sharply deteriorating trading position by dishonest accounting, thereby avoiding pressure on the share price and enabling the senior executives to exercise their own stock options and sell the resulting shares into an unsuspecting and unrealistically buoyant market. In Peter's view, the accounting practices should have taken even a newly qualified CA no more than a few hours to detect and he felt that the damage to his profession would have a long-term impact on its standing and credibility.

Nevertheless, he could not resist some of the new definitions of accountancy acronyms that began to circulate and he forwarded one set to CIR in Vancouver.

- EBITDA, normally "earnings before interest, taxes, depreciation and amortization," became "earnings before I tricked the dumb auditor";
- EBIT, "earnings before interest and tax," became "earnings before irregularities and tampering";
- The more commonplace CEO was "chief embezzlement officer";
- CFO, "corporate fraud officer"; and
- EPS, the humble "earnings per share," became "eventual prison sentence."

The reality was sobering rather than funny, and led to the demise of the huge Arthur Andersen practice before year-end – which would have been almost unthinkable before the event. Despite the fall-out of the scandal in North American markets, however, Japan and the other Asian markets remained firm. And since Peter was nursing a significant cash pile in the funds, he was more jubilant than down-hearted and could congratulate himself on resisting considerable pressure to unwind his U.S. option hedges.

———————————

In a buoyant mood he set off with Joanie for their annual hiking holiday in Interlaken, and then returned to Aspen, where they celebrated her sixty-eighth birthday and Peter ran a half marathon in a new pair of Descente shoes, in which he achieved his best ever time of 1.41.

However there were darkening clouds on the horizon. The shaking of Peter's left hand worsened noticeably, and Joanie consulted her doctor about a constant irritation in her lower diaphragm. Not overly concerned, he had prescribed indigestion tablets and suggested a barium meal "just to check out what's going on." Peter left for Vancouver to spend a week in the office there and catch up with Steph, whom he had not seen all summer.

A visit to his doctor while he was there reiterated, after some tests, that Peter was indeed in peak condition and that his tremor was benign. But Joanie soon called to say that the barium had picked up a one-inch lump on her liver and that the blood tests were threatening: *Then my life changed. Joanie said that her blood test and scans showed that she has lots of cancer. The same as her mother. She is scared and I'm on my way to Aspen.*

When Peter reached Aspen, Joanie had decided to move back to Canyon Ranch as soon as possible, and he felt she was preparing for never returning, although hoping against hope that she would. They said very little, were warm and close, and stuck to routines like walking the dogs. Indeed, little could be said or done before the biopsy the following week. *I am trying to think of alternative scenarios. I will play it straight. It all depends on the severity of the cancer. She continues to lose weight. Soon we shall have a judgement. For the first time I am frightened for her.*

Peter returned to Vancouver to await events. She called to say that the biopsy had been easy and painless. Four days later she had the result: *The oncologist in Denver says she has 9–12 months to live. The only good thing is that she will probably not have chemo, radiation or surgery and she'll lead a normal life. I wonder. She is in shock.*

Returning to the new house in Canyon Ranch for the first time, he found it *full of peace and comfort*. It seemed a good sign that the two dogs and Emmie the cat had settled in at once and that there were lots of Mexican Birds of Paradise, both blue and yellow, in the garden – a good omen, according to the gardener. Joanie seemed calm, not in much pain and, although desperately thin, strong enough to go for walks.

Then the weather changed. Snakes and tarantulas scurried around the garden instead of the birds, and a massive Arizona storm broke with rolling black clouds, tearing winds and massive bolts of lightning. Joanie began to suffer considerable pain and confessed to moments of stark terror. She could feel the growth of the rogue cells, she said, and desperately wished for a miracle. Peter found it hard to cope with his helplessness; rubbing her back and writing her love notes was just not enough. Eventually, he persuaded her to seek a second opinion, to which she agreed only reluctantly, fearing that it would lead to a recommendation for the surgery she dreaded. Peter was glad to be able to busy himself with the practicalities of organizing the consultation and hiring a Lear jet to fly them to Houston.

The specialist there was more encouraging. He merely adjusted the medication, added something to relieve the pain, and offered a grain of hope. His view was that beating cancer had as much to do with willpower and a positive attitude as with medical treatment. It was music to their ears, perhaps especially to Peter, familiar as he was with Joanie's steely determination and reserves of fortitude. They returned to Canyon

Ranch, hoping at least that Joanie might shrink her tumour and return to perfect health.

Having generated this mood of optimism, Peter felt able to escape to London with Joanie's blessing. She was the ultimate pragmatist and knew full well how badly he tolerated any kind of confinement, especially when associated with illness. Her daughter Evelyn, her son Roger, the animals and the housekeeper would be at hand, and she knew that Peter, feeling slightly guilty, would keep in close touch. His flight to Heathrow on the anniversary of 9/11 was decidedly light on passengers.

On arrival at his new apartment at the Savoy, he changed into his smartest suit and strolled over to White's for a drink with James Hambro and Michael St Aldwyn to further his candidacy. *Louise came for a drink and then we dined at Simpson's in the Strand, right beside the Savoy – so old-fashioned that it could almost be a club. I love the atmosphere and the no-nonsense food ... I drank my first martini in some time and had a cigar. I shed a tear for Joanie and L was sweetly comforting.*

Peter slipped seamlessly into his London routines – dinner parties, Annabel's, his local standbys, a cocktail party at the magnificent house of Robert Tchenguiz, the Iraqi/Iranian Jewish entrepreneur to whom he had been introduced through Lady Khadouri in Hong Kong, and a concert at St Martin-in-the-Fields, where the program of Elgar and Tchaikovsky delighted him – perhaps partly because his pew placed him *practically in the lap of the very attractive and well-endowed first viola player.*

The Descente running shoes had regular outings: *Ran for an hour and a half in my Descente slippers. Felt strong ... Later called J. Her cancer count is way down. She's burning calories in the fight but eating well. Felt fully alive for the first time in several weeks.*

From London Peter went on to Toronto to discuss with Jim Hunter the next stage of the transfer of the Cundill Group's administrative functions over to Mackenzie – a process Peter was extremely keen to move forward. He took the opportunity to have a late night on the town with the Mackenzie gang. But he carried on with his routines. *I ran seven miles in the morning. Thought it would be difficult. "Au contraire," I was strong throughout and felt vitalized ... Later thought of J. My marriage is unconventionally conventional. She is my rock and my anchor. My angst is because I fear that I am about to be set loose. I have a desperate sense of malaise sometimes – turn sadness into joy. The doorman at the Four Seasons owns Cundill Value Fund!!*

In Vancouver again to press ahead with the admin transfer, he was very happy, for the moment, to be integrated into Steph's life. They played lots of tennis, took golf lessons together and saw old mutual friends – and he met Steph's parents. She was gentle and comforting as well as being stimulating company, and he was truly grateful. But it must have been obvious to him that she at least thought she was preparing the ground for a permanent relationship.

At the end of October Peter returned for a week at Canyon Ranch. However, he was nursing a cold and the doctor advised that, although he could see Joanie, it was best not to stay in the house until he was clear. *J looks just fine. I am upset that my cold prevents me from staying in the house. I asked her whether she ever gets scared. She says she's determined to beat it. Bravo! In fact she is worried. Her reaction to my cold is not overly concerning, although a real sensitivity. I brought up potential nursing care and her Will. Later she called me and suggested I loosen up and not panic. Rather unfair. We are in uncharted waters.*

Two days later, he was allowed back into the house. At the same time Joanie's cancer markers had dropped to 575 from a starting point at 10,000. *Hot bath and bed beside J. Lovely to be back in the conjugal bed. We said meaningful "I love you's" – she looks so graceful and calm in repose. She feels she can extend her life. Oh, I hope so.*

However, Peter soon became restless, and it was without enormous regret that Joanie said goodbye to him as he left for Tokyo. By mid-November he was in Hong Kong and just recovering from a spirited evening out with old friends when he received a heartbreaking call: *J was in hospital, having undergone major surgery on her colon. Constipation caused by the chemo blew up her insides. I called Evie on her cell. She was with J who, in spite of everything sounded strong ... I arranged to leave HK early and get to Vancouver to be closer to her.*

On the long flight Peter marshalled his thoughts, trying to accept the idea that Joanie's death was inevitable and likely soon. *I think that you can lose your fear of death by acknowledging that you are already dying from the moment you emerge from your mother's womb. Your body is a form that has no permanence. I find that I can only deal with the prospect of J's passing by sticking to ALL my routines as far as possible, reprehensible as some would feel this is. However, I am embarrassed to say that any respite from these falling markets pumps me up, and my concerns about J fall away a bit.*

When he arrived in Vancouver, he called Joanie and found her brave but in bad shape, and decided to continue right on to Tucson. At the Tucson Medical Centre he found Joanie with Evelyn and her husband, Mark. *Sometimes we talked, mostly she slept and I watched over her. I kept notes. Later she stood for a second or two. Sweet melancholy. Evie sad – no game face – J is dying! That night in our bed the dogs joined me.*

Unlikely as it had seemed, Joanie was strong enough to return home a week later and was walking on her own with a stick. Once again Peter felt he could leave, to attend the Cundill Board of Governors meeting in Toronto. On the plane, a passage from Roy Thomson's autobiography *After I Was Sixty* caught his eye: "After sixty I always had a restless feeling, a suspicion that I might be stagnating. Being a widower and my children settled I would have retired to loneliness. In any case, life was too exciting to retire. The brain is like a very sophisticated computer. My advice is to allow it to work, as it were, unattended. It will use your bank of experience and reach lateral conclusions, and otherwise obscure connections, intuitively. Intuition, emotion and intelligence are inextricably linked" (MW Books, 1975).

Back in Vancouver, he addressed a gathering of 650 distributors of Cundill products in the ballroom of the Four Seasons, where he was rapturously received. But later in the day he got news that Joanie's weight had dropped to 91 pounds – no more than a pre-pubescent child. After an evening with Steph, he returned to Canyon Ranch. He was struggling. *I am going through a personal maelstrom. Use the notebook to even out your feelings. Be aware of the unity of mind, body and spirit, keep to process, have measured responses. Try to find a degree of meaning in J's illness. Be never-endingly curious.*

He found Joanie incredibly gaunt but still in command of herself, although a vacant expression sometimes darkened her face. Intermittently she was in great pain. For Christmas Eve Peter arranged for a group of carollers to sing all the traditionals, and Joanie sang along with grandson Charlie, surrounded by the dogs. On Christmas day there was present opening with champagne, and Peter noted that Joanie had made a special effort to look her best. He was tearful, knowing that this would be the last and her time was short. Nevertheless, on Boxing Day he still left for London.

They're talking of another operation on J's stomach. The last thing she needs is another operation. She must just be allowed to slip away as painlessly as possible. I suspect it won't be a long wait. A sense of relief to be away from impending death for a bit. Spoke to J – weak and a bit frightened. Things are closing down.

By New Year's Day Joanie had begun to fade. Her son, Roger, relayed the grave news that she was entering a hospice state. Having made a tearful inventory of Joanie's few belongings at the Savoy apartment, Peter made his way to Heathrow and onto a flight to Phoenix.

Read a lot on the flight and began to think about alternatives, including what I do after J goes. Reflected gently on our life together. It's been pretty bloody good. When I arrived J was compos mentis – told me not to "hover"! Roger and his wife went out, and I spent several hours giggling with J before I faded, although there were some serious and memorable moments. I told her how she had taken care of me. She said I had given her a wonderful life. I shall treasure the exchange. She wants to stay with the pain rather than give in.

During the night Joanie awoke frightened of the wind. Peter held her tightly until she slept again and then walked the dogs in the dark. And so another week crept by with the phone ringing constantly and Peter occupying himself with administration while Joanie slept. *Worked on estate matters. I cancelled J's monthly allowance, which will save me $160,000 Cdn a year. The law of unintended consequences. For some reason my spirits were lifted ... When all this is done I will be a wealthy man with no responsibilities. More giving may be in order.*

At the end of the week Joanie had a completely lucid evening quietly reminiscing with Peter before falling asleep. He went out to the local steakhouse, where he found Evelyn and Mark: *Martini, steak, warmth, love and more reminiscence. I broke down into racking sobs. They were all very caring – a cathartic moment I hope.*

When he returned, Joanie appeared to be asleep but with shakes and dry heaves of her chest. She awoke very anxious, and Peter held her hand for five hours as she slipped into a coma: *In her coma J caressed my face which was wet with tears and my body was throbbing.*

There was a recording of the fourth Sunday in advent Christmas service playing. I hope J could hear it. Nurse Alma was there as her blood pressure plunged but she lasted the night. I was up again at 7.40. Roger said that the death process had begun ... It was not pretty. We took turns being on vigil. Was she frightened, in pain, or determined? Her spasms increased. Evie and I needed time away. We were in the exercise room when Roger rushed in to say that she had died ...

We worked on the details of death. I set off on the Canyon route in a relaxed and determined way, thinking how beautiful J had been in repose. I wanted to do it in less than an hour. Success, I did it for J. I did love her and I'm happy I told her so with the utmost conviction.

PART · FIVE ·

33

A Bachelor Again

PETER'S FIRST NOTEBOOK after Joanie's death reveals much about his state of mind and how he saw his future without her. *This is a journal of renewal and life.* On the journey from Canyon Ranch to Whistler he read very little, pondering instead the mental disciplines he knew would be essential in order to transform the experience of her death and the permanency of the loss into something positive. How might it be possible to turn the void created by her absence into a renewed fascination with life and bereavement into spiritual growth? Mere acceptance was not enough; an active effort to re-centre was required, and only positive action could alter the outcome favourably. He decided to grieve quietly and below the surface, although if tears came at unexpected moments that would be fine too:

I feel as though I am breaking out of the shell of my old life and emerging into a new awareness where the clarity of my present vision is merged with memory; at one with the universe, which is an orderly place governed by the immutable laws of nature. Death ... can be yet another triumph of the human spirit, as it was with J, who never lost her sense of dignity and courage. I am preparing for great adventures with a sometimes joyous heart.

Another consolation was the passion with which he had always approached his investment life, and he never lost his capacity for immersing himself in it. And then there were his ladies. So far, it had been possible to keep at bay those who might have had matrimonial aspirations. Peter had nearly always been unequivocal about his determination never to seek a divorce from Joanie. It was non-negotiable; his other companions either liked it or lumped it. Now, however, his status had changed and he failed at first to appreciate its full implications. Until January 14 he had been able to shelter behind his one permanent relationship, but this was no longer possible and he was vulnerable to pressure at the precise juncture in his life when his age and his health were making him less able to remain detached.

At lunch in London with two of his most loyal old friends, John Talbot and Jenny Bingham, he was full of bravado, boasting that he was now the most eligible bachelor in Britain and was going to make the most of it. Neither one was impressed. Jenny counselled caution: Peter might be wiser to see himself as a rich old man rather than an eligible Don Juan. Both she and John had a premonition that there was trouble ahead in which they, as his trustees, were likely to become embroiled. They little suspected to what extent.

The first intimations were not long in coming. When Peter returned to Vancouver Stephanie Nicolls was again his companion of choice and once more a loyal source of comfort, particularly after Maureen Crocker, his favourite and most confidential assistant, had died within two weeks of Joanie. Stephanie was no gold digger, but expectations had risen steadily – and not just in her own mind. Vancouver society is quite small, and she and Peter had been seen together for some time: there was a certain anticipation of a dénouement. She may not have been imagining imminent wedding bells, but she was seeking reassurance and at least some statement of commitment. When it was not forthcoming, she expressed concern about their relationship.

Back in London and at one remove from her, he wrote: *Steph says she's worried about* US *and where we're going. She feels I have been withdrawing from her. She has been incredibly helpful in both death and the healing process. From my point of view the question is open. I think a lot about J and how irreplaceable she is in almost every point. Considering that we are made up of energy particles, I wonder whether the impulses could ever be picked up and as it were reconstructed. I am quietly getting back into my old routines. Will I want to change them?*

He quickly realized the answer was no, but was considerably slower in conveying the message to other interested parties.

Peter's candidacy for White's was moving ahead satisfactorily and he was discovering that the club harboured a disproportionate number of Old Etonians in all their diversity. He was especially intrigued to discover that George Orwell, the socialist writer and satirist of the totalitarian state, although not a member of White's, had also been an Etonian. Reflections were prompted:

I see Orwell as a kindred spirit in many ways. He believed in the authenticity of the actual experience and he was obsessive about his work. He once described himself as a graphomaniac (good shorthand for a writer who's a workaholic). He was symbolic of that complete independence from convention that is one of the most attractive qualities of many Etonians ...

The physical violence of actual death is greatly on my mind ... I recently read [that] the Romans, and therefore certainly the Greeks before them, knew that hearing is the last of the faculties to be lost in the process of dying. They didn't verify decease by searching for a pulse but by calling the person's name loudly three times. If there was no response, the beckoner intoned the phrase "conclamatum est" – "he or she has been called." This pronouncement was considered to be the definitive assertion of death. Playing music to the dying, or to those in comas and continuing to talk to them must be a comfort and right to do. Equally, discussing the dying person or speaking as though they were no longer present could be very disturbing for them.

Meanwhile, the Stephanie saga continued. She called Peter in London, sick and in some distress. Fearing a resurgence of her earlier cancer, he hot-footed it back to Vancouver to see her. It was just a bad viral infection; nevertheless, the reunion was warm and Peter was especially sympathetic when he learned that she was a kindred sufferer from depressions. Still, the writing was already on the wall. He found the time to call another old friend to ask her out, and was rather put out when she declined because she was in another relationship. She, at any rate, had immediately divined that he had not suggested the outing just for old times' sake. She may also have been aware of Peter's involvement with Stephanie. However, what probably sealed Stephanie's fate was the revelation that she was in considerable financial difficulty: *Steph and I had tea together. I offered to help her out financially – I think this may be the beginning of the end. Maybe not. I care about her. She has been such a comfort.*

Once back in London, he went straight out to dine with one of his London flames at Sketch, the latest restaurant sensation in town. The lady in question evidently understood just how to pique the interest of aging Lotharios like Peter: she was under thirty and had told him he turned her on more than any other man. Pleased as he was, he was not impressed by Sketch, where the bill was an eye-popping £990 for two. This admittedly included a bottle of white wine for £395, but Peter disdainfully remarked that the sommelier had been idiotic to decant it, that the place had far too many hovering staff, and had the effrontery to charge £59 a portion for a starter of langoustines. However, he was still preening himself over the flattery on his way into the City the next day.

Returning to the Savoy, Peter walked past St Paul's Cathedral. On the spur of the moment he went in and knelt for a few minutes to *commune with J*. Very softly he murmured the epitaph he had composed for her. It says a great deal about the reality of their relationship, or at least what it had been in Peter's mind:

My beauty
My strength
My Fair lady
My laughter
My good sense
My Mama bear
My companion
My True Love
My Bird of Paradise.

As he rose to leave, he noticed a memorial plaque that bore a quotation from the Beatitudes: "Blessed are they that mourn for they shall be comforted."

Back at the apartment good news awaited him: he had been elected to White's. There was also a "very serious" fax from Steph giving him his "marching orders": *I suspect that we are into the end game. I think that she's wise. I have no idea how I shall react.* After which Peter poured himself a glass of champagne and settled down to watch the bombardment of Baghdad.

Although the tremor in Peter's left hand was not continuous, he had noticed that the attacks, when they came, were more severe each time. Peter took himself off once more to see Dr Michael Gormley in search of a diagnosis or at least some further reassurance that this was not the onset of Parkinson's. The response was unchanged – "benign tremor" – and Peter was momentarily elated. However, he nursed a nagging sense that this was not the end of the story: *I am beginning to feel a sense of mortality that I never felt before. The speeds are slower, the hangovers*

*last a bit longer – no joy, just duty. That's not really true but I suppose
that I have a lurking suspicion that I'm waiting for Godot.*

From an investment standpoint, 2003 was shaping up to be a bumper
year. He was especially optimistic about developments in Japan, where
the Central Bank was making strenuous efforts to kick start the economy
out of the long deflationary slump that had persisted since 1990. Interest
rates were being maintained at zero and liquidity was being pumped into
the system; unemployment was low and, perhaps most important in
Peter's view, Sino-Japanese economic relations were developing just as
he had foreseen. The Japanese were investing heavily in China, setting
up manufacturing facilities that employed cheap Chinese labour, and the
profits were flowing back into corporate Japan. In this context Peter sent
a memo to the Cundill Investment Research team in Vancouver:

The Hiraki Shoe Company had a heel-making factory in Ikino, a
small town not far from Kyoto. Once a thriving silver mining town,
the ore ran out in 1973, at about the same time as Japan's economic
miracle. Ikono's population plunged from 15,000 to 5,000 (we have
many such examples in Canada). This year Hiraki, whose facility
had taken up some of the slack, closed it down, at the same time
ending any manufacturing production anywhere in Japan. However,
Hiraki is still selling shoes, plenty of them, but they're made in
China and shipped into the spanking state of the art China port at
Kobe. Huge forty-foot containers are then trucked to Hiraki's enormous warehouse from which the shoes are sold by mail order – 10
million of them every year and growing ...

What's the explanation? Employing a factory worker in Japan
costs roughly $700 a week, $300 in Taiwan and just $25 in China
... Of course, there is no doubt that this differential will shrink and
largely disappear over a decade or so, but in the meantime both the
Japanese and the Chinese economies will have been transformed – in
fact the transformation will impact right across Asia Pacific. We
shall do well in the region. For us as value investors, flux usually
spells opportunity.

Another memo followed in quick succession, striking a note of caution about the housing bubble in the U.S.:

> The absolute fixation over consumer-price inflation that possesses most Central Banks is leading them to ignore some other important signs of financial imbalance. As a consequence the Fed has paid little heed to the sharp expansion of excess liquidity in the system ... There now seems to be a willingness among financial institutions to fund this bubble in the housing market on ever more questionable terms. Unless the Fed takes action this spells major trouble down the road. I have reflected that during Japan's much vaunted property bubble, which collapsed in 1991 and heralded the long period of recession and stagnation, the rise was only 36% in real terms in the housing market over the seven preceding years – considerably less than has been the case so far in the U.S. People are going to get hurt and so will institutions. I am certain that we are right to be emphasizing Japan and Asia in our portfolios and we need to be doubly cautious in our investment selections in the U.S.

———————————

Peter shared the news of Joanie's death with Chantale Joseph, his friend from Trader Vic's. CJ, as she shortly became known, was a tall Nigerian lady by then in her early thirties. She told him that she came from an influential and aristocratic Nigerian family forced by political persecution to seek asylum in Sweden, where she had been brought up until, at the age of nineteen, she had been spotted on the streets of Stockholm by a modelling agent and brought to London. Her exotic glamour attracted him and he found her deep voice with its pronounced Nigerian intonations alluring. She became a regular visitor.

As a result Peter's interest in the history of the "Dark Continent" rose by a notch or two: *I am always intrigued by tales of "reversal of fortune," either individual, like that of my Cundill grandfather, or collective ... I have been reading an account of the origins of Rwanda's genocide. It would appear that it was not an ethnic cleansing in a true sense since both the Hutus and the Tutsis are ethnically the same, speak the same language and follow the same native religious practices ... Intrinsically this was revolution not genocide per se, however disgusting. I wonder if the same sort of thing could occur in Nigeria. In any event it is an illustration of how vital it is to have a thorough understanding of history without which workable solutions are impossible to achieve. The colonial powers have consistently failed to appreciate the historical background in constructing the legacy systems that they imposed as they left.*

Early in the summer Peter flew out to Las Vegas to attend the Manulife Financial Corporation's conference, where he met David Ben, a Toronto tax lawyer who had resigned from his tax practice to become a magician. Any *volte-face* of that nature fascinated Peter and he struck up a friendship with Ben, ending up on stage with him, "lending a hand." Afterward, Ben gave Peter a copy of his book *Advantage Play*:

To CIR –
As you know I have made friends with David Ben, a most remarkable man and an amazing magician. I have just begun reading his book and his description of what's needed to solve problems caught my eye so I thought I would share it with you: "Persistence, diligence, grace under pressure and management of resources." Hopefully that's us!

He went on to New York to attend the Association for Investment Management and Research conference on international equities:

Discussion centred on equity valuation in a global context. One of my sadnesses is how homogenized global financial statements are becoming. One of our proprietary skills has been having the know-how to translate the differences for our own purposes. The use of EBITDA [earnings before interest, taxation, depreciation and amortization] methodology is dangerous and sometimes reckless. Why, in the face of plentiful evidence that it is a marginal analytical tool, do we use it? I, of course, would stick with P/E's [price to earnings ratios] and free cash flow analysis. Old man that I am!

There was no discussion of balance sheets. I tried to come up with something that would draw this analytical focus away from the statement of profit and loss with its forecasts of earnings and introduce some form of terminal value forecasting based on liquidation or SOP [Sales and Operations Planning] forecasting. The answer is, of course, that we are doing this already with much skill and discipline. Perhaps what we should be doing is tidying up our various method-ologies into a complete process and contributing it to the academic journals. Volunteers, please!

———————————

Having lectured his research team once again on the subject of margins of safety, Peter himself flew back to London to undertake that year's scary adventure. Early one fine morning his driver picked him up to motor him to Royal Air Force Weston-on-the-Green just north of Oxford. Peter takes up the account:

I found my instructor ... in an old hangar where the other "free-fallers" were getting ready .... Our party was ten, of whom ... most were in their twenties and thirties – one man of 45 and then me, the grandfather. My "pilot," with whom, as a first time free-faller, I was to make the descent in a tandem parachute, was called Darryl, an RAF instructor. We circled up to 12,000 feet into thin, high cloud cover. We were last out. High fives and a knuckle touch for luck. My instructions were to let Darryl bear my weight. I was to cross my legs and keep my arms folded .... For 40 sec-onds, which seemed much longer, we descended in free fall before the parachute jerked open. The feeling is somewhere between floating and falling. One is face down. Flying through the wispy cloud, I had an eerie sensation of what it might be like to be an angel and then a really exhil-arating feeling, such as might have tempted Icarus to climb toward the sun. I moved my arms akimbo after the chute opened. Dropping from 12,000 feet to 5,000, I did 360s to see the world and watch the quilted patchwork of the fields unfold. Then we seemed to accelerate, with the ground leaping up at us. At 800 feet Darryl began to position us and he landed us perfectly on flat ground. The whole drop took only five minutes but my heart stayed pumped for a good half hour afterward and the adrenalin rush lasted for the rest of the day ... I felt as though I was embracing the beauty of rural England with my heart in my mouth. I went to bed feeling fulfilled.

Deciding it was time to end the affair with Stephanie, Peter wrote her a farewell note. The decision was likely prompted by the fact that he had met a very attractive Canadian alternative in Montreal – Josée Nadeau, a young French Canadian painter with talent in the impressionist style that so captivated Peter. She was beautiful, and also recently divorced. On the evening they met, she invited Peter to her studio where they *drank a little wine and smoked a little grass* and he lingered until nearly four a.m. The next morning took them to the Montreal Museum of Fine Arts for an exhibition of Vuillard, a French post-impressionist painter with whose work Peter was not familiar. Josée enthusiastically took care of that deficiency, treating him to an animated critique on colour. Peter was enchanted once again.

On a flight on a private aircraft to Cap à l'Aigle the next morning, he pondered his latest conquest: *I thought of Josée and I'm really looking forward to seeing her again. I admire her continuous artistic struggle to perfect her work. I should be doing the same with the same level of intensity. Is this a one-day infatuation or something else?*

At Cap à l'Aigle the lilac was still in full bloom, a good three months later than in London. Peter put up at the Auberge de la Pinsonnière, a Relais & Château hotel that looked directly out across the great sweep of the St Lawrence. At the Sunday service in St Peter's on the Rock, he sat beside an old family friend and admired the new roof that he had made possible. The weather was balmy with a light breeze coming off the river as he walked back along the cliffs to visit Frank Cabot's world-famous "Four Winds" garden. The garden is a complete experience, combining classical music with stunning views of the river and the mountain landscape behind. It rises steadily back into the hills from the cliffs, and includes a lake, a Japanese garden with a tea-house, an ornamental French vegetable garden, and a garden enclosed by tall, thick hedgerows that surround a magnificent eighteenth-century dovecote. As Peter knew, it was Cabot's life's work, and although they did not particularly like each other, it was impossible not to admire the achievement, made all the more remarkable by the challenges of the near-arctic winter climate.

He dined alone in the rather overly grand restaurant at the Auberge but he had Cabot's lavishly illustrated book to keep him company: *The book, "The Greater Perfection" is superb. Cynthia Ryan, who was my senior Banquo in that Macbeth production here years ago, also plays a role in this story. I gather Frank has the Governor General staying this weekend. I smoked my cigar on the deck with a glass of champagne. The river views at dusk are extraordinary, especially "entre chien et loup" – just before nightfall when you can't distinguish a dog from a wolf. There is that hint of being on an uncertain threshold, between the familiar and the comfortable and the unknown and the dangerous – between hope and fear.*

When Peter got back to Montreal he called Josée and left a message: *Josée finally called back – I was there in 15 minutes. We hugged and talked. I had intended just a brief visit but I stayed for over three hours. She says she has been influenced by our visit to the Vuillard – so have I – but I worry about the wine and the grass. It could be an impediment.*

It was: *Josée came to meet me at the Ritz. We had a wonderful fun lunch. She swam in the pool and we spent the afternoon and evening together. She said she would come to the airport to see me off on the trek to Aspen. I waited until the last minute to leave the hotel. I couldn't reach Josée. I'm disappointed. She is impulsive and unreliable and she drinks and smokes too much. Although I'm fond of her she's erratic. Is it magic? Maybe not. Too bad.*

———————

The memorial for Joanie in Aspen was attended by about forty close family and friends. Joanie's children, Evelyn and Roger, both spoke with humour and affection. Peter spoke of how grief and emptiness can be transformed into fond remembrance. His theme clearly struck a chord because several moments of silence passed before the clapping began. The flowers were sensational, favouring Peter's preferred colour, blue, and the music was Bach and Vivaldi, Joanie's favourites. At first light the next morning Peter, Evelyn, and Roger drove up Aspen mountain to a tent beside the Gondola, where Roger scattered his mother's ashes. *It was a sort of closure. The mountains became stark as we drove down again. Ashes weigh more than I'd imagined.*

From Aspen, he had made arrangements to have lunch with Stephanie in Vancouver at the weekend. The conclusion was that the affair was not in fact over and Peter invited her to join him in New York as his companion before his annual conference and the annual Aspen Institute dinner. In the interim he headed back to London. For the moment he had decided that his interest in CJ was not something about which he wanted to go public. Meanwhile, he had begun to feel that he wanted a London companion who would not particularly attract attention at the Royal Opera House, Harry's Bar, or the Caprice. He had just been introduced to Jane Dobson, a very attractive, elegant and eminently suitable divorcee. She was warm and charming and lived in a pretty flat on Pont Street in Knightsbridge. They quickly became close and Peter invited her to spend the New Year with him in Hong Kong, knowing she would fit in perfectly with his friends there.

Back in New York Peter settled in at the Pierre to await Stephanie's arrival: *I got a tumultuous welcome. Steph in great form. We had a long walk in Central Park and went to the Met to look at Jackson Pollock and the El Greco drawings. We had supper in the suite. David Feather called to say we were chosen as fund manager of the year. Lovely sense of companionship. Steph got me to focus on her life rather than mine. A fulsome day.*

Peter got to Hong Kong in time to attend the "Legends" Christmas Lunch at the Hong Kong Club, for which about twenty of the island's great and good assemble annually to celebrate the season. Percy Weatherall, the then Taipan of Jardine Matheson, was present, and he and Peter got along famously. (Taipan – "big shot" in Cantonese – is the traditional title accorded in Hong Kong to the heads of the two great trading houses, Jardine's and Swire's.). He spent Christmas Day with Carol and Allan Murray at the home of Sir Sydney Gordon overlooking Repulse Bay, and on Boxing Day the Murrays drove him over to the famous golf club at Shek-O, where Weatherall re-introduced him to Sir Adrian Swire, the other Taipan. New Year in Hong Kong with Jane was a success. As Peter had anticipated, she fitted seamlessly into Hong Kong society. No eyebrows were raised.

Jane and I went to the HK Club to meet Carol and Allan Murray. We were a party of 13 hosted by Lester and Kelly Kwon. It was an elaborate meal with a choice selection of wines. There was a great cabaret and

music. All very lively. Cried a little at midnight. Jane v kind. We trans-
ferred our flag eventually to the 48th floor at Jardine House. More danc-
ing – lots of hilarity, some inanity – usual sort of stuff. We left early at
3.30 am! My first raucous New Year in many years. Nevertheless, I enjoyed
the Joanie years of early to bed.

34

Time Present

FROM AN INVESTMENT standpoint 2003 had been an outstanding year, turning in a 35% increase in the Value Fund. However, among the senior portfolio managers within the Cundill Investment Research group, there was some dissatisfaction. Much of the gain had stemmed from Japan, where 40% of the fund's assets were invested, and a further 10% in other Asian markets had performed equally well. Consequently, the stars of the team were those involved with Far Eastern investments, and the North American end was feeling somewhat under-appreciated. This was particularly true for Tim McElvaine.

For several years it had been vaguely assumed that Peter's mantle would eventually pass to McElvaine, but there had been no formal statement to that effect; nor had there been any significant restructuring of the control of the business. Peter remained paramount both in terms of ownership and management. As a result McElvaine, who was inclined with some justification to regard himself as a star in his own right, had become increasingly restless, satisfied neither with his position within the firm nor with his ability to build up significant personal wealth through owning equity in the business.

For Peter the question was clouded by personal feelings. He had always believed he would be able to run the company he had created until he was well into his eighties. He had longevity in his genes, and was supremely fit, having always enjoyed perfect health. What's more, he had models in Warren Buffet, Irving Kahn, and Al Gordon. Appointing a chief executive in waiting would be tantamount to admitting that his tremor was serious. Furthermore, he resisted any plan that might involve a significant dilution of his personal equity interest. This reluctance was fatal to the relationship with McElvaine, who finally resigned in order to start up a fund management business of his own.

Peter immediately recognized the significance of the loss: *I'm now going to be forced to do something concrete about a successor. I suppose*

Tim's continued presence shielded me from that pressure ... In any case
do we not have internal strengths that we can draw on when it really
does become necessary? In my view it's entirely premature.

There was a streak of petulance in the precipitate manner of
McElvaine's departure that he subsequently came to regret, and he discovered that life outside the "Cundill family" was not quite as easy as he
had anticipated. Nevertheless, he received active and generous support
from Peter in the new enterprise, and his old mentor rapidly became one
of his largest clients.

The relationship with McElvaine was not the only one that was limp-
ing to a close. Although a reunion with Stephanie Nicolls in Vancouver
at the end of January had begun well, it steadily deteriorated as she perceived a certain detachment on Peter's part. A few days after his return
to London he received a fax from her, the like of which he had never
experienced before. It did not make for comfortable reading:

> I think I had a reasonably calm statement of facts on the phone
> today when you called me from your new home in yet another
> 5-star hotel. That is, until it declined into an inane, stupid, Peter-
> centred conversation about how many minutes you pumped weight
> for, or stretched before your daily run.
>
> I don't feel special, or loved, or cherished by you. I used to. You
> used to say that I was the most wonderful woman you had ever met,
> that you were quite *bouleversé*. By the end of today's conversation
> you became really quite tongue-tied. Why? ... Were you being honest
> with me? Once again you swore up and down that there was no one
> else. You said these aren't the kind of weekends where we could be
> together because you are working very hard. I challenged you on
> that one and asked you what difference that made ... we could still
> be together. I feel distanced from you because of the shallow level
> that you now seem to operate on with me.
>
> I don't understand how, aged almost 66, you do not want to
> treasure and hang on to the best thing that ever happened to you in
> your life – that would be me. You had the gall to tell me you were
> very fond of me (which is pretty much how people feel about freshly
> squeezed orange juice or gravy with their Yorkshire pudding). You
> told me that you would always be there for me in any way I needed

no matter what happens. I don't want that unless we are staying together. Even if it were what I wanted, it is cold comfort. Why would "being there" for me start now at the end of the relationship?

Perhaps for a man having such a deep (though unnecessary) need to remain forever youthful in your own physicality, requiring such constant reassurance about how flat your lovely tummy is, it is only to be expected that you would have a misguided concept of love. Love gets better and deeper the more you give it to your lover. I am in love with a man who cannot bear to face his own mortality. The measure of a man is the congruency of his words with his actions, his kindness, his confidence and his decisiveness about who he is in the world and who he wants to continue to be. For the sake of our friendship at least be honest with me.

Shortly after this bombshell, Stephanie again fell ill with another viral infection and had to be hospitalized. Coincidentally Peter's regular health check and comprehensive blood test revealed that he was a carrier of amoebic dysentery, although without symptoms. Could Stephanie's illness be related? Although he was told it was highly unlikely, and unnecessary to disclose, knowing that amoebic dysentery is notoriously unpleasant and hard to cure, he promptly informed her. In that mood of concern, he had walked over to the Temple Church, knelt quietly in the peaceful medieval atmosphere and said a prayer for her. As it turned out, the infection was not at all related.

Strangely, his reaction to Stephanie's robust fax had been fairly muted: *Read SN's note – a bit wounding and hurtful, but I understand. I feel rather empty as this comes to a close.*

They met for what he termed an "exit interview." *Semi-candid on my part. I told her that I do not love her enough, but omitted to say that I lost all my ardour when she was ill and that I'm now physically turned off. However I don't want to hurt her. My old life is unravelling in a way and my new one is embryonic. I had a dream where Joanie cheated on me. Is this closure? It is something I knew and yet did not want to know.*

If Peter was expecting closure from the "exit interview," he was to be disappointed. Stephanie was in serious financial difficulty, in part because she had made herself available to Peter to the detriment of her livelihood. The uncertainties of the relationship had undoubtedly also contributed to her health problems. Of course Peter did help, but he did not feel the case merited a pension for life: *I'm having a continuing sad dialogue with SN. I am now not only out of love, I'm having trouble with like.*

The "dialogue" descended into recriminations and eventually into threats which, empty as they may have been, did worry Peter from the point of view of public perception. Eventually they reached a financial settlement – which ought to have served as a caveat to him against future developments.

His lack of candour with Stephanie was in his insistence that there was no one else in his life and that he was "just a bit of a lone wolf." Nothing could have been further from the truth; he was in fact an extremely merry widower. Besides the ships that passed in the night, there were two other ladies in Vancouver, at least three in London, and a new friend in Toronto.

He had met Phyllis Ellis in the lobby of the Four Seasons. She had dropped her cellphone without noticing and Peter gallantly retrieved it. Since she was most attractive, he proffered it with a small flourish and rather a good line: "Now you can just say thank you to me and then we'll both go our separate ways, or you can treat this as an opportunity and have a glass of champagne with me."

Phyllis, a divorcee in her mid-forties, was a professional comedienne who often appeared on television performing her own material. She was extremely intelligent, with a mischievous sense of fun, and had been a considerable athlete until suffering a back injury. She had a strong sense of social responsibility, devoting time and energy to charitable projects mainly related to addressing delinquency among Toronto's urban youth. In this respect she differed from the majority of Peter's other attachments and he was pleased to take an interest because he was reassessing the direction of his own philanthropy. Above all Phyllis was a great companion with a mind of her own, and was ready to challenge and to tease. She had a strong streak of the feminist that refused to tolerate the domineering male, and Peter found this refreshing, especially as he quickly discovered that she could still be dazzled.

In London, meanwhile, Chantale Joseph was fast becoming Peter's local girlfriend of choice. There was, of course, the usual round of fine dining and dancing at Annabel's. But there was also a subtle change in Peter's routines. As Stephanie had discovered, Peter had the habit of excluding female company, other than Joanie, when he was working or just disinclined to have a late night. Now CJ was allowed to be around from time to time, watching "soaps" on television while Peter read, and they would occasionally watch videos together over supper on the sofa. She was promoting an element of domesticity in the relationship, which she could see Peter quite enjoyed.

In due course, the six weeks that Peter had spent in the Far East early in the year elicited a classic Cundill memo entitled "China and Japan: An Unconscious Partnership Unfolds":

Hong Kong was mostly fun and very social. My friend Allan Murray of Jardine's bravely acted "in loco parentis." His outline of my schedule came with the instruction to bring my dinner jacket and my liver. I did. I used both!

The entire Hong Kong establishment passes through Allan's dining room, so there was plenty of well-informed gossip and apposite insights to be had. The current Governor is disliked to a degree which reminds me of the waning months of the Mulroney years. At the same time there is a general view that there is good governance, so I am a little puzzled ... The city is suffering from a recession that has been festering since 1997, mostly related to real estate. The turnaround actually began while I was there. It was sudden and dramatic.

I did a day trip to Shenzhen. When I last passed through some years ago it was a construction zone. Now ... the central area feels like Hong Kong ... The purpose of my visit was to research one of our positions in the Recovery Fund, Sinolink. The holding company is controlled by one Thomas Ou, aged forty-one who ... spent his youth behind a horse-drawn plough before getting out to Hong Kong. In 1991 he committed to buy some 86 acres of Shenzhen from an arm of the municipality – the kind of "cosy" arrangement for which the PRC is becoming well known ...

I wanted to explore the capacity of the management and the sanctity of the accounts. Sinolink is listed in Hong Kong and has well-known accountants and lawyers. My sense of the financials is that they are in order ... I judge the management to be honest and competent so I am content to stay with the holding and build on the relationship ...

In Tokyo what was a general move toward investment in China has turned into a stampede. Among our pet holdings Nipponkoa has set up a joint venture with AIG to sell insurance to Japanese expatriates. Horipro, our talent manager, is promoting Japanese singers in China. This is most surprising given the general assumption that Chinese antipathy towards all things Japanese is unrelenting and universal. Descente, our luxury sporting goods producer, is manufacturing in the PRC and opening retail outlets there. The beat goes on.

The combined GNP of Japan and China is now not that far off the U.S.A. Once this partnership gets its full legs (and it will) the U.S.'s global leadership is going to be challenged. The economic self-interest of both is clearly going to override the tensions of recent history. After all, we Canadians burnt down the White House and we seem to have been forgiven. Well, sort of.

One of the ways to buy into China is to buy Japan, which we will continue to do.

The Benjamin Graham symposium at the Penn Club in New York was packed with old friends and associates. But Peter chiefly spent time with Walter Schloss, a doyen of the value-investing community who began his career as a runner on Wall Street in 1934. He had no college education but took Graham's investment course at the New York Stock Exchange Institute, alongside Gus Levy, who later became chairman of Goldman Sachs. After working in the Graham-Newman partnership, he began managing money on his own, and from 1955 until closing his fund in 2000, he produced a compound return of 15.3%. Schloss was recognized in Warren Buffett's article "The Superinvestors of Graham-and-Doddsville": "He knows how to identify securities that sell at considerably less than their value to a private owner. And that's all he does ... I don't seem to have much influence on Walter. That is one of his strengths; no-one has much influence on him." One could be pardoned for supposing that this was a description of Peter.

Peter was soon back in London again. However his frenetic round of activity clearly concealed an underlying apprehension. Striving for eternal youth was exhausting, and he could no longer ignore the realities of aging. Without any religious conviction, it had become impossible to believe he was journeying toward a meaningful afterlife; his *modus vivendi* was to lurch uncomfortably between a kind of stoical acceptance of the brevity of personal existence and a form of highly charged Epicureanism.

In this mood of uncertainty he chanced upon a poem by the English poet Philip Larkin: *I read some Larkin yesterday and was much struck with "Aubade" ... It is filled with unwavering honesty and an absolute willingness to face the truth, no matter how uncomfortable. It is witty in that iconoclastic Larkin vein, but stark too:*

I work all day, and get half-drunk at night.
Waking at four to soundless dark, I stare.
In time the curtain-edges will grow light.
Till then I see what's really always there:
Unresting death, a whole day nearer now,
Making all thought impossible but how
And where and when I shall myself die.
Arid interrogation: yet the dread
Of dying, and being dead,
Flashes afresh to hold and horrify.

I can identify with every single strand of his thought and imagery. I could have written the poem [which extends to five verses] myself, had I known how. It is on those dark nights of the soul that it is most easeful to turn to another human body breathing peacefully, cushioning one's darkness against warm, yielding flesh.

His relationship with CJ was becoming more intense. She gave him a fine silver-framed full-length photograph of herself, with which Peter was enchanted and it was displayed prominently. Peter was acutely conscious that as a recognized companion in his life she might provoke adverse reaction from colleagues, professional associates, and friends. Nevertheless, CJ was very keen that the forthcoming Cundill conference in London that November should be the occasion of her coming out. For

Peter this was as yet a step too far, but he conceded that she should attend the grand closing dinner at Somerset House, although not as his date and not at his table.

Still in doubt as to how he wanted to proceed with CJ, he invited Phyllis to join him for Christmas at Canyon Ranch, where he realized he was likely to be scrutinized by some of Joanie's oldest friends. Like the previous year in Hong Kong with Jane Dobson, Phyllis's visit was eminently successful: *Phyl may be the ideal companion – stimulating, amusing talk, though not as exotic as CJ, and well able to occupy herself. The certainty of death is overcome by the possibilities of life! Make this decade count. Face down the inexorable fact of age!*

From an email Phyllis sent Peter after Canyon Ranch it is easy to understand the pleasure he took in her company and her fascination with him. Did he but realize it, age was not much of an issue:

> It was a freezing bleak afternoon. She had left him early that morning rushing out of the hotel and back to life. Her time with him was spent often in bed, punctuated with meaningful conversation. For the most part bed meant sex, deeply satisfying lovemaking, on demand. Twenty years and oceans apart, the sex defied all gaps in perception.
>
> Theirs began quite by chance after a black-tie affair. She dropped her cell phone, he picked it up and said, "You can either take this and say thank you OR see it as a wonderful opportunity." After two bottles of champagne she pondered the latter and so it began.
>
> He lived abroad, she lived at home. He widowed, she divorced and while he had lost the love of his life, she was waiting for hers. After 45 years and as many suitors, she approached the possibilities with consternation.
>
> He surpassed her in intelligence and she found her total ineptitude for his world of finance a mystery. She wondered if a section of her brain were injured at birth because for her, numbers usually implied "insufficient funds." It was a personal source of great shame and humiliation and of amusement only to her loved ones. She accepted this not as a challenge but as a fact. He was in control and she was willing to follow his lead, even if it was the "emotionally unavailable" leading the "emotionally detached." Somehow that union

made for excellent bed-mates, which in her mind added up ...

And the story continues ...

Back in London after the holidays, Peter was compelled to acknowledge that his "benign tremor" was becoming increasingly severe. At Canyon Ranch he'd had a bad, bruising fall while out running – an indication that his balance was now affected.

Nevertheless, irrespective of his general health, Peter was planning his annual challenge – a "fire walk." It was to take place at an uninspiring venue, a shopping centre in Milton Keynes, a dormitory city north of London with a reputation as the most boring town in Britain. Peter joined a group of twenty-five, the majority of whom were in their late twenties, making him the oldest by several decades. The fire pit had been constructed in the plaza of the shopping centre, and the training session took place in the conference hall of one of the supermarket chains.

I was a mixture of apprehension and anticipation. My balance continues to be a bit ropey. All I could think about is what would happen if I fell over. The instructor was ... a Martial Arts expert who had picked up this craft in India. He was most direct, with a tendency towards profanity; there were no mantras. However ... he had never had anyone who did not proceed with the event and no-one had ever suffered any form of injury – always a first time I thought! ...

He began helpfully by pointing out how hot the fire was with lots of white burning embers. He discussed the nature of burning and the physiology of our feet. Then he drew us together by having us role-play emotions from depression to euphoria, with lots of shouting and cheering. It worked. By the time we hit the pit we were a unit ...

There were about a hundred and fifty spectators ringing the fire. The pit was perhaps ten yards long. One of the other instructors pre-ran the course. Then we lined up. Martin asked us if we were ready. I was second in line. I was very focused – not surprisingly. There was no pain, nor even a hint of it. The time elapsed can have been no more than five seconds. I moved quickly and yelled. Breathing is important. We cheered the rest on as they came through.

I had to wash the ash off the soles of my feet when I got back to London. The experience is the real thing. The group dynamics are important. Would it still be riskless if one extended the course? I just don't know. I'm glad I did it.

Peter, of course, was quite aware of the intellectual disparity between Phyllis and CJ, who were now his two principal girlfriends. At some level he found CJ's lack of sophistication endearing and felt that, combined with the obvious power of money, it gave him the upper hand in their relationship. This turned out to be a grave miscalculation. At the same time Peter's own intellectual capacity was in no sense on the wane. His curiosity and sensitivity were as lively as ever, as his journal entry about the 2004 tsunami in the Indian Ocean attests:

The tsunami is being heralded as the world's worst-ever disaster and the death toll is continuing to climb. Nevertheless other earthquakes have undoubtedly caused more fatalities. 500 thousand died in Bangladesh in 1970 and many more in China in 1976 ... The thing about this one that has so shocked the world is the direct visual exposure to the tragedy through real-time footage taken on thousands of cell phones and camcorders. All of these images underlined the tsunami's universality in claiming victims and whole families from across the entire globe as they holidayed far from home, basking in the Christmas sunshine, oblivious of impending doom. It is often the smallest details that engage our emotions and our compassion – the half-eaten breakfast on the table in Pompeii and, in this instance, a baby's tiny body bobbing in the water among the flotsam.

Coincident with Peter's aggravated trembling and unreliable balance, a new chief executive arrived at Mackenzie. That Charlie Sims was an accountant by profession immediately recommended him to Peter, as did the fact that his career to date had been successfully spent almost entirely within the Franklin Templeton group to which Sir John Templeton, Peter's friend and mentor, had sold his own business before retiring. By

now the Cundill stable of funds was the jewel in the Mackenzie crown
and Peter, as its head, was recognized and admired throughout Canada
and internationally.

But Mackenzie did not own Cundill Investment Research, which held
the management contract for all the funds and was still controlled by
Peter. Consequently Mackenzie, although it enjoyed considerable influence through the marketing agreements, did not have ultimate sanction.
In addition to which, although Peter's professional faculties remained
unimpaired, it was evident that his health was likely to become a problem. Succession required addressing sooner rather than later, but Peter
was continuing to drag his heels and Mackenzie could do little about it.
It did not take Sims long to conclude that the solution might lie in
Mackenzie making an outright purchase of CIR that would enable him
to insist on a serious search for Peter's successor. He also felt that, if successful, the acquisition would be something of a feather in his cap.

Preliminary discussions proceeded almost immediately, with Peter
playing his cards fairly close to his chest – *not particularly keen but might
perhaps be persuaded by an outstandingly good offer*. The reality was
somewhat different. Beneath the surface Peter was seriously worried
about his condition and was coming to the view that the problem was
anything but benign. Sims was unwittingly pushing at a door that was
already ajar.

As might have been expected, Peter's questionable physical state
seemed to him to have equally serious implications for his personal relationships. For all his surface confidence and bravado, he was afraid of
finding himself bereft of companionship if a transformation were to take
place from a supremely athletic middle age to some form of terminal disability. In considering the question of a female companion who would
be prepared to see him through, the options now appeared much more
limited than in the months after Joanie's death. The evident candidates
were now Phyllis and CJ.

At about this juncture I had lunch with him. The conversation began
with Peter giving an impressive account of his "romantic" rampages
around the globe. However, it gradually concentrated on the gap that
Joanie had left in his life and his need for a substitute, although he could
not imagine anyone who would be as tolerant of his life style as she had
been. He could see clearly that Phyllis was more suitable from a conventional

standpoint – she would be loyal and could be trusted implicitly – but she would insist on being a wife in the full sense. His wings would inevitably have to be clipped or he would lose her.

CJ was another matter; he thought that she could perhaps be controlled through the purse strings. Marriage in her case might not be essential and possibly not in fact desirable. I was fairly sure Peter was looking for a friendly ear rather than advice, which it would in any case have been unwise to give without knowing either of the candidates. However, Peter did offer some account of CJ's temperament, and he shared a short email he had received from Phyllis:

> Peter, you are a curious polymath ...
>
> What you have has not only legs but mountains, oceans, love, success, failure, perspective, compassion, philanthropy, family, apogee, brio, balance, passion, heroes, parables, responsibility, loss, winning, contribution, metaphor, allegory, enrolment, leadership, succession, game, flight, inamoratas, secrets.
>
> Not bad for an accountant ... Life is a story.

35

Triumph and Disaster

SHORTLY AFTER JOANIE had died, Peter copied out some extracts from Garrison Keillor's collection of stories, *The Book of Guys*. Perhaps significantly, it was not in Peter's journal but in his investment analysis/action notebooks. The piece is an imagined, somewhat tongue-in-cheek conversation between Mozart's arch-seducer character Don Giovanni and the unashamedly uxorious Figaro of *The Marriage of Figaro*. It probably expresses what Peter fundamentally felt about his priorities better than he could have articulated it himself. His comments are in square brackets:

Marriage takes too much out of a man, said the old seducer through a cloud of cigar smoke ... Figaro, my friend, a man owes it to himself to stop and consider the three advantages of the single life.

One, if you're single, you can think. Two, you can act. Three, you can feel. Probably there are other advantages, but those three are important, yes? ...You come and go, you eat when you're hungry, [and you eat what you want] you stay up late, you get drunk as it pleases you, and you have two or three terrific lovers who visit only when you invite them and stay about the right length of time ...

Some men should have two lovers, some three, it depends on the man, the Don said. Never limit yourself to one: monogamy leads to matrimony, and marriage, my boy, is pure struggle. Of course the single life has problems – having two lovers is a scheduling problem, and three is a real test of a man's organizational ability [I'll say!] and yet those are the very problems a man hopes for, Figaro ... Think of having three like that at once, their eyes alight at the sight of you, their lips moist, the flush of desire on their cheeks? Sound good? My, yes. The Don smiled at the thought.

"No woman would accept such an arrangement. [Joanie more or less did but she was probably unique.] You would have to lie to her," said Figaro.

Yes, certainly, said the Don.

"To lie to three women at once? To keep inventing stories about where you went? Is that nice?" [You have to practise selfishness with integrity, i.e., look after them.] ...

"But to be so selfish – what if everyone were? What if your parents had been?"

I am selfish, Figaro, because I have a larger capacity for pleasure than other people do. Pleasure is only a hobby to them and to me it is a true vocation.

As one might imagine from this, Peter's preoccupations remained substantially unchanged – in his case his greatest pleasure was his business, and as always it came first – followed, of course, by female companionship. However, the seeds of doubt were growing. The deterioration in his tremor was now apparent to all. Friends commented on it and he had a strong intuition that colleagues and staff were whispering about it, wondering what the future might hold for him and how long his intellectual capacity would remain sufficiently intact for him to continue running the business effectively.

At the 2005 conference in Bermuda Peter confronted the issue head on, realizing that trying to ignore it or brushing it off were no longer options. He chose the end of his "Pete's Morning" presentation as the moment to go public in a most original way. He had written a poem for the occasion:

Ode to a Fractious Left Hand

The hand wobbles, except on contact with a tennis ball,
It responds to massage, acupuncture and deep relaxation,
With tension there's exacerbation.
The medics say nothing can be done at all,
Stay tuned, we're doing more and more research,
So far we haven't hit the Wall.

It was a brave attempt and drew the expected applause, perhaps mainly on that account, although Peter was in thoroughly confident form: *The 26th Pete's Morning went off splendidly. Our numbers are so good. I was able to be the teacher not the zealot. My Ode was well received.* However, there was no disguising the fact that the condition was worsening, and it remained undiagnosed. The suggestion that it was early-stage Parkinson's was becoming untenable because medication for that condition was not helping. In fact he reacted so badly to trying it that he refused to continue.

Nevertheless, the transparency of Peter's health problems had an upside: it lent impetus to Charlie Sims's determination to buy out CIR. The negotiations, which could easily have become bogged down in detail, were driven forward by Sims himself, who overrode the reservations of some senior executives at Mackenzie Financial. Any lingering doubts about Peter's intellectual capacity at the time would have been set aside by the stream of memos and observations that winged their way to the CIR team from all corners of the globe – missives that attest to the extraordinary breadth and intelligence of Peter's reading, his constant rejection of professional complacency, and his gift for lateral, "outside the box" thinking.

From *The Economist*, which was running a series of articles on financial trades entitled "Why Didn't I Think of That?" he picked two examples from the John Templeton corpus.

In 1939 Hitler's invasion of Poland convinced the young Templeton that at the very least a European war was imminent. Not one might say an especially percipient observation but Templeton's thought process led him a step further and he concluded that the oversupply of commodities, which had been an unbroken feature of world markets ever since the great depression, would now go rapidly into reverse. The brilliant part was the step he took to take advantage of this logic. He bought shares in 104 almost worthless and in some cases actually bankrupt New York stock and commodity brokers. Three years later he was looking at very substantial profits on all but 4 of these ...

For good measure he included an account of the trade that won Templeton the prize.

Sixty years later, now Sir John Templeton and aged 77, he correctly foresaw the bursting of the technology and internet bubble. Again there were quite a number who could also see that the smash was inevitable, but the route that Templeton chose ... to exploit this prediction was the mark of his genius. He was aware that the market was awash with high tech and internet flotations in which the insiders were subject to "lock up" periods before they were permitted to sell any of their shares. Templeton reasoned that these insiders were in a better position than anyone else to know that very few companies in this crop of listings were likely to be long-term survivors so that the only way in which they would be able to salt away some capital would be to sell their shares immediately the "lock up" period came to an end. Templeton's next step was systematically to short sell these issues just prior to the end of the "lock up." On 84 transactions representing a total bet of $185 million, he made $92 million in just over a year.

Peter's accompanying comment, if complex, is brilliantly incisive:

We do not generally make macro predictions, or at least we do not allow our macro opinions to influence us in the execution of the value investment process, which is firmly based on the existence of "the margin of safety" in every security we own. However, I would suggest that where there appears to be a coincidence of a glaringly obvious sectoral antithesis of value combined with a reasonable expectation of a macro-economic downdraft and/or general market turmoil, or the reverse, an intelligently constructed short or long bet is within our remit. The trick lies in the mechanism through which we choose to exploit such opportunities and this was where Templeton excelled, as I think does Soros. Keep your eyes peeled, turmoil may not be far off!

————————

His condition notwithstanding, Peter continued to globetrot in the search for value. In the summer of 2005 he paid a visit to Romania for the first time. The Bucharest stock market had slumped by nearly 30% in the first five months of the year:

I half expected difficulties at the airport over immigration and money declaration forms, the way it always used to be in third world countries. Instead, no hassles and a modern airport. In 20 years so much in the world has changed for the better. The ... buildings en route modern, interspersed with attractive old residences. One forgets that Romania was extremely prosperous between the wars. A sense of the residual wealth comes through ...

The country is in transition. Like many of the eastern European countries, it has no history of democracy ... There is no real separation of public and private interests ... Ties to Western Europe are still tenuous and a recent poll says that 50% of Romanians are unhappy with the market economy. My sense is that this will change.

I paid four calls to brokerage firms. All were bright and knowledgeable. More women than men. There are 6,000 securities. The stats of the top 60 are attached. A series of privatizations is scheduled to be done. The market was up 100% last year but has corrected substantially. The average volume is $5 million a day! The total market capitalization is about $10 billion, a scale of assets similar to CIR. That does not absolutely rule out investment for us but with the limited liquidity we would need to be super cautious about the margin of safety. We have not been shy of limited liquidity in the past and nor should we be beginning to be so now – being aware is the thing.

From mid-2005 to mid-2007 there was a 150% rise in the Bucharest index.

At the beginning of August Peter made his way to St Petersburg where, despite his increasingly unreliable balance, he joined a B&R biking tour. As always, he took ample opportunity to assess the state of play in Russia from an investment standpoint:

The key economic issue here is who is going to control the excess revenues from $60 and probably higher oil prices. In early 2004 the Russian government passed a law through the Duma which provided that 90% of the incremental revenue above $28 per barrel would accrue to the state. I understand that Mikhail Khodorkovsky of Yukos tried to influence parliament to block the bill. This led to the demise of Yukos and Mr Khodorkovsky himself who was imprisoned for "tax evasion" – a charge no doubt reserved only for those who fail to support the incumbent in the Kremlin …

Russian equities are near record highs … There is not a lot of margin of safety unless we predicate a much higher oil price and even then the upside must be severely limited by the 90% law. At Lukoil, which is well run with reasonable corporate governance, all cell phones had to be checked into lockers before proceeding through security. The argument was that most phones now have built in cameras. This is a no-no …

In Suzdal we stayed at The Hot Springs Hotel, a clean if spartan inn recently opened. I used the shoe brush for my hair! The biking … modest distances on reasonably level terrain. I was very strong on both days but developed the "wobbles." The second day I abandoned the bike and ran the rest of the way.

The Russian stock market, like that of Bucharest, continued upward to the stratosphere until the sub-prime crisis struck, and in the event one of the Cundill Group's best investments was a Russian oil company with a huge – and very necessary – margin of safety, Sibir.

———————————

Peter's shaking and his uncertain balance were now of heightened concern. Dr Jon Stoessl of the Parkinson's clinic at the University of British Columbia was convinced that Peter was not suffering from Parkinson's and Peter was inclined to agree. However, so far there was no alternative diagnosis to explain the symptoms. It was already a struggle to keep up with writing his journals because his left hand often shook so uncontrollably that his writing wandered across the page as a virtually indecipherable series of squiggles. Peter commented rather forlornly on one of the better days: *Samuel Pepys had to give up his diaries on account of bad eyesight. He was bereft. I would be as well.*

Finally, just before his 67th birthday, Peter was booked in to see Dr Susan Bressman at the renowned neurodiagnostic department in the Beth Israel Medical Center in New York for a day of tests. This time the results were conclusive. He was suffering from a very rare genetic neurological, progressively degenerative, disorder known as Fragile x-associated Tremor/Ataxia Syndrome (FXTAS), for which there was no known cure and little effective palliative medication. In fact, beyond its identification, which had proved difficult enough, almost nothing could be said, even by the specialist neurological community, about what might be anticipated in the evolution of the disease. In many respects Peter was to find himself in the role of guinea pig for the medical profession and the outlook was uncomfortably opaque for quite some time. The one thing of which he was certain through *listening to his body and doing self-assessment on his cognitive capacity* was that the disease was not in a static or remissionary phase. There were good days and less good days, but the good days were becoming perceptibly less frequent, and the symptoms on worse days were gradually increasing in intensity.

Nevertheless, Peter allowed himself no let-up in his routines. His exercise programs remained almost unchanged, except for tennis: he had to resort to an underarm service. Professionally, as we shall see, he was still as sharp as ever and his travelling schedule might have been regarded as unsustainable by a man half his age. In January he made his first visit to Uganda:

As anticipated it is fascinating and brave and troubled. The scenery is rich and majestic. There is much pollution, it is politically unstable but a democracy nevertheless, at the same time chaotic and peaceful ... The roads are reminiscent of Quebec – full of potholes. I felt quite at home. The soil is a deep ox-blood red and it leaves powdery traces on everything, everywhere.

Museveni, the current president, who has done a lot for investment and the country's growing middle class, is in the process of trying to change the constitution so that he can run for a third term. So far he has managed to incarcerate the leader of the opposition twice in the last month. Tony Blair warned that if he did not let him out the forthcoming Commonwealth Conference scheduled for Kampala would be relocated ...

I do seriously wonder whether Uganda has any kind of a secure future. I would not consider investing here, although the friends I was staying with certainly have. Jonathan Wright is a white Ugandan, born and brought up here and he knows his way around. His wife Pam is a Montrealer. Together they have recently opened the best hotel in the capital ... I was pleased to see that the restaurant, which boasts a gourmet chef, was always full of Ugandans and not just the super rich. One lunchtime I was the only white person. The beautiful Queen of Buganda was there on my last night and every celebrity who passes through stays and eats here.

I went for a five-hour hike [in Semliki National Park] up into the mountains to look for chimpanzees and baboons. I was by myself with two game wardens ... We hid in the undergrowth and waited. They knew the meaning of every sound of twig or rustle of leaves and showed me the droppings just left by our quarry. At last we found a Ficus tree filled with chattering chimps and there were two baboons on the ground. We had seen a lot of monkeys around the camp – including the handsome black and white Colobus with their long tails, which unfortunately are so decorative that they are heavily poached so that the tails can be sold as fly whisks.

In an even more glamorous safari camp in the north [I saw] water buffalo, elephants and giraffe in the distance as well as several varieties of gazelle, including the tiny delicate Oribi with its distinctive black beauty spot beneath each eye. The most entertaining creatures are the wart hogs and their piglets which run with their tails sticking straight up in the air. They are at the same time cute and ugly but they have an endearingly comic expression ...

I achieved my great ambition; to see the source of the Nile and Lake Victoria, which brought back vividly all the books I read in my youth about those incredible Victorian explorers – Livingstone, Speke, Grant, and my particular hero Sir Richard Burton.

For me Kampala was a bit of a disaster, overcrowded, polluted with traffic jams as immovable as in Bangkok or Cairo and all that noise of horns honking uselessly. I was knocked over by two youths on a scooter dodging the traffic as though they were doing a slalom ...

It was a memorable three weeks of Africa and I learned a great deal, as much as anything from the table talk at night. There was a constant passage of interesting people that passed through the camps and joined the communal table. The most captivating were perhaps two men, old friends who went into the wilds together every year to hunt for botanical species. Maurizio, an Italian, was a camel vet in Eritrea and his friend was an old Brit colonial from Kenya – a rancher and farmer of his 1000 acres. He was charming, urbane, sun hardened and thorn torn. They both had fascinating tales of survival in Africa's heartland among wild and still naked tribes. I almost felt that I was listening to Burton and Speke, which was more than anything else what I had wanted out of the trip.

But behind my delight it was impossible to ignore the grim reality that we of colonist races are the cause of so many of the problems of this great continent ... But there is hope between the micro intervention of such as the Wrights and the mega efforts of the Gates' Foundation. We talked much of what I might do (supposing that my health permits). We shall see.

Peter's mind was clearly engaged with the question of philanthropy and how to set about giving in an organized, meaningful way, and above all in what direction. Given the uncertainties of his health outlook, however, the extent of any personal involvement was unknown. Even though now fully occupied with running the business, he could foresee a time when he might take a role as non-executive chair, freeing himself up to become active in charitable work, while still investing his own fortune. A basic structure was already in place in Bermuda and disbursing substantial sums on a slightly "ad hoc" basis, the largest recipient being the Aspen Institute, which arguably had more of a business than a philanthropic rationale. It had at least been ascertained that at Peter's death the greater part of his wealth would accrue to his charitable foundation.

Later that year, the question was given added impetus as it became clear that the Mackenzie buyout of Cundill Investment Research was actually going ahead and would add approximately $130 million to Peter's pot. He attended very few of the meetings at which the details of the deal were thrashed out, judging it preferable to remain in the background and give the impression that it was of no consequence to him.

However there was one meeting at which he and David Feather were both present. As it drew to a close and the discussion reverted to social matters, reference was made to one of the Mackenzie Financial people who had recently travelled to Tokyo and had visited a certain rather private night club. Peter was suddenly all attention and the relevant card of the establishment was produced for his perusal. He stared at it for a moment, then slowly took off his glasses and looked up as the famously penetrating blue eyes flashed animatedly around the room and he exclaimed, "This guy's a serious player!"

Once the Fragile X diagnosis had been definitively pronounced, Peter was relieved, although he was less reassured to discover that, little being known about the disease, prognosis was extremely difficult and treatment

even more so. However, he addressed the problem with his habitual decisiveness, putting himself in the day-to-day care of Dr James Pozzi, a
charming, very professional Australian who was also a keen athlete.
Through Pozzi he made contact with one of London's most eminent neurologists, Professor Andrew Lees, who headed up the National Hospital
for Neurology and Neurosurgery in Queen Square. While Lees' experience with FXTAS was at that time limited, his overall clinical abilities in
neurology were second to none and he was prepared to work together
with Peter and Pozzi in a semi-experimental fashion to develop a palliative treatment regime by combining different forms of known drugs. As
a preliminary, Peter spent two days undergoing comprehensive tests to
set a benchmark from which it would be possible to monitor the evolution of the condition in the hope of making an informed prognosis and
observing the effectiveness of the drugs that Peter would be trying. At
the same time they would search the clinical world for any existing repos-
itory of knowledge about FXTAS and its treatment.

At this juncture Peter's abundant curiosity came strongly into play. He
saw the exercise as a challenge that would occupy him in a pragmatic
and almost detached way, and could at least make a pioneering and
meaningful contribution. That said, he was undergoing considerable
internal commotion. Coming to accept that he would no longer be among
the fittest 10 percent of the male population for his age proved hard and
he was beginning to have doubts about his eventual ability to hold on to
his favoured female companions, particularly CJ. It is no coincidence that
he chose this moment to copy out "El Desdichado" ("The Disinherited")
by Gerard de Nerval, the nineteenth-century French symbolist poet:

I am the darkness – the widower – the unconsoled,
The prince of Aquitaine in the ruined tower;
My sole *star* is dead – and my star-studded lute
Now bears the black *sun* of *Melancholy*.

You who consoled me in the funereal night,
Give me back Posillipo and the sea of Italy,
The flower that so delighted my grieving heart,
And the trellis where the vine entwines the rose …

However, there still remained enough of the old Peter spirit for him to be determined not to forgo his annual scary adventure. Accordingly, at the end of May he descended on Fort Lauderdale:

"An Astronaut to Be"

I made my appearance at the Hard Rock Casino to join twenty-seven other would-be astronauts. We were briefed by the Zero-G flight team, which included a real live astronaut, Bob Springer ... We had a mantra drummed into us, "Feet Down" when in weightless mode and nearing the point of return to gravity. Failure to observe this could result in a nasty bump on the head ... We had all been issued with jump-suits. There on the tarmac our Boeing 727, a modified cargo plane, awaited us. We entered at the tail end to the seating arrangements of a normal commercial aircraft but three quarters of the fuselage was completely empty. Having taken off, we settled at 24,000 feet and began to fly in parabolic curves. In the first five there was still some gravity. The next eleven followed the same pattern – nose up at a 45-degree angle for twenty seconds, level out for fifteen seconds, then nose down for a loose thirty seconds, when the somersaults, the swimming and the jumps happened. I would define the feeling as active floating. After the first two passes it all seemed very natural. But towards the end I was very glad that I'd taken an anti-motion tablet beforehand ...

In physical terms, this was probably the least challenging of all my adventures but there was still that sense of nervous anticipation in confronting the unknown.

Although there was little prior knowledge about FXTAS, Peter did quickly learn that there was some consensus of opinion about its outlook. It was not an immediate killer but a degenerative condition that would in due course lead to severe physical disabilities, including significantly impaired mobility and serious deterioration in cognitive capacity. It was a grim outlook that Peter faced with great courage and a complete absence of self-pity. He was of course extremely fortunate to be wealthy enough not to have to rely on public care. He realized at once that it was essential to put measures for his ongoing care in place immediately against the moment when he might no longer be able to make rational decisions. He made a Living Will, giving instructions that no medical team was to undertake any extraordinary measures to prolong his life or resuscitate him. Even more significant, he appointed two trustees under a Lasting Power of Attorney-Personal Welfare who were to be responsible for his care and well-being in all aspects of his life, including his financial affairs, in the event of his incapacity.

The attorneys that he chose for this role were Jennifer Bingham, with whom he had worked for well over twenty years, and Fiona O'Driscoll, his personal assistant. The role carried a huge weight of responsibility, but Peter could not have chosen better. The two ladies worked together tirelessly for his benefit, with tact and discretion in a spirit governed by their deep sympathy and affection for him, until the day he died and indeed after. As will become apparent, what might have been quite a straightforward undertaking was to turn into something of a nightmare as the disease took greater hold of Peter. With the completion of Mackenzie's acquisition of Cundill Investment Research, Peter's assets had roughly doubled, adding to the weight of that responsibility.

The Cundill Conference for 2006 was held in Shanghai, as a reflection of Peter's growing conviction that the Chinese dragon was well and truly out of its cage and was now the dominant economic force in the Far East, in which region the Value Fund had over half of its assets invested. On the way to Shanghai, Peter made a short stop-off in Dubai, where he remarked on the construction frenzy and drew conclusions based on his "crane test": *It's been a long time since I have seen as many cranes as this. It will inevitably lead to a traumatic slowdown and a collapse in the real estate market. The Dubai stock market is mainly composed of realtors, banks who finance real estate, insurance companies whose principal business is real estate insurance, and suppliers to the construction industry. We should consider shorting this index.*

Within a month the prediction proved correct on a dizzying scale, with a 60% plunge in the stock market. The new regime of Mackenzie compliance was not quite nimble enough to facilitate the trade in time, so the opportunity was unfortunately missed.

Peter went on to visit Sri Lanka for the first time. Despite the effects of twenty-five years of civil war and the 2004 tsunami, which had claimed another 35,000 lives, the economy had shown great resilience.

He took a seaplane to the resort town of Galle, the nexus point for the tsunami, where 4,000 had been killed and 50,000 left homeless. After a rapid reconstruction, tourists were just beginning to return when the Tamil Tigers had attacked the harbour and there had been an hour-long gun battle barely a month before Peter arrived. It was hardly surprising that he found himself the sole occupant of a very opulent hotel, with staff falling over themselves to look after him and minister to his every whim.

Back in Colombo, Peter called on Dialogue Telecom and Distilleries. *I sense that we are in the initial stages of a cellular boom here [this was absolutely correct. The cellular phone market in Sri Lanka grew by 550% between 2006 and 2009]. Dialogue Telecom is run by John Keels who I have met in Hong Kong. Both that company and Distilleries have moved up substantially but are not outrageously expensive. The* MARKET P/E RATIO *is about 13 times. Price to Book Value is 4 times. Dividend yield is over 4% and inflation 12%." Sri Lanka is both dangerous and prosperous. We should maintain a careful watching brief. If the market should break we need to be ready.*

He was still on top of his investment game.

36

The Turn of the Screw

AS 2007 BEGAN, Peter was deeply concerned that an unprecedented financial crisis was in the making. Mortgages had been a specialty of his since the Greenshields days when he had helped set up the Mortgage Investment Company of Canada. Later on, he had made money buying undervalued mortgage-related stocks, starting with Crédit Foncier. This time, however, Peter felt that the exceptional levels of leverage and the prolific distribution of packages of mortgages of distinctly dubious quality, dressed up as top-rated securities, represented a precarious and lethal combination that could plunge the entire global financial system into a default-engendered downward spiral. Such a crisis might be extraordinarily difficult to contain, as it would require governments and central banks worldwide to act in concert to avert a collapse on the scale of the Great Depression.

As he put it in a note to CIR:

First we had mortgages and then mortgage-backed securities, and now we have another species called a Collateralized Debt Obligation, which could only have been dreamt up by a particularly wicked sprite determined to prey upon a few innocent victims and a great many who ought to know better ... I would feel marginally more comfortable if I had any faith in the fact that the federal banking regulators understand the monster over whose unleashing they have presided. I do not. What I do understand is that these CDO's are just piles of debt on both the asset and the liability side of the balance sheet. One might imagine them as quasi-banks but without depositors and without the normal dividing lines between what constitutes an asset and what is a liability; nor are they regulated! They are in fact just a jumble of highly speculative loans that have been transformed by alchemy, masquerading as mathematics, into investment grade instruments, more than three quarters of which have been rated as double or triple A. The implosion of all this is not going to be pretty.

Peter had a long practice of considering systemic risk within the financial system with a coterie whose professional view he esteemed – luminaries such Anatole Kaletsky, the *London Times* economic columnist, Lord Rees-Mogg, ex-editor of *The Times*, and George Soros of Quantum Fund. But perhaps his closest confidant on the subject was Prem Watsa of Fairfax Financial. It was through Watsa that Peter arrived at a strategy to protect the assets under his management from what he was convinced would be a major and now unavoidable collapse in credit markets.

The last decade of the twentieth century had seen the development of a new instrument known as a Credit Default Swap, by means of which it was possible to buy insurance against the default of any institution, including CDO's. Generally speaking CDS's would be purchased against an instrument that an investor actually owned, thereby providing the holder with protection against a default of that instrument. The strategy Peter and Watsa were mulling over took this a step further. They proposed to purchase a package of naked CDS's, that is to say CDS's covering instruments they did not own. Their logic was that, as soon as the credit crunch began to bite, the value of the CDS's would take a quantum leap, fuelled by panic, as investors scrambled to buy protection at any price.

For Watsa, putting this strategy into action was merely a question of giving the orders. For Peter it was not so simple; he was no longer an independent operator. Cundill Investment Research was now a wholly owned subsidiary of Mackenzie Financial, and transactions of the kind that Peter was proposing had to be submitted to Mackenzie's compliance department and its legal advisers. The application to purchase CDS's in the Value Fund was put forward in mid-March, making the point that the fund had already been involved in non-deliverable (i.e. naked) swaps for some years. After three months of no noticeable progress in obtaining approval, Peter became impatient. When the matter was pressed, the following response came through from Mackenzie's head of compliance:

Hi Wade [Wade Burton] and Andrew [Andy Massie],
I realize that you are anxious to use CDS's and it must be frustrating to get held up when you see the investment opportunity and want to move forward immediately. However I'd like to make you aware of a few things –
First, as I think you know, our funds have never before used CDS's and no-one here currently has a high level of expertise regarding

these instruments. We are trying to get up to speed internally, but this will take time.

The email agreed that it was perfectly possible for Canadian mutual funds to use CDS's but then cited problems with valuation and a lack of an agreement to proceed, as well as contractual complications. Hence, there would still be significant delay in obtaining approval. The message concluded: "You cannot expect that you can call us at the drop of a hat and expect that we have the capacity to deal with something like this on an immediate basis unless the situation is of the most urgent nature, given our workloads and priorities. It is simply not possible."

Clearly the writer did not share Peter's urgent sense that a crisis was looming. Obstruction of this kind continued until at last it was too late. The opportunity loss was only partially mitigated by adding to the investment holdings of Fairfax, which offered at least some exposure by proxy to the CDS strategy. It was the greatest disaster of Peter's career. Left to his own devices, he would have constructed a naked CDS package on approximately the scale of what constituted a full position in the Value Fund at the time, between $400 and $500 million, covering in excess of $20 billion in nominal amount. The resulting gain would on its own have turned the 25% loss that the Value Fund suffered in the stock market collapse of 2008 into a substantial profit, and the positive impact on the brand value of Mackenzie-Cundill would have been incalculable. New money would undoubtedly have poured in, providing massive cash firepower at the perfect juncture – the bottom of the worst bear market since 1929. It is moot whether, had Peter's energy levels not been affected by the onslaught of FXTAS, he might have intervened personally on the issue with Charlie Sims.

––––––––

Peter had always been a careful – some might think obsessive – observer and recorder of his own physical condition. His note to himself on "the state of play" at the beginning of 2007 is a testament to the quality of the man:

My balance is unreliable. I sometimes suffer extreme fatigue. Is this a side effect of the medication, the progression of the disease or, as is most probable, a combination? My strength is slipping away, almost imperceptibly but enough that I notice it from week to week … I have always needed a lot of sleep. I now find solace in sleep, which I never did until now – except in periods of depression – and I am not depressed. I have continued my routines. Sometimes I struggle to keep up with them. Perhaps they are just becoming boring and I need to jazz them up a bit. Work on this … There seem to be some clear alternatives – fight or give up? I know the answer. Spend or save? This is a different question. I do not want to deprive myself of the fruits of my labours but at the same time I want to leave a material legacy. There must be a balance in this. Retirement is simply a death warrant; hang on, you're still contributing strategically …

In the search for new digs in London you need to consider what the future may hold and the staff with which you will need to surround yourself. Do not look back. Look forward! My mental capacity is mostly I think as sharp as ever but there are moments of fogginess and my ability to concentrate for long periods is less reliable. I'm getting stiffer and my finger dexterity is very poor. Sight and hearing so far OK. Weight stable. Do I smile less?

The question of spend or save was quickly answered. He planned more innovative charitable giving, not just the ad hoc approach that had generally been used to date. The friend in need still found an open door, but the lunches where "so and so hit me up for x" became much less frequent, and gifts made under such circumstances were nominal in relation to Peter's wealth. David Feather, now a very close friend, tells the story of a dinner with Peter at which he pitched him for a contribution to a worthy charity for which he was raising funds. Peter did not react, and the two went on to Annabel's without further reference to the question. The following day Feather received an email from Peter undertaking to make a donation of $10,000. Feather was quietly pleased with his success and called Peter to thank him. The response was laconic to say the least: "That's quite all right, Dave. I am not interested in your charity, I just didn't want you to look like a loser!"

However, a serious initiative was germinating in Peter's mind in discussion with Michael Meighen. Since failing the history module at McGill, at the cost of a summer of painting fences, he had developed a passion for the subject. Peter realized, as many had done before, that in order to understand the present and form an intelligent assessment of future prospects, a study of the past is essential. His enormous admiration for Winston Churchill, who expounded this view most persuasively, was a major factor in whetting his insatiable appetite for reading history in its broadest sense, from serious academic works on periods such as the French Revolution and the Napoleonic Wars, which particularly interested him, to historical biography, country-specific histories, and historical novels. From the 1960s onward, Peter never failed to "bone up" on the history of any country or region he was visiting for the first time.

What he envisioned was a major annual international history prize, modelled broadly on Sir John Templeton's prize for research or discoveries about spiritual realities. He was inspired to go back to the starting point of his own historical journey, McGill itself. The practical structuring of the prize was left largely to Meighen and by the summer of 2007 the memorandum of agreement for establishing the Cundill International Prize and Lecture in History at McGill University was signed. The prize was to be awarded for a newly published work judged to have "a profound, literary, social and academic impact in the area of history." It was axiomatic that the work should appeal not just to academe but to the general reader. No dust was allowed to settle and in October 2008 by far the largest history prize in the world was awarded for the first time, to Stuart Schwarz, professor of history at Yale, for *All Can Be Saved: Religious Tolerance and Salvation in the Iberian Atlantic World*.

Having read the book, Peter wrote to Professor Schwarz:

> I was delighted to receive a copy of "All Can Be Saved" and, now that I have read it, I am equally delighted by the judges' decision to award it the Cundill History Prize. I believe there are always certain periods and themes from our past which have particular relevance to current events and the issues, whether political or spiritual, which are preoccupying us at any given juncture.
>
> It seems to me that your book is just such an example in both respects. Tolerance and the conviction that there is an infinity of routes to grace and salvation, each of which is deserving of respect, is perhaps more vital at this moment than at any time in the recent past. What you have done is to make some very important points about how tolerance emerges, drawn from the Iberian multi-racial,

multi-religious and multi-cultural experience over several centuries.

As you examine the records of that most unjust and repressive of institutions, the Holy Inquisition, what becomes clear is that tolerance stems from the innate goodness and common sense of ordinary folk who are intelligent enough, even though possibly illiterate, to question dogma and reject its tyranny in favour of harmonious human relations. At the same time you make the important reflection that, while intellectual enlightenment and liberal philosophy may have been the means of enunciating the moral principles in favour of tolerance, its true practitioners always turn out in reality to be the Piers Plowmans of the world.

These are valuable insights and I congratulate you on a remarkable and most enjoyable book.

Naturally, Schwarz responded most enthusiastically.[1]

Shortly before the history prize became a reality, Peter received a surprise boost to his confidence. Charles Munger, Warren Buffet's long-time partner in Berkshire Hathaway, was about to retire – unlike Mr Buffett, who had no intention of stepping down. The search was on for a new chief investment officer for Berkshire's $100 billion portfolio. At the company's

---

1 Professor Schwarz's successors have been equally distinguished: Professor Lisa Jardine of London University for *Going Dutch*, a complete reappraisal of the accession of William of Orange to the English throne; Professor Sir Diarmaid MacCullough of Oxford for *The History of Christianity: The First Three Thousand Years*; the Italian scholar Sergio Luzzatto for his account *Padre Pio. Miracoli e politica nell'Italia del Novecento*; Stephen Platt of the University of Massachusetts for *Autumn in the Heavenly Kingdom*, a spellbinding and impeccably researched narrative of the barely known Taiping Rebellion in nineteenth-century China and most recently Anne Applebaum for *Iron Curtain: The Crushing of Eastern Europe, 1944–1956*, a searing account of the Soviet annexations following the collapse of the third reich. This latest award was made after the panel had read nearly 200 works submitted by publishers the world over, all of which emphasizes the truly international character of the prize and its faithful adherence to Peter's intention. The original gift was to be funded for five years, but Peter would be gratified to know that since his death the Peter Cundill Foundation has endowed the prize in perpetuity. The idea has proven truly visionary.

annual meeting, Buffett was asked if he would consider looking beyond the U.S. border for the right individual. He responded that he would not rule out a Canadian candidate – "someone like a Peter Cundill." He was not in negotiations with Peter, he added, but implied that if Peter were to apply he would find an automatic place on the shortlist. What sort of person was he looking for? Someone from outside Berkshire Hathaway who might see things from a different perspective, and whose exemplary long-term record demonstrated a capacity for looking beyond just equities and a thorough grasp of bonds, foreign exchange, and derivatives. Graham's principles of deep value would of course be a prerequisite. It was, as near as could be imagined, an exact description of Peter. The comments were picked up in the Canadian press and Peter responded:

> Dear Warren,
> Thank you very much for your comments. You do wonderful things for my psyche!
> Sadly, I am unable to put my name forward for one of the most challenging positions in the financial world. My reasons are:
> · At 68 I think I am too old for the job.
> · I have potential health issues.
> · I have a really tough non-compete clause.
> If I had $5 billion to invest today, I would keep it in CD's – 50% in U.S. dollars and the remainder in a basket of currencies to be chosen. I would buy credit default swaps. Corporate spreads are much too narrow these days.
> I would then await events.
> I hope our paths cross. Thank you for your thoughts.

As Buffet was contemplating the 40% decline in Berkshire's share price just over a year later, he must have regretted not following Peter's formula to the letter. Nevertheless, for Peter the accolade from Buffett remained his most treasured public recognition.

Peter soon paid another visit to Professor Lees's neurological clinic in Queen Square, this time to test the levels and the characteristics of dopamine in his brain. A connection between a loss of dopamine and the development of Parkinson's disease, whose symptoms, especially tremor and cognitive impairment, closely resemble FXTAS, was already established, and the use of dopamine supplements had proven effective in treating Parkinson's. Perhaps the same medication might be beneficial to Peter's condition.

The general lack of familiarity with FXTAS among medical experts meant that Peter was an unusually interesting subject, and he agreed to be examined by a group of senior neurological consultants who foregathered in the Queen Square lecture hall for the purpose. Most patients would have hated the experience and undergone the ordeal only in the interests of the greater good. Not so Peter, who was in his element: *There was a wealth of knowledge, intelligence and practical clinical know-how in the room. I was able to ask questions to my heart's content. I enjoyed the debate and I insisted on getting a layman's translation whenever I was unable to follow the technical language. It was an interesting and stimulating experience.*

Sadly, dopamine supplements offered no improvement and made Peter so nauseous that they were eventually abandoned. Three months later he penned a rather sombre little memo: *It is not a straight line graph; however ground lost is never entirely regained. I am sometimes deeply fatigued. My gait and my balance are unreliable. My strength is much diminished. On occasion I feel as though I were in a fog. I am losing part of my capacity to absorb information … I find myself dozing during the day which I have never been in the habit of doing. On the other hand I am still trying new solutions. I exercise almost every day, I am not unhappy. I would so much welcome a moment of equilibrium!*

Of course, the question of deterioration is a relative one. As Professor Lees remarked in his report after Peter's visit to Queen Square, this was a man still capable of completing the *New York Times* crossword puzzle on most days, who ran regularly although (by his own standards) slowly, who could write detailed, closely argued memos on credit default swaps, and was able to hold his own in an exchange with a group of the most highly qualified neurologists in the kingdom. Nevertheless, because Peter's mind was still so clear and incisive, he had an ever more vivid perception of what might lie in store as the disease ran its course. It was not an appealing prospect.

Faced with the lack of a credible medical program, Peter turned increasingly to the "alternative" world, which he had always instinctively distrusted. Through his friends Ian and Victoria Watson, he was familiar with the Institute of Noetic Sciences founded by the American astronaut Edgar Dean Mitchell, the pilot on NASA's Apollo 14 mission and the sixth man to walk on the moon. He was a distinguished physicist and mathematician, seemingly completely grounded in scientific skepticism. However, as Apollo 14 was approaching the earth, Mitchell had an out-of-body experience in which he became overpowered by an inner conviction that the earth forms part of a living system comprising a harmonious whole with the entire universe. The experience prompted him to found the institute, which devotes itself to exploring the nature and power of the human mind and spirit and its connections with the universe. Some of these investigations led to the work of Adam McLeod, a micro-biologist who claimed to be able to use the healing powers he had personally developed to treat and eradicate illnesses in third parties from a distance, without necessarily meeting the patient. In the face of such a fantastical claim, Peter would probably have recoiled like a scalded cat. But it was hard to ignore the endorsement of Mitchell himself, who had to be taken seriously and stated categorically that McLeod had cured him of a kidney carcinoma. Perhaps even more compelling was the account of rock musician Ronnie Hawkins who, having been diagnosed with inoperable pancreatic cancer (which Peter knew from Joanie's experience usually triggers palliative care), turned to McLeod in desperation. Following eight months of "treatment" from a distance of over three thousand miles, during which McLeod worked solely with a photograph of Hawkins, the cancer had gone.

Peter read McLeod's book and, somewhat to his surprise, found threads in it that meshed quite closely with his own thinking. *You can focus on self-healing using your own particular strengths to advantage. Healing is a focused kind of telepathy which utilizes a collective energy that is universal. The receptivity of the healee is a vital ingredient. It has a lot to do with attitude. One needs passion and perseverance ... The healing force is harnessed by tapping into this universal energy using your imagination. Healing needs to be visualized.*

And so on a rainy summer's day Peter found himself in the Great Hall of London's Imperial College with Victoria Watson, listening to McLeod and participating in a six-hour seminar on healing technique. His carefully observed account of the day perhaps evinces more longing than real conviction: *Adam is very young and certainly gifted – part guru, part boy ... Through his father he has a North American Indian heritage. Does that explain the spirituality? We were encouraged to use visualization techniques. My picture was to move dopamine into my brain. I felt energized. I think there is something there. Perhaps combine "faith healing" with conventional medicine. Appropriately, given the guru context, we dined at Memories of India.*

A few weeks later Peter took another step in the alternative direction by attending a service at London's Holy Trinity Brompton Church. Once again he scrutinized the experience with a certain detachment: *It is the heartland of the Anglican evangelical movement ... It was a half-hour performance with the odd prayer and a fine talk by Nicky Gumble, who developed the enormously successful Alpha Course as an outreach program. It explores the "meaning of life" but very quickly engages the participant in the Christian evangelical viewpoint. I doubt whether Darwin gets much of a mention. Gumble is a powerful speaker. A form of communion followed. Members of the congregation came forward and were prayed over in a one on one situation. My seatmate led me forward ... It was uplifting and a unique moment in my life.*

Uplifting though it may have been, neither experiment was ever repeated, despite numerous attempts at persuasion.

PART · SIX ·

37

A Brief Respite

EFFORTS HAD MEANWHILE continued to find an organization with some understanding of FXTAS and its treatment. Eventually, through one of Peter's Californian contacts, the MIND (Medical Investigation of Neuro-developmental Disorders) Institute at the University of California in Sacramento was mentioned, and Fiona O'Driscoll at once made contact. The institute has a clinic that treats patients with FXTAS as well as a laboratory that undertakes research and develops remedial drugs in its investigation of autism and related genetic disorders. It was then the only facility of its kind in the world. For Peter it was like stumbling upon the Holy Grail. A formal referral was immediately arranged through Professor Lees and a private jet was chartered.

The journey to Sacramento began auspiciously from Farnborough airport, where the joys of "going private" were immediately evident and Peter was pampered to his heart's content. At their refuelling stop in Goose Bay, Newfoundland, Peter, Fiona, and CJ were welcomed into a pretty log cabin with a roaring fire and served hot drinks, while the immigration officer came to visit them. Peter went straight into Canadian mode, rapidly demolishing two of his favourite Oreo ice creams.

The program at the MIND institute was the most thorough that Peter had yet undergone and the level of knowledge about FXTAS reassuringly impressive, but it was exhausting for him. One of the most interesting things they learned was that, as with autism, a carrier of FXTAS who eventually becomes symptomatic will have been affected by the disorder from birth, often evincing obsessive tendencies and difficulties in conducting normal emotional and sexual relationships. Their consequent single-mindedness often results in sufferers being extremely high achievers. It would be hard to conjure a more accurate vignette of Peter, and it goes a long way toward explaining what otherwise might be seen as fundamental character flaws.

In regard to treatment, obviously at the top of Peter's agenda, the news was not encouraging. The key to successful treatment apparently lies in early diagnosis, and in his case the disease was in an advanced stage. Although medication might offer some hope of slowing its progress and alleviating symptoms, especially cognitive deterioration and tremor, it was too late for an outright cure. The eventual report on Peter by Professor Randi Hagerman at the MIND Institute confirmed that in addition to evident physical symptoms, Peter now had significant cognitive deficiencies, especially in the area of executive function (decision making) and concentration. However, Hagerman offered hope of some remission with radical new medication combined with vitamin supplements and antioxidants. Peter seized on the proposals with enthusiasm. After about three months, signs of real improvement appeared for the first time. The tremor was less pronounced thanks to a course of Botox injections prescribed in Sacramento, the sense of fatigue less extreme, the impression of sometimes living in a fog lifted, and his ability to concentrate revived.

The respite freed Peter to turn his mind to other pressing issues. Nominally, he still occupied the position of chief investment officer of the Mackenzie Cundill Value Fund as well as all the other investment products and accounts that came under the CIR umbrella. However, he was no longer able to direct day-to-day investment policy. His intuitive grasp of risk in financial markets was unimpaired but, with his energy reduced, his grip on overall strategic structuring was weaker. For all the accuracy of his predictions about the financial crisis, the funds under management had suffered their worst year ever in 2008. The missed opportunity of the Credit Default Swaps did not explain why, in spite of Peter's repeated warnings to his portfolio managers, the build-up of cash in the funds had not been nearly as high as should have been expected. Expressed in terms of the Dow Jones Industrial Average, which quite accurately mirrored performance everywhere at the time, markets peaked in October 2007. From the standpoint of a deep-value investor, valuations had been getting increasingly speculative for a good six months prior to this. Normally, this should have led to an automatic accretion of cash as overvalued positions were sold and other investments with adequate margins of safety became scarcer. (Actually, in light of Peter's pessimistic outlook, one would have anticipated that an even more rigorous approach to the margin of safety would have been applied, but it was not). From October 2007 until February 2008, markets fell by just over 12% and then rallied until the beginning of May.

In early March Peter sent a general memo to the team at CIR: "I draw your attention to an article in this month's edition of the *Financial Analyst's Journal* called 'Black Monday, Black Swans.' It is a series of remarkable insights and it points out the dangers inherent in a financial system that is beginning to dwarf the real economic enterprises."

One could make a case that the reason Peter's repeatedly expressed forebodings and insistence on special rigour with regard to value were largely ignored was that he could not pursue his point with his erstwhile vigour. It is true that he did not issue specific instructions as to sales, but that had never been his style. The real reason is more likely to have been a culture change within CIR following its acquisition by Mackenzie. Although highly respected, Peter was no longer the chief executive and owner of the business, but simply an employee like everyone else. By contrast with Peter's lifelong career as an unashamed contrarian, Mackenzie's culture was essentially sales-driven, and any fund that nursed large pools of uninvested cash and ran short positions would be harder for the sales force to market to the retail clientele who were Mackenzie's bread and butter. In light of their delaying over the CDS proposal, it seems probable that some of this predominantly long only and fully invested culture had begun to rub off on the CIR team.

Given Peter's conviction that financial turmoil on a scale far exceeding that of 1987 was unavoidable, the portfolio managers at CIR ought to have anticipated a major bear market. The decline of 12% from the October peak did not qualify as a bear market at all, let alone a major one. (A bear market is usually defined as a fall of at least 20%). The conclusion that the recovery from February to April was a bear market rally, offering an ideal selling opportunity with which to raise liquidity, should have been inescapable. Again, an opportunity was missed. The really damaging precipitous decline in markets began only in May 2008.

By the time markets finally bottomed out in June 2009, they had fallen by a staggering 53% from their all-time high in February 2007, and by 48% from the peak of the bear market rally that had ended in May the following year. However, by this time Peter was no longer even nominally at the helm. His successor, Jim Thompson, was formally appointed in February 2009, although he had been effectively running the show for some months. In April 2009 Peter officially retired with the honorary title of chairman emeritus of Mackenzie Cundill. During the "interregnum" Peter had, with perfect correctness, not sought in any way to overshadow Thompson. He merely expressed his views if and when asked. Nevertheless, we have a very clear indication of his thinking from the way his personal investments were run. At the end of February 2009 the cash content in Peter's accounts was over 50% of total assets. By that spring, Peter was convinced that the worst was over, that a meltdown of the financial system had been averted, if only narrowly, and enough had been done globally by way of rescue to ensure a gradual economic recovery. It was therefore high time to reinvest.

Since he had already substantially added to his investment position in James Morton's Cundill International Company, which had been especially hard hit in the bear market, Peter considered that his direct exposure to equity markets was probably sufficient for the moment. What struck him was that corporate debt markets had been uniformly massacred as equity markets fell. Consequently, the corporate debt of many companies with sound balance sheets and healthy prospects even in an anaemic economic upturn were offering yields in excess of 20%. Nothing remotely approaching such fixed interest returns had been seen since the mid-1970s. This time around, Peter was certain he could anticipate a prolonged period of modest inflation and almost unprecedentedly low interest rates. But the window of opportunity might be short because the negligible returns offered for cash on deposit or on high-grade bonds would inevitably drive investors seeking income toward higher-yielding blue chip equities and, of course, corporate bonds. It was thus with a sense of extreme urgency that Peter asked Jenny Bingham to present the idea to the trustees with the suggestion that a third of total assets should be committed to it.

The trustees had appointed Peter's friend and fellow value investor Richard Oldfield of Oldfield Partners as their investment advisor. However, Oldfield's expertise lay in equities rather than bonds; and he lacked the in-house resources to engage in the exhaustive balance sheet analysis essential for running a sizeable international portfolio in distressed corporate debt. As a result, the trustees turned to another member of Peter's investment network, Mark Coombs of the Ashmore Group. A deal was struck almost immediately. The documentation was rushed through in three weeks and the funds were fully committed a month later.

The return in the first twelve months was over 40%, which more than repaired any damage inflicted during the financial crisis.

The other matter to which Peter now gave renewed attention was the writing of his book – in concept partly an autobiography and partly a more specific account of his investment life. He had discussed the idea with Mackenzie, especially with David Feather, who enthusiastically supported the project. As a group, Mackenzie agreed in principle to purchase a large number of copies to give to the more substantial holders of Mackenzie Cundill products and their distributors. Even after the redemptions that had accompanied the crisis, unit-holders of the Value Fund still numbered well over a million.

Obviously Peter would require help with his book, but deciding what kind of help was not entirely straightforward. Had it simply been an autobiography, he could have engaged a well-known journalist to ghost write it, but his conception of the book meant that the helper would also need considerable financial and investment knowledge. In addition, Peter's handwritten journals would have to be transcribed and edited. His earlier attempts to get this done had failed owing to the difficulty of deciphering his tiny, spidery script and his habit of using people's initials instead of their full names. Unless the transcriber were familiar both with the topics and the characters involved, the job posed real problems.

Peter really needed an "insider," and he invited me – CR-G, as I was always referred to in Peter's journal – to lunch. Since we had been friends for over thirty years, for twelve of which I had served on the board of the Value Fund, I filled the "insider" requirement. What's more, I had a degree in economics, had been an investment banker, a "risk arbitrageur," and a fund manager, had already written a book, and was as familiar with the work of Ben Graham and Peter's own "deep value" practices as I was with the main features of Peter's private life. Although I had been in touch with Peter I had not actually seen him for over two years.

When the lunch date was arranged, Fiona warned me that I would see a big physical change in him, but nothing she could have said would have prepared me adequately. As I was ushered into the hall I could see through to the master bedroom where Peter was standing next to the window. I was speechless. The contrast with the lithe athletic figure I had last encountered, in whom the only sign of illness was the merest tremor of the left hand, was so extreme that I was on the verge of tears. Peter caught sight of me and began to walk unsteadily toward me in welcome. Fixing me with those startling blue eyes and patting my hand he said, "It's all right, Christopher. Take a deep breath. It's not as bad as it looks." Unfortunately it was.

Once I recovered, we had the kind of fulsome discussion over lunch that we had always had. It included a very frank resumé of where matters stood with CJ and how it might be possible to ring the changes. After lunch we sat in the bay window overlooking Kensington Gardens while I read back to Peter the journal account of the shooting trip we had made to Hungary together years before. There was then a little wistful reminiscence about the night life in Budapest before we shook hands over Peter's proposal.

The book project could not have come at a better time. After ten years of success in my latest career incarnation as a maker of corporate films, the financial crisis had brought that market to a halt. Work on the book began almost immediately. I was to operate from the Kensington apartment at a desk in a bedroom next to Peter's study. We began by my reviewing all the Cundill Value Fund annual reports to determine what might make good investment stories. Then we turned our attention to the journals, of which there are nearly three hundred, going back to 1963. After a tense week despairing of Peter's idiosyncratic handwriting and thinking of Samuel Pepys, who wrote his diary in a code that no one managed to decipher for nearly three hundred years, the penny at last dropped, and the characters began to slip into fluid readability. I realized that the material was original, frank and quite eccentric, and that the venture was actually going to be fun.

Our routines soon became established. After reading that day's papers and periodicals, Peter stretched out on the bed beside my desk to assess what had been done and what needed doing. I quickly discovered that there was nothing at all wrong with his memory. He had pretty well perfect recall, right back to his early childhood, and in investment matters still had all the detail at his fingertips. Despite the Sacramento report, his ability to concentrate seemed largely unimpaired, at least when the subject interested him and he was not stressed. During his morning "nap," he frequently opened his eyes to comment or add some information, demonstrating that he had been thinking rather than sleeping.

Lunch together – usually finger food which Peter could still manage to eat on his own – became the high point of his day. Between mouthfuls I would read what I had transcribed in the past twenty-four hours. As Peter put it, in an extraordinary way it enabled him to relive his "wonderful life." For me the exercise was invaluable because the readings often prompted him to explain or expand on the journal. Revisiting the youthful Peter Cundill was often very funny, and laughter echoed round the apartment as it had not done in a while. *Routines and Orgies* was Peter's chosen title, taken from a rather obscure travel book called *Beyond the Mexique Bay* by Aldous Huxley. He had read it at that highly impressionable age when a young man knows what an orgy is and is ardently hoping one will come his way. The full sentence actually reads, "The commonest, one might call it the natural rhythm of human life, is routine punctuated by orgies." Huxley goes on to make it quite clear that he is not necessarily referring to "orgies" in the Roman sense. Peter told me that he had no intention of implying that either. My immediate response was to tell him "to pull the other one," after which we understood each other perfectly, and he chuckled away to himself on and off for an hour or so.

Peter was keen to get some chapters down on paper as quickly as possible so that extracts could be shared with Mackenzie and Charlie Sims's approval on its general direction could be canvassed. Within six months, about a third of it was done to Peter's satisfaction and extracts were duly sent off. After three weeks, feeling the silence was a little ominous, Peter e-mailed Charlie to enquire. In their ensuing conversation, it emerged that Charlie had hated the title, fearing it might create entirely the wrong impression among the Mackenzie clientele, and after reading the extracts he was entirely convinced that it would. Back to the drawing-board. In order to secure Mackenzie's participation and its financial commitment to the project, the book would have to focus primarily on Peter's investment life, touching only lightly on the personal side. There were definitely to be no orgies and there was to be a new working title. When the laughter subsided, Peter's first question was whether I could manage to write such a book and still make it entertaining rather than morphing it into some kind of textbook. I was confident that I could, and the project moved ahead.

38

The Tide Turns Again

THUS FAR PETER HAD BEEN comfortable spending the night on his own after the housekeeper had served his supper. Unfortunately, by then he was no longer completely safe on his legs. I became aware of this problem one afternoon upon hearing a heavy thud from Peter's study next door. I found him on the floor quite unable to get up by himself. He was unhurt, although his head had narrowly missed the corner of the desk, but it had taken all my strength to haul him back onto his feet. Peter dismissed the incident as a one-off stumble and swore me to secrecy. But his fall on the way to the bathroom in the middle of the night was potentially more serious. Once again he was fortunately not hurt, but spent the next three hours on the floor, before managing to drag himself close enough to the telephone to dislodge it and make contact with the porter on duty.

This time it could not be kept under wraps. For Fiona O'Driscoll it was the signal to put twenty-four-hour care in place. The proposal faced huge resistance from Peter, for whom any reduction in independence simply underlined the writing on the wall. However, the new night carers turned out to be a great success with Peter. Roza Pawlowska was a particular hit – very tall and good-looking with curly blonde hair, a warm smile and a generous, affectionate nature. She undoubtedly brightened up his evenings, bringing along good movies that they watched together, and she offered interesting, intelligent conversation with some original views on life. Her slightly hysterical Slavic personality and hero worship of things Polish rather appealed to Peter's taste for the dramatic. As Peter's mobility decreased, he felt his world shrinking around him. Even travelling by private plane was becoming awkward. This was in fact more of an attitude of mind than a reality.

At the same time Peter was embarrassed by his physical decline and reluctant to be seen at any of his old haunts. He had always taken a certain delight in being envied and had a horror of being pitied. His unavoidable early retirement had caused him great anguish. Of course he maintained a lively interest in his personal investments, but this could never replace the swashbuckling glamour associated with being the head of a large and influential group of mutual funds. He deeply missed the cut and thrust of daily business life and, like so many before him, found that after retirement it was not quite so easy to pick up the phone and get straight through to the chief executive of a major corporation.

In retirement the frequency of guests would have fallen off somewhat anyway but somehow the perception was that too many visitors were not really welcome. In fact, having been present at some of Peter's meetings, I soon discovered that, far from tiring Peter out, a lively exchange reanimated him and made him forget to be ill. Naturally his faithful coterie of old friends from both sides of the Atlantic and beyond never allowed themselves to be discouraged, and among the London residents he received frequent, regular visits from Peter Darling, Ian Steers, Ian Watson, James Morton, and David Nabarro in particular.

What Peter had been lacking was the imagination to see himself in the supremely fortunate position of being able to recreate a fulfilling life within the limitations of his disease. Work on the book now provided the stimulation that his job had previously offered, and he was just as passionately interested in that. The fear of loneliness was receding. He was enjoying regular companionship: with his carers; with Carla Williams, his charming masseuse, who brought music along and even got him dancing with her on his wobbly pins; with Jake, his physiotherapist; and with some of his old flames, including Louise Somers, who had been co-opted as a research assistant on the book; and with me and his family office entourage. A feeling was emerging that Peter could be weaned from leading a dull, reclusive life if he would only consent to use a wheelchair – a proposal that he stubbornly resisted because he saw it as a public admission of his invalid status, and his pride revolted at the idea.

He was still able, it was true, to include a routine daily walk unsupported, for which he was invariably attired only in skimpy shorts, his treasured Descente running shoes without socks, a short-sleeved singlet and, if it was very cold, a flimsy blue windbreaker zipped up half way. Anything more was just sissy. In this gear he would parade along Kensington High Street toward the Albert Hall in the company of his walker of the day – a kind porter from the Thorney Court apartments, Fiona, Jake, or myself, each on tenterhooks lest Peter should stumble. Like royalty he walked a step or two in front, keeping an eye out for pretty girls, of whom there were usually plenty along that well-trodden tourist beat. His usual form, whenever such a one was approaching, was to break into a little jog. The spectacle of this tall, painfully gaunt figure, displaying strawberry red knees in colder weather – seemingly hardly capable of hobbling, far less managing a sort of extended lope – rarely failed to attract attention, often accompanied by a smile and an encouraging wave, always graciously returned by Peter.

Entertaining as the walks were, they represented less than half an hour of the day and could never have compensated adequately for full access to the world of culture that lay at his doorstep in one of the planet's greatest cities. It was a world that Peter truly missed. The sight of him rather pathetically leafing through *The Week*, the best of London's "what's going on" digests, was more than sad; it was irritating. Although he could no longer manage anything more than a short distance on a route without steps, wheelchair access could certainly be arranged at every theatre, cinema and art gallery in the capital, even on London's buses, although there was little likelihood that he'd take that option. In the event, it took a very attractive lady and a rather unusual circumstance to persuade him to cross the Rubicon and get the wheels rolling.

He received a visit from a Russian lady, Yulia Naily, one of the Annabel's crowd, recently divorced from her Lebanese husband and now in the final stages of a degree course at Central St Martin's, one of London's most prestigious art colleges. Her spoken English was excellent but in the course of conversation she confessed that she was having difficulty with expressing herself effectively in writing. Helpful as ever, Peter said he didn't understand a word of what she was trying to explain anyway but he knew a man who would know what it was all about and could help her. Yulia was duly introduced to me. A few days later she arrived for tea armed with the draft of her thesis which, at Peter's behest, I agreed to review and correct. During the tea party there was an animated discussion about art in which Yulia evinced a pretty sound knowledge of contemporary art but a woeful deficiency in anything much earlier than the 1970s. After she left, Peter rather wistfully mused that he wished he were able to take her to the Wallace Collection for an eye-opener with me as their guide.

Here was the wheelchair opportunity. I said I was very willing, but that I agreed it would not be possible for Peter unless it were in a wheelchair. I suggested that he call Yulia and invite her, mentioning *en passant* that he would probably have to be in a chair and ask her whether she would mind. Peter was dubious until I made the point that going around the museum even in a wheelchair with a glamorous companion like Yulia ministering to him had a certain unique cachet, and if she agreed to go he ought just to sit back and enjoy the envious glances. Yulia was in fact entranced by the idea, hitting exactly the right note by telling Peter she would be delighted to be seen with a handsome chap like him whether in wheelchair or not. The expedition went forward with one addition: lunch in the central courtyard at the Wallace. We would be ravenous after all the art appreciation, Yulia said, and pooh-poohed the idea that having to eat so clumsily in public would embarrass Peter. She undertook to feed him herself if that would make him more comfortable. Peter agreed that it certainly would.

The morning of the visit was warm and sunny. Yulia arrived punctually, long legs in the snuggest of blue jeans, a pair of St Tropez style espadrilles, a blouse that made a rather poor attempt at disguising what lay beneath, a little cardigan draped over her shoulders and a silk bandana tied tightly round her blonde curls. The lipstick was red but not excessively so. She could have stepped right out of *Vogue*. Peter was agog – as was I. The wheelchair had been stowed in the waiting car so that Peter could arrive downstairs walking with Yulia on his arm. All the porters on duty, who had evidently been equally smitten by this visitor, had lined up to open doors and fuss around while Peter basked in the reflected glory. As arranged, the car whisked our party straight through the courtyard to the front entrance of the museum, where Peter transferred to the wheelchair and the tour began. I pushed the chair and talked them along, while Yulia walked beside Peter holding his hand. When we came to a room panelled with Boucher's extremely buxom, naked nymphs, she burst into fits of laughter. Did Peter have a taste for that kind of figure? she asked. If so, she would start today eating only cakes and keep going for six months until she got there, but he would have to buy her a new pair of jeans – probably a whole new wardrobe.

At lunch she was as good as her word, feeding Peter with oysters, champagne and smoked salmon sandwiches, interspersed with the odd mildly flirtatious peck on the cheek, and interesting, occasionally slightly risqué, comments on what we had been viewing. There was plenty of laughter. The wheelchair had been discreetly tucked away so that Peter just appeared to be seated quite normally. It was the only discreet aspect. The surrounding guests found it hard to keep their eyes off the unfolding spectacle. Peter was in seventh heaven. The visit was an enormous hit, as was the wheelchair, and it ushered in a new – albeit brief – era.

39

The Spark of Life Regained

PETER WAS NOW feeling well enough to plan on attending the various trust meetings that took place in Bermuda. Although the care he required was readily available on the island, he was still keen to take a companion. Louise Somers was persuaded to take on the role and with the trip in the offing, Peter was very much in a holiday frame of mind, focused, energized, walking much better and looking forward to the meetings as well as the sunshine. The wheelchair stayed in its cupboard at Thorney Court and Peter climbed the steps into the private jet unaided. At the Hamilton Princess Hotel he had a ground floor suite that opened onto the garden and the swimming pool. The weather was ideal, warm and sunny but not humid. He took plenty of exercise, going for walks with Louise and swimming. He ate and slept well without seeming to need the frequent naps that had recently become a feature of his day. He surprised everybody by attending all the meetings, for which he had read and digested the papers, and he participated fully.

Christmas was approaching when Peter returned from Bermuda and he was keen that there should be what he called a Cundill family office Christmas lunch with Jenny Bingham, Fiona O'Driscoll, and me. It was to be another experimental outing to a restaurant and his preference was for Chinese. It was arranged at Ming Jiang, perhaps the best Chinese in London, with its splendid location at the top of the Royal Garden Hotel, which gives it panoramic views of Kensington Palace and Gardens. It was no more than a brisk five-minute walk from Peter's apartment and so he was determined that the wheelchair remain where it was and he would go on foot. The outward journey there was uneventful. Jenny arrived with party hats, the table was slap in the middle with the optimum view, Peter drank pink champagne through a straw and polished off a large helping of his favourite sweet and sour pork with the ladies taking turns feeding him.

However, by the time we finished lunch snow was lying thick on the ground in the park and there was no doubt that the pavements would be treacherous and slippery. A taxi appeared to be the obvious solution but Peter would have none of it. He had arrived on foot and he would go home by the same locomotion. The short journey back was utterly hair-raising with Peter lurching and slithering along, shaking uncontrollably and brushing off all attempts at assistance from either the home team or from good natured passers-by. As he finally staggered through the entrance at Thorney Court he wobbled around to face the rest of the party with a broad smile as if to say, "You didn't think I could do it, but I did it in spite of you." Finishing a marathon could hardly have given him more satisfaction.

Peter now had much to occupy him. His acceptance of the wheelchair had suddenly reopened vistas of opportunity that had seemed closed to him forever. Although he did not know it, this was to be the last year of his life, and what a year it was. As he said to me, it had been one of the best in his life, "and as you know better than most there've been plenty of great ones." Forlornly browsing through *The Week* was a thing of the past. Now he was keen as mustard to get out there and take cultural London by the scruff the neck once more. Over that final twelve months he made almost thirty visits to the theatre, the ballet, the major art exhibitions, concerts, and museums. It was a complete transformation from the reclusive life he had begun to lead. It enthused everyone around him, initiating a stream of ideas about where he might go and what he might do. Fiona was a great source of suggestions, and her days once again became caught up with booking tickets and organizing cars.

Peter made his inaugural trip to the theatre in my company. For years he had been a life benefactor of the National Theatre on the South Bank, and the staff there was delighted to welcome him back to the audience, devoting time and effort to ensuring that his wheelchair experience was as smooth and agreeable as possible. Nothing gave Peter greater pleasure than to be treated as a VIP; being greeted and guided to his place by an attractive young lady from the Corporate Office got things off to an excellent start. Chatting to the girl distracted his attention from the occasional glance by other theatre-goers at his rather emaciated, shaking frame.

The play was a production of Ted Hughes's translation of *Phèdre*, Racine's great classical tragedy in verse, with Helen Mirren in the title role, and it was first class. Having enthusiastically transferred from the wheelchair to a seat, Peter devoured the program and then sat rapt throughout the performance. He ate two vanilla ice creams in the interval and would have eaten a third had there been time. On the way out, people were beginning to arrive for the evening shows, the musicians were playing in the foyer and the bars were busy. Peter asked to be wheeled around to see the action. In the car on the way home he turned to me and said, "You know, I enjoyed the play very much indeed but the best thing about it was feeling a part of it all again – that and driving through the London streets I so often ran through." After that there was no stopping him. The wheelchair access facilities of London's major theatres were put thoroughly to the test and passed with flying colours. One particularly attractive, and largely unmodernized, Victorian theatre even laid out special planking and had two of its staff on hand to do the extra pushing up a steep slope.

Apart from his deep interest in history in its more academic sense, Peter was a great aficionado of the historical novel as a genre that can make history significantly more approachable to a wide audience. Because he gobbled up the works of his favourite authors, such as Bernard Cornwall and Conn Iggulden, as fast as their books came out, he was always on the look-out for alternatives. With this in mind I introduced him to the historical novels of Daphne du Maurier, which he took to instantly. They are all set in Cornwall, the most westerly of the English counties and one that Peter had never visited. Its north coast is wild and romantic, lashed by the ocean, exposed to its gales and home to the sweeping open terrain of Bodmin Moor, whereas the south coast on the English Channel is sheltered and temperate, in some places sub-tropical.

Once he was hooked by du Maurier's books, Peter wanted to visit Cornwall, and Fiona began investigating possibilities. Getting there was no problem, with the international airport at Newquay open to private flights but, rather surprisingly, accommodation that matched his standards was. The county could offer nothing better than a four-star hotel, and disabled access was pretty poor. The other difficulty was how to arrange the sight-seeing. Road travel along deeply banked lanes with no view was clearly impractical. Fiona hit on the obvious answer – a helicopter, which also meant that staying at a hotel in Cornwall was not essential.

When he mentioned his Cornwall project to CJ she evinced no interest whatever. However Fiona had now found a wonderful hotel, complete with a helipad, which would certainly work. Lucknam Park near Bath is definitely five-star; a beautiful Georgian country mansion, built in the distinctive honey-coloured limestone of the Cotswolds, surrounded by five hundred acres of parkland and offering a Michelin-starred restaurant, a spa and a beauty centre. The question of possible companions then arose in earnest. Unfortunately Yulia, who might have been delighted to join Peter on a holiday, was going to be busy with exams and Louise could not then be spared from the research work that she was doing for me. However Peter's old address book turned out to be a sterling resource well stocked as it remained with erstwhile dining and dancing partners, many of whom still made efforts to keep in touch. Peter eventually invited Emily Clarke, an amusing and attractive lady with an extremely kind heart.

Emily came to visit with Peter well in advance of the trip so that he could give her copies of Daphne du Maurier's novels and discuss the details of the planned excursions. Despite Fiona's warning, she was shocked by Peter's appearance but, as was invariably the case she quickly forgot about it between the spell of Peter's charm and a natural sympathy for him. She seemed inclined to mother him a little and consequently very soon had him purring; at the same time she was sensitive enough not to fuss over him too much, which he would have hated.

As the plans for the trip matured the sightseeing program was expanded to include all the major attractions of Cornwall as well as Bath and the Scilly Isles, making full use of the scope of the helicopter. It was agreed that Fiona would accompany the party to get them settled in at Lucknam and then return to London. They made it to Lucknam in forty minutes. Their reception was all it should have been; the ground floor suite was magnificent and gave them perfect wheelchair access to the garden and the public rooms. The heli-tourism made it possible for them to accomplish an enormous amount with very little effort, with the perfect view and no crowds. Afterward Captain Richardson forwarded a copy of his log to Peter. It gives an amazing account of what they managed to see in nine and a half hours of flying time. Historic and pre-historic sites and literary legends rolled out under them. Peter now had the bug, and it was to be heli-tourism from now on wherever possible. Here is one day's overview:

August 4
The Westbury White Horse, Stonehenge, Old Sarum Castle, Salisbury Cathedral, Sandbanks, with its multi million pound seaside houses, Cerne Man (the biggest prick in the world), Lyme Regis, Exmouth, Plymouth, over the Hoe where Drake calmly played bowls as the Spanish Armada approached, crossed the Tamar over Fowey and up the river to Menabilly (du Maurier's home and the model for Manderley in *Rebecca*), Polkerris, Mevagissey, Falmouth, over and around St Mawes and Pendennis castles and the spectacular St Michael's Mount. Bude, Clovelly and Westward Ho! Across over Doone Valley (location for Blackmore's historical novel *Lorna Doone*).

40

Living in the Moment

AS NEWS ABOUT Peter's condition spread he was receiving a steady stream of visitors. In addition to old friends and colleagues, fellow value investors and fund managers with whom the trust had investments, a number of people seeking financial help for personal reasons, or for some charity or project, found his door open. Among them was the British journalist and media personality Kate Spicer. She had learned from a mutual friend that Peter was suffering from Fragile X, as was her younger brother Tom, who had been afflicted from birth. Naturally Peter was deeply sympathetic and he quickly discovered that Kate was far more knowledgeable about FXTAS than any of the doctors he had seen, other than the team in Sacramento.

She had come to canvas Peter's support for a unique and highly ambitious project related to Tom, who from his early teens had been a huge fan of the iconic American heavy metal band Metallica and, above all, of their drummer Lars Ulrich. For years he had badgered Kate to take him to Los Angeles to hear the band play live and to meet Ulrich – no small ambition, especially given the band's commitments and their enormous fan club. However, it seemed to Kate that this was so important to Tom that she and her other brother, Will, a filmmaker, had to pull it off somehow. Her idea was to film the whole expedition and turn the footage into a documentary to raise public awareness of Fragile X and secure more funding toward the search for a cure. She had already contacted Ulrich and found him sympathetic and willing in principle to lend his support. Now she needed help financing the project.

Peter, of course, had never heard of Lars Ulrich or Metallica and would undoubtedly have hated the band's music, but he was excited by the imaginative approach and the long-term possibilities of Kate's scheme. Above all he was moved at the thought of what a young man like Tom had endured so far and what a dire future seemed in store for him. As Peter saw it, realizing this ambition might be the high point of Tom's life – something he could always look back on with pleasure. He contributed most generously. The film is moving and tender as well as exuberantly funny and completely engaging. It would have had Peter in tears, as it did many in the audience when it debuted at the British Academy of Film and Television Arts in Piccadilly. At least he did see a rough cut. *Mission to Lars* has since been shown to great acclaim all over the world. It actually transcends the topic of Fragile X, It emerges as a celebration of the triumph of the human spirit over seemingly insuperable odds, facilitated by many acts of spontaneous generosity, especially from Ulrich, who has become something of a folk hero as a result.

Another visitor was Peter's old friend Prem Watsa, who had kindly agreed to write the foreword to *There's Always Something to Do,* the book about Peter's investment life on which I was then working. Prem had visited the previous year and had particularly asked to be warned if there was a feeling that the end might be in sight. I had duly called Prem to warn him that it might not be that far off. However remarkable the recent improvement might have appeared to those who saw Peter every day, for Prem the deterioration that he now witnessed was a big shock. Before leaving he suggested hosting a dinner in Toronto in Peter's honour. It was agreed there and then that it would need to be soon. Peter was delighted with the plan and Prem wasted no time. With Charlie Sims of Mackenzie as the joint sponsor, they fixed a date in September at the Toronto Club and Peter was asked to provide a list of friends he would like to be invited.

In the meantime another visit to Bermuda for trust meetings was in the offing. This time Peter had decided to ask Phyllis Ellis to come from Toronto to act as his companion. Her account of this visit to Bermuda is touching and funny, but it gives a stark picture of the realities of Peter's condition. Only his indomitable spirit could have held him together and still made it possible, against all the odds, to live life and enjoy it in the face of an apparently overwhelming and humiliating debility. This is Phyllis's account:

Bermuda Bound
Toronto was already turning hot and humid when Peter placed his regular Sunday "check in" call, surprising me with an invitation to

Bermuda. Of course I would go. I always took the opportunity to see him when he "summoned," or in Peter's case, "when it suited." In many ways I had become his "go-to girl," a friend, confidante and jester. Long gone were the days when "lover" was part of the equation, which suited me perfectly. But I remained a constant in his life and with the large pond between us, was excited to see him ...

The trip was an odd and fractured comedy of errors.

Peter immediately rejected the hired nurse (a frail seventy-year-old woman) who herself needed an afternoon nap and couldn't lift him from his wheelchair. He demanded that I take over the role of care-giver, chief bottle washer, changer of diapers, showerer and shaver, feeder of vanilla ice cream, wiper of drool, TV channel surfer, Kindle operator, dresser (a.m. and p.m.); basically, his full-time nurse. He was almost completely incapacitated, shaking beyond belief, weak and frail. "Not doing well physically" had been a gross understatement.

Oh yes, and if he choked, there was a battery-powered machine to prevent him from ... well, choking. Wonderful! I had already dropped all soaking, six feet of him as he stumbled out of the shower, slipping through my arms like a wet fish and missing a seri-ous head injury on the porcelain by inches. He just burst into laugh-ter and then so did I. Crisis averted for the moment, my next nursely duty was mastering the electric pump apparatus. Directions: Remove from hard case, quickly shove rubber pipe down throat, hoping not to puncture anything and press on. And of course, at dinner, he did choke, turning blue. With the directions in my hand and out of my mind for fear that I might perforate his oesophagus, I rushed the procedure and cleared his throat but succeeded in suctioning his en-tire bottom lip into the tube of the machine. Unfortunately how to prise bottom lip from tube is not in the instructions.

A wonderful reason why Bermuda was a perfect place for Peter was the weather, and he loved our daily swims. About mid-week, we struggled to the pool (he refusing his wheelchair) to begin what he called his "laps" – walking in circles at the shallow end. Having been a great sports woman myself, I took pleasure in the notion that although he couldn't walk, was beginning to find speech more difficult, and could no longer dance, he still wanted to do his "work

out." That morning was no different. I was in the lead almost running on the spot slowly in the water with Peter pulling up the rear.
There were a couple of pretty women sitting in the sun and I noticed
him paddling with a little more purpose than the day before. Funny
how pretty women motivated him. With my back to Peter, and the
pretty women, I heard a loud scream. As I turned around, Peter was
gone. I looked down and there he was, still paddling his arms, but at
the bottom of the pool. I dived down, pulled him up, dragged him
lifeguard-style (I'd seen it in movies) to the side of the pool. After his
choking subsided, I asked him furiously what the hell he thought he
was doing, was he trying to give me a heart attack! He grinned and
whispered with a crooked smile, "the backstroke."

I can make light of my Florence Nightingale-esque week with
Peter in Bermuda. But it wasn't really funny. Not really funny at all.
He was a shadow of himself, no less selfish or demanding but somehow childlike in his utter dependency, almost like an infant. He
hated being like it, but he tried to make the best of it. I hated it too.
Not the idea of helping my dearest friend or reading to him or rubbing his back when he shook himself to sleep. But the idea that I
was alone and responsible for him and although I tell the story
with humour, on a couple of occasions the near misses could have
been fatal.

"You could have died!" I said as I sat on the floor with him after
he smashed into the corner of the bureau. He smiled, a trickle of
blood rolling from his forehead and said "Well my dear, you are
missing the point; at least I would have been with you."

I'm not sure loved ones should be "that responsible person," especially when someone is so compromised. Of course you'll do it,
you'd do anything for them, but as the shadows circle and the end is
inevitable, the time together might be more meaningfully spent in
sharing stories, memories and love and having someone else do the
chores.

But not so fast, this is Peter Cundill we're talking about – a man
who could move mountains in his professional life, but also a man
who had the emotional intelligence of a spoiled child having a temper tantrum. But that's who he was, a wonderful dichotomy.

Fiona O'Driscoll and I went with Peter on the flight to Toronto for the dinner in his honour, but he was to be without a carer until we reached Canada. By this time Peter could only walk with support and although emaciated, was still very heavy. There was no question of his climbing up into the cabin; instead he was carried bodily up the gangway by a muscular stalwart in a sort of fireman's lift that left his torso dangling over his porter's back. He evidently enjoyed it, chuckling away and attempting to wave to Fiona and me, watching slightly apprehensively from below.

The aircraft interior was superbly equipped, with a proper full-length bed, and the hostess took charge of feeding Peter. Nevertheless, ministering to his needs was still a full-time job; turning the pages for him, persuading him to drink water, blowing his nose, wiping away the dribbles and especially getting him to the toilet and back – not an operation that could be undertaken single-handed. His frequent visits proved extremely taxing although, as always with Peter, there was a comic side to it all that he entered into fully. The remarkable thing was that even through the humiliating indignities of helplessness and failing bodily functions Peter held onto his sense of humour and his delightful appreciation of the absurdities of life – incredibly, his personal dignity actually remained intact.

The visit got off to an auspicious start in the limousine on the way into town. Fiona remarked that the staff at the Four Seasons would be looking forward to welcoming Peter Cundill back. At the next red light the driver turned round to look at Peter and asked, "Are you really the famous Peter Cundill?" Peter nodded and the driver went on. "It's fantastic to have you in my car. I've owned your fund for years and it's been the best investment I've ever had." Nothing could have delighted Peter more.

His reception at the Four Seasons exceeded every expectation. Liloo, the diminutive head concierge, ran around from her desk to embrace him as he tottered across the lobby – he had refused to make his grand entrance in the wheelchair. He fell, almost literally, into her arms and for a split second it looked as if they were both going to end up on the floor together. She only just managed to hold him up, staving off disaster. For the next few days Peter held court in his suite. He immediately established a routine for the day that began with his constitutional along Yorkville Avenue, down Old York Lane and back along Cumberland Street, accompanied by an entourage, generally consisting of Fiona, Jenny Bingham, and me. He seemed revitalized. He had asked Phyllis to be his date for the party and she spent as much time as she could with him in the preceding days. She wrote an endearingly frank account:

> The dinner at The Toronto Club was an extraordinary event. It was the perfect thing to do for Peter and also very important for all his closest friends and colleagues to honour him, have a visit and reminisce. He was excited, pleased and proud but also rather nervous. It was like a Fragile X coming out party, as many of the guests hadn't seen him since the disease had ravaged him so.
>
> He wanted to be in good form, to look dapper and receive his guests with panache. So we practised … smiling, standing with purpose and we even ran a few firm handshakes. Over the past year I had mastered the seamless dinner routine to make it look less like feeding a baby and more like he was some great king who couldn't be bothered feeding himself. That's where Peter and I had so much fun, when he'd expose his insecurities, his fears and secrets. As the keeper of so many Peter Cundill secrets, I knew first-hand how worried he really was about seeing everyone at the event. Would he stumble or drool or choke? But we laughed about it and put measures in place to contend with all potential mishaps.
>
> I would be close, Kleenex in hand, and with our practised choreography and a subtle brush, keep him fresh and, as he said, "drool-free." I'd stand close and if he faltered, doing his famous bob and weave, I'd grab his elbow and give him a peck on the cheek to make it look as if I couldn't wait to get back to his hotel room to give the impression – in his words – that he was still a stallion in bed.
>
> The evening was spectacular for him. He loved receiving his dry martini (another choreographed moment) avec the ever-important straw, but was a little fussy when it was delivered at the wrong moment. He addressed each of his guests with wise whispers of brilliance and I watched as young and older hung on his every word. This was pure joy for him.

The speeches, the revealing of his portrait, the honouring of him both as a man and as a genius puffed up his chest in a way I hadn't seen since he had become so ill. He even had a little nap halfway through the event so he could hang in a little longer, as anything north of 7 p.m. was much past his bedtime.

When we arrived back to the hotel, I expected a little download of all the reconnects, the wonderful words, and everyone honouring him in this way. But he just looked at me and stuttered, "Well Phyl, better to be alive and hear all the nice things people say about you, than dead and never know."

Nonetheless Peter knew it would be his last visit.

He had made no attempt at a speech; however, at the end of the dinner his glass was tapped for silence and the microphone was held for him as he spoke the three famous words from the lines penned by Catullus after his brother's death, "Ave atque vale" – "Hail and farewell." There was a moment of complete silence while its import dawned, and then rapturous, prolonged applause.

That was undoubtedly the high point of the entire trip, although it was very nearly equalled two days later when Phil Cunningham and David Feather took Peter out to lunch in the wheelchair. It was a warm, sunny, early fall day. Instead of going to a restaurant they bought hot dogs and Dairy Queen sundaes from a vendor stand and ate them in the park as they told stories.

No matter how enfeebled Peter's physical condition, there was no allowing the grass to grow under the wheelchair. In the first two weeks after getting back to London he went to see the American Dance Company at Sadler's Wells, attended the Battle of Britain 50th anniversary concert at the Albert Hall, went to the National Theatre to see *Danton's Death* and to the Royal Academy to visit the Gauguin exhibition. At the same time he was planning an excursion to Sicily for a week – another adventure in heli-tourism.

On this occasion Peter was very keen to see whether he could rustle up a friend who spoke Italian to be his companion on the expedition which was to last for a week and indeed he did know a young woman film director, perhaps from the MOA days, called Michaela Vignard. As it turned out she was just finishing shooting a film in France and welcomed the prospect of a break and a bit of an adventure. Owing to her filming commitment she was unable to join the group, which included Fiona and me, who were flying with Peter to Palermo, but would meet us there for the helicopter flight to Trapani on the south coast of Sicily.

On arrival in Palermo we were met by the helicopter pilot, a little Sicilian, with a jaunty air, and driven across to his plane. About ten minutes later an airport vehicle came screaming across the tarmac and skidded to a halt beside us. Michaela had arrived. Seeing Peter again in his present condition must have been quite a shock, but she carried it off and bore the pilot's slightly quizzical eye with admirable disdain. She was very slim, with long black hair that fluttered in the wind, gauzily attired in a most tasteful way and wearing a picture hat. Peter was obviously pleased to see her and at his most charming as she began to fuss over him a little. The dwarf-sized pilot must have been a champion weight lifter. He picked Peter up as if he were a toddler and swung him up into his seat. He looked as if he was about to do the same with Michaela but she hopped up nimbly on her own, giving Peter a peck on the cheek as she settled beside him. Peter was shaking away as usual but busy being genial to Michaela and started telling her about his pilot's license and that he could easily fly the helicopter. An expression of complete horror and naked terror crossed her face – was he really proposing to fly us all? Peter chuckled away as he patted her hand to calm her down.

The flight took us over the Greek temple at Segesta, basking majestically in the sunshine, its honey-coloured stone glowing hypnotically, almost untouched by the centuries. The hotel was slightly inland, in the midst of orange and lemon groves, shaped like a renaissance palazzo with two wings projecting from the centre surrounding a swimming pool the size of a small lake. Peter's corner suite had a private Jacuzzi on its terrace. He had visions of lazing in it with Michaela smoking a cigar and quaffing glasses of champagne. There was, however, a slight drawback – the Jacuzzi was accessed by steep steps. How to get Peter in and out? Michaela seemed quite game in principle, but she was not in the same muscular league as the pilot. Undaunted, Simon, the resourceful concierge, solved the problem by offering the services of the gardeners to do the hoisting. As he said, it would be more entertaining for them than clipping hedges.

The two local carers who were to be in charge of the practicalities of nursing the invalid were completely unphased by Peter's condition. In fact they very quickly got to grips with the situation. With Peter and Michaela contentedly settled and ordering their supper and the carers in charge, Fiona and I repaired to the bar for a stiff cocktail, leaving them to dine together in the suite and catch up.

During the night a rain storm flooded the hotel terraces and the water was being sluiced out of the marble-floored lobby when I came down early to set off across the fields for a constitutional walk in the watery sunshine. My choice of route was a glorious mistake. I arrived back an hour later muddied up to the knees but carrying a selection of freshly picked fruit and wild flowers for the breakfast table – oranges, tangerines, pomegranates, grapes, and figs still damp from the rain. With this offering in a basket, I arrived in Peter's suite to find him breakfasting with one of the carers. He explained to me with a mischievous smile that Michaela had intended to have a sleep in because she was completely exhausted, at which statement the carer looked mightily impressed, as Peter probably intended.

Over the next few days they certainly covered a lot of ground together, flying over Mount Etna, visiting Horatio Nelson's Sicilian estate at Bronte, and following the line of advance of the British 8th Army in their 1943 campaign. Michaela turned out to be as well informed as Peter on the island's history so they got along famously. As he also discovered she was deeply religious and a committed Roman Catholic as well as a strong believer in faith healing. She made a great effort to persuade Peter to visit a healer in Madrid who had effected a miraculous cure of her mother. In this she failed completely but she was genuinely tender-hearted and from then on kept in regular touch with Peter.

Fiona and I had returned to London the day after the party arrived, but Fiona was able to keep abreast of events through the carers and with Simon, who made it his particular business to see that Peter and his guest enjoyed a thoroughly good time. His efforts did not go unnoticed or unrewarded. As soon as Peter learned that Simon would be out of a job in the winter, when the hotel is closed, he sent him $10,000 to tide him over.

41

Fast Lane to the Finish

BY THE TIME PETER got back from Sicily he was already planning Christmas in a warm and luxurious spot that offered a new experience. After a great deal of deliberation he zeroed in on Egypt, which had always intrigued him as the most populous and only secular Arab state of real consequence. He had been closely following the recent upheaval in Tunisia and at this point his acute antennae were beginning to sense that Egypt might now also be on the brink of a seminal transition toward parliamentary democracy. If this were so, the evolution was unlikely to be peaceful because the oligarchy would almost certainly cling to power. Potentially this was the stuff out of which investment opportunities are born. True to old habit, Peter was keen to sniff the air.

Naturally Egypt's investment potential was not the sole attraction. Peter had always been fascinated with the country's extraordinarily long, uninterrupted history, rivalled only by that of China. He had been particularly struck years earlier by a visit to the great temple complex at Philae, just above the Nile's first cataract, near Aswan. His guide had taken him down into a kind of crypt to see a primitive statue of the pre-dynastic god Min, the god of reproduction and fecundity, represented as the figure of a man with an outsized, erect penis, polished by the hands of thousands of generations of sterile women who had come, and still came, to petition his aid. While Peter stood in amazement a woman in Muslim garb went through the ancient rite, paying no attention to the onlooker and not evincing the slightest sign of embarrassment. Min's worship had been continuous among women of all faiths for well over seven thousand years.

Its sheer antiquity was a part of the country's magic for Peter, as was its remarkable ability to accommodate an endless flow of different invasions, civilizations, cultures, and religions without losing its unique identity. Since his visit to the Orthodox Primate in Istanbul, Peter had hoped one day to visit Saint Catherine's Monastery at the foot of Mount Sinai. It is the oldest monastery in the world and has never been pillaged or sacked since its foundation by the great Byzantine Emperor Justinian, who also built Hagia Sophia. It interested Peter especially on account of one particular manuscript known as the "Achtiname," a document of the Prophet Mohamed giving his protection to the monastery in perpetuity. What Peter found compelling about it was its content, which contravened any claim to legitimacy on the part of Islamic Jihad. This is the section he had in mind:

> This is a message from Mohammed bin Abdullah, as a covenant to those who adopt Christianity near and far, we are with them. Verily I, the servants, the helpers and my followers defend them, because Christians are my citizens and by Allah I hold out against anything that displeases them. No compulsion is to be on them. Neither are their judges to be removed from their jobs, nor their monks from their monasteries. No one is to destroy a house of their religion, to damage it, or to carry anything from it to the Muslims' houses. Should anyone take away any of these, he would spoil God's covenant and disobey His Prophet ... No one of the Nation is to disobey this covenant until the Last Day.

There are of course disputes about the manuscript's authenticity but it is impossible to ignore that Saint Catherine's, rich though it was, has remained free from any form of violation for over fourteen centuries. It was endorsed and respected by every successive Islamic regime under whose governance the monastery happened to fall, right up to the present governor of Sinai. Peter's plan was to make one of his helicopter descents on Saint Catherine's. The next step was to find a five-star hotel within striking distance. Sharm El-Sheikh, the playground of the Moubarak regime at the top of the Gulf of Aqaba on the Red Sea, was an ideal location, to which it was perfectly practicable to fly privately from London. Fiona O'Driscoll found a Four Seasons Hotel there, and Christmas began to take shape.

In the meantime Peter's old and dear friends George and Anne MacLaren from Montreal had decided not to defer a farewell visit to him in London until the spring just in case it should be too late. By this time, although Peter loved visitors, he was finding that an hour at a time was all he could take. That said, if it was an exhibition or a matinee performance that gripped him, he could still manage hours without a break. He was keen to see Tate Britain's exhibition "The Romantics: Art and the Sublime," which had caught his imagination. It was to include two of his favourite paintings by John Martin, *The Great Day of His Wrath* and *The Plains of Heaven*, as well as paintings on epic themes and major turbulences of nature – and Shakespeare, with Henry Fuseli's *Lady Macbeth Seizing the Bloody Daggers* as one of the centrepieces. Peter could hardly wait. It was as though he was expecting vicariously to relive some of his own high-risk adventures from the confines of his wheelchair, and *Macbeth* had been his favourite Shakespeare since his performance as Banquo at Cap à l'Aigle. He decided that the MacLarens would be ideal companions for this experience, and so it proved. It was a memorable morning, during which the party experienced every nuance, from the storms and avalanches and the "derring-do" of epic heroes to Napoleon's retreat from Moscow and the battle of Waterloo. It was a stirring farewell.

———————

The Christmas visit to Egypt was to last almost two weeks. Peter had invited CJ to join him for the last few days, which would include Christmas Day itself. Somewhat to his surprise, she accepted; but he was still concerned with whom he could invite as a congenial companion for the outward journey and the major part of the excursion. Once again Yulia, who might have been a possibility, was going to be absent in Russia and he found Michaela's reiterated attempts to enthuse him about faith healing a little tiresome. However Yulia had a friend, a mature student from Ukraine, who was studying hard to complete her master's thesis and who, so she thought, might be delighted to keep Peter company in Egypt as long as it was alright to bring along her books and she could count on having plenty of time for her studies. In principle this was a perfectly workable arrangement from Peter's point of view since he slept so much anyway, and Karine Iumukian was duly invited to tea with Yulia. She was a little shy but she was bright and attractive. Peter and she were soon chatting away as though they had known each other for years and the discovery that Karine had a major interest in the Byzantine and Ottoman Empires clinched it.

The most significant danger to Peter's immediate health stemmed from his inability to cough strongly enough to clear his throat and prevent food particles from slipping down into his lungs. He had suffered several bouts of resulting infection over the past year, which had been successfully treated with antibiotics. Peter's physician, James Pozzi, was both a good friend and a pragmatist. He well knew that Peter had deliberately refused the option of being fed through a tube, which would have avoided that danger. However, he was anxious about the projected visit to Egypt, which is not noted either for its hygiene or for its medical facilities. On one of his routine visits, which were usually conducted in Peter's bedroom and consisted mostly of general conversation with much laughter, he found Peter stretched out on his bed listening to music on his iPod. Pozzi obliged by turning the music off so they could enjoy their usual chat. Nevertheless, before leaving he used the occasion to voice his concerns about Egypt. Peter listened politely and then said, "James, you and I both know that I haven't much time left and I've nothing to lose. Something's going to carry me off in the not too distant future whatever I do, and I intend to make the most of my time in the interim." Then, with a wicked smile, he added, "So why don't you just fuck off home now and turn the Sinatra back on before you go." This exchange has remained one of Pozzi's most treasured memories of Peter.

Then the question of the changeover of companions in Egypt needed a solution. Peter had decided it would be best handled by having two Christmases with two batches of presents, the first before Karine's departure on Christmas Eve and the second with CJ on Christmas Day. The slightly awkward matter of briefing the hotel staff and the two full-time Egyptian carers was to be left to Fiona who was accompanying the party to see them get settled in and to instruct the local medical team and the carers about Peter's medical and dietary requirements. I was also to be a member of the party in order to work with Peter on an interview that he was giving for David Berman's "Report on Business" in the Toronto *Globe and Mail*.

Things began well. The same crew as for the Sicilian jaunt greeted Peter enthusiastically, and the brawny stalwarts were waiting on the tarmac ready to lift him into the aircraft. Karine seemed a little confused as to what to do, evidently not certain that turning pages, administering drinks, spoon feeding, or lavatory attendance fell within her remit as a guest. Peter was paying rather more attention to the delightful air hostess, laughing and joking with her as she plied him with ice cream and encouraged him to drink his nourishing soup. Karine eventually gave up on her slightly ineffectual efforts to be companionable and retired to read until lunchtime, when she perked up considerably, tucking in with an impressive gusto that belied her slim lines. By the end of the flight Peter had begun to tire visibly, having slept very little.

The welcoming committee at the VIP terminal at Sharm El-Sheikh was an unhelpful irritation. The group was kept waiting for nearly an hour in the lounge while the staff rushed around ineffectually with the passports. Constant offers of tea and coffee were no consolation for the delay in getting to the Four Seasons. There was worse to come. Another welcoming committee was waiting for us at the resort, including the doctor and the two Egyptian carers. By this time Peter was in no mood to be meeting and greeting; all he wanted to do was to get to the accommodation, watch some baseball while he ate his supper, and go to bed. But the accommodation was a disaster.

Despite Fiona's absolute stipulation that there could not be any stairs, it was on multiple levels and not even the front door could be reached without going up and down. Nor were there any wheelchair ramps. By this time Peter's mood had reached the decidedly grumpy stage. While Fiona and I were engaged in an interminable meeting with the medical team, Peter and Karine were waiting for room service to appear with some sustenance. Peter asked Karine to switch on the TV to see if she could find the channel with the baseball. She spent the next quarter of an hour flicking through channel after channel, occasionally stopping at a film or a soap show. Finally, and most uncharacteristically, Peter exploded and told her to stop fiddling with the channel changer and get someone who was competent. She ran off in tears and shut herself up in her room.

Having said goodnight to the medical team, with the exception of the night carer, Fiona managed to find the right channel and sat with Peter while he ate his supper. I set off with two glasses of wine to talk to Karine, who I eventually coaxed out of her bedroom, although still in tears. She was ready to gather up her bags and return to London. It took three quarters of an hour out on the patio and all my powers of persuasion, with repeated assurances that Peter was really a very kind, charming and gentlemanly man, to convince her to stay. By this time, general exhaustion had set in and everyone retired to their quarters leaving the night carer to deal with Peter until the morning.

Fiona and I were acutely aware that there was no possible way we could leave matters as they stood. The next morning we would have to insist on a change of accommodation. After an early visit to the duty manager to express extreme dissatisfaction with the arrangements and with the hotel's incomprehensible failure to act on the explicit requirements laid out at the time of booking, a meeting was arranged for later, so that Fiona and I could view the alternatives.

Back at the house the atmosphere when we returned was far better than expected. Peter, Karine, and Samar Mohammed, the night carer, were breakfasting peacefully by the pool in the early morning sunshine. Karine was appealingly groomed, wearing a most tasteful bikini underneath a gauzy *pareo* – a combination that showed her to advantage. Peter was paying her plenty of attention, and at his most winsomely charming. She was responding animatedly, laughing and joking and discussing plans. A night's rest and an attractive lady to breakfast with had banished the blues. Karine had obviously decided to make the best of things and was beginning once again to enjoy Peter's company. Peter and Samar, a Muslim lady with a lively sense of humour, seemed already to be old friends.

Fiona and I met with the director of rooms, and explained the situation again. Together we visited two other possibilities, neither of them ideal. When I insisted that, since cost was not an issue, they simply must be able to do better, things changed. Indeed, there were all sorts of splendid stand-alone villas scattered across the property. Given that the sea in the vicinity was internationally known to be out of bounds owing to recent shark attacks, perhaps one of them was unoccupied. Half an hour later he called to recommend the Presidential Suite, a huge domed bungalow with practically no steps, standing alone in its own garden, surrounded by lawns and festooned with jasmine and bougainvillea. Its panoramic view stretched out uninterrupted across the sea to Tiran Island. This was it at last.

Peter was at first reluctant to undergo the upheaval, but finally saw that he need only sit in the sunshine with a hat on and read his new book, *Democracy Prevention: The Politics of the U.S.-Egyptian Alliance*. The transfer was, of course, a complete sell-out and not just for Peter; Karine too was evidently enchanted by the charm of the new surroundings and now entering fully into the spirit of what was, after all, an amazing holiday. After yet another meeting with the charismatic and super-conscientious Dr Nagla, whom Peter had very reluctantly agreed to see briefly, Fiona felt satisfied that her work was done and she could make her way to the airport and back home. Peter's other carer, Nagwa Bestavros, an independently minded lady in her mid-forties, was a mine of information about Egyptian politics, feminist issues, and the unique culture of the country's Coptic community, all of which fascinated Peter. The routine that the two carers established was that whoever was doing day duty would arrive early in the morning in time to help with Peter's ablutions and get him dressed. The three of them would then have breakfast together outside, in the early morning sunshine, while Karine, who was not an early riser, remained asleep. Under their tutelage Peter went native for this meal, eating a "Bedouin breakfast" of sweet mint tea, spicy falafel, a fresh curd cheese, Bedouin-style flat bread, honey, and halva.

Although neither of the carers could swim, they agreed to take Peter into the pool as long as he stayed within their depth. They were both tiny. For the occasion they turned up swathed in voluminous robes which were in fact more revealing than bathing suits as they clung to the body as soon as they got wet. However, it made for quite a party; the tall skeletal figure of Peter gambolling with the two little ladies, one of whom was quite plump, who squealed and shrieked with laughter in the water. As a follow-up, I was persuaded to give the ladies a swimming lesson in the afternoon. This consisted in dragging them up and down the pool by their hands, while they more or less kept afloat by kicking their legs – until they dissolved into giggles and forgot to kick. Toward the end of the afternoon swim, Karine also appeared wearing a thoroughly non-Islamic bathing suit and gave an elegant demonstration of the breaststroke.

I had expected to fly back to London that day, but the flight had been cancelled because of heavy snow at Heathrow. Peter was sympathetic, although quietly rather pleased, hoping that the delay might be further prolonged so that I could join the excursion to Saint Catherine's monastery. A helicopter trip had been ruled out because the Egyptian military had closed the airspace over Sinai to all helicopter traffic except for the army and politicos, but an air-conditioned limousine was quite feasible. As a consolation for the delay Peter insisted that I should dine that evening in the grandest of the Four Seasons' restaurants and provide myself with a large cigar that I was to smoke "for Peter" on the lawn of the villa in the moonlight, cradling a brandy glass. Nothing loath, I fulfilled these instructions to the letter and it was indeed a memorably beautiful night – crystal clear with stars peppering the sky.

By the next day flights to London were restored and I was able to head for home and Christmas with my family in the knowledge that I was leaving Peter in fine form and surrounded with excellent care. Both Samar and Nagwa had derived considerable amusement from the prospect of the second Christmas that was to follow CJ's arrival. All went according to plan. Karine travelled back to London on Christmas Eve and CJ arrived. Christmas Day went by peacefully enough and presents were opened and crackers pulled for the second time. But unfortunately on Boxing Day the old trouble of bronchial pneumonia caused by food particles returned with a vengeance. By the evening Peter was running a high temperature and having difficulty breathing. Dr Nagla wanted to transfer him immediately to the nearby military hospital for intravenous antibiotic treatment but Peter was resolute about sticking to the scheduled date for his return to London, come what may. And return he did. The course of antibiotics did its work but the infection had undone all the good of the holiday and visibly weakened him.

By this time Peter's investment book *There's Always Something to Do* was fully edited and awaiting its first print run. No sooner was he back than he asked me pointedly when he could expect to see a copy. I replied that it would likely not be before the end of February. Peter then fixed me with his mesmeric blue eyes and replied very quietly, "That's not soon enough." The implication was inescapable. For the first time I had to face the reality that his days were now really numbered. That afternoon I put in a call to Philip Cercone, the chief executive of McGill-Queen's University Press, to explain the urgency. Cercone is a most human and sympathetic person. He understood at once and agreed to pull out all the stops to accelerate the printing.

Sombre though that brief conversation was, no gloom prevailed at Thorney Court. Peter remained as keen as ever to make the most of the time left to him, with cultural expeditions still very much on the agenda. He had noticed that the Dulwich Picture Gallery's two-hundredth anniversary celebrations included an exhibition of the work of the great American illustrator Norman Rockwell, who had produced so many iconic front covers for the *Saturday Evening Post*. Peter had always been an admirer of his work, on top of which he had never before been to the Dulwich Gallery, which is home to one of the world's finest collections of sixteenth and seventeenth-century European paintings.

Hence, on a freezing mid-January morning, Peter and I were driven across London to Dulwich. Peter was enchanted, immediately taking an interest in its attractive, village-like high street and handsome Georgian houses. The gallery itself is a fine, purpose-built edifice designed by Sir John Soane in 1811. The Rockwell show brought together the original paintings for the *Post* covers, which had been such a nostalgic part of Peter's youth. Above all though, he was so impressed by the gallery itself that he asked to see the curator, Ian Dejardin, there and then. Unfortunately Dejardin was out, but Peter took away a copy of the annual report and accounts from his assistant, which he combed through as soon as he got home with the idea of becoming a benefactor, or perhaps sponsoring an exhibition that might have a Canadian flavour to it.

During the next week Peter's physical deterioration was very rapid. So much so that I called Philip Cercone again, anxious to know how things stood in the printing process. Cercone suggested that printed copies of the book could probably be available by month end. I was very much afraid that this would be too late, and Philip responded magnificently. He arranged for a digital copy to be sent from Canada to printers in Oxford who would produce a special run of five copies by the end of the week and have them couriered up to London immediately.

By mid-week Peter's condition was such that the doctor was pressing for him to be hospitalized. However, he was still adamant that he wanted to remain at home. On Friday evening, under a long-standing arrangement, CJ arrived to spend the weekend at Thorney Court. I slipped quietly off home, but as I stepped off the underground my cellphone rang. It was CJ in a state of total panic; Peter was having terrible difficulty breathing and Roza, his favourite professional night carer, was seriously concerned. I told CJ to instruct Roza to call the emergency services at once and called Fiona in Surrey before making my way back to Peter's apartment. As soon as I arrived the paramedics explained that unless Peter went into hospital without delay he was unlikely to survive the night. Peter was still refusing and, although Fiona, who had the authority to insist, was already on her way, time was of the essence. I wheedled and cajoled until Peter gave in.

The ambulance raced headlong, the siren sounding at full blast, to the Chelsea and Westminster Hospital. Fiona arrived from Surrey moments ahead of the ambulance, having driven in at breakneck speed. The gravity of Peter's condition was immediately underlined by the urgency with which the medical team went into action. An hour later, while Fiona was completing the paperwork, I stood in front of the xrays of Peter's lungs with the senior registrar. "Would you show me where you can see the pneumonia?" The registrar paused for moment: "I'm sorry to say that it's easier to show you where I can't see it. We'll have to see how he responds to the intravenous antibiotics, but I wouldn't put the chances at better than 30 percent because he's already so weak." Having digested this informal prognosis, I called Philip Cercone again and received the welcome news that the promised copies of the book would arrive first thing in the morning.

Amazingly, now that he had had some oxygen and liquid glucose, Peter's breathing was much less laboured and he was just conscious. By midnight he was installed in an intensive-care ward. CJ had been pressing for him to be transferred to a private hospital; however the medical advice was that he was not well enough to be moved and that the care that he would receive from the National Health Service at Chelsea was likely to be considerably better, if not as luxurious, than could be expected privately. At this point chintz curtains, gourmet cuisine, high-definition TV and Bose music systems were not an issue. Nevertheless, Peter was promised a private room in the hospital should one became available. At this point there seemed nothing useful left to do. CJ was reluctant to leave and was clearly still in shock, but the ward staff intimated that remaining any longer was not really an option. (She was eventually persuaded to go home and get some sleep, as did the rest of us.)

Fiona, Jenny Bingham, and I arrived back at the hospital a little before six in the morning to find Peter awake and perfectly lucid, although frequently drifting back to sleep owing to the sedation. At ten I called the front desk at Thorney Court and learned that the package from Oxford had arrived as promised. As soon as a copy was presented to Peter, a seraphic smile beamed out. He asked to read the table of contents. He picked out the first chapter of the book entitled "The Eureka Moment" and the one on the subject of Mississippi bonds, so that they could be read to him. After this, he asked for his book to be propped up at the foot of the bed so that he could see it when he woke up.

To the three visitors there seemed to be reason for some optimism, but the consultation later that morning with the senior doctor responsible was anything but encouraging. Peter was not responding and barring a significant improvement in the next thirty-six hours there was no hope. He put the chances of this at 20 percent or less. By the end of the morning Peter's brother, Grier, was on his way from Oregon, John Talbot was to travel from Bermuda, and David Feather from Toronto. Peter Webster was already in London and Peter's closest friends had all been warned. CJ arrived in the afternoon, as did the faithful Roza, who managed to persuade the staff to allow her to remain with Peter for the night. Under protest from Peter, an attempt was made to insert a tube down his throat so that he could be fed, but he made it crystal clear that he refused to allow any invasive intervention whatever.

The same group of visitors arrived early Sunday morning. Peter had passed a feverish night and Roza had spent a good deal of it mopping his brow with cool cloths, but he was now awake, alert and asking for newspapers. As soon as the newsagents opened I went out to fetch Peter's usual papers: *The Sunday Times*, *The Observer*, *The Independent*, the now defunct *News of the World*, colloquially known as the *News of the Screws*, and, of course, *The Sunday Telegraph*. On my return with this bulky selection, which amounted to about half of Britain's entire Sunday press, Peter asked me to read him the headlines so that he could choose those that grabbed his attention to be read to him. It was an eclectic collection.

There was an article about the Arab Spring in Tunisia with a photograph of the fugitive president Zine Ben Ali's prized Ferrari sports car impaled on a forklift truck. Peter looked at it carefully and croaked, "He's lucky it wasn't him. Egypt won't be far behind." He was right on the money; the riots in Tahrir Square began two days later. He listened to an entire piece on Li Ka Shing, the Hong Kong billionaire whom he knew personally, talking about his interest in acquiring Irish government assets, including ports and the electricity company. When it was finished he looked across at Jenny and said, "We'd better get on with that trip to Ireland to look at real estate." He found a story about Silvio Berlusconi's love of sex and prostitutes irresistible, especially since it reported that Berlusconi's tastes in this direction were being publicly defended and applauded by a certain Rocco Siffredi, a well-known Italian stud and porn star, who was quoted as saying, "Italians understand all this; the voters will forgive him, you'll see," at which Peter nodded sagely.

News of the Wasps' victory over Toulouse in the Heineken Cup was enthusiastically received, rugby football being one of Peter's favourite sports and the Heineken particularly so because of his friend Michel de Carvalho. However, possibly the two star attractions were from the *News of the World*. There was a photograph with a story about a Neapolitan motorist attempting a 180-degree turn in one of its narrowest one-way streets and naturally getting stuck, with catastrophic consequences for the city's traffic flow. And finally, a feature on Anna Nicole Smith, whose huge breast enhancements had led her from obscurity to marriage with a billionaire and now to becoming the subject of an eponymous opera shortly to be performed by the Royal Opera House in Covent Garden. After all that, Peter was rather tired again, but his delightfully eccentric *tour d'horizon* of current affairs had lifted the spirits of the whole group, who could only marvel at it under present circumstances.

Nevertheless, the candle was guttering. By this time Grier had arrived. The doctors reported that there was no real improvement and that Peter's breathing would steadily become more laboured. They recommended that he be placed in palliative care, which meant doing nothing but hydrating him by drip, increasing the morphine and maintaining the oxygen for his comfort. It was an emotional decision but Peter had made it absolutely clear, both verbally and in writing, that come the day he forbade any extraordinary attempts at intervention or resuscitation. Peter had been offered the spiritual consolation of a visit from the Anglican chaplain, which he had politely declined. He was not afraid of death, whatever that state might hold in store, although his rational conclusion had for some time been that there was no afterlife. By the afternoon he was clearly sinking quickly and had lost the power of speech. Ian and

Victoria Watson visited and although he was unable to speak he was still conscious. Before leaving, Ian leaned over and whispered to him, "I bet you had a good time in Egypt," at which Peter's eyes flickered with animation and there was a wisp of his old impish smile.

Grier and Roza spent the night largely engaged in moistening his lips and tongue, since he was receiving "nil by mouth" for fear of causing vomiting. In the morning John Talbot and David Feather arrived in time to make their farewells, as did his friends Richard Oldfield and Louise Somers. Mid-morning, two lady doctors from the palliative care unit arrived to say that with Fiona's and Grier's consent they felt that the time had come to increase the dosage of morphine significantly and switch off the oxygen. They were sweet and gentle, promising that they would ensure that Peter did not suffer. The curtains around the bed were drawn, Grier put his arms around Peter, and Fiona and I held his long-fingered hands, which were warm and soft. The oxygen was switched off and within five minutes, with one small heave of the chest, he was gone.

The feeling of bereavement was immediate and powerful, and the tears flowed, but there was work to do. Peter's instructions were that his brain and spinal cord were to be given to Professor Lees's research unit at Queen Square, for which paperwork needed to be completed, and there were many calls to make. I was assigned the task of informing CJ, and David Feather and I escorted her to see Peter.

That evening, instead of everyone moping their way home or back to their respective hotels, John and Jenny decided to host a dinner to celebrate Peter's life in a style of which he would have approved. The chosen venue was Clarke's in Kensington Church Street. On a Monday evening in January the group had the restaurant to themselves by nine o'clock. Peter was toasted in dry martinis as reminiscences began to flow. Peter Webster provided cigars, which the smokers were invited to puff outside in the patio garden, fortified against the cold by some good cognac and a choice selection of Peter stories.

Peter's private cremation was a far more melancholy affair. It took place on a damp, freezing, and gloomy morning, lightened only by the loveliness of the flowers that covered the coffin and the faint scent of the rosemary that formed part of the arrangement. But whatever is read, said, or sung there remains an awful finality as the box disappears. A few days later two urns containing the ashes were delivered to Thorney Court.

They were to be entrusted to Fiona's safekeeping until their journey to Canada. When she arrived to collect them, she put her head round the door of the room where I was working and asked, "Where've you put Peter?" Without thinking I replied, "Oh, he's sitting on the table in the hall." Then the absurdity of the exchange struck us and we burst out laughing.

Epilogue

OF COURSE PETER'S STORY did not come to an abrupt end with his death. Obituaries had to be written and disseminated and there were memorial services – three of them – to be planned and organized – each in a style to suit the likely attendance in London, Toronto, and Vancouver. The London memorial was a formal service with organist and a full choir in Peter's chosen venue, the lovely St Martin-in-the-Fields, which sits in Trafalgar Square, looking across to Nelson's column, the National Gallery and coincidentally, Canada House. It is renowned for its music, which was what had been its attraction for Peter, although he had never been a worshipper there.

Fiona therefore had slight misgivings about meeting the vicar and asked me if I would offer support. We were greeted by Reverend Nick Holtam (now Bishop of Salisbury) and immediately put at ease. Although totally professional, he was relaxed and informal, and possessed of a lively sense of humour. He was also genuinely interested in Peter and happened to be a friend of Diarmaid MacCulloch, the most recent winner of the Cundill History Prize. Naturally, he did not omit the obvious question about Peter's connection with his church. Fiona hesitated for a second and then looked at me for help. I took the plunge and explained that Peter had been a frequent attendee at St Martin's twilight concerts, after which he would customarily hightail it over to Annabel's for a glass or two of champagne, and it was there that he was wont to spend the rest of his evening. Fortunately I had not mistaken my man. This account drew a broad smile and a chuckle from Holtam, who at once agreed to conduct the service and give the address. With that in mind he asked if he might receive a copy of Peter's book so that he could learn a little more about him.

Although the service appeared to follow tradition to the letter, it thoroughly expressed some of the more unconventional aspects of Peter's character. The flowers were spectacular. The music was certainly beautiful and splendid – organ concertos and a toccata and fugue by J.S. Bach, an anthem, "Ye Boundless Realms of Joy" by Handel, and Mozart's "Laudate Dominum." The prayers were what one would expect, as were the hymns – beginning with Bunyan's "Who Would True Valour See" and ending with "Jerusalem."

It was in the variety of the readings that Peter's individuality was expressed. The first, from Montaigne's *Essays*, was read by James Pozzi: "The value of life lies not in the length of days but in the use made of those days. It is quite possible to have lived a long time and yet not to have lived at all."

Ian Watson read from T.S. Eliot's *Four Quartets*:

> Then a cloud passed and the pool was empty.
> Go, said the bird, for the leaves were full of children,
> Hidden excitedly, containing laughter.
> Go, go, go, said the bird: human kind
> Cannot bear very much reality.
> Time past and time future
> What might have been and what has been
> Point to one end, which is always present.

Pozzi followed with an extract from Auden's poem "Death's Echo":

> Dance, dance, for the figure is easy,
> The tune is catching and will not stop;
> Dance till the stars come down from the rafters;
> Dance, dance, dance till you drop.

Grier Cundill concluded with four lines from Kipling's *Just So Stories*, which were a virtual mantra for Peter's view of the importance of curiosity throughout life:

> I keep six honest serving-men:
> (They taught me all I knew)
> Their names are What and Where and When,
> And How and Why and Who.

After this, Michael Meighen movingly and affectionately lifted the lid a little further with his tribute:

With the death of Francis Peter Cundill, Canada lost one of its most remarkable individuals and the investment world one of its most distinguished practitioners. And I, and countless others, have lost a cherished friend.

Peter had a profound and positive impact on the Canadian investment industry, as is witnessed by his many accolades. For almost thirty years he hosted a conference replete with investment gurus, political and journalistic movers and shakers as well as entertaining speakers on "off-beat" topics. Needless to say, an invitation became a much sought-after item. And what a show Peter himself put on – in form and substance – culminating with "this lean and bald figure with piercing blue eyes," striding about the floor during "Pete's Morning," wearing his trademark blue sleeveless sweater.

Integrity was a hallmark of his investment style. At his annual general meeting in 1985 he astonished a packed hall when he cautioned: "We are having a difficult time finding anything we want to buy. Don't send me your money!"

Patience – which Disraeli once characterized as "a necessary ingredient of genius" – was another. In his last interview, Peter's advice for regular investors is quoted as follows: "The mantra is patience, patience and more patience. Think long term and remember that the big rewards accrue with compound annual rates of return."

Peter loved his work and imparted an infectious dynamism and joie de vivre. After the 1987 stock market crash, Peter told those assembled at his AGM: "How do I feel about the situation?" Holding his thumb and forefinger half an inch apart he answered "About this far from euphoria!" Peter happily travelled the lonely road and did so without doubts or regrets – "There is no need for self-flagellation," he often counselled.

But Peter Cundill was in no sense a one-dimensional man. Springing from his wonderful curiosity and openness to new ways of thinking, his interests were eclectic. He was a voracious reader on a wide range of subjects, a faithful diarist, an inveterate and adventurous traveller, a generous philanthropist and a devoted runner of twenty-two marathons. Peter relished sports and physical challenges of every kind: tennis, handball, squash, rugby, skiing, hiking – Peter did them all with enthusiasm and skill. Thankfully, Peter gave up driving early on, having demonstrated beyond the shadow of a

doubt that this was an activity which was not just dangerous to his
own health!

The iron discipline employed in his professional life was generally
replicated in his personal habits – cigars? Yes ... but only on Thurs-
days ... And martinis? Yes ... but only on Fridays! However, Peter's
self-discipline did not extend to junk food and ice cream, for which
he had an irrepressible craving!

And for a long period, he annually selected a new skill such as
piano playing, or skydiving, which he sought to master before his
curiosity about the world and life drove him on to the next. I often
urged Peter to choose proficiency in French as a goal, but he invariably demurred, insisting that his fluency was entirely adequate and
that in any event, it grew in direct proportion to the amount of fine
French wine consumed! I was always inclined to agree.

Peter had a fascination with history, arising – some would say –
from failing a history course at McGill. His penance was a job painting the university's fence on Sherbrooke Street instead of a trip to
Europe, before he retook and passed. This trauma apart, the more
likely explanation for his captivation by history was his belief that it
is only possible to comprehend the present and arrive at a measured
perspective about the future if we understand the past.

As a result, in 2008, Peter founded the Cundill International Prize
in History at McGill, the largest in the world, and designed to encourage the writing of history for a general audience. He closely followed the progress of this inspired initiative, reading the winning
books, corresponding with the authors and in the case of the 2009
winner, Professor Lisa Jardine, meeting and chatting with her over tea.

In a cruel twist of fate for such a fitness devotee, Peter was diagnosed in 2006 with an untreatable genetic condition known as Fragile X. But not surprisingly for those who knew him, he never once
complained, much less wallowed in self-pity. Rather, he embraced
the challenge of his condition with unwavering cheerfulness and a
determination to lead as full a life as possible and to continue to
guide and support all those within his wide reach in a personal and
professional sense.

After the death of his beloved wife, Joanie, and especially towards the
end of his life, Peter was supported by devoted friends and colleagues.

I think in particular of Jenny Bingham, Fiona O'Driscoll, and Christopher Risso-Gill, whose loyalty, support and constant presence were of the greatest comfort to him. Christopher, of course, was the one responsible for making Peter's dream of a book a reality.

There's Always Something to Do: The Peter Cundill Investment Approach will stand as his enduring legacy and, to his immense delight, he received the first copy just before his death.

While Peter Cundill has left us, his influence will continue to be felt for many years to come through his contributions to the financial world, to philanthropy and to the broader community. In the words of one of his long-time associates: "He was a true global person and a renaissance man." While he will be widely missed and mourned, I feel fortunate to have known this unusual and extraordinary individual for as long and as well as I did.

Au revoir, mon ami. You have made such a difference.

The lid continued to be lifted in the three "Personal Reflections" that followed: "Peter the Sportsman" given by Victor Emery, "Peter the Philanthropist" by David Feather, and "Peter the Investor" by Peter Darling, for which I have the text:

"My work is my play," Peter once said, and it was to him one of life's great pleasures. If Friday evening was a time to celebrate with a martini or two, and Saturday was reserved for a party or dinner with friends, then Sunday was for getting stuck into a raft of balance sheets in search of companies whose shares were selling for less than their net asset values. That, to borrow from Noel Coward, was more fun than fun. Unless, perhaps, there was an opportunity for a conversation with an attractive member of the opposite sex.

The full story of Peter's phenomenal achievements as an investment manager, and how he did it, is set out in Christopher Risso-Gill's fascinating book, launched last Friday, *There's Always Something to Do: The Peter Cundill Investment Approach*. I probably shouldn't be talking about money in this beautiful and historic church, but let me just record that $10,000 invested in Cundill Value Fund when Peter started it in 1975 was worth over $1 million when he stopped running it thirty-two years later.

Peter had a number of qualities common to all the great investors: infinite curiosity, acute intuition, a huge appetite for reading, a long-term horizon and the patience to stick with it, and a passion for detailed analysis.

But I'd like to mention a few qualities which differentiated his investment style from the others, each reflecting some of his highly individual personal characteristics.

First, his generosity, and not just his philanthropic activities. There were many acts of personal kindness, as I know from personal experience. More important, he was generous with his time. There was nothing Peter liked more than to teach his craft to others who wanted to learn the Cundill way. And he was never reluctant to share the fruits of his labours with lazier and less-gifted people who wanted the benefit of his investment ideas for free.

Then there was Peter the explorer. He loved to travel, liked hotels, and was equally at home in Toronto, London, New York, Tokyo or Hong Kong, just as his investments had no country bias, provided the securities in question met his value criteria. He was intrigued by the unusual or offbeat, and liked exploring far away places. Who else would go to Ecuador, or Gabon, or Siberia in search of under-valued investments, or would sue the State of Mississippi for repayment of bonds on which they had defaulted in 1841?

He relished danger in his personal life: hang gliding, deep sea diving, walking on hot coals, and so on. No wonder he related to Indiana Jones, a sort of American James Bond but with an intellect. Peter's courage, of course, was never in doubt, as was so clear during his illness. So it should be no surprise that *Barron's*, a leading American financial weekly, described him as "the bravest of the value investors." By definition a value investor is a contrarian, someone who has the courage to buy the shares no one else wants, the "fallen angels." I once heard someone telling Peter all the reasons he should *not* buy a certain share. "That's what I like about it," was Peter's reply.

In his apartment in Kensington, Peter had a larger-than-life bust of his great hero, Winston Churchill. He shared with Churchill an indomitable spirit, a wonderful sense of humour and a capacity to live life to the full. No one better personified Churchill's mantra, "Never Give Up." Despite the increasingly disabling illness, he kept on travelling – he was in Egypt at Christmas, he continued to read, had outings to the theatre and was following the markets even in his last days. An unforgettable character. What an example he has set for us.

The final reading by James Morton was of one of Peter's favourite poems. "Abou ben Adhem" by Leigh Hunt expresses the essence of what being a humanist, and not being religious, meant for him.

Abou Ben Adam (may his tribe increase!)
Awoke one night from a deep dream of peace,
And saw, within the moonlight in his room,
Making it rich, and like a lily in bloom,
An angel writing in a book of gold:
Exceeding peace had made Ben Adhem bold,
And to the presence in the room he said,
"What writest thou?" The vision raised its head,
And with a look made of all sweet accord,
Answered, "The names of those who love the Lord."
"And is mine one?" said Abou, "Nay, not so,"
Replied the angel. Abou spoke more low,
But cheerly still; and said, "I pray thee, then,
Write me as one who loves his fellow-men."

The angel wrote, and vanished. The next night
It came again, with a great wakening light,
And showed the names whom love of God had blest,
And lo! Ben Adhem's name led all the rest.

Some readers will have noticed that there was scant reference to Peter the ladies' man. Apart from the obvious necessity of circumspection in a consecrated place of worship, it would have been awkward, given that at least five of his girlfriends were present in the congregation. Suffice it to say that the topic was not entirely disregarded, either at the reception at Brooks's Club after the service, or at the dinner that followed later. However, as a postscript, à propos of Peter's effect on ladies in general – of whatever nationality, creed, or station in life – let me simply quote the reply that Fiona received from Samar, one of his two Egyptian carers, after she received the news of his death:

> You really make me sad and crying. He was a very good one. I'm glad I met him in my life. He wasn't a patient for me. He was such a DAD and friend. This was my feeling towards him. God bless his soul. Please if you go to visit him [she meant "to take flowers"], just tell him that and tell him that I'm really sad and for sure love him. My Consolation to all of you.

Not inappropriately, Peter's last journey was a transatlantic one, in the two separate urns. He had instructed that his ashes be scattered equally: at the top of Whistler Mountain in British Columbia and in the St Lawrence River at Cap à l'Aigle in Quebec. Fiona's job as courier coincided with the memorials in Toronto and Vancouver, which she was organizing. Their format was completely different from the one in London and entirely secular – a reception and drinks at the Toronto Club, and subsequently at the Vancouver Club, with Michael Meighen's tribute forming the principal speech and myself finishing with a reading of "Abou Ben Adhem," after which I repeated the Latin tag from Catullus that Peter had spoken at his dinner in Toronto the previous year, adding three words of my own: *Ave atque vale amicus meus carissimus*, "Hail and farewell my very dear friend." In Toronto Peter's stepdaughter, Evelyn, contributed a memento that was both touching and funny – with several anecdotes about Peter's lamentable performances with a motor car that included running over the family cat, hitting the neighbours' garbage bins at dawn, and squashing Evelyn's favourite doll. Later in the evening she took Fiona aside and asked if she might have some of Peter's ashes to scatter over her mother's grave. Fiona of course said yes, but the practicality of arranging this was less straightforward. After unpacking the urns in Vancouver she retired to her bathroom armed with a plastic bag and opened one of them over the washbasin. Using a dessert spoon she ladled some of Peter laboriously into the bag. Unfortunately, she got the giggles while doing so, spilling some in the process, which she then had to wash down the sink. She reflected that at least it would eventually end up in the British Columbia

water table along with the Whistler deposit. The following day this seg-
ment of Peter was dispatched to Evelyn by Fedex.

Although already mid-April, there was still plenty of snow at Whistler,
so the group for the scattering had to go up the mountain in a large snowcat with an enclosed cabin. The party was led by Grier and Peter's friend
William Roberts, as chaplain to the resort, with Fiona and her husband
Sean, myself, Grier's wife, Nancy, and John Fraser, the retired Speaker of
the Canadian House of Commons. The view from the chosen spot was
magnificent, looking down from the mountain across the valley with
flickers of sunshine in the distance and looming snow clouds in between.
The ceremony was extremely short and yet most moving. After a very
short prayer from the chaplain and a few words from Grier, came a poem
written by Fiona, which I read:

> To our dear friend Peter,
> Who faced his fate with courage
> And found a way of keeping his dignity.
>
> Among other things
> He brought us new friendships
> New sights and new sounds.
>
> We travelled to far-flung places
> With body and mind.
> He touched our lives
> And enriched them.
> Thank you, Peter.

On the way back down, the snowcat driver took the vehicle to the top
of the Olympic downhill course – so that we could enjoy the view and
appreciate the challenge, we supposed. However, far from stopping at the
edge of the descent, the snowcat plunged straight down what appeared
to be an almost vertical slope. The magnificently frightening experience
would have delighted Peter. It was as though he had planned it.

Several weeks later an even smaller group, made up of the Grier
Cundills, Michael Meighen, David Feather, and yours truly, foregathered
at the Hôtel La Pinsonnière in Cap à l'Aigle, where Peter had stayed on

his last visit. The lilac was everywhere in full bloom, scenting the air, and the sunset over the great river, softened by a slight mist creeping in, was like a Turner landscape.

In the morning, the views were completely shrouded by a persistent downpour, as the small party set off for St Peter's on the Rock – fortunately not far down the road. Once inside the little wooden church there was no smell of damp, only of pine – Peter's gift of funds to repair the roof had been well spent. Grier rang the church bell several times, after which we trooped out again into the drizzle to the little enclosed plot, surrounding a tall granite cross where a small carved slab, set flat into the grass, marks the spot where Peter's father, Frank, is interred. Armed with the urn and an ice-cream scoop (without doubt the most appropriate instrument to use for Peter), Grier ladled out a little circle of ashes around the slab. After this it was onward for the main event. The whole group, by now distinctly damp, set off again for the beach below Granny Cundill's old house, following Grier down the tangled cliff path. In spite of the weather, it was beginning to be quite fun. Once we reached the beach, Grier took off his shoes and socks, rolled up his trousers, and waded out into the river, while the rest of us stood on the shoreline mouthing our "bon voyage's" as the skein of Peter's ashes was caught by the current and drifted away on its journey to the sea. After hugs all round, we tramped back to the hotel for a very fine, and for some quite boozy, lunch – entirely after Peter's heart.

Peter had never been interested in immortality in any of its guises but he was nevertheless passionately interested in legacy. This took two forms, the first being his professional legacy, which he saw as having been secured with the publication of the book on his investment approach. The second, and perhaps even more important, was his philanthropic legacy. Consequently, he had long wished that the lion's share of the fruits of his investment success would pass on his death to a charitable foundation that would exist in perpetuity. His intention was realized in early 2012 with the formation of The Peter Cundill Foundation, based in Bermuda.

The foundation's primary focus is to be pro-active in promoting youth welfare on a global basis and in its broadest sense through its gifting. Its values have been carefully aligned with Peter's: absolute integrity, no cutting of corners in the evaluation of projects; an insistence on full accountability and a willingness to engage, which means giving help with time as well as money. The objective is to make a difference with its giving, whether small or large, recognizing that Peter was a firm believer in the axiom that judicious small gifts can often deliver disproportionately large results.

Peter never made substantial gifts where the funds would simply be swallowed up in the general inflow, and he insisted on the vital importance of monitoring the effectiveness of each gift. The foundation is pursuing the same approach, with a hand-picked team that includes a number of the main characters who appear in this biography. The flair, imagination and sense of personal responsibility that they bring to the management of this very substantial endowment and the foundation's gifting policies will be instrumental in fulfilling Peter's dream of a worthwhile and enduring legacy.

· APPENDICES ·

Appendix A

NET-NET WORK SHEET

The example from 1996 shown here is Neue Zuricher Zeitung (NZZ), a tightly held Swiss newspaper group, chosen to illustrate the adaptability of the process to any stock market under any conditions. On two sides of A4, it offers a comprehensive snapshot of the company's capital structure, its earnings progression, its return on equity, its stock market trading history, and most important of all, its financial health as revealed in the balance sheet. The two most significant sets of numbers are boxed and set in bold so that the reader can see easily that, by comparison with NZZ's then share price of EU 54,500, although it is not trading at a discount to its Net-Net Working Capital Per Share of EU 25,001, there is significant value in the fixed assets, resulting in Shareholder's Equity Per Share of EU 75,580. This premium over the share price represents "the margin of safety."

The Value Fund's position was bought out by the NZZ management a year later at a significant premium to cost.

Peter Cundill & Associates Ltd.
INVESTMENT APPRAISAL FORM -- NET NET
24-Apr-96

Analyst:	FPC/TM/AWM	Contact:	Dr JC Matherly	Symbol:	OTC listed

Company·   **Neue Zuricher Zeitung**   Currency·   Sfr

Current Price: 54,500   Total Mkt Value: 218.0   Year End: Dec 95

				Dec95	Dec94
Business:	Premier German newspaper in Switzerland		Registered shares	4,000	4,000

Sedol #·

Major Shareholders:
Swiss Residents - 80%

EPS		Dec95	Dec94	Dec93	Dec92	Dec91
	1					
	2					
	3					
	4	4,880	6,105	2,760	651	1,204

PROFIT & LOSS ANALYSIS
(In: MILLIONS   )

	Dec95	Dec94	Dec93	Dec92	Dec91
Revenues	355.3	336.7	319.1	170.5	179.3
Inc before x-ord	19.5	24.4	11.0	2.6	4.8
Net Income	19.5	24.4	11.0	2.6	4.8
EPS (before x-ord)	4,880	6,105	2,760	651	1,204
EPS (incl x-ord)	4,880	6,105	2,760	651	1,204
Dividend P.S.	330	330	300	na	na
Price Range:					
High	50,000	39,500	33,000	NA	NA
Low	40,250	32,500	29,750	NA	NA
Volume		NA	NA	NA	NA

BALANCE SHEET
(In: MILLIONS   )

	Dec95	Dec94	Dec93	Dec92	Dec91
Cash and securities	27.2	40.7	30.9	30.9	47.6
Other current assets	66.3	55.4	50.0	28.3	31.2
Current Liabil.	(62.2)	(50.7)	(49.4)	(51.0)	(54.3)
Working Capital	31.4	45.4	31 4	8.2	24.5
Less: LT Debt	(45.5)	(71.2)	(89.8)	(21.9)	(21.9)
Pension liab	0.0	0.0	0.0	0.0	0.0
Other	0.0	0.0	0.0	0.0	0.0
Add: Equity invest. (cost)	118.2	107.9	102.3	0.0	0.0
Other investments	0.0	0.0	0.0	113.0	86.5
Net Net Working Capital	104.0	82.1	43.9	99.3	89.1
Net Net Working Capital P.S.	26,011	20,525	10,983	24,827	22,268
Add: Net Fixed Assets	276.7	290.6	300.4	89.1	98.2
Int. Ass (incl def chgs)	0.5	1.0	1 4	0.0	0.0
Other Assets	0.0	0.0	0.0	0.0	0.0
Less: Def. Inc. Tax	0.0	0.0	0.0	0.0	0.0
Min. Int.	(20.1)	(19.7)	(18.2)	0.0	0.0
Untaxed reserves	0.0	0.0	0.0	0.0	0.0
Allow. and provisions	(58.8)	(60.5)	(56.3)	(88.3)	(93.8)
Shrhldrs Equity	302.3	293.5	271 4	100.1	93.5
Shareholders Equity P.S.	75,580	73,375	67,840	25,031	23,383

CASH FLOW ANALYSIS
(In: MILLIONS   )

	Dec95	Dec94	Dec93	Dec92	Dec91
Net Profit	19.5	24.4	11.0	2.6	4.8
Deprec & Amort	25.8	24.9	24.8	13.6	12.5
Other non-cash	0.0	0.0	0.0	0.0	0.0
Gross Cash Flow	45.3	49.3	35.8	16.2	17.3
Gross Cash Flow P.S.	11,330	12,320	8,960	4,061	4,329
CAPEX	12.4	18.4			

Neue Zuricher Zeitung

OTHER DATA

Employees	1,602
Shareholders	1,356
Debt/Equity Ratio	15.1%
Return on Sales	5.5%
Return on S.E.	6.5%
Return on Price Paid	22.7%
Price/Earnings	11.2
Price/cashflow	4.8
Current Yield	0.6%

	Dec95	Dec94	Dec93	Dec92	Dec91
INSURANCE VALUE PER DR MATHERLY					
Market				147.0	
Cost				0.0	
Diff				147.0	
Per Sh.				36,750.00	
Stated insurance values	462.0	430.0	406.0		
PENSION FUND					
Assets	NA	NA	NA	NA	NA
Accum Bene Oblig					
Proj Bene Oblig					
Amount on B/S					
Invest ROR					
LIFO					
Amount	NA	NA	NA	NA	NA
Per Share	NA	NA	NA	NA	NA
NOL					
Amount	NA	NA	NA	NA	NA
Per Share	NA	NA	NA	NA	NA

Other Comments:

	Dec95	Dec94	Dec93	Dec92	Dec91
Days of invent.	15	12	12	NA	NA
Days of rec'ls	47	45	40	NA	NA

Voting/Registration:

Each shareholder is restricted to a maximum of 30 votes. 17.6% of shareholders are not registered. Registration requirements are somewhat draconian, residence in certain Swiss cantons and membership in any Swiss liberal party (this is somewhat relaxed from the past).

Dividends:

Dividends are only paid out to registered shareholders. We have not been able to collect. Unpaid dividends remain in retained earnings.

Appendix B

NOTES FROM A BATTLE-SCARRED WARRIOR

PRINCIPLES

Our investment approach utilizes time-tested principles of intelligent investing. Achieving a superior track record is a lot harder than most people think, and developing investment wisdom comes from both direct experience and a willingness to absorb lessons from others. We have been fortunate to learn from the experiences and writings of super-investors such as Benjamin Graham, Warren Buffett, Charlie Munger, and others.

Over time we have identified the following principles, which we judiciously apply to all of our investment efforts:

- Think about stocks as part ownership of a business. When we buy stocks for our unit-holders, we have a mindset similar to that if we were buying into a private business.
- Maintain the proper emotional attitude. It is often the case that fear and greed drive stock market prices. We strive to tune out the daily noise that is swirling about and attempt to use market fluctuations to our advantage.
- Insist on a margin of safety. We only make purchases when we judge that the companies we are interested in are available at prices significantly below their intrinsic value.
- Do not diversify excessively. We believe in concentrating our holdings in a limited number of companies in the belief that we will have a chance at superior results only if we take risks intelligently. Good investment ideas are rare and when we find one, we prefer to make a significant commitment.
- Invest for the long term. Attempting to invest based on guessing short-term swings in individual stocks or the overall stock market is not likely to produce consistently good results. Furthermore, frequent trading in stocks can have two major disadvantages: transaction

costs and taxes. We believe that investment capital will grow more rapidly if the interruptions for commissions and taxes are kept to an absolute minimum.

ACTIVITIES

The investment mandates for our two funds contain few restrictions. While this enables us to invest in any viable opportunity that presents itself, our principal focus is on the following investment activities:
- The purchase of securities at significantly less than their intrinsic value to be held as long-term positions.
- Participation in arbitrage and workout situations
- Holding fixed income instruments when we have excess capital.

INVESTMENT POSITIONS

In accumulating our long-term positions we are guided by the following criteria:
- Can we understand it?
  We fully acknowledge that we are incapable of understanding every business and its prospects. While we constantly study businesses to expand our knowledge and improve our insights over time, a key component to our success has been the ability to stay within our circle of competence in selecting investments for purchase.

- Does it possess favourable business economics?
  We look for businesses that possess a sustainable competitive advantage. Over time we have found that excellent businesses will possess many of the following attributes:
  - High returns on equity
  - A strong balance sheet with minimal debt
  - Attractive operating and profit margins
  - A dominant position in its industry
  - Significant brand recognition
  - Pricing power for its products
  - Growing revenues and earnings over time
  - Consistent free cash flow generation

- Does it have honest capable management?
  Making judgements about the integrity and ability of people is an important, even a vital, component in our approach. We want to align ourselves with the principled managers of proven ability who think and act like owners. We have found over time that it pays to invest in companies where the managers have made a significant investment in the company with their own capital on the same basis as us. We look for reasonable compensation practices and managers who are effective at deploying excess capital.

- Can it be purchased at an attractive price?
  The price you pay matters. Even the world's greatest business is not a good investment if you pay too much. An attractive purchase price creates a margin of safety in the event that the business encounters unexpected difficulties. The value of any business is equal to the net present value of all the cash it will generate for the owners over time. In practice, this value is difficult to calculate with any certainty. In making judgements about what price we can pay for an investment, we consider the ratio of price to earnings and price to free cash flow. We also compare the earnings yield of a company to that available from investment alternatives such as risk free government or high quality corporate bonds.

We strive to be disciplined in the application of our stated investment criteria to all purchase decisions. We also recognize that another key component to long-term investing is when to sell opportunistically. While we agree with Warren Buffett when he says that his favourite holding period is forever, we understand that there are times when it may be appropriate to sell some or all of an investment position in order to maximize our returns.

We will normally dispose of an investment position in the following circumstances:
- When we deem the market price to be significantly in excess of its underlying intrinsic value.
- If we see evidence of factors that are likely to significantly lessen its sustainable competitive advantage.

- Where we believe that we have been intentionally deceived by company management whether through their comments or in the financial statements.
- In circumstances where we find a new investment idea that we judge to be better than an investment position that we already own and where we have no excess capital available for deployment.

ARBITRAGE AND WORKOUT SITUATIONS

While our long-term investment positions generally account for the largest portion of the capital in both of our funds, participation in arbitrage and work-out situations has been a significant part of our operations. Often, such activity is undertaken as an alternative to holding short-term fixed instruments.

Arbitrage and workout investing involves the pursuit of profit from an announced corporate event such as the sale, merger, recapitalization, or liquidation of a company. Financial results from this kind of operation depend more on a specific corporate action than on overall stock market behaviour. This activity features securities with a timetable where we can predict, within a reasonable probability, when the investment will be realized, how much we will receive and what might prevent that from happening. Essentially to evaluate an arbitrage or work-out situation we must answer four questions:

- How likely is it that the promised event will indeed occur?
- How long will our capital be tied up?
- What chance is there that something still better will transpire (an example would be the emergence of a competing takeover bid)
- What will happen if the event does not take place? (Examples would include antitrust action or financing glitches).

We only participate in arbitrage and workout situations that have been publicly announced. Also, where possible, we attempt to reduce risk through some sort of hedge. An example of this would occur in the situation where an acquiring company is offering some form of exchange of its shares with the target company. In such a situation, we may sell short the proper ratio of shares to be received from the acquiring company in order to lock in a spread.

The gross profits from most arbitrage and workout investments are normally quite small. However, the predictability of the return coupled with the short holding period usually produces acceptable rates of return. Arbitrage and workout investing typically produces more consistent profits from year to year than our long term investment positions because the returns are to a large extent independent of the course of stock market averages.

FIXED INCOME INSTRUMENTS
While it is our least preferred option for allocating capital in most circumstances, from time to time we find ourselves with more capital than good ideas. Rather than deploying our capital into opportunities that we would consider to be of inferior quality, or with unfavourable risk reward characteristics, we will park such excess capital in various fixed income instruments, usually short term treasury bills, while we continue to search for superior return opportunities into which to allocate capital. When holding fixed income instruments, our overriding concern is both to minimize the interest rate risk and credit risk to the greatest extent possible.

SOME FINAL THOUGHTS
We have had many years of experience in applying this investment philosophy for our unit-holders. We know that proper execution of this approach will lead to satisfactory results over time. That is not to say that we don't seek continuous improvement in our ability to analyze and select investments. We set incredibly high standards for ourselves and are never totally satisfied with our results. We owe our investors nothing less.

Index